Aristotle

De Caelo

Aristotle

De Caelo

Translated
With an Introduction and Notes
By

C. D. C. Reeve

Hackett Publishing Company, Inc.
Indianapolis/Cambridge

23 22 21 20   1 2 3 4 5 6 7

For further information, please address
   Hackett Publishing Company, Inc.
   P.O. Box 44937
   Indianapolis, Indiana 46244-0937

   www.hackettpublishing.com

Cover design by Deborah Wilkes
Interior design by E.L. Wilson
Composition by Aptara, Inc.

Library of Congress Control Number: 2019952374

ISBN-13: 978-1-62466-881-4 (cloth)
ISBN-13: 978-1-62466-856-2 (pbk.)

The paper used in this publication meets the minimum requirements of
American National Standard for Information Sciences—Permanence of Paper
for Printed Library Materials, ANSI Z39.48–1984.

∞

For

Carrie

Contents

De Caelo

Book I

Book II

Book III

Preface

A reliable translation of *De Caelo* needs to be accurate and consistent. No surprise there. It also needs to be accompanied by sufficient annotation to make it intelligible. Some of this can take the form, as it does here, of texts selected from other works by Aristotle himself, so that, while traveling through the region of the Aristotelian world *De Caelo* describes, the reader can also travel through other regions of it, acquiring an ever widening and deepening grasp of the whole picture—something that is crucial, in my view, to understanding any part of it adequately. But much commentary must simply be explanatory, clarificatory, and interpretative.

To make the journey as convenient as possible, footnotes and glossary entries are replaced by sequentially numbered endnotes, so the information most needed at each juncture is available in a single place. The non-sequential reader, interested in a particular passage, will find in the detailed Index a guide to places at which focused discussion of a term or notion occurs. The Introduction describes the book that lies ahead, explaining what it is about, what it is trying to do, how it goes about doing it, and what sort of audience it presupposes. It is not a comprehensive discussion of every aspect of *De Caelo*, nor is it, I should add, an expression of scholarly consensus on the issues it does discuss—insofar as such a thing exists—but my own take on them. The same goes for many of the more interpretative notes. They are a place to start, not a place to finish—a first step in the vast dialectical enterprise of coming to understand Aristotle for oneself.

Some readers will, I have assumed, be somewhat new to Aristotle, so I have tried to keep their needs in mind. But it is the resolute reader that Aristotle most repays, and it is such a reader, of whatever level of knowledge or sophistication, that I most wish to serve.

I have benefited greatly from the work of previous translators and commentators, especially that of Catherine Dalimier and Pierre Pellegrin; Paul Moraux; J. L. Stocks; and, in the case of Books I and II, Stuart Leggatt; and of Book III, Theokritos Kouremenos. Also extremely useful were the translations included in the Ancient Commentators on Aristotle series edition of Simplicius, as was the commentary of Simplicius himself, which I have re-translated to be consistent with the translation of *De Caelo*.

Abraham Bos generously twice read the final draft, detecting many errors, typographical and otherwise, and raising important questions of interpretation. I am in his debt for the care and attention he has paid to my work, and I thank him warmly. My greatest debt, however, is to István Bodnár, who made his enviable knowledge of *De Caelo* available to me in the form of extensive comments and corrections, resulting in very many changes for the better. I am lucky to have been met with such generosity, as I am to have had Philip Bold to help with correcting the page proofs.

I renew my thanks to ΔKE, the first fraternity in the United States to endow a professorial chair, and to the University of North Carolina for awarding it to me. The generous research funds, among other things that the endowment makes available each year, have allowed me to travel to conferences and to acquire books, computers, and other research materials and assistance, without which my work would have been much more difficult.

Lastly, I again very warmly thank Deborah Wilkes for her enthusiastic support of my work and of the New Hackett Aristotle Series.

Abbreviations

Aristotle

Citations of Aristotle's works are made to Immanuel Bekker, *Aristotelis Opera* (Berlin, 1831 [1970]), in the canonical form of abbreviated title, book number (when the work is divided into books), chapter number, page number, column letter, and line number. An * indicates a work whose authenticity has been seriously questioned, ** indicates a work attributed to Aristotle but generally agreed not to be by him (similarly in the case of Plato). The abbreviations used are as follows:

APo.	*Posterior Analytics*
APr.	*Prior Analytics*
Cael.	*De Caelo (On the Heavens)*
Cat.	*Categories*
DA	*De Anima (On the Soul)*
Div. Somn.	*On Divination in Sleep* (Ross)
EE	*Eudemian Ethics*
GA	*Generation of Animals*
GC	*De Generatione et Corruptione (On Coming to Be and Passing Away)* (Rashed)
HA	*History of Animals* (Balme)
IA	*De Incessu Animalium (Progression of Animals)*
Int.	*De Interpretatione*
LI	*On Indivisible Lines***
Long.	*On Length and Shortness of Life* (Ross)
MA	*Movement of Animals* (Nussbaum)
Met.	*Metaphysics*
MM	*Magna Moralia** (Susemihl)

Mete.	*Meteorology* (Fobes)
NE	*Nicomachean Ethics*
PA	*Parts of Animals*
Ph.	*Physics*
Plant.	*On Plants***
Po.	*Poetics*
Pol.	*Politics*
Pr.	*Problems**
Protr.	*Protrepticus* (Düring)
Resp.	*On Respiration***
Rh.	*Rhetoric*
SE	*Sophistical Refutations*
Sens.	*Sense and Sensibilia*
Somn.	*On Sleep*
Top.	*Topics*
Xen.	*On Melissus, Xenophanes, and Gorgias***

I cite and translate the *Oxford Classical Texts* (OCT) editions of these works, where available, otherwise Bekker or the editions noted:

Balme, D. *Aristotle: Historia Animalium* (Cambridge, 2002).

Düring, I. *Aristotle's Protrepticus: An Attempt at Reconstruction* (Göteborg, 1961).

Fobes, F. H. *Aristotelis Meterologicorum Libri Quattor* (Cambridge, Mass., 1919).

Mayhew, R. *Aristotle: Problems* (Cambridge, Mass., 2011).

Nussbaum, M. *Aristotle's De Motu Animalium: Text with Translation, Commentary, and Interpretative Essays* (Princeton, 1978).

Rashed, M. *De la Génération et Corruption* (Paris, 2005).

Ross, D. *Aristotle Parva Naturalia* (Oxford, 1955).

Susemihl, F. *Aristotelis Magna Moralia* (Leipzig, 1883).

Plato

Chrm.	*Charmides*
Crat.	*Cratylus*
Def.	*Definitions***
Epin.	*Epinomis*
Euthphr.	*Euthyphro*
Lg.	*Laws*
Phd.	*Phaedo*
Phdr.	*Phaedrus*
Rep.	*Republic*
Smp.	*Symposium*
Tht.	*Theaetetus*
Ti.	*Timaeus*

Translations of Plato in the notes are based on those in J. M. Cooper, ed. *Plato: Complete Works* (Indianapolis, 1997) and on my *The Trials of Socrates* (Indianapolis, 2002) and *Plato: Republic* (Indianapolis, 2004).

Other Abbreviations and Symbols

Allan = D. J. Allan, *Aristotelis De Caelo* (Oxford, 1955).

Alex. *In. Metaph.* = Haydruck, M. ed. *Alexandri Aphrodisiensis in Aristotelis Metaphysica Commentaria* (Berlin, 1891).

Baksa = I. Baksa, "*Meteorology* I.3 340^{b}6–10: An Ambiguous Passage." *Rhizomata* 2 (2) (2014): 234–245.

Barnes = J. Barnes, *The Complete Works of Aristotle: The Revised Oxford Translation* (Princeton, 1984).

Betegh = G. Betegh, *The Derveni Papyrus: Cosmology, Theology, and Interpretation* (Cambridge, 2004).

Betegh, Pedriali, Pfeiffer = G. Betegh, F. Pedriali, and C. Pfeiffer, "The Perfection of Bodies: Aristotle, *De Caelo* I.1." *Rhizomata* 1 (2013): 30–62.

Bodnár = I. Bodnár, "Aristotle's Planetary Observations." In D. Føllesdal and J. Woods (eds.), *Logos and Language: Essays in Honour of Julius Moravcsik* (London, 2008), pp. 243–250.

Bos = A. Bos, *Cosmic and Meta-Cosmic Theology in Aristotle's Lost Dialogues* (Leiden, 1989).

Braunlich = A. Braunlich, "'To the Right' in Homer and Attic Greek." *American Journal of Philology* 57 (1936): 245–260.

Chantraine = P. Chantraine, *Dictionnaire Étymologique de la Langue Grecque* (Paris, 1968).

Collinge = N. Collinge, "The Senate and the Essence: γερουσία and οὐσία." *Glotta* 49 (3/4) (1971): 218–229.

Cornford = F. Cornford, *Plato's Cosmology* (London, 1952).

DK = H. Diels and W. Kranz, eds. *Die Fragmente der Vorsokratiker*, 6th ed. (Berlin, 1951).

DP = C. Dalimier and P. Pellegrin, *Aristote: Traité du Ciel* (Paris, 2004).

Easterling = H. Easterling, "Homocentric Spheres in De Caelo." *Phronesis* VI (1961): 138–153.

Elders = L. Elders, *Aristotle's Cosmology: A Commentary on the De Caelo* (Assen, 1965).

FP = M. Frede and G. Patzig, *Aristoteles Metaphysik Z: Text, Übersetzung und Kommentar* (München, 1988).

Gill = M. Gill, "The Theory of the Elements in De Caelo 3 and 4." In A. Bowen and C. Wildberg (eds.), *New Perspectives on Aristotle's De Caelo* (Leiden, 2009), pp. 139–161.

Guthrie = W. Guthrie, *Aristotle: On the Heavens* (Cambridge, Mass., 1939).

Hankinson = R. Hankinson, *Simplicius: On Aristotle's On the Heavens I. 1–4* (Ithaca, 2002); *I.5–9* (Ithaca, 2004); *I.10–12* (Ithaca, 2006).

Heath-1 = T. Heath, *A History of Greek Mathematics*, vols. I and II (Oxford, 1921).

Heath-2 = T. Heath, *Mathematics in Aristotle* (Oxford, 1949).

Huffman-1 = C. Huffman, *Philolaus of Croton* (Cambridge, 1993).

Huffman-2 = C. Huffman, *Archytas of Tarentum: Pythagorean, Philosopher and Mathematician King* (Cambridge, 2005).

Isnardi = M. Isnardi Parente and T. Dorandi, *Senocrate e Ermodoro, Testimonianze e Frammenti* (Pisa, 2012).

Jori = A. Jori, *Aristotele: Il Cielo* (Milan, 2002).

Judson = L. Judson, "Eternity and Necessity in De Caelo I. 12: A Discussion of S. Waterlow, Passage and Possibility: A Study of Aristotle's Modal Concepts." *Oxford Studies in Ancient Philosophy* I (1983): 217–255.

Kouremenos = T. Kouremenos, *Aristotle's De Caelo* Γ: *Introduction, Translation and Commentary* (Stuttgart, 2013).

Lagarais = J. Lagarais, *Packing Space with Regular Tetrahedra* (www.math.lsa.umich.edu/~lagarias/TALK-SLIDES/icerm-clay2015apr.pdf).

Leggatt = S. Leggatt, *Aristotle: On the Heavens I & II* (Warminster, 1995).

Longo = O. Longo, *Aristotele, De Caelo: Introduzione, Testo Critico, Traduzione e Noti* (Florence, 1961).

Longrigg = J. Longrigg, "Review of Paul Moraux: *Aristote: Du Ciel*." *Classical Review* 20 (1970): 171–174.

Madigan = A. Madigan SJ, *Alexander of Aphrodisias, On Aristotle's Metaphysics 4* (Ithaca, 1993).

Maso = S. Maso, C. Natali, and G. Seel (eds.), *Reading Aristotle's Physics VII.3: What Is Alteration?* (Las Vegas, 2012).

Matthen = M. Matthen, "Why Does the Earth Move to the Center? An Examination of Some Explanatory Strategies in Aristotle's Cosmology." In A. Bowen and C. Wildberg, *New Perspectives on Aristotle's De Caelo* (Leiden, 2009), pp. 119–138.

Moraux = P. Moraux, *Aristote: Du Ciel* (Paris, 1965).

Mueller = I. Mueller, *Simplicius: On Aristotle's On the Heavens 2. 1–9* (Ithaca, 2004); *2.10–14* (Ithaca, 2005).

Prince = S. Prince, *Antisthenes of Athens: Texts, Translations, and Commentary* (Ann Arbor, 2015).

PNC = Principle of Non-Contradiction.

R^3 = Rose, V., *Aristotelis Fragmenta* 3rd ed. (Leipzig, 1886).

Ross = D. Ross, *Aristotle's Physics: A Revised Text with Introduction and Commentary* (Oxford, 1936).

Schiefsky = M. Schiefsky, *Hippocrates on Ancient Medicine: Translated with an Introduction and Commentary* (Leiden, 2005).

Senechal = M. Senechal, "Which Tetrahedra Fill Space?" *Mathematical Magazine* 54 (1981): 227–243.

Simp. = Simplicius, *In Aristotelis De Caelo Commentaria* (Berlin, 1893).

Stocks = J. Stocks, *De Caelo*, in D. Ross (ed.), *The Works of Aristotle* Vol. II (Oxford, 1930).

TEGP = D. W. Graham, *The Texts of Early Greek Philosophy: The Complete Fragments and Selected Testimonies of the Major Presocratics* (Cambridge, 2010).

Verdenius = W. Verdenius, "Critical and Exegetical Notes on *De Caelo*." In I. Düring (ed.), *Naturphilosophie bei Aristoteles und Theophrast* (Heidelberg, 1969).

Wildberg = C. Wildberg, *Philoponus: Against Aristotle, On the Eternity of the World* (London, 1987).

Wilson = M. Wilson, *Structure and Method in Aristotle's Meteorologica* (Cambridge, 2013).

A = B = A is identical to (equivalent to) B.

A ≈ B = A is roughly the same as or roughly equivalent or analogous to B.

A ⊃ B = If A then B, or A implies B.

Introduction

Life and Works

Aristotle was born in 384 BC to a well-off family living in the small town of Stagira in northern Greece. His father, Nicomachus, who died while Aristotle was still quite young, was allegedly doctor to King Amyntas of Macedon. His mother, Phaestis, was wealthy in her own right. When Aristotle was seventeen his guardian, Proxenus, sent him to study at Plato's Academy in Athens. He remained there for twenty years, initially as a student, eventually as a researcher and teacher.

When Plato died in 347, leaving the Academy in the hands of his nephew Speusippus, Aristotle left Athens for Assos in Asia Minor, where the ruler, Hermias, was a patron of philosophy. He married Hermias' niece (or ward) Pythias and had a daughter by her, also named Pythias. Three years later, in 345, after Hermias had been killed by the Persians, Aristotle moved to Mytilene on the island of Lesbos, where he met Theophrastus, who was to become his best student and closest colleague.

In 343 Aristotle seems to have been invited by Philip of Macedon to be tutor to the latter's thirteen-year-old son, Alexander, later called "the Great." In 335 Aristotle returned to Athens and founded his own institute, the Lyceum. While he was there his wife died and he established a relationship with Herpyllis, also a native of Stagira. Their son, Nicomachus, was named for Aristotle's father, and the *Nicomachean Ethics* may, in turn, have been named for him or transcribed by him. In 323 Alexander the Great died, with the result that anti-Macedonian feeling in Athens grew stronger. Perhaps threatened with a formal charge of impiety (*NE* X 7 1177^{b}33), Aristotle left for Chalcis in Euboea, where he died twelve months later, in 322, at the age of sixty-two.

Legend has it that Aristotle had slender calves, small eyes, spoke with a lisp, and was "conspicuous by his attire, his rings, and the cut of his hair." His will reveals that he had a sizable estate, a domestic partner, two children, a considerable library, and a large circle of friends. In it Aristotle asks his executors to take special care of Herpyllis. He directs that his slaves be freed "when they come of age" and that the bones of his wife, Pythias, be mixed with his "as she instructed."

Although the surviving writings of Aristotle occupy almost 2,500 tightly printed pages in English, most of them are not works polished for publication but sometimes incomplete lecture notes and working papers. This accounts for some, though not all, of their legendary difficulty. It is unfair to complain, as a Platonist opponent did, that Aristotle "escapes refutation by clothing a perplexing subject in obscure language, using darkness like a squid to make himself hard to catch," but there is darkness and obscurity enough for anyone, even if none of it is intentional. There is also a staggering breadth and depth of intellect. Aristotle made fundamental contributions to a vast range of disciplines, including logic, metaphysics, epistemology, psychology, ethics, politics, rhetoric, aesthetics, zoology, biology, physics, and philosophical and political history. When Dante called him "the master of those who know," he was scarcely exaggerating.

What De Caelo Is

One thing we might mean by *De Caelo* is what we now find inscribed on the pages that make up Paul Moraux's Budé edition of the Greek text (which is the one available in the *Thesaurus Linguae Graecae* and in DP), first published in 1965, which is the basis of the present translation. This is the descendant of texts derived—via manuscripts copied in the Byzantine period (from the tenth to the fifteenth centuries AD)—from manuscripts that derive from the edition of Aristotle's works produced by Andronicus of Rhodes in the first century BC. Its more precise transmission is discussed in Moraux's Introduction, pp. clviii–cxc.

Moraux's edition, like most other modern editions, records in the textual apparatus at the bottom of the page various manuscript readings alternative to the one he prints in the body of his text. In some cases, I have preferred one of these readings and have, when they seem important, indicated so in the notes. Divisions of the text into books and chapters are the work of editors, not of Aristotle himself. Also present in Moraux's text are the page numbers of Bekker, *Aristotelis Opera*. These appear here in the margins of the printed version and enclosed in || in the electronic one at the end of the line to which they apply. Occasional material in square brackets in the text is my addition.

The second thing we might mean, and are perhaps more likely to mean, is the work itself—that more abstract thing that is embodied in a good Greek text and (ideally) in any translations. It is clear from the beginning that its distinctive focus, at any rate, is not primarily or exclusively on the world of sublunary nature (*phusis*), consisting canonically of matter-form compounds, whose material component involves the elements (earth, water, air, and fire), but on the superlunary or *super*-natural realm, *ho ouranos* ("the heaven"), as Aristotle calls it, consisting of celestial spheres, composed of primary body or ether (*Cael.* I 3 270^{b}21), as well as the stars and planets affixed to them. Nonetheless, if its scope is more catholic than a strictly natural science, much of what it discusses, for example, the sublunary elements, heaviness and lightness, up and down, has obvious application in the sublunary realm. Some topics belonging to the superlunary one (to super-nature), indeed, are included in natural science's purview:

> The next thing to get a theoretical grasp on [is] . . . whether astronomy is distinct from natural science or a part of it. For if it belongs to the natural scientist to know what the sun or the moon is, for him not to know their intrinsic coincidents would be absurd—especially since it is evident that those who speak about nature discuss the shapes of the sun and the moon, and in particular whether the earth and the cosmos are spherical or not. (*Ph.* II 2 193^{b}22–30)

Finally, and perhaps most tellingly, the evidentiary basis of the science in *De Caelo* is that of natural science:

> The result [of making natural bodies be composed of planes] is that people speaking about the things that appear to be so say things that are not in agreement with the things that appear to be so. And the cause of this is not correctly grasping the primary starting-points, but instead wishing to lead everything back to certain definite beliefs. For presumably the starting-points of perceptible things must be perceptible, of eternal ones eternal, of things capable of passing away things capable of passing away, and, in general, each must be of the same genus (*homogenês*) as what falls under it. But out of love for these beliefs of theirs they seem to do the same thing as those defending their theses in [dialectical] arguments. For they accept a consequence on the supposition of its having true starting-points, as if starting-points must not sometimes be judged on the basis of what follows from them, and most of all on the basis of their ends. And the end in the case of productive science is the work, and in that of natural science what appears to be so to perception has the controlling vote in every case. (*Cael.* III 7 306^{a}5–17)

That is why it is "experience in astronomy" that must provide the starting-points of astronomical science (*APr.* I 30 46ᵃ19–20). It could hardly be clearer that however we are to conceive of the super-natural it cannot be as a realm entirely different in kind from the natural one. Super-nature, to put it this way, is a sort of nature, not a sort of something else.

In *GC*, likewise, we are reminded that the discussion must be conducted *phusikôs*—in a way appropriate to natural science (see I 2 316ᵃ11, II 9 335ᵇ25) and that perception is not something reason (theory) should overstep or disregard (I 8 325ᵃ13–14), but should be in agreement with our arguments (II 10 336ᵇ15–17). Indeed, if it fails in this regard, it is reason that must go:

> On the basis of reason (*logos*), then, and on the basis of what seem to be the facts about them, matters having to do with generation of bees appear to be this way. The facts, though, have certainly not been sufficiently grasped, but if at some time they are, one should take perception rather than reasonings to be what must carry conviction, and reasonings [only] if what they show agrees with what appears to be the case. (*GA* III 10 760ᵇ27–33)

Conviction even on such fundamental matters as the four causal factors distinguished for the elements in *GC* II 1–6 is "based on induction" (*Mete.* IV 1 378ᵇ10–14). The lab, to be anachronistic, not the armchair, has pride of place, even if there is also much that can be done in that more cozy place: "We consider that we have adequately demonstrated in accord with reason (*logos*) things unapparent to perception if we have led things back to what is possible" (*Mete.* I 7 344ᵃ5–7). This has obvious application not just to astronomical objects inaccessible in the absence of telescopes, but to cellular structure and the like that are similarly inaccessible in the absence of microscopes.

Now if the various bodies, natural and super-natural, were the only substances, the only primary beings, the science of them would be the science that the *Metaphysics* proposes to investigate, and which it refers to as theoretical wisdom, the science of being qua being, and as primary science or primary philosophy.

> That natural science is a theoretical science, then, is evident from these considerations. Mathematics too is a theoretical one, but whether its objects are immovable and separable is not now clear; however, it is clear that *some* parts of mathematics get a theoretical grasp on their objects insofar as they are immovable

and insofar as they are separable. But if there is something that is eternal and immovable and separable, it is evident that knowledge of it belongs to a theoretical science—not, however, to *natural* science (for natural science is concerned with certain moveable things) nor to mathematics, but to something prior to both. For natural science is concerned with things that are inseparable but not immovable, while certain parts of mathematics are concerned with things that are immovable and not separable but as in matter. The primary science, by contrast, is concerned with things that are both separable and immovable. Now all causes are necessarily eternal, and these most of all. For they are the causes of the divine beings that are perceptible.* There must, then, be three theoretical philosophies, mathematical, natural, and theological, since it is quite clear that if the divine belongs anywhere, it belongs in a nature of this sort.** And of these, the most estimable must be concerned with the most estimable genus. Thus, the theoretical are the more choiceworthy of the various sciences, and this of the theoretical. . . . If, then, there is no other substance beyond those composed by nature, natural science will be the primary science. But if there is some immovable substance, this [that is, theological philosophy] will be prior and will be primary philosophy. (*Met.* VI 1 1026^{a}6–30)

That there is a substance that is eternal and immovable is argued in *Physics* VIII, and that the gods, including in particular *the* god, are among them is presupposed from quite early on in the *Metaphysics*. Thus in *Met.* I 2 we hear that theoretical wisdom is the science of this god, both in having him as its subject matter and in being the science that is in some sense *his* science. When it is argued in XII 9 that he must be "the active understanding [that] is active understanding of active understanding" (1074^{b}34–35), we see how much his it actually is, since actively understanding itself—contemplating itself in an exercise of theoretical wisdom—is just what Aristotle's god *is*.

With just this much on the table there is already a puzzle whose difficulty is increased by special doctrine. Aristotle usually divides the bodies

---

*These divine beings are the stars and heavenly bodies (*Cael.* II 2 285^{a}29–30, *Met.* XII 7 1072^{a}26–30, 8 1073^{a}23–^{b}1), whose causes are their immovable movers (XII 8).

**The three theoretical philosophies are referred to as theoretical sciences at *Met.* XI 7 1064^{b}1–3.

of knowledge he refers to as "sciences" (*epistêmai*) into three types: theoretical, practical, and productive (crafts). When he is being especially careful, he also distinguishes within the theoretical sciences between the *strictly theoretical* ones (astronomy, theology), as we may call them, and the *natural* ones, which are like the strictly theoretical ones in being neither practical nor productive but unlike them in consisting of propositions that—though necessary and universal in some sense—hold for the most part rather than without exception:

> If all thought is either practical or productive or theoretical, natural science would have to be some sort of theoretical science—but a theoretical science that is concerned with such being as is capable of being moved and with the substance that in accord with its account holds for the most part only, because it is not separable. (*Met.* VI 1 1025^{b}25–28; compare *Ph.* II 9 200^{a}30–^{b}9)

Psychology, as a result, has an interestingly mixed status, part strictly theoretical (because it deals with understanding, which is something divine), part natural (because it deals with perception and memory and other capacities that require a body):

> It is clear that the affections of the soul are enmattered accounts. So their definitions will be of this sort, for example: "Being angry is a sort of movement of such-and-such a sort of body, or of a part or a capacity, as a result of something for the sake of something." And this is why it already belongs to the natural scientist to get a theoretical grasp on the soul, either all soul or this sort of soul. But a natural scientist and a dialectician would define each of these differently—for example, what anger is. For a dialectician it is a desire for retaliation or something like that, whereas for a natural scientist it is a boiling of the blood and hot stuff around the heart. Of these, the scientist gives the matter, whereas the dialectician gives the form and the account. For this is the account of the thing, although it must be in matter of such-and-such a sort if it is to exist. And so of a house the account is this, that it is a shelter to prevent destruction by winds, rain, and heat. But one person will say that it is stones, bricks, and timbers, and another that it is the form in them for the sake of these other things. Which of these people, then, is the natural scientist? Is it the one concerned with the matter but ignorant of the account, or the one concerned with the account alone? Or is it rather the one concerned with what is composed

of both? Who, then, is each of the others? Or isn't it that there is no one who is concerned with the attributes of the matter that are not separable and insofar as they are not separable? And isn't it, rather, the natural scientist who is concerned with everything that is a function or attribute of this sort of body and this sort of matter? And isn't anything not of this sort the concern of someone else, in some cases a craftsman, if there happens to be one, such as a builder or a doctor? And aren't those things that are not actually separable, but are considered insofar as they are not attributes of this sort of body and in abstraction from it, the concern of the mathematician? And insofar as they are actually separable, that of the primary philosopher? (*DA* I 1 403ᵃ25–ᵇ16)

Psychology has a theological dimension, then, as well as a more naturalistic biological or psychological one.

With all this before us, we are in a position to say something further about the science of *De Caelo*. That it is not a work of strictly natural science, but rather of super-natural science, we know. That it is theoretical rather than productive or practical is plain. But what sort of theoretical science is it exactly? Insofar as it is a work of astronomy (or what we would probably call cosmology), we at least know where Aristotle himself puts it, since he refers to it as "the mathematical science that is most akin to philosophy" (*Met.* XII 8 1073ᵇ4–5). Yet it is not a branch of pure mathematics but rather something closer to what we would call applied mathematics:

Odd and even, straight and curved, and furthermore number, line, and figure will be without movement, whereas flesh, bone, and human will not, but rather all of them are said of things just as snub nose is and not as curved is. This is also clear from the more natural-science-like parts of mathematics, such as optics, harmonics, and astronomy. For these are in a way the reverse of geometry. For whereas geometry investigates natural lines, but not insofar as they are natural, optics investigates mathematical lines, but not insofar as they are mathematical. (*Ph.* II 2 194ᵃ3–12)*

A mathematical science, then, but a more natural-scientific one than one pure or abstract.

---

*Also, "Mathematical beings are without movement, except for those with which astronomy is concerned" (*Met.* I 8 989ᵇ32–33).

At the same time, Aristotle tell us too that while we think about "the stars as bodies only, that is, as units having a certain order, altogether inanimate," we should in fact "conceive of them as participating in action and life" (*Cael.* II 12 292ª18–21) and of their action itself as being "like that of animals and plants" (292ᵇ1–2). And the complexity does not end there. For he also includes the primary heaven, the sphere of the fixed stars, as among things divine:

> The activity of a god is immortality, and this is eternal living. So it is necessary that eternal movement belongs to the god. And since the heaven is such (for it is a certain divine body), because of this it has a circular body, which by nature always moves in a circle. (*Cael.* II 3 286ª9–12)*

Apparently, then, the science to which *De Caelo* contributes is at once a natural-scientific branch of mathematics, a biological science, and a theological one.

When science receives its focused discussion in the *Nicomachean Ethics*, however, Aristotle is explicit that if we are "to speak in an exact way and not be guided by mere similarities" (VI 3 1139ᵇ19), we should not call anything a science unless it deals with eternal, entirely exceptionless facts about universals that are wholly necessary and do not at all admit of being otherwise (1139ᵇ20–21). Since he is here explicitly epitomizing his more detailed discussion of science in the *Posterior Analytics* (as 1139ᵇ27 tells us), we should take the latter too as primarily a discussion of science in the exact sense, which it calls *epistêmê haplôs*—unconditional scientific knowledge. It follows that only the strictly theoretical sciences are sciences in this sense. It is on these that the others should be modeled to the extent that they can: "it is the things that are always in the same state and never undergo change that we must make our basis when pursuing the truth, and this is the sort of thing that the heavenly bodies are" (*Met.* XI 6 1063ª13–15).

Having made the acknowledgment, though, we must also register the fact that Aristotle himself mostly does not speak in the exact way but instead persistently refers to bodies of knowledge other than the strictly theoretical sciences as *epistêmai*. His division of the *epistêmai* into theoretical, practical, and productive is a dramatic case in point. But so too is his use of the term *epistêmê*, which we first encounter in the *Metaphysics*, for example, as a near synonym of *technê* or craft knowledge, which is productive not theoretical (I 1 981ª3).

---

*For more details see the notes to this text.

An Aristotelian science, although a state of the soul rather than a set of propositions in a textbook, nonetheless does involve an affirmational grasp of a set of true propositions (*NE* VI 3 1139^{b}14–16). Some of these propositions are indemonstrable starting-points or first principles (*archai*), which are or are expressed in definitions, and others are theorems demonstrable from these starting-points. We can have scientific knowledge only of the theorems, since—exactly speaking—only what is demonstrable can be scientifically known (VI 6). Yet—in what is clearly another lapse from exact speaking—Aristotle characterizes "the most exact of the sciences," which is theoretical wisdom (*sophia*), as also involving a grasp by understanding (*nous*) of the truth where the starting-points themselves are concerned (VI 7 1141^{a}16–18). He does the same thing in the *Metaphysics,* where theoretical wisdom is the *epistêmê* that provides "a theoretical grasp of the primary starting-points and causes"—among which are included "the good or the for-the-sake-of-which" (*Met.* I 2 982^{b}7–10). It is for this reason that the god's grasp of himself through understanding is an exercise of scientific knowledge.

Now each of these sciences, regardless of what group it falls into, must—for reasons having to do with the nature of definition and demonstration—be restricted in scope to a single genus of beings (*Cael.* I 1 268^{a}1n). Since being is not itself a genus (*APo.* II 7 92^{b}14), as Aristotle goes out of his way not just to acknowledge but to prove (*Met.* IV 2), it apparently follows that there should be no such science as the science of being qua being—as theoretical wisdom. To show that there is one thus takes some work. By the same token, there should be no such science as natural science, but only a collection of distinct sciences, each focused exclusively on its own distinct genus of natural beings.

It is a cliché of the history of philosophy that Aristotle is an empiricist and Plato a rationalist, and like all clichés there is some truth in it. In fact, Aristotle is not just an empiricist at the level of the sciences we call empirical, he is an empiricist at all levels. To see what I mean, think of each of the special, genus-specific sciences—the *first-order* sciences—as giving us a picture of a piece of the universe, a region of being. Then ask, what is the universe like that these sciences collectively portray? What is the nature of reality as a whole—of being as a whole? If there is no answer besides the collection of special answers, the universe is, as Aristotle puts is, episodic—like a bad tragedy (*Met.* XII 10 1076^{a}1, XIV 3 1090^{b}20). But if there is an answer, it should emerge from a meta-level empirical investigation of the special sciences themselves. As each of these looks for universals (natural kinds) that stand in demonstrative causal relations to each other, so this meta-level investigation looks for higher-level universals that reveal the presence of common structures of explanation in diverse sciences:

The causes and starting-points of distinct things are distinct in a way, but in a way—if we are to speak universally and analogically—they are the same for all. . . . For example, the elements of perceptible bodies are presumably: as *form*, the hot and, in another way, the cold, which is the *lack* [of form]; and, as *matter*, what is potentially these directly and intrinsically. And both these and the things composed of them are substances, of which these are the starting-points (that is, anything that comes to be from the hot and the cold that is one [something-or-other], such as flesh or bone), since what comes to be from these must be distinct from them. These things, then, have the same elements and starting-points (although distinct things have distinct ones). But that all things have the same ones is not something we can say just like that, although *by analogy* they do. That is, we might say that there are three starting-points—the form and the lack and the matter. But each of these is distinct for each category (*genos*)—for example, in colors they are white, black, and surface, or light, darkness, and air, out of which day and night come to be. (*Met.* XII 4 1070ᵃ31–ᵇ21)

The genus-specific sciences show the presence in the universe of a variety of *different* explanatory structures. The trans-generic sciences, by finding commonalities between these structures, show the equally robust presence there of the *same* explanatory structure: form, lack of form, matter.

The science to which form, lack of form, and matter belong is, in the first instance, trans-generic or universal natural science. It is the one that would be the primary science, as we saw, were there no eternal immovable substances separable from the natural ones. But there is also a trans-generic— or universal—mathematical science:

We might raise a puzzle indeed as to whether the primary philosophy is universal or concerned with a particular genus and one particular nature. For it is not the same way even in the mathematical sciences, but rather geometry and astronomy are concerned with a particular nature, whereas universal mathematics is common to all. (*Met.* VI 1 1026ᵃ23–27)*

---

*Many theorems in mathematics are special to some branch of it, such as arithmetic or geometry, but there are also "certain mathematical theorems of a universal character" (*Met.* XIII 2 1077ᵃ9–10). Here is an example: "That proportionals alternate might be thought to apply to numbers qua numbers, lines qua lines, solids qua solids, and times qua times, as used to be demonstrated of these separately,

The introduction of intelligible matter (*Met.* VII 10 1036ª11–12), as the matter of abstract mathematical objects, allows us to see a commonality in explanatory structure between the mathematical sciences and the natural ones. Between these two trans-generic sciences and the theological one (VI 1 1026ª19), on the other hand, the point of commonality lies not in matter, since the objects of theological science have no matter (XII 6 1071ᵇ20–21), but rather in form. For what the objects of theology, namely, divine substances (which include human understanding or *nous*), have in common with those of mathematics and natural science is that they are forms, though—and this is the crucial point of difference—not forms in any sort of matter whatsoever. That form should be a focal topic of investigation for the science of being qua being is thus the result of an inductive or empirical investigation of the various genus-specific sciences, and then of the various trans-generic ones, which shows form to be the explanatory feature common to all their objects—to all beings.

It is a nice question, but one now within reach of an answer, as to how the science of *De Caelo* is to be incorporated into this uniform explanatory

---

although it is possible to show it of all cases by a single demonstration. But because all these things—numbers, lengths, times, solids—do not constitute a single named [kind] and differ in form from one another, they were treated separately. But now it is demonstrated universally: for what is supposed to hold of them universally does not hold of them qua lines or qua numbers but qua this [unnamed kind]" (*APo.* I 5 74ª17–25). Nonetheless, the universality of the demonstration is open to challenge on the grounds that lines and numbers differ in genus. For "it is necessary for the extreme and middle terms in a demonstration to come from the same genus" (I 7 75ᵇ10–11), so that trans-generic demonstrations are ruled out: "it is impossible that what is shown should cross from one genus to another" (I 23 84ᵇ17–18). Hence "the why [that is, why the theorem about proportionals holds in the case of lines and of numbers] is different" (II 17 99ª8–9), and so separate demonstrations seem to be needed in the case of each. Nonetheless, "qua such-and-such an increase in quantity" (99ª9–10) the demonstration is the same, so that the theorem "holds in common of all *quantities*" (*Met.* XI 4 1061ᵇ19–21). For "while the genera of the beings are different, some attributes belong to quantities and others to qualities alone, with the help of which we can show things" (*APo.* II 32 88ᵇ1–3). But though the universal theorem holds of all quantities, it does so *by analogy*: "Of the items used in the demonstrative sciences some are special to each science and others common—but common by analogy, since they are only useful insofar as they bear on the genus falling under the science. Proper—for example that a line is such-and-such, and straight so-and-so. Common—for example, that if equals are taken from equals, the remainders are equal" (I 10 76ª37–41). Thus, the kind to which lines, numbers, and so on belong, which is the ontological correlate of a theorem of universal mathematics, is not a first-order genus, but a higher-order unity—a quantity.

structure. But it is perhaps enough to notice that its objects of study are matter-form compounds, like those of natural science, but with this one difference: their matter is primary body (ether) rather than earth, water, fire, and air in some combination or other. And because the difference this makes is that astronomical objects, though in many cases biological, are amenable to being studied by an applied mathematical science, it must be that primary body is relevantly similar to intelligible matter. It must be like it in not deforming geometrical shapes, unlike it in being concrete rather than abstract: a sphere made of earth (say) cannot be a perfect sphere; a sphere made of primary body can. Result: the heavenly bodies are perfect or exact models of geometrical theorems, while sublunary bodies are no better than imperfect ones. Hence the need to take account of the margin of error. Thus super-natural science of the *De Caelo* variety enters the uniform explanatory structure required for the existence of the science of being qua being by doors already opened by natural and mathematical science.

It is all this that provides the science of being qua being with a genuine trans-generic object of study, thereby legitimating it as every bit as much a science as any generic-specific one. The science of being qua being is accordingly a science of form. The question now is how can that science at the same time be theology, the science of divine substance? And to it Aristotle gives a succinct answer:

> If there is some immovable substance, this [that is, theological philosophy] will be prior and will be primary philosophy, and it will be universal in this way, namely, because it is primary. And it will belong to it to get a theoretical grasp on being qua being, both what it is and the things that belong to it qua being. (*Met.* VI 1 1026ᵃ23–32)

So the primacy of theology, which is based on the fact that theology deals with substance that is eternal, immovable, and separable, is supposedly what justifies us in treating it as the universal science of being qua being.

To get a handle on what this primacy is, we need to turn to being and its structure. The first thing to grasp is that beings are divided into categories: substance, quality, quantity, relation, and so on (see *Cael.* I 12 281ᵃ32n). But of these, only beings in the category of substance are separable, so that they alone enjoy a sort of ontological priority that is both existential and explanatory (9 278ᵃ17n). Other beings are attributes or affections of different sorts, which exist only by belonging to some substance. So if we want to explain what a quality is, for example, we have to say what sort of attribute it is and ultimately what in a substance is receptive of it. It is this fact that gives one sort of unity to beings: they are all either substances or attributes of substances. Hence the famous claim:

> Indeed, the question that was asked long ago, is now, and always will be asked, and is always raising puzzles—namely, What is being?—is just the question, What is substance? . . . And that is why we too must most of all, primarily, and (one might almost say) exclusively get a theoretical grasp on what it is that is a being in this [substantial] way. (*Met.* VII 1 1028^{b}2–7)

The starting-points and causes of the beings qua beings, then, must be substances. Thus while something is said to be in as many ways as there are categories, they are all so-said "with reference to one thing and one nature" (*Met.* IV 2 1003^{a}33–34)—substance. It could still be the case, of course, that the universe is episodic like a bad tragedy, made up of lots of separate substances having little ontologically to do with each other, but the number of episodes has at least been systematically reduced.

Before turning to the next phase in being's unification, we need to look more closely at substance itself as it gets investigated and analyzed in *Met.* VII–IX. The analysis begins with a *legomenon*—with something said and accepted quite widely.

> Something is said to be (*legetai*) substance, if not in more ways, at any rate most of all in four. For the essence, the universal, and the genus seem to be the substance of each thing, and fourth of these, the underlying subject. (*Met.* VII 3 1028^{b}33–36)

Since "the primary underlying subject seems most of all to be substance" (*Met.* VII 3 1029^{a}1–2), because what is said or predicated of it depends on it, the investigation begins with this subject, quickly isolating three candidates: the matter, the compound of matter and form, and the form itself (1029^{a}2–3), which is identical to the essence (7 1032^{b}1–2). Almost as quickly (3 1029^{a}7–32), the first two candidates are at least provisionally excluded, leaving form alone as the most promising candidate for being substance. But form is "most puzzling" (1029^{a}33) and requires extraordinary ingenuity and resources to explore.

Aristotle begins the investigation into it with the most familiar and widely recognized case, which is the form or essence present in sublunary matter-form compounds. This investigation is announced in *Met.* VII 3 1029^{b}3–12, but not begun till some chapters later and not really completed till the end of IX 5. By then the various other candidates for being substance have been eliminated or reconceived, and actuality and potentiality have come to prominence. Hence in IX 6 it is with actuality or activity—*entelecheia* or *energeia* (*Cael.* I 12 281ᵇ22n)—that form, and so substance, is identified, and matter with potentiality.

Precisely because actuality and potentiality are the ultimate explanatory factors, however, they themselves cannot be given an explanatory definition in yet more basic terms. Instead we must grasp them by means of an analogy:

> What we wish to say is clear from the particular cases by induction, and we must not look for a definition of everything, but be able to comprehend the analogy, namely, that as what is building is in relation to what is capable of building, and what is awake is in relation to what is asleep, and what is seeing is in relation to what has its eyes closed but has sight, and what has been shaped out of the matter is in relation to the matter, and what has been finished off is to the unfinished. Of the difference exemplified in this analogy let the activity be marked off by the first part, the potentiality by the second. (*Met.* IX 6 1048ᵃ35–ᵇ6)

What is common to matter-form compounds, mathematical objects, and divine substances, then, is actuality. In the case of matter-form compounds and numbers, the actuality is accompanied by potentiality—perceptual sublunary matter in the first case, intelligible matter in the second. In the case of divine substances and other such unmoved movers, it is not. They are "pure" activities or actualities, wholly actual at each moment. Matter-form compounds, by contrast, are never wholly actual—they are always in some way potential. You are actually reading this now, not reading *Much Ado About Nothing*, but you could be reading *Much Ado About Nothing*, since you have the presently un-actualized capacity (or potential) to read it.

The science of being qua being can legitimately focus on form, or actuality, as the factor common to divine substances, matter-form compounds, and mathematical objects. But unless it can be shown that there is some explanatory connection between the forms in these different beings the non-episodic nature of being itself will still not have been established, and the pictures given to us by the natural, mathematical, and theological sciences will, so to speak, be separate pictures, the being they collectively portray, divided.

The next stage in the unification of being, and the legitimation of the science dealing with it qua being, is effected by an argument that trades, unsurprisingly, on the identification of form and matter with actuality and potentiality. Part of the argument is given in *Met.* IX 8–9, where the various sorts of priority requisite in a substance are argued to belong to actuality rather than potentiality. But it is in XII 6 that the pertinent consequences are most decisively drawn:

> If there is something that is capable of moving things or acting on them, but that is not actively doing so, there will not [necessarily] be movement, since it is possible for what has a capacity not to activate it. There is no benefit, therefore, in positing eternal substances, as those who accept the Forms do, unless there is to be present in them some starting-point that is capable of causing change. Moreover, even this is not enough, and neither is another substance beyond the Forms. For if it will not be active, there will not be movement. Further, even if it will be active, it is not enough, if the substance of it is a capacity. For then there will not be *eternal* movement, since what is potentially may possibly not be. There must, therefore, be such a starting-point, the very substance of which is activity. Further, accordingly, these substances must be without matter. For they must be eternal, if indeed *anything* else is eternal. Therefore they must be activity. (*Met.* XII 6 1071^{b}12–22)

Matter-form compounds are, as such, capable of movement and change. The canonical examples of them—perhaps the only genuine or fully fledged ones—are living metabolizing beings (*Met.* VII 17 1041^{b}29–30). But if these beings are to be actual, there must be substances whose very essence is activity—substances that do not need to be activated by something else.

With matter-form compounds shown to be dependent on substantial activities for their actual being, a further element of vertical unification is introduced into beings, since layer-wise the two sorts of substances belong together. Laterally, though, disunity continues to threaten. For as yet nothing has been done to exclude the possibility that each compound substance has a distinct substantial activity as its own unique activator. Being, in that case, would be a set of ordered pairs, the first member of which was a substantial activity, the second a matter-form compound, with all its dependent attributes.

In *Met.* XII 8 Aristotle initially takes a step in the direction of such a bipartite picture. He asks how many substantial activities are required to explain astronomical phenomena, such as the movements of the stars and planets, and answers that there must be forty-nine of them (1074^{a}16). But these forty-nine are visibly coordinated with each other so as to form a system. And what enables them to do so, and so to constitute a single heaven, is that there is a single prime mover of all of them:

> It is evident that there is but one heaven. For if there are many, as there are many humans, the starting-point for each will be one in form but in number many. But all things that are many in number have matter, for one and the same account applies to many, for example, humans, whereas Socrates is one. But the primary essence does not have matter, since it is an actuality. The primary immovable mover, therefore, is one both in account and in number. And so, therefore, is what is moved always and continuously. Therefore, there is only one heaven. (*Met.* II 8 1074ᵃ31–38; also *Cael.* I 8)

The argument is puzzling, to be sure, since the immateriality that ensures the uniqueness of the prime mover would seem to threaten the multiplicity of the forty-nine movers, since they are also immaterial; nonetheless the point of it is clear enough: what accounts for the unity of the heaven is that the movements in it are traceable back to a single cause—the prime or primary mover.

Leaving aside the question of just how this primary mover moves what it moves directly, which is left unanswered (as not belonging to natural science) in the *Physics* and *De Caelo* but discussed in *Met.* XII 7, the next phase in the unification of beings is the one in which the sublunary world is integrated with the already unified superlunary one studied by astronomy. This takes place in *Met.* XII 10, although elements of it have emerged earlier. One obvious indication of this unification is the dependence of the reproductive cycles of plants and animals on the seasons, and their dependence, in turn, on the movements of the sun and moon:

> The cause of a human is both his elements, fire and earth as matter and the special form [as form], and furthermore some other external thing, such as the father, and beyond these the sun and its movement in an inclined circle. (*Met.* XII 10 1071ᵃ13–16)

And beyond even this there is the unity of the natural world itself, which is manifested in the ways in which its inhabitants are adapted to each other:

> All things are jointly organized in a way, although not in the same way—even swimming creatures, flying creatures, and plants. And the organization is not such that one thing has no relation to another but rather there is a relation. For all things are jointly organized in relation to one thing—but it is as in a household, where the free men least of all do things at random, but all or most of the things they do are organized, while

the slaves and beasts can do a little for the common thing, but mostly do things at random. For this is the sort of starting-point that the nature is of each of them. I mean, for example, that all must at least come to be disaggregated [into their elements]; and similarly there are other things which they all share for the whole. (*Met.* XII 10 1075ᵃ16–25)

Just how much unity all this results in—just what it means to speak of "the nature of the whole" (*Met.* XII 10 1075ᵃ11) or of the universe as having "one ruler" (1076ᵃ4)—is a matter of dispute. The fact remains, though, that the sublunary realm is sufficiently integrated with the superlunary one that we can speak of them as jointly having a nature and a ruler, and as being analogous not to Heraclitus' "heap of random sweepings" (DK B124), but to an army (1075ᵃ13) and a household (1075ᵃ22).

We may agree, then, that the divine substances in the superlunary realm and the compound substances in the sublunary one have prima facie been vertically integrated into a single explanatory system. When we look at the form of a sublunary matter-form compound, then, we will find in it the mark of a superlunary activator, just as we do in the case of the various heavenly bodies, and, as in the line of its efficient causes, we find "the sun and its movement in an inclined circle" (*Met.* XII 7 1071ᵃ15–16). Still awaiting integration, though, are the mathematical objects, and their next of kin, Platonic Forms.

That there is mathematical structure present in the universe can seem to be especially clear in the case of the superlunary realm, just as mathematics itself, with its rigorous proofs and necessary and certain truths, can seem the very paradigm of scientific knowledge. So it is hardly surprising that some of Aristotle's predecessors, especially Pythagoreans and Platonists, thought that the primary causes and starting-points of beings are to be found in the part of reality that is mathematics friendly, or in some way mathematizable. For example, some Platonists (Plato among them, in Aristotle's much disputed view) held that for each kind of sublunary (or perceptible) thing there was an eternal intelligible Form or Idea to which it owed its being, and which owed its own being, in turn, to "the one," as its substance, and the so-called indefinite dyad of the great and the small, as its matter. So when we ask what makes a man a man, the answer will be, because it participates in the Form or Idea of a man, which owes its being to the way it is constructed or generated from the indefinite dyad and the one (*Ph.* IV 2 209ᵇ7–16, 209ᵇ33–210ᵃ2). And because the Forms are so constructed, Aristotle says (anyway on one reading of the text) that "the Forms are the numbers" (*Met.* I 6 987ᵇ20–22). Between these so-called Form (or Ideal) numbers, in addition, are the numbers that are the objects of mathematics: the intermediates. This elaborate system of, as I put it, mathematics-friendly objects, then, are the substances—the ultimate starting-points and causes of beings qua beings.

Against these objects and the ontological role assigned to them, Aristotle launches a host of arguments (thirty-two or so in *Met.* I 9, twenty-four in XIII 8–9, and many others elsewhere), proposing in their place an entirely different account of mathematical objects, which treats them not as substantial starting-points and causes but as abstractions from perceptible sublunary beings—dependent entities, in other words, rather that self-subsistent or intrinsic ones:

> The mathematician too busies himself about these things [planes, solids, lines, and points], although not insofar as each of them is the limit of a natural body, nor does he get a theoretical grasp on the coincidents of natural bodies insofar as they are such. That is why he separates them. For they are separable in the understanding from movement, and so their being separated makes no difference, nor does any falsehood result from it. (*Ph.* II 2 193^{b}31–35)

This completes the vertical and horizontal unification of being: attributes depend on substances, substantial matter-form compounds depend on substantial forms, or activities, numbers depend on matter-form compounds.

Beings are not said to be "in accord with one thing," then, as they would be if they formed a single genus, but "with reference to one thing"—namely, a divine substance that is in essence an activity. And it is this more complex unity, compatible with generic diversity, and a genuine multiplicity of distinct genus-specific sciences, but just as robust and well grounded as the simpler genus-based sort of unity, that grounds and legitimates the science of being qua being as a single science dealing with a genuine object of study (*Met.* IV 2 1003^{b}11–16). The long argument that leads to this conclusion is thus a sort of existence proof of the science on which the *Metaphysics* focuses.

It is the priority of a divine substance with that science that justifies each of the following descriptions of what the *Metaphysics* is about:

> If, then, there is no other substance beyond those composed by nature, natural science will be the primary science. But if there is some immovable substance, this [that is, theological philosophy] will be prior and will be primary philosophy, and it will be universal in this way, namely, because it is primary. And it will belong to it to get a theoretical grasp on being qua being, both

what it is and the things that belong to it qua being. (*Met.* VI 1 1026ᵃ27–32)

Whether there is, beyond the matter of these sorts of substances, another sort of matter, and whether to look for another sort of substance, such as numbers or something of this sort, must be investigated later. For it is for the sake of this that we are trying to make some determinations about the perceptible substances, since in a certain way it is the function of natural science and second philosophy to have a theory about the perceptible substances. (*Met.* VII 11 1037ᵃ10–16)

Since we have spoken about the capacity [or potentiality] that is said [of things] with reference to movement, let us make some distinctions concerning activity, both concerning what it is and what sort of thing. For the capable too will at the same time become clear as we make our determinations, because we do not say only of that which naturally moves something else, or is moved by something else, that it is capable, whether unconditionally or in a certain way, but also use the term in a different way, which is why in the course of our inquiry we went through the former. (*Met.* IX 6 1048ᵃ25–30)

Concerning the primary starting-points and the primary causes and elements, however, some of what is said by those who speak only about perceptible substance has been discussed in our works on nature, while some does not belong to the present method of inquiry. But what is said by those who assert that there are other substances beyond the perceptible ones is something we need to get a theoretical grasp on next after what we have just discussed. (*Met.* XIII 9 1086ᵃ21–26)

The science of being qua being is a sort of theology, as *Met.* II 2 already told us it was, but it is a sort of theology only because of the special role of the primary god among beings.

Is the Investigation in De Caelo *a Scientific One?*

If we think of a science in the exact sense as consisting exclusively of what is demonstrable, as we saw Aristotle himself sometimes does, we will be right to conclude that a treatise without demonstrations cannot be scientific. But if, as he also does, we include knowledge of starting-points as parts of science, we will not be right, since a treatise could contribute to a science not by demonstrating anything but by arguing to the starting-points themselves—an enterprise which could not without circularity consist of demonstrations *from* those starting-points. Arguments leading *from* starting-points and arguments leading *to* starting-points are different, we are invited not to forget (*NE* I 4 1095ᵃ30–32), just as we are told that because establishing starting-points is "more than half the whole" (I 7 1098ᵇ7), we should "make very serious efforts to define them correctly" (1098ᵇ5–6). We might reasonably infer, therefore, that *De Caelo* is a contribution to astronomy (cosmology), *at least in part* by establishing the correct definition of its starting-points: primary body (ether), which is the distinctive matter of the heaven (I 2–7); up, down, left, and right (II 2); heavy and light (IV 1); and so on.

In our investigation of starting-points, "we must," Aristotle says, "start from things known *to us*" (*NE* I 4 1095ᵇ3–4). For the sake of clarity, let us call these *raw starting-points*. These are the ones we start from when we are arguing to *explanatory scientific starting-points*. It is important not to confuse the two. In the case of the special sciences the *explanatory starting-points* include, in particular, definitions that specify the genus and differentiae of the real (as opposed to nominal) universal essences of the beings with which the science deals (*APo.* II 10 93ᵇ29–94ᵃ19). Since scientific definitions must be apt starting-points of demonstrations, this implies, Aristotle thinks, that the "extremes and the middle terms must come from the same genus" (I 7 75ᵇ10–11). As a result a single canonical science must deal with a single genus (I 28 87ᵃ38–39). To reach these definitions from *raw starting-points*, we first have to have the raw starting-points at hand. Aristotle is clear about this, as he is indeed about what is supposed to happen next:

> The method (*hodos*) is the same in all cases, in philosophy as well as in the crafts or any sort of learning whatsoever. For one must observe for both terms what belongs to them and what they belong to, and be supplied with as many of these terms as possible, and one must investigate them by means of the three terms [in a syllogism], in one way when refuting, in another way when establishing something. When it is in accord with truth, it must be from the terms that are catalogued (*diagegrammenôn*) as truly belonging, but in dialectical deductions it must be from premises that are in accord with [reputable] belief. . . . Most of the starting-points, however, are special to each science.

That is why experience must provide us with the starting-points where each is concerned—I mean, for example, that experience in astronomy must do so in the case of astronomical science. For when the things that appear to be so had been adequately grasped, the demonstrations in astronomy were found in the way we described. And it is the same way where any other craft or science whatsoever is concerned. Hence if what belongs to each thing has been grasped, at that point we can readily exhibit the demonstrations. For if nothing that truly belongs to the relevant things has been omitted from the collection, then concerning everything, if a demonstration of it exists we will be able to find it and give the demonstration, and if it is by nature indemonstrable, we will be able to make that evident. (*APr.* I 30 46ᵃ3–27)

Once we have a catalogue of the *raw starting-points*, then, the demonstrative explanation of them from explanatory scientific starting-points is supposedly fairly routine. We should not, however, demand "the cause [or explanation] in all cases alike. Rather, in some it will be adequate if the fact that they are so has been correctly shown (*deiknunai*) as it is indeed where starting-points are concerned" (*NE* I 8 1098ᵃ33–ᵇ2). But what exactly is it to show a starting-point correctly or adequately?

The science of *De Caelo*, as we saw, is a branch of theoretical philosophy or science, and to the explanatory scientific starting-points of philosophical sciences, Aristotle claims, there is a unique route:

Dialectic is useful in the philosophical sciences because the capacity to go through the puzzles on both sides of a question will make it easier to judge what is true and what is false in each. Furthermore, dialectic is useful in relation to the primary [starting-points] (*ta prôta*) in each science. For it is impossible to say anything about these based on the starting-points properly belonging to the science in question, since these starting-points are, of all of them, the primary ones, and it is through reputable beliefs (*endoxa*) about each that it is necessary to discuss them. This, though, is a task special to, or most characteristic of, dialectic. For because of its ability to stand outside and examine (*exetastikê*), it has a route toward the starting-points of all methods of inquiry. (*Top.* I 2 101ᵃ34–ᵇ4)

And this is repeated almost word for word in the *Physics* with reference to the concept of place, which is a natural scientific starting-point:

> We must try to make our investigation in such a way that the
> what-it-is is given an account of, so that the puzzles are resolved,
> the things that are believed to belong to place will in fact belong
> to it, and furthermore, so that the cause of the difficulty and of
> the puzzles concerning it will be evident, since this is the best
> way of showing each thing. (*Ph.* IV 4 211^{a}7–11)

We might notice in this regard that the verb *deiknunai* occurs around
thirty times in *De Caelo*, where twelve or so puzzles are explicitly identified
as such.* Prima facie, then, *De Caelo* should correctly show the explanatory starting-points of astronomy (cosmology) by going through puzzles
and solving these by appeal to reputable beliefs and perceptual evidence.
But before we rush off to see whether that is what we do find, we need to be
clearer about what exactly we should be looking for.

Dialectic is recognizably a descendant of the Socratic elenchus, which
famously begins with a question like this: *Ti esti to kalon?* What is the
noble, or the nobly beautiful? The respondent, sometimes after a bit of
nudging, comes up with a universal definition, what is noble is what all
the gods love, or whatever it might be (I adapt a well-known answer from
Plato's *Euthyphro*). Socrates then puts this definition to the test by drawing attention to some things that seem true to the respondent himself but
which conflict with his definition. The puzzle or *aporia* that results from
this conflict then remains for the respondent to try to solve, usually by
reformulating or rejecting his definition. Aristotle understood this process
in terms that show its relationship to his own:

> Socrates, on the other hand, busied himself about the virtues of
> character, and in connection with them was the first to inquire
> about universal definition. . . . It was reasonable, though, that
> Socrates was inquiring about the what-it-is. For he was inquir-
> ing in order to deduce, and the what-it-is is a starting-point of
> deductions. For at that time there was not yet the strength in
> dialectic that enables people, and separately from the what-it-
> is, to investigate contraries, and whether the same science is
> a science of contraries. For there are two things that may be
> fairly ascribed to Socrates—inductive arguments and univer-
> sal definition, both of which are concerned with a starting-
> point of scientific knowledge. (*Met.* XIII 4 1078^{b}17–30; also I
> 6 987^{b}1–4)

---

*These are listed in the Index.

In Plato too dialectic is primarily concerned with scientific starting-points, such as those of mathematics, and seems to consist in some sort of elenchus-like process of reformulating definitions in the face of conflicting evidence so as to render them puzzle free (*Rep.* 532a–533d). Aristotle can reasonably be seen, then, as continuing a line of thought about dialectic, while contributing greatly to its exploration, systemization, and elaboration in works such as *Topics* and *Sophistical Refutations*.

Consider now the respondent's first answer, his first definition: what is noble is what the gods love. Although it is soon shown to be incorrect, there is something quite remarkable about its very existence. Through experience shaped by acculturation and habituation involving the learning of a natural language, the respondent is confident that he can say what nobility is. He has learned to apply the word "noble" to particular people, actions, and so on correctly enough to pass muster as knowing its meaning, knowing how to use it. From these particular cases he has reached a putative universal, something the particular cases have in common. But when he tries to define that universal in words, he gets it wrong, as Socrates shows. Here is Aristotle registering the significance of this: "The things that are knowable and primary for particular groups of people are often only slightly knowable and have little or nothing of the being in them. Nonetheless, beginning from things that are poorly known but known to ourselves, we must try to know the ones that are wholly knowable, proceeding, as has just been said, through the former" (*Met.* VII 3 1029^{b}8–12).

The route by which the respondent reaches the universal that he is unable to define correctly is what Aristotle calls induction (*epagôgê*) (mentioned at *Cael.* I 7 276^{a}15). This begins with (1) perception of particulars, which leads to (2) retention of perceptual contents in memory, and, when many such contents have been retained, to (3) an experience, so that for the first time "there is a universal in the soul" (*APo.* II 19 100^{a}3–16). The universal reached at stage (3), which is the one the respondent reaches, is described as "rather confused" and "more knowable by perception" (*Ph.* I 1 184^{a}22–25). It is the sort of universal, often quite complex, that constitutes a nominal essence corresponding to the nominal definition or meaning of a general term. Finally, (4) from experience come craft knowledge and scientific knowledge, when "from many intelligible objects arising from experience one universal supposition about similar objects is produced" (*Met.* I 1 981^{a}5–7).*

---

*Compare: "Unconditionally, what is prior is more knowable than what is posterior—for example, a point than a line, a line than a plane, and a plane than a solid, just as a unit is more so than a number, since it is prior to and a starting-point of all number. Similarly, a letter is more so than a syllable. To us, on the other

The *nominal* (or analytic, meaning-based) definition of the general term "thunder," for example, might pick out the universal *loud noise in the clouds*. When science investigates the things that have this nominal essence, it may find that they also have a real essence or nature in terms of which their other features can be scientifically explained:

> Since a definition is said to be an account of what something is, it is evident that one sort will be an account of what its name, or some other name-like account, signifies—for example, what triangle signifies. . . . Another sort of definition is an account that makes clear why it exists. So the former sort signifies something but does not show it, whereas the latter will evidently be like a demonstration of what it is, differing in arrangement from a demonstration. For there is a difference between saying why it thunders and saying what thunder is. In the first case you will say: because fire is being extinguished in the clouds. And what is thunder? The loud noise of fire being extinguished in the clouds. Hence the same account is given in different ways. In one way it is a continuous demonstration, in the other a definition. Further, a definition of thunder is a noise in the clouds, and this is a conclusion of the demonstration of what it is. The definition of an immediate item, though, is an indemonstrable positing (*thesis*) of what it is. (*APo.* II 10 93ᵇ29–94ᵃ10; compare *DA* II 2 413ᵃ13–20)

A real (or synthetic, fact-based) definition, which analyzes this real essence into its "elements and starting-points" (*Ph.* I 1 184ᵃ23), which will be definable but indemonstrable within the science, makes intrinsically clear what the nominal definition made clear only by enabling us to recognize instances of thunder in a fairly—but imperfectly—reliable way. As a result, thunder itself, now clearly a natural and not just a conventional kind, becomes better known not just to us but entirely or unconditionally. These analyzed universals, which are the sort reached at stage (4), are the ones suited to serve as starting-points of the sciences and crafts: "experienced people know the that but do not know the why, whereas craftsmen know the why, that is, the cause" (*Met.* I 1 981ᵃ28–30).

---

hand, it sometimes happens that the reverse is the case. For the solid falls most under perception, the plane more than the line, line more than point. For ordinary people know things of the former sort earlier. For to learn them is a task for random thought, whereas to learn the others is a task for exact and extraordinary thought" (*Top.* VI 4 141ᵇ5–14).

Socrates too, we see, wanted definitions that were not just empirically adequate but also explanatory: in telling Euthyphro what he wants, he says that he is seeking the form itself *in virtue of which* all the noble things are noble (*Euthphr.* 6d). That is why he rejects the definition of the noble as being what all the gods love. This definition is in one way correct, presumably, in that if something is pious it must be loved by the gods and vice versa, but it is not explanatory, since it does not tell us what it is about noble things that makes all the gods love them, and so does not identify the form in virtue of which they are noble (9e–11b).

Let us go back. We wanted to know what was involved in showing a scientific starting-point. We were told how we could *not* do this, namely, by demonstrating it from scientific starting-points. Next we learned that dialectic had a route to it from reputable beliefs. At the same time, we were told that induction had a route to it as well—something the *Nicomachean Ethics* also tells us: "we get a theoretical grasp of some starting-points through induction, some through perception, some through some sort of habituation, and others through other means" (I 7 1098^{b}3–4). This suggests that induction and dialectic are in some way or other related processes.

What shows a Socratic respondent to be wrong is an example that his definition does not fit. The presentation of the example might be quite indirect, however. It might take quite a bit of stage setting, elicited by the asking of many questions, to bring out a puzzle. But if it does succeed in doing so, it shows that the universal grasped by the respondent and the definition of it produced by him are not entirely or unconditionally knowable and that his state is not one of clear-eyed understanding:

> A puzzle in thought makes manifest a knot in the subject matter. For insofar as thought is puzzled it is like people who are tied up, since in both cases it is impossible to move forward. That is why we must get a theoretical grasp on all the difficulties beforehand, both for these reasons and because those who inquire without first going through the puzzles are like people who do not know where they have to go. And, in addition, a person [who has not already grasped the puzzles] does not even know whether he has found what he is inquiring into. For to someone like that the end is not clear, whereas to a person who has already grasped the puzzles it is clear. (*Met.* II 1 995^{a}30–^{b}2)

But lack of such clear-eyed understanding of a scientific starting-point has serious downstream consequences:

> If we are to have scientific knowledge through demonstration, . . . we must know the starting-points better and be better persuaded of them than of what is being shown, but we must also not find anything more persuasive or better known among things opposed to the starting-points from which a contrary mistaken conclusion may be deduced, since someone who has unconditional scientific knowledge must be incapable of being persuaded out of it. (*APo.* I 2 72ª37–ᵇ4)

If dialectical examination brings to light a puzzle in a respondent's thought about a scientific starting-point, then, he cannot have any unconditional scientific knowledge even of what he may well be able to demonstrate correctly from it. Contrariwise, if dialectical examination brings to light no such puzzle, he apparently does have clear-eyed understanding, and his route to what he can demonstrate is free of obstacles.

At the heart of dialectic, as Aristotle understands it, is the dialectical deduction (*dialektikos sullogismos*). This is the argument lying behind the questioner's questions, partly dictating their order and content and partly determining the strategy of his examination. In the following passage it is defined and contrasted with two relevant others:

> Dialectical arguments are those that deduce from reputable beliefs in a way that reaches a contradiction; peirastic arguments are those that deduce from those beliefs of the respondent that anyone must know (*eidenai*) who pretends to possess scientific knowledge . . . ; contentious (*eristikos*) arguments are those that deduce or appear to deduce from what appear to be reputable beliefs but are not really such. (*SE* 2 165ᵇ3–8)

If we think of dialectical deductions in this way, a dialectician, in contrast to a contender, is an honest questioner, appealing to genuinely reputable beliefs and employing valid deductions. "Contenders and sophists use the same arguments," Aristotle says, "but not to achieve the same goal. . . . If the goal is apparent victory, the argument is contentious; if it is apparent wisdom, sophistic" (*SE* 11 171ᵇ27–29). Nonetheless, he does also use the term *dialektikê* as the name for the craft that honest dialecticians and sophists both use: "In dialectic a sophist is so called in virtue of his deliberate choice, and a dialectician is so called not in virtue of his deliberate choice, but in virtue of the capacity he has" (*Rh.* I 1 1355ᵇ20–21). If dialectic is understood in this way, a dialectician who deliberately chooses to employ contentious arguments is a sophist

(I 1 1355ᵃ24–ᵇ7).* We need to be careful, therefore, to distinguish *honest dialectic* from what we may call *plain dialectic*, which—like all crafts— can be used for good or ill (*NE* V 1 1129ᵃ13–17).

The canonical occasion for the practice of the Socratic elenchus, obviously, is the examination of someone else. But there is nothing to prevent a person from practicing it on himself: "How could you think," Socrates asks Critias, "that I would refute you for any reason other than the one for which I would refute myself, fearing lest I might inadvertently think I know something when I don't know it?" (*Chrm.* 166c–d). Dialectic is no different in this regard:

> But the philosopher, who is investigating by himself, does not care whether, though the things through which his deduction proceeds are true and knowable, the answerer does not concede them, because they are close to what was proposed at the start, and he foresees what is going to result, but rather is presumably eager for his claims to be as knowable and as close to it as possible. For it is from things of this sort that scientific deductions proceed. (*Top.* VIII 1 155ᵇ10–16; compare *Ph.* VIII 8 263ᵃ15–23)

> An inquiry with another person is carried out by means of words (*logôn*), whereas an inquiry by oneself is carried out no less by means of the things at issue themselves. (*SE* 7 169ᵃ38–40)

What we are to imagine, then, is that the philosopher surveys the raw scientific starting-points, constructing detailed catalogues of these. He then tries to formulate definitions of the various universals involved in them that seem to be candidate scientific starting-points, testing these against the raw scientific starting-points by trying to construct demonstrations from them. But these definitions will often be no more than partial: the philosopher is only on his way to complete definitional starting-points, just as the demonstrations will often be no more than proto or nascent demonstrations. The often rudimentary demonstrations that we find in Aristotle's scientific treatises are surely parts of this process of arguing *to* not *from* starting-points. We argue to these in part by seeing whether or to what

---

*Compare: "There are some things that cannot be put in only one genus—for example, the cheat and the slanderer. For neither the one with the deliberate choice to do it but without the capacity, nor the one with the capacity but not the deliberate choice, is a slanderer or a cheat, but rather the one with both" (*Top.* IV 5 126ᵇ8–11).

extent we could demonstrate from them. There are many such arguments in *De Caelo*, but they are typically arguments that show, not arguments that demonstrate. But that we must not overwork the distinction is clear:

> It is no less possible to state a deduction or an enthymeme based on it about matters of justice than it is about matters of natural science, or about anything else whatsoever, even though these things differ in species. Special [topics] on the other hand are the ones based on premises concerning a given species and genus. For example, there are premises concerning natural things on which neither an enthymeme nor a deduction can be based concerning ethical things, and about the latter there are others on which none can be based concerning natural ones. And the same holds in all cases. The common ones will not make some-one wise about any genus, since they are not concerned with any underlying subject. But as to the special ones, the better someone is at selecting premises,* [the more] he will without noticing it produce a science that is distinct from dialectic and rhetoric. For if he hits upon starting-points, it will no longer be dialectic or rhetoric, but instead will be that science whose starting-points he possesses. (*Rh.* I 2 1358ᵃ14–26).

The two instances (and there are only two) in *De Caelo* where Aristotle refers to something he has shown (or takes himself to have shown) as something that has been demonstrated, namely, I 3 269ᵇ18 (*apodedeiktai*), 6 273ᵇ24 (*apodeixin*), are probably best seen in this light.

So: First, we have the important distinction between dialectic proper, which includes the use of what appear to be deductions from what appear to be reputable beliefs, and honest dialectic, which uses only genuine deductions from genuine reputable beliefs. Second, we have the equally important distinction between the use of dialectic in examining a

---

*Retaining τὰς προτάσεις ("premises"); OCT secludes. Compare: "Unconditionally, then, it is better to try to make what is posterior known through what is prior. For proceeding in this way is more scientific. Nevertheless, in relation to those who cannot know through things of the latter sort it is presumably necessary to produce the account through things knowable to them. . . . One must not fail to notice, however, that it is not possible for those who define in this way to make clear the essence of the definiendum, *unless it so happens that the same thing is more knowable both to us and also unconditionally more knowable*, if indeed a correct definition must define through the genus and the differentiae, and these are among the things that are unconditionally more knowable than the species and prior to it" (*Top.* VI 4 141ᵇ15–28).

potentially hostile respondent and its use by the philosopher in a perhaps private pursuit of the truth. Third, we have an important contrast between honest dialectical premises and philosophical ones or scientific ones: honest dialectical premises are reputable beliefs, philosophical and scientific premises must be true and knowable. Fourth, we have two apparently equivalent routes to scientific starting-points, one inductive, which starts from raw starting-points, and the other dialectic, which starts from reputable beliefs.

According to the official definition, reputable beliefs are "things that are believed by everyone, by the majority, or by the wise—either by all of them, or by most, or by the most well known and most reputable" (*Top.* I 1 100^{b}21–23). Just as the scientist should have a catalogue of scientific (often perception-based) truths at hand from which to select the premises of his demonstrations, so a dialectician ought also to select premises "from arguments that have been written down and produce catalogues (*diagraphas*) of them concerning each kind of subject, putting them under separate headings—for example, 'Concerned with good,' 'Concerned with life'" (*Top.* I 14 105^{b}12–15). But for obvious reasons reputable beliefs in outré subjects like astronomy and cosmology (unlike in ethics and politics) are likely to have predominantly expert rather than non-expert sources. Thus the views that are reputable beliefs because they are those of other thinkers about astronomy loom larger in *De Caelo* than beliefs that are reputable because they are held by ordinary people rather than the wise. By the same token things that appear to be so on the basis of astronomical observation should figure along with these beliefs (notice *tôn endoxôn kai tôn phainomenôn* at III 4 303^{a}22–23), since these, as we saw, have the controlling vote in astronomy.

Clearly, then, there will be considerable overlap between the scientist's catalogue of raw starting-points and the honest dialectician's catalogue of reputable beliefs. For, first, things that are believed by reputably wise people are themselves reputable beliefs, and, second, any respondent would accept "the beliefs of those who have investigated the subjects in question—for example, on a question of medicine he will agree with a doctor, and on a question of geometry with a geometer" (*Top.* I 10 104^{a}8–37). The catalogues also differ, however, in that not all reputable beliefs need be true. If a proposition is a reputable belief, if it would be accepted by all or most people, it is everything an honest dialectician could ask for in a premise, since his goal is simply this: to show by honest deductions that a definition offered by any respondent whatsoever conflicts—if it does—with other beliefs the respondent has. That is why having a complete or fairly complete catalogue of reputable beliefs is such an important resource for a dialectician. It is because dialectic deals with things only "in relation to belief," then, and not as philosophy and science do, "in relation to truth" (I 14 105^{b}30–31), that it needs nothing more than reputable *beliefs*.

Nonetheless, the fact that all or most people believe something leads us "to trust it as something in accord with experience" (*Div. Somn.* 1 426^{b}14–16), and—since human beings "are naturally adequate as regards the truth and for the most part happen upon it" (*Rh.* I 1 1355^{a}15–17)—as containing some truth. That is why having catalogued some of the things that people believe happiness to be, Aristotle writes: "Some of these views are held by many and are of long standing, while others are held by a few reputable men. And it is not reasonable to suppose that either group is entirely wrong, but rather that they are right on one point at least or even on most of them" (*NE* I 8 1098^{b}27–29). Later he generalizes the claim: "things that seem to be so to everyone, these, we say, are" (X 2 1172^{b}36–1173^{a}1). Raw starting-points are just that—raw. But when refined some shred of truth is likely to be found in them. So likely, indeed, that if none is found, this will itself be a surprising fact needing to be explained: "when a reasonable explanation is given of why an untrue view appears true, this makes us more convinced of the true view" (VII 14 1154^{a}24–25).* It is the grain of truth enclosed in a reputable belief that a philosopher or scientist is interested in, then, not in the general acceptability of the surrounding husk, much of which he may discard.

The process of refinement in the case of a candidate explanatory starting-point is that of testing a definition of it against reputable beliefs and perceptual evidence. This may result in the definition being accepted as it stands or in its being altered or modified: when a definition is non-perspicuous, Aristotle tells us at *Top.* VI 13 151^{b}7–8, it must be "corrected and reconfigured (*sundiorthôsanta kai suschêmatisanta*)" until it is made clear. The same process applies to the reputable beliefs and perceptual evidence themselves, since they may conflict not only with the definition but also with each other. Again, this may result in their being modified, often by uncovering ambiguities within them or in the argument supporting them, or by drawing distinctions that uncover complexities in these, or they may be rejected entirely, provided that their appearance of truth is explained away—*Cael.* IV 4 310^{b}24–31 is a nice example.

The canonical occasion for the use of honest dialectic, as of the Socratic elenchus and plain dialectic, is the examination of a respondent. The relevant premises for the questioner to use, therefore, are the reputable beliefs

---

*Compare: "What we are about to say will also be more convincing to people who have previously heard the pleas of the arguments disputing them" (*Cael.* I 10 279^{b}7–9); "refutations of those who dispute them are demonstrations of the contrary arguments" (*EE* I 3 1215^{a}6–7).

in his catalogue that his respondent will accept. Just how wide this set of beliefs is in a given case depends naturally on how accessible to untrained respondents the subject matter is on which he is being examined. We may all have some beliefs about thunder and other phenomena readily perceptible to everyone and which are—for that very reason—reputable. But, as we mentioned earlier, about fundamental explanatory notions in an esoteric science we may have none at all.

When a scientist is investigating by himself, the class of premises he will select from is the catalogue of *all* the raw starting-points of his science, despite a natural human inclination to do otherwise:

> [People] seem to inquire up to a certain point, but not as far as it is possible to take the puzzle. For it is customary for all of us to make our inquiry not with an eye to the thing at hand but with an eye to the person who says the contrary. For a person even inquires within himself up to the point at which he is no longer able to argue against himself. That is why a person who is going to inquire well must be capable of objecting by means of objections proper to the relevant genus, and this comes from having a theoretical grasp on all the differentiae. (*Cael.* II 13 294^{b}6–13)

Hence a scientist will want to err on the side of excess, adding any reputable belief, any perceptual evidence, that appears to have any relevance whatsoever to his catalogue. When he formulates definitions of candidate scientific starting-points from which he thinks he can demonstrate the raw ones, he must then examine himself to see whether he really does have the scientific knowledge of it that he thinks he does. If he is investigating together with fellow scientists, others may examine him: we all do better with the aid of co-workers (*NE* X 7 1177^{a}34). What he is doing is using honest dialectic on himself or having it used on him. But this, we see, is little different from the final stage—stage (4)—of the induction we looked at earlier. Induction, as we might put it, is in its final stage (possibly self-directed) honest dialectic.

In a well-known and much-debated passage, Aristotle writes:

> We must, as in the other cases, set out the things that appear to be so, and first go through the puzzles, and, in that way, show preferably all the reputable beliefs about these ways of being affected, or, if not all of them, then most of them and the ones with the most authority. For if the objections are refuted and the reputable beliefs are left standing, that would be an adequate showing. (*NE* VII 1 1145^{b}2–7)

The specific topic of the comment is "these ways of being affected," which are self-control and its lack as well as resilience and softness, as in the parallel passage about place (*Ph.* IV 4 211ª7–11) we examined. Some people think that it applies only to this topic and should not be generalized, even though "as in the other cases" surely suggests a wider scope. And, as we can now see that scope *is* in fact entirely general, since it describes the honest dialectical or inductive route to the starting-points of *all* the sciences and methods of inquiry, with *tithenai ta phainomena* ("setting out the things that appear to be so") describing the initial phase in which the raw starting-points are collected and catalogued.

Now that we know what it means for honest dialectic of the sort employed by the philosopher to provide a route to the explanatory starting-points of the philosophical sciences, we are in a position to see that it is just such a route that *De Caelo* takes to those of astronomy (cosmology). Since this route is the sort any science must take to show its explanatory starting-points, the investigation it undertakes is indeed a scientific one. It is not, to be sure, a demonstration from starting points (the word *apodeixis*, as we saw, occurs only three times in it), but rather a showing of the starting-points themselves, which, if successful, allows us to achieve the sort of puzzle-free grasp on them that comes with genuine understanding.*

The Audience for De Caelo

In the *Nicomachean Ethics*, Aristotle famously tells us that it is not a work for young or immature people, inexperienced in the practical matters with which it deals:

> But each person correctly judges the things he knows and is a good judge of these. Hence a person well educated in a given area is a good judge *in that area*, while a person well educated in all areas is an unconditionally good judge. That is why a young person is not a suitable audience for politics. For he has no experience of the actions of life, and the accounts are in accord with these and concerned with these. (*NE* I 3 1094ᵇ25–1095ª4)

---

*For further argument bearing on the scientific status of *De Caelo*, see A. Falcon and M. Leunissen, "The Scientific Role of *Eulogos* in Aristotle's *Cael* II 12." In D. Ebrey (ed.), *Theory and Practice in Aristotle's Natural Science* (Cambridge, 2015), pp. 217–240.

Though less often recognized, he issues a similar warning in the *Metaphysics*, and there as in the *Ethics*, he makes being well educated a prerequisite:

> That is why we should already have been well educated in what way to accept each argument, since it is absurd to look for scientific knowledge and for the way characteristic of scientific knowledge at the same time—and it is not easy to get hold of either. Accordingly, we should not demand the argumentative exactness of mathematics in all cases but only in the case of things that include no matter. (II 3 995ᵃ12–16)

But whereas in the case of ethics and politics the relevant experience is practical, in metaphysics it is theoretical. There we need experience in life. Here we need experience in the sciences. And in both we need the sort of training in honest dialectic, as in logic and what we would call the philosophy of science, for which the treatises in the so-called *Organon* (*Categories, De Interpretatione, Prior and Posterior Analytics, Topics,* and *Sophistical Refutations*) might serve—or might once have served—as a textbook.

Now it is true that there is no comparable warning to be found within the *Physics* itself, which never mentions its intended audience or what it requires of them. But in a passage in the *Nicomachean Ethics* a requirement is explicitly mentioned:

> While young people become geometers and mathematicians and wise in such things, they do not seem to become practically-wise. The explanation is that practical wisdom is concerned also with particulars, knowledge of which comes from experience. But there is no young person who is experienced, since it is quantity of time that produces experience. (Indeed, we might also investigate why it is that a child can become a mathematician but not a theoretically-wise person or a natural scientist. Or isn't it that the objects in mathematics are given through abstraction, while the starting-points in theoretical wisdom or natural science come from experience, so that the young lack conviction there but only talk the talk, whereas in mathematics it is quite clear to them what each of the objects is? (*NE* VI 8 1142ᵃ13–29)

The *Physics*, then, is no more for the inexperienced than the *Nicomachean Ethics* or the *Metaphysics*, although in its case the experience is presumably in the genus-specific natural sciences, Aristotle's own philosophy of science, and in dialectic. The following two passages indicate as much:

We shall next argue that this is also the only way to resolve the puzzle of the ancient thinkers. For those who were the first to inquire philosophically into the truth and the nature of beings were turned aside, and as it were diverted from their route, by their inexperience, and say that none of the beings either comes to be or passes away, because what comes to be must come to be either from what is or from what is not, both of which are impossible. (*Ph.* I 8 191ᵃ23–29)

For even if things are truly in this state, as certain people assert, and being is unlimited and immovable, at least it does not at all appear to be that way according to perception, but instead many beings appear to be in movement. If indeed, then, there is false belief, or belief at all, or even if there is imagination, or if things seem to be sometimes one way and sometimes another way, there is also movement. For imagination and belief seem to be sorts of movements. But to investigate this question at all, and to seek an argument when we are too well off to need an argument, is to be a bad judge of what is better and what is worse, and what is trustworthy and what is not trustworthy, and what is a starting-point and what is not a starting-point. (*Ph.* VIII 3 254ᵃ24–33)

Hence there is much in the *Physics* that its readers are supposed to know already. When it is simply information or arguments that are at issue, notes can provide what we need. But there is more to being well educated than being well informed; we must also be the intellectual equivalent of morally virtuous.

What, then, of *De Caelo*? Well, we have only to notice in how many cases it refers us to the *Physics* for supporting argument to infer that it presupposes that we already have it under our belt, and so have it in that same good epistemic place that the *Physics*, in turn, presupposes.

When dialectic has done its testing of the opposing sides of a puzzle, we hear in the *Topics*, it "only remains to make a correct choice of one of them" (VIII 14 163ᵇ11–12). And what enables us to make such a choice is the "naturally good disposition (*euphuia*)" that enables people to "judge correctly what is best by a correct love or hatred of what is set before them" (163ᵇ15–16). The reference to "what is best" suggests that this disposition is the *euphuia* also referred to in the following passage:

His seeking of the end in question is not self-chosen, rather, we must be born possessed of a sort of sight by which to judge correctly and choose what is truly good, and a person in whom this by nature operates correctly is naturally well disposed (*euphuês*). For this is what is greatest and noblest and is not the sort of thing we can get from someone else or learn but the sort of thing whose condition at birth is the one in which it will later be possessed and, when it is naturally such as to be in a good and noble condition, will be the naturally good disposition (*euphuia*) in its complete and true form. (*NE* III 5 1114^{b}5–12)

And that, in fact, is what the distinction between philosophy and sophistry, which uses all of plain dialectic's resources, might lead us to expect, since "philosophy differs from dialectic in the way its capacity is employed, and from sophistic in the life it deliberately choses" (*Met.* IV 2 1004^{b}23–25).

Now a deliberate choice of how to live is at bottom a choice of an ultimate end or target for our life: "everyone who can live in accord with his own deliberate choice should adopt some target for the noble life, whether honor, reputation, wealth, or education, which he will look to in all his actions" (*EE* I 2 1214^{b}6–9). And what "teaches *correct* belief" about this end or target, thereby ensuring that the deliberate choice of it is correct, is "natural or habituated virtue of character" (*NE* VII 8 1151^{a}18–19). It is this, we may infer, in which the naturally good disposition under discussion consists. Hence if we possess it, and it has been properly developed by a good upbringing and education, when we hear from ethics that the starting-point it posits as the correct target for a human life is "activity of the soul in accord with virtue, and if there are more virtues than one, in accord with the best and most complete" (I 7 1098^{a}16–18), we will accept it as true, and so strive to clear away the puzzles in such a way as to sustain its truth. If we do not possess it, we will reject this starting-point, so that in our choice between the conflicting sides of these puzzles, we will go for the wrong ones: "the truth in practical matters must be judged from the facts of our life, since these are what have the controlling vote. When we examine what has been previously said, then, it must be judged by bringing it to bear on the facts of our life, and if it is in harmony with the facts, we should accept it, but if it clashes, we should suppose it mere words" (X 8 1179^{a}17–22).

In the *Rhetoric*, we learn of an apparently different sort of good natural disposition which might seem from the company it keeps to be an exclusively intellectual trait: "good natural disposition, good memory, readiness to learn, quick-wittedness . . . are all productive of good things" (I 6 1362^{b}24–25). When it comes to solving dialectical problems bearing on "truth and knowledge," we might conclude, such apparently intellectual good natural disposition is all we need, even if, when it comes to those bearing on "pursuit and avoidance" (*Top.* I 11 104^{b}1–2), we also need its apparently more ethical namesake. It would be a mistake, though, to rush to this conclusion. For the ultimate starting-point and cause that the *Metaphysics* finally uncovers, which is at once the active understanding of active understanding, the prime unmoved mover, and the primary god, is the ultimate cause and starting-point for beings qua beings—*all of them*. And that means that it is our ultimate starting-point and cause too.

When we look at our lives from the outside, so to speak, from the theoretical point of view, if the *Metaphysics* is right, we see something amazing, namely, that the heavenly bodies, those bright denizens of the starry heavens above, are living beings who, like us, are moved by a desire for the best good—for the god (XII 7). It is the conclusion for which *De Caelo* II 1, like *Physics* VII 10, prepares us. When we view our lives from the inside, from that perspective from which "the truth in practical matters" can alone be judged, the *Ethics* tells us that we will find that we are moved by the same thing—that as the good for the heavenly bodies consists in contemplating the primary god, so too does our happiness: "The activity of a god, superior as it is in blessedness, will be contemplative. And so the activity of humans, then, that is most akin to this will most bear the stamp of happiness" (*NE* X 8 1178^{b}21–23). But Aristotle's hand is tipped also within the *Metaphysics* itself:

> [Active understanding rather than receptive understanding] seems to be the divine element that understanding possesses, and contemplation seems to be most pleasant and best. If, then, that good state [of activity], which we are sometimes in, the [primary] god is always in, that is a wonderful thing, and if to a higher degree, that is yet more wonderful. But that is his state. And life too certainly belongs to him. For the activity of understanding is life, and he is that activity; and his intrinsic activity is life that is best and eternal. We say, then, that the god is a living being that is eternal and best, so that living and a continuous and everlasting eternity belong to the god, since this is the god. (*Met.* XII 7 1072^{b}22–30)

That is why "we should not, in accord with the makers of proverbs, 'think human things, since you are human' or 'think mortal things, since you are mortal' but rather we should as far as possible immortalize, and do everything to live in accord with the element in us that is most excellent" (*NE* X 7 1177^{b}31–34), this being our understanding—our divine *nous*.

Aristotle arrives at this great synthesis of theory and practice, as we saw, on empirical grounds, by reflecting on, and drawing inductive conclusions from, the various sciences—theoretical, practical, and productive—as they existed in his day. He is not doing "armchair" philosophy, but rather drawing on his own vast knowledge of these sciences to reach a unified explanatory picture of being as such and our place in it, as practical agents and theorizers. If we followed in his footsteps, drawing on *our* sciences, from theoretical physics to engineering, economics, and ethics, we would not reach his conclusions about the primary starting-points and causes of beings qua beings. If we are to be Aristotelians now it cannot be by parroting Aristotle's theories. Instead, it must be by taking him as a paradigm of how we might be philosophers ourselves—a "paradigm in the heaven," which is what *De Caelo* studies, "for anyone who wishes to look at it and to found himself on the basis of what he sees" (Plato, *Rep.* 592^{b}1–2).

De Caelo

Book I

I 1

It is evident that scientific knowledge about nature is pretty much mostly concerned with bodies and magnitudes, their affections and movements, and, further, with the starting-points, as many as there may be, of this sort of substance.[1] For of the things composed by nature some are bodies and magnitudes, some have body and magnitude, while others are starting-points of things that have these.[2]

The continuous, accordingly, is what is divisible into things that are themselves always divisible, and a body is what is divisible in all ways.[3] A magnitude continuous in one dimension is a line, in two dimensions a plane, in three dimensions a body.[4] And beyond these there is no other magnitude, because the three dimensions are all there are, and so "in three ways" is "in all ways." For, as the Pythagoreans in fact say, the All and all things are defined by [the number] three, since end, middle, and starting-point have the number of the All, and their number is the triad.[5] That is why, having taken these from nature, as if it is one of its laws, we make use of this number even in the worship of the gods.[6] And we assign labels too in this way. For we use "both" of two things and "both" of two people, but we do not use "all," but rather three is the first number with reference to which we use the latter mode of address. And in these domains, as was said, we do so because of following the lead of nature itself.[7] So, since all things, the All, and the complete do not differ from each other with respect to form, but rather, if indeed they do differ, it is with respect to their matter and the things of which they are said, body alone among the magnitudes would be complete.[8] For it alone is defined by [the number] three, and this is All.[9]

Being divisible in three dimensions, body is divisible in all, whereas of the others, one lot is divisible in one, the other lot in two. For as it is with the number they attain, so it is too with their divisibility and continuity. For one is continuous in one dimension, another in two, and this sort in all. All magnitudes, then, that are divisible are also continuous. But whether all that are continuous are also divisible is not yet clear on the basis of the present considerations.

One thing, however, is clear: it is not possible to transition to another genus (*genos*) of magnitude, as we pass from length to surface, and to body from surface.[10] For magnitude of this sort would no longer be complete. For it is necessary that the passage come about in accord

2

with a deficiency. But what is complete cannot be defective. For it is [complete] in all directions.[11]

Bodies, then, that are in the form (*eidos*) of parts are each, according to this account, this sort [of complete].[12] For each has all the dimensions.[13] But each one is defined by contact with what is neighboring. That is why each of the bodies is in a way many. The All of which these are parts, on the other hand, is necessarily complete, and, as its name signifies, in all ways, not in one way so and in another not.[14]

I 2

Where the nature of the All is concerned, whether it is unlimited in magnitude or its total mass is limited must be investigated later.[15] Now, though, we shall speak about the parts of it with respect to form (*eidos*), having made the following our starting-point:[16]

For we say that all natural bodies and magnitudes are intrinsically capable of moving with respect to place.[17] For nature we say is the starting-point of movement for them.[18] Now all movement with respect to place—which we call spatial movement—is either rectilinear or circular or a mixture of these.[19] For these are the only simple movements.[20] And the cause of this is that these magnitudes are the only simple ones, namely, the straight line and the circumference.[21] Circular movement is movement around the center, rectilinear is movement up and down. By "up" I mean away from the center, by "down," toward the center. So it is necessary for all simple spatial movement to be away from the center, toward the center, or around the center. And this seems to follow in accord with the account at the start.[22] For as body found its completion in [the number] three, its movement does too.

Since of bodies some are simple and others composed of these (by "simple" I mean those that in accord with nature have a starting-point of movement—for example, fire and earth, the species of these, and things of the same kind (*suggenês*) as these), it is necessary that their movements too are in some cases simple and in others some sort of mixture—simple in the case of the simple bodies, mixed in the case of the composite ones, but in their case movement is in accord with the predominant component.[23]

[*Argument 1*] If indeed, then, there is simple movement, and circular movement is simple, and simple movement is movement of a simple body (for if the body is composite, its movement will be in accord with the mastering component), it is necessary for there to be some simple body that, in accord with its own nature, naturally moves spatially in a circle. For by force it is possible for it to be that of another, distinct body, but in accord with nature it is impossible, if indeed the movement of each of the simple bodies that is in accord with nature is one movement.[24]

[*Argument 2*] Further, if movement contrary to nature is contrary to movement in accord with nature, and if one thing has one contrary, then, it is necessary, since circular movement is simple, if it is not going to be in accord with the nature of the spatially moving body, that it is contrary to its nature.[25] If, then, fire or something else of this sort is the thing spatially moving in a circle, its spatial movement in accord with nature will be contrary to the circular. But one thing has one contrary, and up and down are contrary to each other.[26] If, on the other hand, it is some distinct body that is the one spatially moving in a circle contrary to nature, there will be some other movement that is in accord with nature. But this is impossible. For if it is up, it will be fire or air, and if it is down, water or earth.

[*Argument 3*] But then too it is necessary for the spatial movement in question to be *primary*. For the complete is prior in nature to the incomplete, and the circle is one of the complete things, whereas no straight line is.[27] For an unlimited one is not complete (for [to be complete (*teleion*)] it would have to have a limit, that is, an end (*telos*)) and neither is any of the limited ones (for all limited ones have something outside them, since any of them can be extended). So if indeed a movement that is prior is movement of a body that is prior in nature, and circular movement is prior to rectilinear, and rectilinear movement is movement of the simple bodies (for example, fire spatially moves in a straight line upward and earthy bodies in a straight line toward the center), it is necessary for circular movement to be the movement of some simple body.[28] For the spatial movement of mixed bodies, we have said, is in accord with the simple body that is the mastering one in the mixture.[29]

On the basis of these considerations, then, it is evident that there is some natural corporeal substance beyond the ones composed here, more divine and prior to all these.[30] [*Argument 4*] And, further, if one were to assume that all movement is either in accord with nature or contrary to nature, and that what is contrary to nature for one thing is in accord with nature for another (for example, as is the case with upward and downward movements, which are contrary to nature and in accord with nature for earth and fire respectively), it would necessarily follow that circular movement too, since it is contrary to nature for these, is in accord with nature for something else.

[*Argument 5*] In addition, if circular spatial movement is in accord with nature for anything, it would clearly be some simple and primary body that in accord with nature spatially moves naturally in a circle, as fire does upward and earth downward. If, on the other hand, the things that spatially move in a circle perform the all-around spatial movement contrary to nature, it would be a wondrous and altogether unreasonable (*alogos*) thing for this movement alone to be continuous and eternal, since it is contrary to nature.[31] For it is evident in other cases that the ones contrary to nature pass away fastest.[32] So if indeed the thing spatially moving [in a circle] is fire, as some people say, this movement will be no less contrary to nature for it than movement downward.[33] For we see that the movement of fire is the rectilinear one away from the center.

This is why a person who makes his deductions on the basis of all these considerations would be convinced that there is some body beyond the ones around us here, separate from them, and having a nature that is more estimable to the extent that it stands farther off from those here.[34]

I 3

Since some of the things that have been said are being assumed while others have been demonstrated, it is evident that not all body has lightness or heaviness. But we must set down what we mean by the light and the heavy—now in a way that is sufficient for our present needs, though later in a more exact one, when we investigate their substance [= essence].[35] Heavy, then, is what naturally moves spatially toward the center, light, away from the center; heaviest, what sinks below all the downward-moving bodies, lightest, what rises above all the upward-moving ones.

It is necessary, then, for everything that moves down or up to have lightness, heaviness, or both—though not in relation to the same thing. For things are heavy and light in relation to each other—for example, air is light in relation to water, whereas water is so in relation to earth. The body, though, that spatially moves in a circle cannot possibly have heaviness or lightness. For neither in accord with nature nor contrary to nature does it admit of moving toward the center or away from the center. For in accord with nature rectilinear spatial movement does not pertain to it. For the movement of each of the simple bodies is, as we saw, one movement, so that the body that spatially moves in a circle will be the same as one of the bodies spatially moving in this way.[36] On the other hand, if it is moved contrary to nature, then if downward movement is contrary to nature, upward will be in accord with nature, and if upward is contrary to nature, downward will be in accord with nature. For we posited that, of contrary movements, if one is contrary to nature for something, the other is in accord with nature.[37]

Since, however, the whole and the part—for example, all of earth and a small clod—spatially move in accord with nature to the same place, it follows, first, that it has neither lightness nor heaviness (for otherwise it would be capable of spatially moving either toward the center or away from the center in accord with its own nature).[38] Next, it follows that it cannot be moved with respect to place by being hauled either up or down. For it does not admit of moving, either in accord with nature or contrary to nature, with a movement other than its own, either itself or any of its parts. For the same argument applies to whole and part.

It is equally reasonable (*eulogos*) to suppose about this body that it is incapable of coming to be and passing away, incapable of increase, and incapable of alteration, because everything that comes to be comes to be from its contrary and from an underlying subject, and passes away similarly, namely, from an underlying subject, because of a contrary, and to a contrary, as was said in our first accounts.[39] Also, contrary spatial movements are of contraries.[40] If, then, this body can have no contrary, because there cannot in fact be a movement contrary to spatial movement in a circle, nature seems to have correctly removed from among the contraries the body that was going to be incapable of coming to be and passing away. For coming to be and passing away belong in the realm of contraries.

But then too everything that increases, increases because of something of the same kind (*suggenous*) being added to it and dissolving into its matter.[41] But there is none from which this body has come to be.[42]

But if it is not capable of either increase or passing away, the same thinking leads us to suppose that it is not capable of alteration either. For alteration is movement with respect to quality, and qualitative states and dispositions—for example, health and disease—do not come about without change with respect to the affections.[43] But all natural bodies that change with respect to an affection we see are subject both to increase and decrease—for example, the bodies of animals and plants and their parts, and also those of the elements.[44] So if indeed the body in circular movement does not admit of either increase or decrease, it is reasonable (*eulogos*) for it to be unalterable as well.

Why, then, the primary body is eternal and not subject to increase or decrease, but rather incapable of aging, incapable of alteration, and unaffectable, is—provided our assumptions are convincing—evident from what has been said.

It seems too that the argument attests to the things that appear to be so, and the things that appear to be so attest to the argument.[45] For all human beings have a supposition about the gods, and all—both barbarians and Greeks, as many as acknowledge gods at all—assign the highest place to the gods, on the assumption, clearly, that immortal is closely linked with immortal, since any other way is impossible.[46] If indeed, then, there is something divine, as indeed there is, the things just now said about the substance that is primary among the bodies were correctly said.

But this result also follows sufficiently enough through perception, at any rate for (one might almost say) merely human conviction.[47] For in all of past time, according to the record people have handed down one to another, nothing appears to have changed either in the whole of the outermost heaven or in the parts proper to it.[48]

And it seems that the name too has been handed down even to the present time by the ancients, who conceived of it in the very way we ourselves speak of it. For one must acknowledge that the same beliefs return to us not once or twice but an unlimited number of times.[49] That is why, on the supposition that the primary body was something distinct, beyond earth, fire, air, and water, they gave the name *aithêr* ("ether") to the uppermost place, positing a name for it from the fact that, throughout eternal time, it is running always (*thein aei*).[50] Anaxagoras, on the other hand, does not use this name correctly, since he uses "*aithêr*" in place of "fire."[51]

It is also evident from what has been said why the number of what are called simple bodies cannot be greater. For it is necessary for the movement of a simple body to be simple, and we say that the following are the only simple movements: circular and rectilinear, the latter having two parts, one away from the center, the other toward the center.[52]

I 4

That there is no other spatial movement contrary to spatial movement in a circle is a conviction one may obtain from many sources.

First, we assume the straight line to be opposed above all to the circular. For concave and convex seem to be opposed not only to each other but also, when they are coupled and taken as put together, to the straight line.[53] So, if indeed there is a contrary movement, it is above all necessary for what is contrary to movement in a circle to be rectilinear movement. But rectilinear movements are opposed to each other because of their places. For up-down is at once a differentia of place and a contrariety.[54]

5   Next, if someone supposes that the very same argument that applies
to rectilinear applies also to spatial movement along a circumference
(for example, that spatial movement from A to B is contrary to that
from B to A), it is [in fact] the rectilinear he is speaking of. For it is
limited, whereas there would be an unlimited number of circular paths
through the same points [Fig. 1].[55]

10   It is the same too in the case of one of the two semicircles—for
example, from C to D and from D to C [Fig. 2]. For it [the spatial
movement] is the same as along the diameter, since we always suppose
the distance between each pair of points to be a straight line.[56]

And it is the same even if one constructed a circle and posited that
the spatial movement along one semicircle was contrary to that along
15   the other—for example, that along the whole circle, the spatial movement along semicircle G from E to F is contrary to that along semicircle H from F to E [Fig. 3]. Even if these were contraries, however, it
in no way follows that the spatial movements along the whole circle are
23   contraries. { . . . }[57] For they will be toward the same point, because it is
necessary for what spatially moves in a circle, wherever it starts from,
25   to return to all the contrary places alike (the contrarieties of place are
up and down, front and back, right and left, and the contrarieties of
28   spatial movement are in accord with the contrarieties of place).

19   But then neither is spatial movement in a circle from A to B contrary to that from A to C [Fig. 4]. For the movement is from the same
and to the same, but a contrary spatial movement was defined as from
22   a contrary to a contrary.[58]

And even if spatial movement in a circle were contrary to spatial
23   movement in a circle, one or the other would be pointless. For if they
were equal, there would be no movement of them, whereas if one of
the movements did the mastering, the other would not exist.[59] So if
30   there were two bodies, one of the two, in not moving with its own
movement, would be pointless. For we say that a shoe is pointless if
it is not being worn.[60] The god and nature, however, make nothing
pointlessly.[61]

I 5

But since we are now clear about these matters, we must investigate the
271^b1   remaining ones, and first whether there is an unlimited body, as most of
the ancient philosophers thought, or whether this is an impossibility.[62]
For its being the former way or the latter way makes no small differ-
5   ence—but rather absolutely all the difference—as regards getting a theoretical grasp on the truth.[63] For this has been and is the starting-point

of pretty much every disagreement among those who have made some pronouncement about nature as a whole, if indeed even a small initial deviation from the truth multiplies itself ten-thousand times. For example, if someone said there is a smallest magnitude, this person, by having introduced the smallest one, would have upset the greatest things in mathematics.[64] The cause of this is that the starting-point is greater in capacity than in magnitude, which is why what is small at the start becomes immensely great at the end.[65] The unlimited, though, has both the capacity of a starting-point and, in quantity, the greatest one. So there is nothing absurd or unreasonable in the fact that the difference that stems from the assumption that there is an unlimited body is a wondrous one. That is why we must speak about it, taking it up from the start.

It is necessary, then, for every body to be either simple or composite, so that the unlimited one will be either simple or composite. But it is also clear, surely, that if the simple ones are limited, it is also necessary for the composite ones to be limited. For what is composed of things that are limited in both number and magnitude is limited in number and magnitude. For it is as great as what it is composed of.

It remains, therefore, to see whether any of the simple bodies can be unlimited in magnitude, or whether this is impossible. When we have discussed the primary one among the bodies, then, let us investigate the remaining ones in the same way.

Now then, that it is necessary for the body that spatially moves in a circle to be limited in its entirety is clear from the following:

[*Argument 1*] For if the body moving spatially in a circle is unlimited, the radii produced from the center will be unlimited.[66] But the interval between unlimited radii is unlimited—by "interval" I mean that outside of which no magnitude in contact with the lines can be found.[67] It is necessary, then, for this to be unlimited. For the interval between limited lines will always be limited. Further, it is always possible to take [an interval] greater than [any] given one, so that just as we say number is unlimited, because there is not a greatest, the same argument also applies to the interval. If, then, it is not possible to traverse the unlimited, and if, of an unlimited body, it is necessary for the intervals to be unlimited, it could not possibly be moving in a circle.[68] But we see the heaven revolving in a circle, and we have also determined by argument that movement in a circle belongs to a certain thing.[69]

[*Argument 2*] Further, if you subtract a limited time from a limited time, it is necessary for the remainder to be limited as well and to have a starting-point. But if the travel time has a starting-point, there is also a starting-point of the movement, and so of the magnitude that has been travelled. Let, then, the line ACE be unlimited in one direction, E, and the line BB be unlimited in both [Fig. 5].⁷⁰ If, then, the line ACE inscribed a circle with C as its center, ACE will at some time spatially move in a circle while cutting BB for a limited time. For the entire time in which the heaven spatially moved in a circle is limited. Therefore, the time subtracted from this, in which it was doing the cutting, is limited as well. Therefore, there will be a starting-point at which ACE first cut BB. But this is impossible. Therefore, it is not possible for the unlimited to revolve in a circle. So neither could the cosmos, if it were unlimited.⁷¹

[*Argument 3*] Further, it is also evident from the following considerations that it is impossible for the unlimited to move. For let the limited line A be spatially moving past the limited line B. It is necessary, then, for A to get clear of B, at the same time as B gets clear of A. For the extent to which one overlaps the other is the same as that to which the other overlaps the one. If, then, both were moving in contrary directions, they would get clear of each other faster, whereas if one were spatially moving past one remaining at rest, they would do so more slowly, provided the one spatially moving is moving at the same speed. But this at least is evident, namely, that it is impossible to traverse an unlimited line in a limited time. Therefore, it must be in an unlimited one. This was shown previously in the discussions concerning movement.⁷² And it makes no difference at all whether the limited line is spatially moving past the unlimited one, or the unlimited one past it. For whenever the one passes the other, the other passes the one, whether it is moving or unmoving, except that they will get clear of each other faster if both are moving. And yet sometimes there is nothing to prevent a moving line from passing one at rest faster than one moving in a contrary direction, if one has made both the lines moving spatially in contrary directions move slowly, but the one passing the one at rest move spatially much faster. It is no impediment to the argument, then, that one line is passing a line that is at rest, since it is possible for a moving A to pass a moving B more slowly. If, then, the time in which a limited moving line gets clear [of an unlimited one] is unlimited, it is necessary for the time in which an unlimited one moves past a limited one to also be unlimited. It is impossible, therefore, for the unlimited to move as a whole. For if it moves even the smallest distance, it is necessary for it to do so in an unlimited time.⁷³ But then the heaven as a whole does go around and revolve in a circle in a limited time, so it goes around any line within it—for example, AB [Fig. 6].⁷⁴ It is impossible, therefore, for the body moving in a circle to be unlimited.

[*Argument 4*] Further, just as a line, in that respect in which is limited, cannot possibly be unlimited (or rather, if indeed it is, it is in length), a plane too, in that respect in which there is a limit, cannot be unlimited, and, if it is a definite one, it cannot be unlimited in any way—for example, a square, a circle, or a sphere cannot be unlimited, any more than a foot-long line can be.[75] If, then, neither a sphere nor a circle can be unlimited, and if there were no circle there would be no spatial movement in a circle, and similarly if there were no unlimited, there would be no unlimited spatial movement, then if there were no unlimited circle, there would be no unlimited body moving in a circle either.[76]

[*Argument 5*] Further, if C is the center, the line AB unlimited, E an unlimited line at right angles to it, and CD a moving line, CD will never get clear of E, but will always be in a situation like that of CE, since it cuts E at F [Fig. 7].[77] The unlimited line, therefore, will not go around the circle.

[*Argument 6*] Further, if the heaven is unlimited, and moves in a circle, it will have traversed the unlimited in a limited time. For let the heaven when remaining at rest be unlimited, and another heaven of equal magnitude be moving within it.[78] So if, being unlimited, it has indeed gone around in a circle, it has traversed an unlimited equal to itself in a limited time. But this, we saw, is impossible.[79]

[*Argument 7*] One can also state it conversely, namely, that if the time in which it has revolved is limited, it is necessary for the magnitude traversed to also be limited.[80] But it has traversed a magnitude equal to itself. Therefore, it too is limited.

That, then, the body moving in a circle is neither unending nor unlimited, but has an end, is evident.

I 6

Moreover, neither what spatially moves toward the center nor what moves away from the center will be unlimited:

[*Argument 1*] For spatial movements upward and downward are contraries, and contrary ones are to contrary places. And if one of two contraries is definite, the other will be definite too. But the center is definite. For wherever the body that sinks down spatially moves from, it cannot go farther than the center.[81] Since, then, the center is definite, the upper place must also be definite. But if the places are definite, that is to say, limited, the bodies will also be limited.[82] Further, if up and down are definite, it is necessary for what is intermediate to be definite too. For if it is not definite, movement would be unlimited. But that this

is impossible was shown previously.[83] Therefore, the middle is definite, so that a body that is in it, or that can come to be in it, is definite as well.[84] Moreover, the bodies spatially moving upward or downward can
20 come to be in it. For the one naturally moves away from the center, the other toward the center.[85] From these considerations, then, it is evident that there cannot possibly be an unlimited body.

[*Argument 2*] Also, in addition to these, if there is no unlimited heaviness, none of these bodies could be unlimited either. For it is necessary for the heaviness of an unlimited body to be unlimited too. (The
25 same argument will also apply in the case of lightness. For if heaviness is unlimited, lightness is as well, if what rises above is unlimited.) This is clear from the following:

For let weight be limited, and take an unlimited body AB, of weight C.[86] Then, let the limited magnitude BD be subtracted from the unlim
30 ited body, and let its weight be E. E then will be smaller than C. For the weight of the smaller body will be smaller. Let the smaller, then, taken as many times as you like, measure out the greater, and, as the smaller
273ᵇ1 weight is to the greater, let BD be to BF. For it is possible to subtract as much as one likes from the unlimited. Accordingly, if the magnitudes are proportional to the weights, and the smaller weight is of the smaller magnitude, the greater would also be of the greater one. Therefore, the
5 weight of the limited one and of the unlimited one will be equal.

Further, if the greater weight is of the greater body, the weight of GB will be greater than that of FB, so that the weight of the limited will be greater than that of the unlimited.[87] Also, the weight of unequal magnitudes will be the same. For the unlimited is equal to the limited.
10 And it makes no difference whether the weights are commensurable or incommensurable.[88] For the same argument will apply even if they are incommensurable. For example, if E, taken three times in measuring C, exceeds it.[89] For then three times the whole weight of the three magnitudes BD will be greater than that of C. So that there will be the same impossibility.[90]

Further, we can however assume them to be commensurable.
15 For it makes no difference whether one starts from the weight or from the magnitude. For example, if weight E is taken to be commensurable with C, and a magnitude, BD, of weight E is subtracted from the unlimited, then as weight is to weight, BD will be to some
20 other magnitude, BF. For if the magnitude is unlimited, it is possible to subtract as much as one likes. For both the magnitudes and the weights of the things taken will be commensurable with each other.

Nor indeed will it make any difference to the demonstration whether the magnitude has its weight uniformly or non-uniformly distributed.[91] For it is always possible to take bodies of equal weight to BD from the unlimited, subtracting or adding whatever one wishes.[92]   25

So it is clear from what has been said that the weight of an unlimited body will not be limited. Therefore, it is unlimited. If, then, this is impossible, it is also impossible for there to be an unlimited body.

[*Argument 3*] But that it is impossible for there to be an unlimited weight is evident from the following. For if a certain weight moves a certain distance in a certain time, a yet greater one will move the same   30 distance in a shorter time, and the proportion the weights have, the times will have in reverse—for example, if half the weight moves in a certain time, twice the weight will do so in half the time. Further, a lim-   274ᵃ1 ited weight will traverse any limited distance in a certain limited time. Therefore, it is necessary on the basis of this that if there is an unlimited weight, it must on the one hand move (insofar as it is as great as a limited one plus yet more), but on the other hand not move (insofar as it must move in proportion to the excess, though in the reverse way,   5 namely, the greater one in the shorter time).—But there is no ratio of the unlimited to the limited, while there is one of the shorter time to the greater limited [weight]. But perhaps [as the weight increases, it moves] in an ever shorter time. Yes, but there is no shortest time. Nor, if there were, would it be of any benefit. For some other limited weight   10 could have been taken in the same ratio in which the unlimited one stood to the other. So the unlimited weight would move the same distance in the same time as the limited one. But this is impossible.

Moreover, it is surely necessary, if indeed an unlimited weight can move in *any* limited time, for there to be another limited weight that will move a certain limited distance in the same time.   15

It is impossible, therefore, for there to be an unlimited heaviness, and similarly there cannot be unlimited lightness either. Therefore, bodies having unlimited heaviness or lightness are also impossible.

I 7

That there can be no unlimited body is clear through getting a theoretical grasp on the particular [simple bodies] in the foregoing way, and by a universal investigation not only in accord with the arguments   20 in our discussions concerning the starting-points (for there we previously determined in universal terms in what way the unlimited exists and in what way it does not exist), but now also in another way.[93] After this we must investigate whether, even if the body of the universe is not unlimited, it may nonetheless be enough for there to be several   25 heavens.[94] For perhaps someone might be puzzled about whether there is anything to prevent there being more than one other, composed just like the cosmos around us, though of course not an *unlimited* number.[95] First, though, let us speak in universal terms about the unlimited.

[*Argument 1*] It is necessary, then, for every body to be either
30   unlimited or limited, and if unlimited, either entirely homoeomerous or non-homoeomerous, and if non-homoeomerous, either composed of a limited number of forms (*eidos*) or of an unlimited number.[96] Now then, that it cannot be composed of an unlimited number is clear, if one will allow our first assumptions to stand.[97] For since the primary
274^{b}1   movements are limited, it is necessary for the forms (*idea*) of the simple bodies to also be limited. For the movement of a simple body is simple, and the simple movements are limited in number, and it is necessary for every natural body to have movement.[98]

5   On the other hand, at any rate if the unlimited is to be composed of a limited number [of forms], it is necessary for each of the parts to be unlimited—I mean, for example, water or fire.[99] But this is impossible. For it has been shown that neither heaviness nor lightness is unlimited.[100]

Further, it is necessary for their places to also be unlimited in magnitude, so that the movements of all of them must be unlimited as well.
10   But this is impossible, if we are to posit that our first assumptions are true, and that what spatially moves downward cannot possibly move without limit, nor, in accord with the same argument, can what spatially moves upward.[101] For it is impossible for what cannot have come to be to be coming to be, alike in quality, quantity, and in place.[102] I mean that if it is impossible for a thing to have come to be white, or a
15   cubit long, or in Egypt, it is also impossible for it to be coming to be any of these things. Therefore, it is impossible even to spatially move toward a place where no spatially moving thing is capable of arriving.

Further, even if they are dispersed, it might nonetheless still be thought possible for what is composed of all the particles [, for example,] of fire to be unlimited.[103] But body, we saw, is what has extension
20   in all ways.[104] So how could there possibly be several dissimilar bodies, each of which is unlimited? For each must be unlimited in all ways.

But then neither can the unlimited body be entirely homoeomerous. For, first, there is no other [rectilinear] movement besides these. It will, then, have one of these. But if this is so, it will follow that there
25   will be either unlimited heaviness or unlimited lightness. But then the body that spatially moves in a circle cannot be unlimited either. For it is impossible for the unlimited to spatially move in a circle. For there is no difference between saying this and saying that the heaven is unlimited, and this has been shown to be impossible.[105]

[*Argument 2*] But then it is in fact not possible for the unlimited to move at all. For it will move either in accord with nature or by force.[106] And if by force, there is also a movement that is in accord with nature for it, so that there will be another place of equal size toward which it will spatially move. But this is impossible.[107]

[*Argument 3*] That it is impossible in general for the unlimited to be affected in any way by the limited, or to affect the limited, is evident from the following. For let A be unlimited, B limited, C the time in which it moves or is moved. If, then, A is heated, pushed, or affected in some other way by B, or is moved in any way in the time C, let D be smaller than B, and let the smaller move a smaller in the same time. Let E be what has been altered by D. Then, as D is to B, E will be to some limited quantity. Let, then, the equal alter an equal in an equal time, the smaller a smaller in an equal one, and the greater a greater one—greater in the same proportion as the greater thing to the smaller one. Therefore, the unlimited will be moved by no limited thing in any time. For a smaller thing will be moved by another smaller one in an equal time, and what is proportional to it will be limited. For the unlimited stands in no ratio (*logos*) to the limited.

But then neither will the unlimited move the unlimited in any time. For let A be unlimited, B limited, and C the time in which [it does so]. Then D will move something smaller than B in C; let it be F. What BF as a whole is to F, then, let E stand in this ratio (*logos*) to D. Therefore, the limited and the unlimited will cause an [equal] alteration in an equal time. But this is impossible. For it was assumed that the greater does so in a shorter time.[108] Whatever time is taken, the result will be the same, so that there will be no time in which the unlimited will move something. But then it cannot move something or be moved in an *unlimited* time either. For it has no limit, whereas affecting and being affected do have one.[109]

Nor, then, can the unlimited be affected by the unlimited in any way. Let A and B be unlimited and CD the time in which B was affected by A. Then, since the whole of B was affected, E, which is a part of the unlimited, will not be affected to the same extent in an equal time. For let it be assumed that the smaller is changed in a shorter time. Let E have been moved by A in D. Then what D is to CD, E is to some limited part of B. Therefore, it is necessary for this to be moved by A in time CD. For let it be assumed that the greater and smaller things will be affected in a longer and a shorter time by the same thing, when they are determined in proportion to the time. Therefore, there is no limited time in which the unlimited can be moved by the unlimited. Therefore, it must be in

30

275ᵃ1

5

10

15

20

25

30

275ᵇ1

an unlimited one. But an unlimited time does not have an end, whereas what has been moved does have [an end of its movement].

Therefore, if every perceptible body has the capacity to affect, or be affected, or both, an unlimited body cannot be perceptible. Moreover, whatever bodies are in a place, at any rate, are also perceptible.[110] Therefore, there is no unlimited body outside the heaven; nor yet is there one that is so up to a certain point.[111] Therefore, there is no body at all outside the heaven. For if it is intelligible, it will be in a place.[112] For "outside" and "inside" signify place.[113] So it will be perceptible. But nothing perceptible is not in a place.

[*Argument 4*] It is also possible to attack the issue in a more logico-linguistic way as follows.[114] For the unlimited, when homoeomerous, cannot move in a circle.[115] For there is no center of the unlimited, whereas what moves in a circle moves around the center. But then neither can the unlimited spatially move in straight line. For there would need to be another just as large (that is, unlimited) place that it will spatially move toward in accord with nature, and a distinct one, just as large, that it will move toward contrary to nature.[116]

[*Argument 5*] Further, whether it has its rectilinear movement by nature or by force, either way there will need to be a mover of unlimited strength to move it. For the unlimited strength is that of the unlimited and the strength of the unlimited is unlimited. So there will also be an unlimited mover (there is an argument in the discussions concerning movement that nothing limited has unlimited capacity and nothing unlimited has limited capacity).[117] If, then, what can be moved in accord with nature can also be moved contrary to nature, there will be two unlimited things, the one that is a mover in this way and the one that is a moved.[118]

[*Argument 6*] Further, what is the mover of the unlimited? If it moves itself, it will be animate.[119] But how is it possible for there to be an unlimited animal? But if its mover is something else, there will be two unlimited things, the mover and the moved, differing in shape and capacity.[120]

If the universe is not continuous, but rather, as Leucippus and Democritus say, divided into particles by the void, it is necessary for there to be one [sort of] movement for all things.[121] For the particles are determined by their shapes [= forms], but, they say, the nature of each of them is one nature, as if each one were a separate piece of gold.[122] Of these, though, as we say, it is necessary for there to be the same [sort of] movement. For where a single clod of earth spatially moves to, the totality of earth does as well, and both the totality of fire and a single spark spatially move to the same place.[123] So none of these bodies will be unconditionally light, if all have heaviness, whereas if all have light-ness, none will be heavy.[124] Further, whether they have heaviness or lightness, there will be some extremity or some center of the universe. But this is impossible if *it* is unlimited.

In general, where there is neither center nor extremity, and neither up nor down, there will be no place for the spatial movement of bodies. And if there is not this, there will not be movement. For it is necessary for things to move either in accord with nature or contrary to nature, and these are determined by their proper places, and by those of the others.

Further, if there is a place where a thing remains at rest or to which it spatially moves contrary to nature, it is necessary for there to be something else for which this place is in accord with nature (one may be convinced of this on the basis of induction).[125] It is necessary, then, that not everything have heaviness (or lightness), but rather for some to have it, and others not to have it.

That the body of the universe is not unlimited, therefore, is evident from these considerations.

<h1 style="text-align:center">I 8</h1>

Let us now say why there cannot be several heavens either. For we said that this must be investigated, in case someone thinks that it has not been shown universally about all bodies that it is impossible for any of them at all to exist outside the cosmos, but that the argument applies only to those with no definite position.[126]

[*Argument 1*] For all things both remain at rest and move both in accord with nature and by force, and, where they remain at rest not by force, they also spatially move to in accord with nature, and where they spatially move to [in accord with nature], they also remain at rest [not by force]; on the other hand, where they remain at rest by force, they also spatially move to by force, and where they spatially move to by force, they also remain at rest by force. Further, if this spatial movement is by force, its contrary is in accord with nature. If, then, earth will spatially move by force from there to the center here, it will spatially move in accord with nature from here to there; and if earth from there remains at rest here not by force, it will spatially move here in accord with nature too.[127] But the spatial movement that is in accord with nature is a single one.[128]

Further, it is necessary for all the cosmoses, being admittedly similar in nature, to be composed of the same bodies.[129] But then it is necessary for each body to have the same capacity—I mean, for example, fire and

276ᵇ1   earth and the ones intermediate between them.¹³⁰ For if these are hom-
          onyms and are not said of things there in accord with the same form
          as those among us, then the universe too would be said to be a cosmos
          homonymously.¹³¹ It is clear, therefore, that one of them must spatially
          move naturally away from the center, while another does so toward the
5   center, if indeed all fire is the same in form as other fire (and also each
          of the others), just as the parts of fire are in this cosmos.

          That this is so of necessity is evident from our hypotheses about
          movement. For the movements are limited, and each of the elements
          is said to be what it is with reference to one of the movements. So if
10   indeed movements are in fact the same, it is necessary for the elements
          too to be everywhere the same.

          [*Argument 2*] Therefore, the parts of earth in another cosmos will
          be naturally such as to spatially move toward the center of this one,
          and fire there toward the extremity of this one. But this is impossible.
          For if this happens, it is necessary for earth in its own cosmos to spa-
15   tially move upward, and fire toward the center. Similarly, the earth
          here will move in accord with nature away from the center in moving
          toward the center there, because of the way the cosmoses are posi-
          tioned in relation to each other. For either we must not posit that the
          simple bodies have the same nature in the several heavens, or in say-
          ing that they do, it is necessary to make a unique center and a unique
20   extremity. But if this is so, there cannot be more than one cosmos.

          But then to think that the nature of the simple bodies is different the
          more or less distant they are from their proper places is unreasonable.
          For what difference will it make to say that they are this distant or that
          distant? They will differ in proportion (*logos*) to the distance, but their
25   form will remain the same.

          [*Argument 3*] Moreover, it is necessary for the simple bodies to
          have some movement. For that they do move is evident. Are we to
          say, then, that all their movements are by force, even contrary ones?
          But what does not naturally move at all cannot be moved by force. If,
          therefore, some movement in accord with nature belongs to them, it
          is necessary for the movement of particular ones that are the same in
30   form to be toward a place that is one in number—for example, toward
          this center and *this* extremity. But if they are toward places that are the
          same in form, but many (because as particulars they are in fact many,
277ᵃ1   but in form each is undifferentiated [from the others]), then there will
          not be such [a place] for one but not for another of the parts, but for
          all alike.¹³² For all are alike undifferentiated in form, although any one
          is distinct in number from any other. What I mean is this: if the parts
          here behave in a similar way both toward each other and toward the

ones in another cosmos, then one taken from here will not behave differently toward the ones in another cosmos than toward those in its own, but in a similar way. So either it is necessary for these assumptions to be altered, or it is necessary for there to be a unique center and a unique extremity. But if this is so, then, by the same proofs and the same necessities, there must also be only one heaven and not several.[133]

[*Argument 4*] That there is a certain place that it is natural for earth to spatially move toward, and also one for fire, is clear from other [sorts of change]. For, in general, what moves changes from something to something, and these—the from which and the to which—differ in form. And all change is limited—for example, what becomes healthy changes from sickness to health, and what increases changes from smallness to largeness.[134] So too for what spatially moves. For it too comes to be somewhere from somewhere. Therefore, what it naturally moves from and to must differ in form, just as what becomes healthy [does not change to] some random destination, nor to whichever one the mover wishes.[135]

Therefore, fire—and earth too—spatially moves not without limit but toward opposite points. But with respect to place up is opposed to down, so that these will be the limits of spatial movement. (Since even spatial movement in a circle has in a way opposite points, namely, the endpoints of its diameter, though to the whole movement nothing is contrary, so even for these the movement is in a certain way toward opposite and limited points.[136]) Therefore, it is necessary for it to have some end and not spatially move without limit.

A proof of there being no spatial movement without limit is that earth, the closer it gets to the center the faster it spatially moves, while fire does so the closer it gets to the upper place.[137] But if the spatial movement were without limit, its speed would be unlimited too, and if the speed were, so too would be the heaviness and the lightness involved. For just as a thing that is lower than another because of its speed is fast because of its heaviness, so if the increase in heaviness were unlimited, the increase in speed would be unlimited as well.[138]

[*Argument 5*] But then neither could they be moved upward and downward by something else, nor by force or by squeezing out, as some people say.[139] For then more fire would move more slowly upward and more earth more slowly downward. As things stand, however, the contrary always happens: more fire, or more earth, spatially moves faster to its own place. Nor would it spatially move faster toward the end if it were by force and squeezing out. For everything spatially moves more

slowly the farther it gets from what did the forcing, and what it spatially moves from by force, it spatially moves to not by force. So by getting a theoretical grasp on these points it is possible to get adequately
convinced about what is being said.

[*Argument 6*] Further, [that there is a unique heaven] might also be
shown by means of the arguments from primary philosophy, and from
movement in a circle, which is necessarily eternal both here and in
other cosmoses as well.¹⁴⁰

[*Argument 7*] It should also be clear to those who investigate in the
following way that it is necessary for there to be a unique heaven. For
since there are three corporeal elements, the places of the elements will
also be three, one around the center for the body that sinks, another
for the body that spatially moves in a circle, which is the extremity,
and a third intermediate between them for the middle body.¹⁴¹ For it is
necessary for what rises above to be in this one. For if it is not in this
one, it will be outside. But it is impossible for it to be outside. For one is
without heaviness, the other has heaviness, and the lower place is that
of the body that has heaviness (if indeed that of what is heavy is toward
the center). Moreover, it could not be so contrary to nature. For then
it will be in accord with nature for another one; but there is, as we saw,
no other one. Therefore, it is necessary for it to be in the intermediate
place. What the differentiae (*diaphora*) of this place are, we shall say
later.¹⁴²

Concerning the bodily elements, then, what sort they are and how
many, and what the place of each is, and further, in general, how many
in number the places are, is clear to us from what has been said.

I 9

That the heaven is not only unique, but that there cannot come to be
more, and, further, that it is eternal, being incapable of coming to be
and of passing away, we should now state, first of all going through
the puzzles about this.¹⁴³

For it might seem to those who investigate in the following way that
there cannot be one, unique heaven. For in everything that is constituted and has come to be by nature or by craft, the shape [= form] taken
intrinsically and the shape mixed together with the matter are distinct.
For example, the form of the sphere and the gold or bronze sphere are
distinct; and, again, the shape of the circle and a brazen or wooden
circle are distinct. For in stating the essence for sphere or for circle we
do not mention bronze or gold in the account, on the supposition that
these are not [parts] of its substance (whereas if we are speaking of the

brazen or golden one, we do mention it, also if we cannot understand   5
or grasp any other, beyond the particular one).[144] For sometimes nothing prevents this from happening—for example, if only one circle were
grasped.[145] For the being for circle will be no less distinct from the being
for this circle, and the one is the form, whereas the other is the form in
the matter, that is, one of the particulars.[146]

Since, then, the heaven is perceptible, it will be one of the particulars.   10
For everything particular is in matter. But if it is one of the particulars,
the being for this heaven and the being for heaven unconditionally will
be distinct. Therefore, this heaven and heaven unconditionally will be
distinct, and the latter as being form and shape, the former as being
mixed with matter. But of what there is a certain shape or form of,
there either is or can come to be many particular instances. For if there   15
are Forms, as some say, it is necessary for this to result—and no less so
if nothing of this sort is separable.[147] For we see in all cases in which
the substance [= essence] is in matter that things of the same form
are several, indeed unlimited in number. So either there are or can be
several heavens.   20

On the basis of these considerations, then, one might suppose either
that there are or that there can be several heavens. We must go back,
however, and investigate which of these is correctly stated and which
incorrectly.

That the account of the shape [= form] without the matter and of the
one in the matter are distinct is correctly stated, and let it be true. But
nonetheless there is no necessity because of this for there to be several   25
cosmoses, nor even that several can come to be, if indeed this one is
composed of the totality of matter, as in fact it is.

What is being said will perhaps be clearer put in the following way.
For if aquilinity is curvature in a nose, or in other words, in flesh, and
if flesh is matter for aquilinity, then if of the totality of flesh one [parcel
of] flesh were to come to be composed, and the aquiline belonged to   30
it, nothing else either would or could be aquiline.[148] Similarly, if fleshes
and bones are matter for what is human, if of the totality of flesh and
of all the bones a human were to come to be composed in a way incapable of dissolution, it would be impossible for another human being
to come to be. And similarly in other cases. For in general, nothing   35
whose substance [= essence] is in some underlying matter can come to   **278ᵇ1**
be without there being some matter.

The heaven is certainly one of the particulars and one of the things
composed of matter. But if it is composed not of a part of matter but of
the totality of it, the being for the heaven itself and for this heaven are   5
distinct, yet it is not the case either that there is another one or even

that several could come to be, because this one includes the totality of the matter. It remains, therefore, to show this: that the heaven is composed of the totality of natural and perceptible body.

Let us first state what we say it is to be a heaven and in how many ways, in order that what we are inquiring into will become clearer to us.[149]

In one way, then, [1] we say that the substance belonging to the outermost revolution of the universe is heaven, or the natural body that is on the outermost revolution of the universe, since more than anything else it is the last upper region that we usually call heaven, the one in which we say that everything divine also has its seat.

In another way, [2] it is the body that is continuous with outermost revolution of the universe, in which we find the moon, the sun, and some of the stars, since we say that these bodies too are in the heaven.

Further, [3] we say that the body that is encompassed by the outermost revolution is heaven, since we are accustomed to say that the whole and the universe is heaven.

Heaven is said, then, in three ways. The whole encompassed by the outermost revolution is of necessity composed of the totality of natural perceptible body, because there neither is nor can be any body outside the heaven.

For if there is a natural body outside the outermost revolution, it is necessary for it to be either one of the simple ones or one of the composite ones, and for it to be there either in accord with nature or contrary to nature. But it could not be one of the simple ones. For it has been shown that the one that spatially moves in a circle cannot change its own place.[150] But then neither can it be the one that moves from the center nor the one that sinks. For they could not be there in accord with nature (for other places are proper for them), while if indeed they are there contrary to nature, the place outside will be natural for some other body. For what is contrary to nature for it is of necessity in accord with nature for something else. But there is, we saw, no other body beyond these.[151] Therefore it is not possible for any of the simple bodies to be outside the heaven. But if none of the simple ones can be, neither can any of the mixed ones. For where a mixed one is, it is necessary for simple ones to be as well.

Moreover, neither can a body come to be there. For it will do so either in accord with nature or contrary to nature, and it will be either simple or mixed, so that, again, the same argument will apply. For it makes no difference whether one investigates if it is, or if it can come to be.

It is evident, therefore, from what has been said that no corporeal mass either is or can come to be outside [the heaven]. For the total cosmos is composed of the totality of its proper matter. For its matter is natural perceptible body.[152] So neither are there now several heavens, nor have there been, nor can there come to be. On the contrary, this   10 heaven is one, unique, and complete.[153]

At the same time it is clear that there is neither place, nor void, nor time outside the heaven. For in every place body can exist; void, they say, is that in which body does not exist, but in which it can; and time is a number of movement, and there is no movement without natural body.[154] But it has been shown that outside the heaven there neither is   15 nor can be body.[155] Therefore it is evident that there is neither place nor void outside it.

That is why things that are there are naturally such as not to be in place, nor does time age them, nor is there any change for any of the things that are stationed above the outermost spatial movement, instead, unalterable and unaffectable, having the best and most self-   20 sufficient life, they are attaining their end throughout all eternity (*aiôn*).[156] —And in fact this name *aiôn* was given utterance by the ancients in a divinely inspired way. For the end that encompasses the time of a given thing's life, outside of which nothing exists in accord with nature, is called the *aiôn* ("lifetime") of it. And by the same argu- ment, the end of the entire heaven too, that is, the end that encom-   25 passes all of time and the unlimited, is *aiôn* ("eternity"), immortal and divine, deriving its name from its always being (*aiei einai*). — From it too derive the being and life for other things, for some in a more exact way, for others in a more obscure one.

And in fact, just as in the philosophical works in circulation   30 about things divine, it is often brought to light by arguments that whatever is divine, whatever is primary and highest, is necessarily unchangeable.[157] The fact that this is so attests to what has been said. For neither is there anything else greater that will move it (for then that thing would be more divine), nor has it any defect, nor does it lack any of the noble things proper to it.[158] That it is moved with an unceasing movement is also reasonable. For everything ceases mov-   279^{b}1 ing when it arrives at its proper place, but, in the case of the body that moves in a circle, the place it starts from and at which it ends are the same.

I 10

Having determined these matters, let us say next whether it is inca- pable of coming to be or capable of coming to be, and incapable of passing away or capable of passing away, having first gone through   5 the suppositions of others.[159] For in the case of contrary ones the demonstrations belonging to one lot are puzzles for the contrary lot.[160] At the same time, what we are about to say will also be more convincing to people who have previously heard the pleas of the arguments disputing them.[161] For then we will less seem to be securing a favorable judgment by default. And in fact those who are going to judge the truth adequately must be arbitrators rather than legal opponents.[162]

Everyone says, then, that it has come to be, but some say that having come to be it is eternal, while others say that it is capable of passing away, just like any of the other things that are put together; still others say that it is alternately sometimes in the one state and other times in the other (passing away), and it continues being like this always, as Empedocles of Acragas and Heraclitus of Ephesus say.[163]

[*Argument 1*] To state that it has come to be but is nonetheless eternal is to state impossible things. For it is reasonable that one must posit only those things that we see to hold in many or in all cases, and in this one it is the contrary that happens. For it is evident that everything that comes to be also passes away.

[*Argument 2*] Further, what has no starting-point of its present state, but rather was incapable of being otherwise throughout the entirety of its previous lifetime, is also incapable of changing. For there is some cause [of its change], and if this had obtained previously, what is incapable of being in another state would have been capable of being in another state.

[*Argument 3*] If the cosmos was composed of things that were previously in another state, if they were always this way, and incapable of being in a different state, it would not have come to be, whereas, if it did come to be, it is clearly also necessary for these things to be capable of being in a different state and cannot always be in the same one. So what has been composed will be dissolved and was composed of things that were in a state of dissolution beforehand. And this either has taken place, or is capable of having taken place, an unlimited number of times. But if this is so, it will not be incapable of passing away, whether it was in another state at some time or capable of being in another state.

[*Argument 4*] The aid with which some of those who say that the cosmos came to be but is incapable of passing away attempt to support their case is not a true one.[164] For they say that they speak about coming to be in a similar way to those who draw geometrical diagrams, not as of something coming to be at some time, but rather for the sake of teaching, on the supposition that it makes things easier to come to know, just as the diagram does for those who see it coming to be. But the two cases, as we say, are not the same. For in the production of geometrical diagrams, if everything is assumed to exist at the same time, what results is the same, whereas in the demonstrations these people give it is not the same—it cannot be. For the earlier and later assumptions are contrary ones. For they say that ordered things came from disordered ones, yet things cannot be ordered and disordered at the same time. Instead, it is necessary for there to be a process of coming to be separating the two, as well as a period of time. In geometrical diagrams, by contrast, nothing is separated by time. That it is, then, impossible for it [the cosmos] to be at once eternal and have come to be is evident.

[*Argument 5*] Having it be alternately composed and dissolved is doing nothing other than establishing it as eternal but changing its shape, just as if one thought that a man coming to be from a boy or a boy from a man is at one time passing away and at another is in being.[165] For it is clear that, whenever the elements are coming together with each other, it is not any random order and composition that comes to be, but rather the same one, especially according to those who state this account, since they assign to each of the two dispositions [of the elements] a contrary cause.[166] So if the whole body, being continuous, is at one time disposed and ordered in this way and at another in that, and the composition of the whole is a cosmos, that is, a heaven, then the cosmos would not come to be and pass away, but its dispositions would.[167]

[*Argument 6*] And it is impossible that, having come to be, it passed away as a whole, without making a return, since it is one.[168] For before it came to be, the composition before it always existed, and, not having come to be, cannot (we say) change.[169] If there are an unlimited number [of cosmoses], however, this is more possible.[170] Nonetheless, whether even this is impossible or possible will be clear from later considerations.[171]

Indeed, there are some people to whom it seems possible both for something that is incapable of coming to be to pass away, and for something that has come to be to persist, incapable of passing away, as in the *Timaeus*. For there he says that while the heaven came to be, nonetheless it will always be for the remainder of time.[172]

In relation to these [thinkers] we have spoken about the heaven only in natural scientific terms, but when we have investigated everything in universal ones, things will be clear about this issue too.[173]

I 11

But first of all we must distinguish the ways in which we say things are
280^b1 incapable of coming to be, capable of coming to be, capable of passing away, and incapable of passing away.[174] For these are said of things
in many ways, and even if this makes no difference to the argument,
thought will be indefinite if one uses what is divided in many ways as
undivided.[175] For it is unclear with reference to which nature what is
5 said applies to it.[176]

[1a] Something is said in one way to be incapable of coming to
be if it is now but previously was not, without any coming to be or
change, as is the case, some people say, with being in contact and being
in movement.[177] For there is not, they say, a coming to be of being in
contact or being in movement. [1b] In another way, if something can
come to be, or have come to be, but is not. For this too did not come to
10 be, because it can come to be [but did not do so]. [1c] In another way,
something is incapable of coming to be if it is wholly incapable of coming to be, so that it is at one time and is not at another. (For something
is said to be incapable [of this] in two ways: [1c–i] because of its not
being true that it could come to be; or [1c–ii] because of its not doing
so easily, quickly, or well.[178])

It is the same way too with capable of coming to be. [2b] Something
is capable of coming to be in one way if it previously is not but later
15 is: whether having come to be or without coming to be, it is not at one
time, but is at another. [2c] In another, if it is capable [of coming to be],
defining being capable of it either [2c–i] in terms of its being true that
it can, or [2c–ii] in terms of its doing so easily. [2a] In another, if there
is a coming to be of it from not being to being, whether—because of
coming to be—it already is, or is not yet, but can be.

And capable of passing away and incapable of passing away are
20 [said of things] in like manner. For [3] whether something that previously is, later is not, or can not be, we say it is capable of passing
away, whether [3a] it is passing away and changing at some time, or
[3b] not. [3c–i] Sometimes too we say that what—because of passing
away—can not be is capable of passing away, and in a yet other way,
[3c–ii] what easily passes away—what is "prone to passing away," as
one might say.

And the same account applies to incapable of passing away. For
25 it is either [4a] what without passing away is at one time but is not
at another—for example, points of contact, because, without passing
away, these are previously but later are not. Or it is [4b] what is, but
is capable of not being, or what will not be at some time but now is.[179]

For [4b] you and [4a] the point of contact are now; nonetheless, both are capable of passing away, because there will be a time at which it is not true to say that you are, or that these things are making contact. [3c–i] But most strictly speaking [what is incapable of passing away] is what now is and is incapable of passing away in such a way that it now is but later is not or can not be.[180] Or else it is [3b] what has not yet passed away, but can not be later on. And something is also said to be incapable of passing away when [3c–ii] it does not pass away easily.

If these things are indeed so, in what ways we say things are capable and incapable must be investigated.[181] For we say that something is incapable of passing away most strictly speaking because it is incapable of passing away, and cannot at one time be and at another not be. And what is incapable of coming to be is also said to be incapable, that is, not capable of coming to be in such a way that previously it is not and later it is—for example, the commensurable diameter.[182]

But if indeed something is capable of moving, or of lifting a weight, we always say so with reference to the greatest one—for example, of lifting one hundred talents or walking one hundred stades (although it is also capable of doing the parts within it, if indeed it is capable of doing the maximum), as the capacity must be defined in relation to the end, that is, the maximum.[183] It is necessary, then, for what is capable of the maximum to be capable of what is within it—for example, if one is capable of lifting one hundred talents, one is also capable of lifting two, and if capable of walking one hundred stades, one is also capable of walking two. But the capacity is a capacity for the maximum. And if something is incapable of doing so-and-so much, speaking with reference to a maximum, it is also incapable of greater ones—for example, if a person is incapable of walking one thousand stades it is clear that he is also incapable of walking one thousand-and-one.

None of this, though, should trouble us. For let what is capable in the strict sense be defined by the end in the sense of the maximum. For perhaps someone might object that what has been said is not necessarily so. For a person who sees a stade will not also see the magnitudes within it; on the contrary, it is rather the case that a person who is capable of seeing a point or of hearing a small sound will also perceive greater ones. But this makes no difference to the argument. For let the maximum be defined either with respect to the capacity or with respect to the thing [it is a capacity for]. For what is being said is clear: for while sight reaches its maximum in relation to the smallest thing, speed reaches its maximum in relation to the greater distance.

I 12

Having made these determinations, what comes next must be discussed. If, accordingly, some things are capable of being and of not
being, it is necessary that there be some greatest time determined both
for their being and for their not being, I mean, during which the thing
at issue is capable of being and of not being, with respect to any category—for example, [being or not being] human, white, three-cubits
long, or anything else of this sort.[184] For if there will not be a certain
quantity [of time], but always a longer one than any proposed and
none than which it is shorter, the thing will be capable of being for an
unlimited time, and of not being for another unlimited time—but this
is impossible.[185]

[*Argument 1*] Let our starting-point be the following: Impossible
and false do not signify the same thing.[186] However, there is an impossible and possible, a false and a true, that are based on a hypothesis
(I mean, for example, it is impossible for a triangle to contain two
right angles and it is possible for the diameter to be commensurable,
if these things hold).[187] But there are also things that are possible and
impossible, false and true, unconditionally. It is not the same thing,
then, for something to be unconditionally false and to be unconditionally impossible. For to say, when you are not standing, that you
are standing is false, but not impossible. Similarly, to say that a person
playing the lyre, but not singing, is singing is false, but not impossible. But for someone to be standing and sitting at the same time,
and for the diagonal to be commensurable, is not only false, but
also impossible. It is not the same thing, then, to assume something
false and something impossible. But the impossible results from the
impossible.

A person does of course at the same time have the capacity for sitting and for standing, because when he has the one, he also has the
other—not so as to be sitting and standing at the same time, though,
but rather at distinct times. But if something has a capacity for several things for an unlimited time, it cannot be [to do them] at distinct
times, but at the same time.

So if for an unlimited time something is capable of passing away, it
would have the capacity for not being. If, then, it has it for an unlimited time, let what it is capable of doing be realized. At the same time,
therefore, it will actively be and not be at the same time.[188] A falsehood would result, then, because a falsehood was assumed. But if
what was assumed was not impossible, the result would not actually

be impossible. Therefore everything that always is, is unconditionally incapable of passing away.[189]

Similarly, it is also incapable of coming to be. For if it is capable of coming to be, it will be capable of not being at some time. For while a capable of passing away thing is one that is previously, but now is not or can not be at some later time, a capable of coming to be one is one that can previously not be. But there is no time in which what always is, is capable of not being, whether for an unlimited or for a limited one. For it is also capable of being in a limited time, if indeed it is in fact capable of being in an unlimited one. Therefore one and the same thing cannot be capable of being always and of not being always. Moreover, the negation is not possible either, I mean, not always being. Therefore, it is also impossible for something to always be and to be capable of passing away. Neither, similarly, is it capable of coming to be. For of two terms, if it is impossible for the posterior one to hold [of something] without the prior one, and if it is impossible for the prior one to hold, it is also impossible for the posterior one to hold.[190] So if what always is cannot at some time not be, it also cannot be capable of coming to be.

[*Argument 2*] And since the negation of "what is always capable of being" is "what is not always capable of being," while its contrary is "what is always capable of not being," the negation of which is "what is not always capable of not being," it is necessary for the negations of both to belong to the same thing, and that it be intermediate between what always is and what always is not, capable of being and of not being. For the negation of each will belong to it at some time, if not always. So if *what not always is not* will be at some time and not be at some time, clearly *what is capable of not always being but is at some time* will as well, so that it too will not be. Therefore the same thing will be capable of being and of not being, and it is intermediate between the two.

The universal argument is this: Let A and B be incapable of belonging to the same thing, and let A or C and B or D belong to everything.[191] It is then necessary that C and D belong to everything that is neither A nor B. Then let E be intermediate between A and B (for what is neither of two contraries is intermediate). It is necessary, then, for both C and D to belong to it. For A or C belongs to everything, so that one of them will also belong to E. Since, then, it is impossible that A belong to it, C will belong to it. The same argument also applies to D.

Neither what always is, then, nor what always is not is either capable of coming to be or capable of passing away. But it is clear too that if

25

30

282ᵃ1

5

10

15

20

something is capable of coming to be or capable of passing away, it is not eternal. For it will at the same time be capable of always being and capable of not always being; but that this is impossible was shown previously.[192]

Always being   Always not being
     A   B

Capable of coming to be

Not always being   Not always not being
     C   D

[Fig. 8]

[*Argument 3*] If, then, something is incapable of coming to be, but is, is it necessary for it to be eternal, and likewise if something is incapable of passing away, but is? (I mean incapable of coming to be and incapable of passing away strictly speaking: something incapable of coming to be is now and previously it was not true to say that it is not; something incapable of passing away is now and it will not be true to say later that it is not.)

Or, rather, if these things follow along with each other, and what is incapable of coming to be is incapable of passing away and what is incapable of passing away is incapable of coming to be, then it is necessary for eternality to follow along with each of them, and whether something is incapable or incapable of passing away, it is eternal. This is also clear from the definition of them. For necessarily if something is capable of passing away, it is capable of coming to be. For it is either incapable of coming to be or capable of coming to be. But if it is incapable of coming to be, it has been established that it is incapable of passing away.[193] And if it is capable of coming to be, then it is necessarily capable of passing away. For either it is capable of passing away or incapable of passing away. But if it is incapable of passing away, it has been established that it is incapable of coming to be.[194] If, on the other hand, incapable of passing away and incapable of coming to be do not follow along with each other, it is not necessary for either what is incapable of coming to be or what is incapable of passing away to be eternal.

But that it is necessary for them to follow along is evident from the following considerations. For capable of coming to be and capable of passing away follow along with each other. This too is clear from the previous [arguments]. For intermediate between what always is and

what always is not is what follows along with neither of them, and it   10
is what is capable of coming to be and capable of passing away. For
each is capable of being and of not being for a definite time (I mean
each of being for a quantity of time and of not being [for a quantity
of time]).

If, therefore, something is capable of coming to be or capable of
passing away, it is necessary for it to be intermediate. For let A be
what always is, B what always is not, C what is capable of coming to   15
be, and D what is perishable [Fig. 9]. It is necessary, then, for C to be
intermediate between A and B. For there is no time in the direction
of either limit in which either A was not or B was.[195] But for what is
capable of coming to be it is necessary that there be such a time either
actively or potentially, and for A and B there is not one in either way.
Therefore it [= C] will be, and again not be, for some definite quantity   20
of time. And likewise too in the case of D. Therefore each of the two
is capable of coming to be and capable of passing away. Therefore
capable of coming to be and capable of passing away follow along
with each other.

Always being   Capable of coming to be
A   C

Capable of passing away   Always not-being
D   B
[Fig. 9]

Now let E be incapable of coming to be, F be capable of coming to
be, G be incapable of passing away, and H be capable of passing away.
As for F and H, it has been shown that they follow along with each   25
other.[196] But whenever things are established to be related as these are,
such that F and H follow along with each other, and E and F never
belong to the same thing, but one or the other belongs to everything,
and likewise for G and H, then it is also necessary that E and G follow
along with each other. For let E not follow along with G. Therefore F
will follow along with G, since E or F belongs to everything. But then   30
H also belongs to whatever F belongs to. Therefore H will follow along
with G. But it has been established that this is impossible. The same
argument shows too that E follows along with G.   283ᵃ1

Moreover, the same relation holds between what is incapable of
coming to be, E, and what is capable of coming to be, F, as between the

incapable of passing away, G, and what is capable of passing away, H [Fig. 10].

Incapable of coming to be	Capable of coming to be
E	F
Incapable of passing away	Capable of passing away
G	H

[Fig. 10]

To say that nothing prevents something that comes to be from being capable of passing away, or something incapable of coming to be from having passed away, if in the one case coming to be and in the other the passing away occurs only once, is to do away with one of the things that have been granted. For all things are capable either of affecting or of being affected, of being or of not being, for either an unlimited or for some definite quantity of time (and an unlimited one [simply] because of this, namely, because the unlimited is in a way definite, being what nothing is greater than).[197] What is unlimited in some way, then, is neither unlimited nor definite.[198]

Further, what more [cause] did what previously always was have to pass away, or what previously always was not to come to be, at this point [in time than any other]? For if there was no more, and the points are unlimited [in number], it is clear that for an unlimited time something was capable of coming to be and capable of passing away. Therefore, it was capable of not being for an unlimited time. Therefore, it will at the same time have a capacity for not being and for being— beforehand, if it is capable of passing away, afterward if it is capable of coming to be.[199] So if we suppose the things it is capable of to be realized, contraries will belong to it at the same time.

Further, these things will belong to it alike at every point in time, so that for an unlimited time it will have a capacity for not being and for being; but it has been shown that this is impossible.[200]

Further, if the capacity belongs to it prior to its activation, it will belong to it for the entirety of time, even when it had not come to be and was not—the unlimited time in which it is capable of coming to be.[201] At the same time, then, it was not and had a capacity for being, both for being then and later on—therefore, for an unlimited time.

It is also evident in another way that [that the unlimited is incapable of passing away, because it is evident that] it is impossible for what is capable of passing away not to have passed away at some time.[202] For it

will always be at the same time both capable of passing away and not   25
actually passed away.²⁰³ So at the same time it will be capable of always
being and of not always being. Therefore what is capable of passing
away passes away at some time. And if it is capable of coming to be, it
has come to be [at some time]. For it was capable of having come to be,
and therefore of not always being.

It can also be seen in the following way that it is impossible either
for what has come to be at some time to persist, incapable of passing
away, or for what is incapable of coming to be and previously always   30
was to pass away. For nothing can be by chance either incapable of
passing away or incapable of coming to be.²⁰⁴ For what is by chance or
by luck is beyond what always or for the most part either is or comes
to be.²⁰⁵ But what is for an unlimited time, whether unconditionally   283ᵇ1
or from a certain point, belongs either always or for the most part.
Therefore it is necessarily by nature that things of this sort are at some
times and not at others. And in things of this sort the same capacity
is for what is contradictory, and the matter is the cause of their being
and not being.²⁰⁶ So it is necessary for opposites to belong actively too   5
at the same time.²⁰⁷

Moreover, it is not true to say of anything now that it *is* last year, or
of something last year that it *is* now.²⁰⁸ Therefore, it is impossible for
what is not at some time to be eternal at a later one. For later it will also
have the capacity for not being—except not for *not-being*-at-the-time-
when-it-is (for then actively being will belong to it), but last year or
in time past. Let, then, what it is a capacity for belong to it actively. It   10
will, therefore, be true to say of it now that it *is not* last year. But this is
impossible. For there is no capacity for having come to be, but [only]
for being now or being in the future. Likewise, if previously it is eternal and later will not be. For it will have a capacity for something that
actively is not. So if we suppose what it is capable of to be realized, it   15
will be true to say now that it *is* last year and, in general, in time past.

And if we investigate in a natural scientific way, and not in universal
terms, it will be impossible either for something that previously eternally is to pass away later, or for what previously is not to be eternal
later on. For things that are capable of coming to be and capable of
passing away are all alterable as well.²⁰⁹ But they are altered by their   20
contraries, and the things from which natural beings are composed are
also the same ones by which they are caused to pass away.

Book II

II 1

It is possible to obtain the conviction that the entire heaven has neither come to be nor is it possible for it to pass away, as some people say it is, but is one and eternal, having neither starting-point nor end of its entire eternity, on the basis of what has been said, and by means of the doctrine of those who speak otherwise by having it come to be. For if it is possible for things to be as we say, but not possible for them to be in the way described by those who say it comes to be, this should add great weight to the conviction about its being immortal and eternal.

That is why it is well to convince oneself that the ancient accounts, especially those of our forefathers, are true, namely, that there is something immortal and divine among the things that have movement, having movement of such a sort that there is no limit to it, but rather it is the limit of the others. For the limit belongs to what encompasses, and this movement, being complete, encompasses the incomplete movements, which have a limit and a cessation, while it itself has neither a start nor an end, but rather is unceasing throughout unlimited time, and is the cause of the start of the others, and receives their cessation.[210]

The ancients assigned the heaven, that is, the upper place, to the gods on the supposition that it alone is immortal. And the present account testifies to its being incapable of passing away and incapable of coming to be, and, further, to its being unaffectable by all mortal difficulty, and, in addition to these, it is unlabored, because it needs no additional necessary force which restrains it, preventing it from spatially moving in another way that is natural to it.[211] For everything of that sort is laborious, the more so the more eternal it is, and without a share of the best disposition.[212]

That is why one must not suppose it to be in accord with the myth of the ancients, who say that the heaven needs the addition of some Atlas for its preservation.[213] For it seems that the people who composed this account had the same supposition as the later ones. For on the supposition that all bodies have weight and are earthy, they supported the heaven in mythical fashion with an animate necessity.

One should not, then, suppose it to be this way, nor that, because of its whirling's having a spatial movement that is faster than its own balance-weight, the heaven has been preserved [from falling to the earth] for all this time, as Empedocles says.[214]

But then neither is it reasonable that the heaven remains eternal because a soul necessitates it. For it is not possible for this sort of life to be painless and blessedly happy for a soul.[215] For it necessarily, with respect to its movement, involves force—if indeed it moves the primary body in another way than with its natural spatial movement, and moves it continuously—and to be unleisured and deprived of all thought-involving ease, if indeed it does not have, as does the soul of mortal animals, the relaxation of the body that comes about in sleep.[216] Instead, it is necessary that a fate of some Ixion, eternal and indefatigable, restrain it.[217]

If, then, as we said, it is possible for the primary spatial movement to be the way we have stated, not only is it more refined to think this way about its eternity, but also this is the only way to provide harmonious accounts that are in agreement with the prophecy about the god.[218] But let this be enough about these sorts of accounts for now.

II 2

Since, though, there are some people who say that there is some right and left in the heaven, such as those called Pythagoreans (for this account is theirs), we must investigate whether this is the way they say it is, or rather another way, if indeed one must ascribe these starting-points to the body of the universe.[219]

For first of all, if right and left do belong [to the heaven], one must suppose that prior starting-points belong to it in a prior way. These things have been determined in our works on the movement of animals, because they properly belong to the nature of animals.[220] For evidently in some animals it is evident that all parts of this sort belong (I mean, for example, right and left), in others [only] some, while in plants only up and down belong.[221] If, however, one must ascribe some parts of this sort to the heaven as well, it is reasonable that the first one, as we said, that belongs in animals belongs in it too.[222] For there are three [pairs], each of which is a starting-point of a sort. The three I mean are: up and down, front and its opposite, and right and left. For it is reasonable that all these dimensions belong to complete bodies. Up, though, is a starting-point of length, right of breadth, and front of depth. Further, [they are starting-points] in another way, in accord with movements. For I mean by starting-points these things from which the movements first start for the things that have them. Growth, though, starts from the up, movement with respect to place from things right, and perception from the front (for by front I mean what perceptions are directed toward).[223]

30   That is why one must not look for up and down, right and left, and
front and back in every body, but only in those that, being animate,
have a starting-point of movement within them. For in inanimate ones
we do not see the starting-point from which the movement derives
(for some things do not move at all, whereas others, though they do
move, do not do so in every direction alike—for example, fire moves
35   upward only and earth toward the center). On the contrary, in things
285^{a}1   of this sort we speak of up and down and right and left with reference
to ourselves. For we speak of them either with reference to our own
right, as prophets do, or with reference to what is similar to our right,
as with the sides of a statue, or of what has its position in the contrary
5   way, speaking of right with reference to our left, and left with reference
to our right{, and of back with reference to our front}.^{224} In these things
themselves, on the other hand, we do not see any differences, since if
they are turned around, we call their contraries right, left, up, down,
front, and back.

10   That is why one might wonder at the Pythagoreans, because they
said that only two of these, right and left, are starting-points, but omitted the four remaining starting-points, which are no less controlling.^{225}
For in all animals up has no less a difference in relation to down, and
front in relation to back, than things right have in relation to things
15   left. For some of these differ in capacity only, others in their shapes
as well, and all animate things, animals and plants alike, have up and
down, but right and left is not present in plants.^{226}

Further, since length is prior to breadth, if up is a starting-point of
20   length, right of breadth, and the starting-point of what is prior is prior,
up would be prior to right in coming to be (since things are said to be
prior in many ways).^{227}

In addition to these, if up is where movement derives from, right
what it derives from, front what it is directed toward, in this way
too up will have a certain capacity in relation to the other forms [of
dimensionality].

25   It is just, then, to criticize the Pythagoreans because they omitted
the most controlling starting-points, and because they thought that the
starting-points belong alike in all things.^{228}

Since we have determined previously that capacities of this sort
belong in things that have a starting-point of movement, and the
heaven is animate, that is, has a starting-point of movement, it is clear
30   that it also has both up and down and right and left.^{229}

For there is no need to be puzzled, because the shape of the universe is spherical, as to how there can be a right and a left of it when

all its parts are similar and all the time moving. Instead, we should
understand that it is as if it were a thing in which there is a difference
between right and left, even in their shapes, around which someone
has placed a sphere. For it will then have the capacity corresponding
to the difference, but would seem not to because of the uniformity
of its shape. It is the same way with the starting-point of movement.   5
For even if it never began moving, nonetheless it is necessary for it to
have a starting-point from which it would have begun if it had begun
moving, and, if it were to come to a stop, from which it would start
moving again.

I mean by the length of it the interval between its poles, and of the
poles, one is up and the other down. For only in these hemispheres do
we see a difference, because of their poles not moving.[230] At the same   10
time, we are also accustomed to saying that the sides in the cosmos are
not up and down, but rather what is beside the poles, on the supposition that length is this thing [we said it is].[231] For what is to the side is
what is beside what is up or what is down.

Of the poles, however, the one that appears above us is down, the
one invisible to us is up. For we say that the right of a given thing is   15
where the starting-point of its movement with respect to place derives
from. And in the case of the heaven the starting-point of its revolution
is where the stars rise from, so that this would be right, and where they
set would be left. If, then, it starts from the right and revolves to the
right, it is necessary for the non-apparent pole to be up.[232] For if it is   20
the apparent one, the movement will be to the left, which is just what
we say it is not.[233] Therefore it is clear that the non-apparent pole is up,
and the people who dwell there are in the upper hemisphere and near
the right-side things, whereas we are in the lower one and near the
left-side ones, which is contrary to what the Pythagoreans say.[234] For   25
they put us up and in the right [part] and put the people there [in the
other hemisphere] down and in the left one.[235] But the opposite turns
out to be the case.

But with respect to the second revolution, that is, the revolution of
the planets, we are in the upper and in the right [parts], whereas those
others are in lower and in the left ones. For the starting-point of move-   30
ment is the reverse for the planets because their spatial movements are
contrary, so that as a result we are near the starting-point, while they
are near the end-point.

About things relating to the dimensions of the parts [of the cosmos]
and to their definitions with respect to place, let these be the things
that are said.

II 3

Since movement in a circle is not contrary to movement in a circle, let us investigate why there are several spatial movements—even though we have to try to make our inquiry from far away, not far away in place, but much more in that we have perception of altogether few of their coincidental attributes.[236] Nonetheless, let us speak about the issue.

The cause of [there being several spatial movements] must be grasped from the following. Each thing of which there is a function is for the sake of the function.[237] The activity of a god is immortality, and this is eternal living.[238] So it is necessary that eternal movement belongs to the god.[239] And since the heaven is such (for it is a certain divine body), because of this it has a circular body, which by nature always moves in a circle.[240]

Why, then, is the whole body of the cosmos not like this? Because it is necessary for some part of the body spatially moving in a circle to remain at rest, namely, the part at the center.[241] But no part of it can remain at rest either in general or at the center.[242] For then its movement in accord with nature would in fact be toward the center. But by nature it moves in a circle. For [otherwise] its movement would not be eternal. For nothing contrary to nature is eternal.[243] But what is contrary to nature is posterior to what is in accord with nature, and in coming to be what is contrary to nature is a sort of departure from what is in accord with nature.[244] It is necessary, therefore, for there to be earth. For it rests at the center. Let this be assumed for now; later this will be shown about it.[245]

But then if there is earth, it is necessary for there to be fire as well. For if one of two contraries is by nature, it is necessary for the other—if indeed it is a contrary and has some nature—to be by nature as well.[246] For the matter of contraries is the same; the positive is prior to the lack (I mean, for example, that hot is prior to cold); and rest and heaviness are said of things as lack of lightness and movement.[247] But then if indeed there is fire and earth, it is necessary for there also to be the bodies intermediate between them.[248] For each element has a contrariety in relation to each. Let this too be assumed for now; later we must try to show it.[249]

Since these elements exist, it is evident that it is necessary for there to be coming to be, because none of them can be eternal. For contraries are affected by, and affect, each other, and are destructive of each other.[250] Further, it is not reasonable for something moveable, whose movement in accord with nature does not admit of being eternal, to be eternal. But of these there is [such] movement. That it is,

therefore, necessary for there to be coming to be is clear from these
considerations.[251]

But if there is coming to be, it is also necessary for there to be another
spatial movement, either one or many. For with respect to the spatial
movement of the whole, the elements of the bodies necessarily relate to
each other in the same way. We shall speak more perspicuously about
this in what follows.[252]   5

For now, though, this much is clear: due to what cause the circular
bodies are many, namely, because it is necessary for there to be coming to be; and there is coming to be if indeed there is fire; and there is
fire and the other elements if indeed there is earth; and there is earth
because it is necessary for there to be something that always remains
at rest if indeed it is necessary that there be something that is always
in movement.

II 4

It is necessary for the heaven to have a spherical shape. For this most   10
properly belongs to its substance and is by nature primary.[253]

Let us, though, speak in universal terms about shapes, about what
sort is primary, both among plane figures and among solids. Every
plane figure, of course, is either rectilinear or curvilinear. And the rectilinear is encompassed by several lines, the curvilinear by one line.   15
Since in each genus, the one is prior by nature to the many, and the simple to the compound, the circle would be the primary plane figure.[254]

Further, if indeed the complete is that outside which no part of it
can possibly be found, as it was previously defined, and it is always
possible to add to the straight line, but never to that of the circle, it is   20
evident that the one encompassing the circle will be complete.[255] So
that if the complete is prior to the incomplete, because of this too the
circle would be primary among the shapes.[256]

Similarly too the sphere is the primary solid. For it alone is encompassed by one surface, whereas rectilinear solids are encompassed by
several. For as the circle stands among plane figures, so the sphere   25
stands among solids.

Further, even those who divide bodies into plane figures and generate them from plane figures apparently testify to this.[257] For the sphere
is the only solid that they do not divide, because of its not having more
than one surface. For the division into plane figures is not as some-   30
one cutting something into parts would divide the whole, rather it is
divided as someone would who was dividing into things that are distinct in form.[258]

That the sphere is primary among the solids, then, is clear. And it is also most reasonable for those who assign [the shapes] a numerical order to do so by assigning one to the circle, two to the triangle (since it has [interior angles equal to] two right angles).[259] But if one is assigned to the triangle, the circle will no longer be a shape.[260]

[*Argument 1*] Since the primary shape belongs to the primary body, and the body in the outermost revolution is the primary body, the body that revolves in a circle will be spherical.[261] So too, therefore, is the body continuous with it. For what is continuous with something spherical is spherical. And it is the same way with what is at the center of these spheres. For it is necessary for the things circumscribed by things spherical, and in contact with them as wholes, to be spherical. But the things below the sphere of the planets are in contact with the sphere above them. So all of them would be spherical.[262] For everything is in contact and continuous with the spheres.

[*Argument 2*] Further, since the universe appears and is assumed to revolve in a circle, and it has been shown that there is neither void nor place outside the outermost revolution, it is also necessary, because of these things, for it to be spherical.[263] For if it is rectilinear, the result will be that there is space, body, and void outside it.[264] For something rectilinear, turning in a circle, will never occupy the same space, but rather where previously there was body, now there will not be, and where now there is not, there will be one again, because of the changing position of the angles.

Similarly, even if it were to be some other shape not having equal lines from the center—for example, lentil-shaped or ovoid. For in all instances it would result that there is place and void outside its spatial movement, because the whole does not remain in the same space.

[*Argument 3*] Further, if the spatial movement of the heavens is the measure of movements because only it is continuous, regular, and eternal, and what is least in each thing is its measure, and if the fastest movement is the least, it is clear that the movement of the heaven would be the fastest of all movements.[265] Moreover, the line of the circle is the least line from a point to itself, and the fastest movement is that along the shortest line.[266] So if the heaven spatially moves in a circle and moves fastest, it is necessary for it to be spherical.

[*Argument 4*] But it is also possible to obtain this conviction from the bodies situated around the center. For if water surrounds earth, air water, and fire air, the upper bodies will also be in the same ratio (*logos*) (for though they are not continuous with them, they are in contact with them).[267] But the surface of the water is spherical, and what is continuous with what is spherical, or is situated surrounding what is spherical, is necessarily so itself. So it would also be evident from this that the heaven is spherical.

But then that the surface of the water is like this is evident to those who take it as an assumption that water is naturally such as always to flow into what is more hollow. Let, then, the lines AB and AC be drawn from the center, and let them be joined by the line BC [Fig. 11].²⁶⁸ The line AD drawn from the base is less than the ones from the center [AB and AC]. Therefore, the place is more hollow. So let water flow around until it is equalized. But AE is equal to those from the center [namely, AB and AC]. So it is necessary for the water to reach [the ends of] the lines from the center [namely, B, E, and C]. For then it will rest.²⁶⁹ But the line in contact with [the ends of] those from the center is the circumference. Therefore the surface BEC of the water is spherical.

That the cosmos is spherical, then, is clear from these considerations, and that it is rounded so exactly that nothing artificial, nor anything else that appears within sight of our eyes, comes close to it.²⁷⁰ For none of the things from which it gets its composition is capable of receiving a regularity and exactness in the way that the nature of the all-around body is.²⁷¹ For it is clear that they have a proportionality: as water is to earth, so it always is too with the more distant of the co-ordinate ones.²⁷²

II 5

There are two ways of moving in a circle—for example, from A to B and from A to C; that these movements are not contraries has been said previously.²⁷³ But if nothing that is by luck or by chance can possibly be among the eternal things, and the heaven is eternal, as its spatial movement in a circle, due to *what* cause does it spatially move in one direction and not in the other? For it is necessary for this either to be a starting-point or that there be a starting-point of it.²⁷⁴

Now, to try to prove all things, omitting nothing, in the same way as one does certain things would perhaps seem to be a sign of great naivety or of great audaciousness.²⁷⁵ But it is certainly not just to censure in the same way all [who do try]. Instead, one must look to see what the cause is of their saying what they say, and furthermore in what way they have hold of their conviction, whether in a merely human way or something stronger.²⁷⁶ Indeed, when someone hits on necessities that are more exact, then one must show gratitude to the discoverers, for now, though, we must state what appears to be so.²⁷⁷

For if nature always produces the best of the things that are possible, and if, just as in the case of rectilinear spatial movements, that toward the upper place is more estimable (for the upper place is more divine than the lower), and in the same way too forward spatial movement is more estimable than backward, and if indeed [the heaven] has a right and a left, as was said previously (and the puzzle just stated testifies that it does), it has a priority and a posteriority.[278] For this cause resolves the puzzle. For if things are in the best state possible, this would in fact be the cause of what was stated. For it is best to be moved with a simple, unceasing movement, and for this to be in a direction that is more estimable.

II 6

Where the movement of it is concerned, that it is regular and not irregular, is the next issue that should be discussed.[279] I mean this about the primary heaven and about the primary spatial movement. For in the lower [places] several spatial movements have already come together into one.[280]

[*Argument 1*] For if it moves irregularly, it is clear that there will be an acceleration, top-speed, and deceleration of the spatial movement. For every irregular spatial movement has an acceleration, top-speed, and deceleration. And the top-speed occurs either at the point from which a thing moves, at the point to which it moves, or at the mid-point—for example, perhaps for things spatially moving in accord with nature it is at the point to which they move, for those that move contrary to nature it is at the one from which they move, and for projectiles at the mid-point.[281] Of spatial movement in a circle, on the other hand, there is no point from which, point to which, or mid-point. For of it there is simply neither starting-point, limit-point, nor end-point. For in time it is eternal and in length joined in one and unbroken.[282] So if there is no top-speed of its spatial movement, there will be no irregularity either. For irregularity comes about because of deceleration and acceleration.

[*Argument 2*] Further, since everything that moves is moved by something, it is necessary for irregularity of movement to come about either because of the mover, because of the thing moved, or because of both.[283] For if the mover did not move it with the same capacity, or if the thing moved alters and does not remain the same, or if both changed, nothing prevents the thing moved from moving irregularly. But none of these can possibly come about in the case of the heaven. For it has been shown that the thing moved is primary, simple, incapable

of coming to be, and wholly unchangeable.[284] But it is much more rea-　**288ᵇ1**
sonable for the mover to be like this. For the primary one is capable
of moving the primary one, the simple one is capable of moving the
simple one, and the one incapable of passing away and coming to be is
capable of moving the one incapable of passing away and coming to be.
Since, then, the thing moved, which is a body, does not change, neither
will its mover, which is incorporeal, change.[285] So it is also impossible　5
for the spatial movement to be irregular.

[*Argument 3*] For if it becomes irregular, either it changes as a whole
and becomes faster at one time and slower again at another, or its parts
do. Well, that its parts are not irregular is evident. For it would, in the
unlimited time, by now have produced a difference in the distances of
the stars, if one part were moving faster and another slower. But none　10
of these distances is observed to vary.

But neither is it possible for the whole to change. For the deceleration of a given thing results from incapacity, and incapacity is contrary
to nature.[286] For the incapacities in animals are all contrary to nature—
for example, old age and wasting away.[287] For presumably the whole
composition of animals is made up of the sorts of things that differ in　15
their proper places. For none of their parts occupies its own proper
space.

If, then, among the primary things there is nothing contrary to
nature (for they are simple, unmixed, and in their proper space, and
nothing is contrary to them), there would not be any incapacity either,　20
and so no acceleration or deceleration (for if there is acceleration, there
is also deceleration).[288]

[*Argument 4*] Further, it is also unreasonable that the mover is
incapable of doing so for an unlimited time, and capable of doing so
again for another unlimited one. For nothing appears to be contrary to
nature for an unlimited time (and incapacity is contrary to nature),
nor contrary to nature and in accord with nature for an equal time,　25
nor, in general, capable and incapable for an equal time.[289] And it is
necessary, if the movement decelerates, that it do so for an unlimited
time.[290] Moreover, neither is it capable of always accelerating nor again
of always decelerating. For then the movement would be unlimited
and indefinite, but all movement, we say, is from something to something, that is, definite.[291]

[*Argument 5*] Further, if someone assumes there is some least time,　30
which it is not possible for the heaven to move in a lesser one than (for
just as it is not possible to play the lyre or to walk in any time whatsoever, but rather for each action there is a definite least time which
cannot be surpassed, so too it is not possible for the heaven to move in

any time whatsoever)—if, then, this is true, there would not always be an acceleration of movement (and if there is not acceleration, neither is there deceleration, since the same goes for both and each), if indeed it accelerates by identical or increasing increments of speed, and for an unlimited time.

5   [*Argument 6*] It remains, then, to say that the movement is alternately faster and slower. This, though, is entirely unreasonable and like a fabrication.²⁹² Further, if such were the case, it is also more reasonable that it not go unnoticed. For things put next to each other are easier to perceive.²⁹³

     About the fact that there is only one heaven, then, and that it is incapable of coming to be and is eternal, and, further, that it moves in 10 a regular way, let us say this much.

II 7

We should next speak about what are called stars, what they are composed of, in what sorts of shapes, and what their movements are.

     It is most reasonable, then, and follows from what we have said, to make each of the stars be composed of the body in which it has its spa-15 tial movement, since we said that there is something that is of a nature to spatially move in a circle.²⁹⁴ For just as those who declare that the stars are fiery do so because they say that the upper body is fire, and that it is reasonable for each to be composed of what it is in, so we too are speaking in a similar way.²⁹⁵

20   The heat and light from the stars come about when air is chafed by their spatial movement.²⁹⁶ For movement is of a nature to ignite even wood, stones, and iron. It is more reasonable, then, for it to do the same to what is closer to fire, and air is closer to fire—as, for example, in the case of spatially moving missiles. For these are themselves ignited to such an extent that lead balls melt, and, since *these* are ignited, it 25 is necessary for the air around them to be affected in the same way. These missiles themselves, then, are heated up because of their spatial movement in air, which becomes fire because of a blow struck by the movement.²⁹⁷

     Each of the upper things spatially moves in a sphere, so that, though they themselves cannot ignite, the air beneath the sphere of the rotating 30 body is necessarily heated up, especially there where the sun happens to be fixed. That is why heat comes about when the sun gets closer, rises, and is over us.

     About the fact that the stars are neither fiery nor spatially move in 35 fire, then, let us say this much.

II 8

Since both the stars and the whole heaven appear to change position, it is necessary for the change to occur either [1] with both being at rest, [2] both moving, or [3] one being at rest and the other moving.[298]

[1] Now that both be at rest is impossible, if the earth is at rest. For then the things that appear to be the case would not come about. And so let it be assumed that the earth is at rest. It remains, then, that both move, or that one moves and the other is at rest.

[2] If, then, both move, it is unreasonable for the speeds of the stars and of their circles to be the same. For then each star will then be equal in speed to the circle on which it is carried.[299] For they appear to return to the same point at the same time as their circles. The result, then, is that a star has traversed its circle at the same time as its circle has carried out its own spatial movement in traversing its circumference. It is not reasonable, however, for the speeds of the stars and the magnitudes of their circles to stand in the same ratio (*logos*). For there is nothing absurd—rather, it is necessary—for the circles to have speeds proportional to their magnitudes, but for each of the stars in them it is not reasonable at all. For if the star spatially moving in the greater circle will of necessity move faster, it is clear that even if the stars were transferred to each other's circles, one will be faster and the other slower (in this way they would not have their own movement, but they would be carried by their circles). Or, if it happened by chance, it would still not be reasonable for it to happen in such a way that in every case the circle was greater and at the same time the spatial movement of the star on it was faster. For there is nothing absurd about one or two cases being this way, but for all alike to be so seems like a fabrication. At the same time too luck is not found in things that are by nature, and what holds by luck is not what holds everywhere and in all cases.[300]

[3] But then again if the circles remain at rest while the stars themselves move, there will be the same unreasonable results, and in the same way. For the result will be that the outer stars move faster, and that their speeds are in accord with the magnitude of their circles.[301]

Since, therefore, it is not reasonable either that [2] both move or [3] that the star alone does, it remains that the circles move while the stars remain at rest, and, fixed to their circles, are carried around. For in this way alone nothing unreasonable results.[302] For [first] it is reasonable for the speed of the larger circle to be faster where the circles are fixed around the same center. For just as in the case of other things the greater body carries out its own proper spatial movement faster, so it is too in the case of circular bodies.[303] For of arcs cut off by lines from the center, that of the greater circle is greater, so that it is reasonable for the greater circle [and the smaller one] to rotate in an equal time.[304] [Second,] the result is, both because of this and because it has been shown that the whole is continuous, that the heaven is not dispersed.[305]

[*Argument 1*] Further, since the stars are spherical, as others too say, and for us it is consistent to say, generating them as we do from that body [namely, ether], and since of what is spherical there are two intrinsic movements, rolling and rotation, if indeed then the stars move because of themselves, they should move with one or other of these movements.[306] But they appear to move with neither.

For in rotating they would have remained in the same place and not have changed it, which is just what they appear to do and everyone says they do. Further, it is reasonable for all of these to be moved with the same movement, but among the stars only the sun seems to do this in rising and setting, and it seems so not because of itself [rotating], but because of the distance from our sight. For sight, when extended a great distance, wobbles because of its weakness. This is also the very cause, perhaps, of the stars appearing to twinkle, and of the planets not appearing to twinkle. For the planets are close by, so that sight reaches them while it is strong, but when it reaches the fixed stars, it shakes because it is stretched out too far.[307] And its trembling makes the movement seem to be the star's, since it makes no difference whether our sight moves or the thing seen does.

Moreover, it is evident that the stars do not roll either. For it is necessary for a thing that rolls to turn about, but the so-called face of the moon is always visible.

So, since it is reasonable that in moving because of themselves they move with their own proper movements, but they are not observed to move in this way, it is clear that they cannot move because of themselves.

[*Argument 2*] In addition to this, it is unreasonable that nature gave them no instrument for movement (since nature does nothing by luck), and that it should give thought to animals, but overlook such estimable beings.[308] Instead, it seems that nature, as if advisedly, excluded anything by means of which they could move forward by themselves, and set them at the greatest distance from things that have instruments for movement.

That is why it would also seem to be reasonable for the whole heaven and each of the stars to be spherical. For the sphere is the shape best adapted for movement within itself (for as such it can at once move fastest and most of all occupy the same place), whereas for forward movement it is worst adapted.[309] For it is least similar to those things

that move because of themselves. For it has nothing appended or pro-   5
jecting, as in a rectilinear figure, but stands farthest apart from the
shape of bodies capable of perambulation.[310]

Since, then, it is necessary for the heaven to move with a movement
within itself, but for the stars not to move forward because of themselves, it is reasonable for each to be spherical.[311] For most of all as
such, the one will move and the others be at rest.   10

II 9

It is evident from these considerations that the view that a harmony
is produced when [the heavenly bodies] spatially move, since their
sounds are in concord, though stated in an extraordinarily subtle way
by those who express it, does not thereby have any truth to it.[312] For it
seems to certain people that it is necessary for a sound to be produced   15
when such large bodies spatially move, since even in the case of the
ones around us, which do not have equal mass or spatially move with
such a speed, this happens. But when the sun and moon, and furthermore stars of such number and magnitude, spatially move with such
speed, it is impossible for some sound, enormous in magnitude, not to   20
be produced. Assuming these things, as well as that the speeds, based
on the distances, have the ratios (*logos*) of musical concords, they say
that, when the stars spatially move in a circle, the sound is in harmony.
But since it seems unreasonable that we do not at the same time hear
this sound, they say that the cause of this is that the sound is present
straight from our birth, so that it is not distinguishable from the silence   25
contrary to it. For sound and silence are distinguished in relation to
each other. So just to coppersmiths, because of what they are accustomed to, sound and silence do not seem to differ, to human beings too
the same thing happens.

These things, then, as was said earlier, are harmoniously and musi-   30
cally stated, but it is impossible for them to be this way.[313] For it is not
only absurd that nothing is heard (they do try to resolve [the puzzle]
about its cause), it is also absurd that nothing is affected apart from perception.[314] For excessive sounds shatter the masses even of inanimate
bodies—for example, that of thunder splits stones and the toughest of   35
bodies. With so many things spatially moving, and the sound passing   291^{a}1
through being proportional to the spatially moving magnitude, it is
necessary for a magnitude that is many times greater to reach here,
and for the strength of its force to be inconceivable. Well then, it is reasonable [to conclude] that we do not hear it, and that bodies are quite
evidently not affected forcibly by it, because no sound is produced.   5

At the same time the cause of these things is clear, and is testimony to the accounts we have stated. For what puzzled the Pythagoreans and made them say that there is a concord in the moving things is a proof for us.[315]

For whatever things are themselves in spatial movement produce a sound and a blow, whereas whatever things are fixed to or present in a spatially moving thing, such as the parts in a ship, cannot produce a sound, nor could the ship itself if it were carried along on the river. And yet it would be possible to come forth with the same arguments, saying that it is absurd if, when spatially moving, the mast and the stern of so large a ship do not produce a sound, or again the ship itself when it is spatially moving. But though when something spatially moves in something not spatially moving, it does produce a sound, when it is in, and continuous with, something spatially moving and does not produce a blow, it cannot produce a sound.[316] So in the present case one must say that if indeed the bodies of the stars are moving either in a quantity of air or of fire spread through the universe, as everyone says, it is necessary for them to produce a sound of enormous magnitude, and if this happens, it reaches here and shatters things.[317] So, since it is evident that this does not result, none of the stars could be spatially moving with either an animate or a forced spatial movement, as if nature foresaw the future, namely, that if they did not have their movement in this way, nothing in the place around here would be the same.

That, then, the stars are spherical and that they do not move because of themselves, has now been stated.

II 10

As to their order—the way in which each is positioned, some being prior and some posterior, that is, how they are related to each other with respect to their distances—let a theoretical grasp be got on it on the basis of astronomical accounts. For they speak adequately about it.[318] And it turns out that the movements of each are in proportion (*logos*) to their distances, one lot being faster and the other slower. For since the outermost revolution of the heaven is assumed to be at once simple and fastest, while those of the others are slower and more numerous (for each is carried on its own circle in a direction contrary to the heaven), it is reasonable immediately that the one closest to the simple and primary revolution traverse its own circle in the longest time, the farthest away in the shortest, and in the case of the others, always the closer in a longer time, the farther away in a shorter one.

For the closest is most of all controlled by the primary locomotion, the farthest away least of all, because of its distance, and the intermediate ones in proportion (*logos*) to their distance—as the mathematicians also show.[319]

II 11

The shape, though, of each of the stars one would most reasonably assume to be spherical. For since it has been shown that they are not naturally such as to move because of themselves, and nature produces nothing unreasonably or pointlessly, it is clear that it also gave to these unmoving things a shape that is least capable of movement.[320] But the sphere is least capable of movement because it has no instrument for movement. So it is clear that the stars will be spherical in mass.

Further, it is similarly so for one and all. The moon, on the other hand, shows itself to be spherical by the evidence of sight. For otherwise it would not be mostly crescent-shaped or gibbous in the greater part of its waxing and waning, and only at one time semicircular.[321] And, again, [it is shown] through astronomy that eclipses of the sun would not be crescent-shaped [if the moon were not spherical].[322] So, if indeed one star is like this, it is clear that the others too would be spherical.

II 12

There are two puzzles, which it makes perfect sense for anyone to puzzle over, about which we must try to state what appears to be so, thinking such audaciousness to be reverence rather than rashness, if someone, because of his thirst for philosophy, is content to become a little more puzzle-free concerning the things about which we have the greatest puzzlement.[323]

[*Puzzle 1*] Among the many things of this sort, not the least wondrous is what the cause is due to which it is not those bodies that are more distant from the primary spatial movement that always have more movements, but rather the intermediate ones have the most. For it would seem reasonable, since the primary body has one spatial movement, for what is closest to it to move with the fewest movements—for example, two, the next three, or that there be some other order of this sort. But as things stand, the contrary is the case. For the sun and the moon move with fewer movements than some of the wandering stars.[324] And yet these are farther away from the center and closer to the primary body. And in some cases this has even been made

clear by sight. For we have seen the moon, when half-full, move under
the star of Ares [Mars], which was occulted by the dark half of the
moon, and come out on its light and bright side.[325] The ancient Egyp-
tians and Babylonians, who have kept a close watch for the most years,
speak similarly about the other stars as well, and from them we have
acquired many convictions about each of the stars.

[*Puzzle 2*] One might justly raise this puzzle and also what the cause
is due to which the multitude of stars in the primary spatial movement
is so great that their whole order seems to be uncountable, whereas
each of the others has one separate star, and two or more do not appear
fixed on the same spatial movement.

[*Resolution of Puzzle 1*] Where these issues are concerned, then, it is
well to seek to increase our comprehension, even though we have few
things to start from and are at such a great distance from what happens
concerning them.[326] Nonetheless, for those who get their theoretical
grasp on the basis of things of the following sort what is presently puzzling would not seem to be at all unreasonable. We think about these
stars as bodies only, that is, as units having a certain order, altogether
inanimate. But we should conceive of them as participating in action
and life.[327] For in this way what happens will not seem at all contrary
to reason.[328] For it seems that the good belongs without action to what
is in the best state, to what is closest by means of one small action, and
to what is farther away by means of several actions.[329] It is just as in
the case of the body: one is in a good state without exercising, another
by walking around a little, a third needs running, wrestling, and hard
training, while to another again this good would not yet belong no matter how much exertion he undergoes, but rather a distinct one.[330]

It is difficult, though, to attain success either in all things or often—
for example, to make ten-thousand Chian throws at knucklebones
is inconceivable, but one or two is comparatively easy.[331] And, again,
when it is necessary that one do this for the sake of that, and that for
the sake of something else, it is easy to succeed at one stage or two, but
when it is through a greater number, it is more difficult.[332]

That is why one should think the action of the stars to be like that
of animals and plants. For here the actions of human beings are in fact
most numerous, since it is possible to attain many goods, so that it is
possible to do many things in action, and for the sake of other ones.
(What is in the best state, by contrast, has no need of action, since it is
itself the for-the-sake-of which; action, though, is always in two [vari-
eties], namely, when it is the for-the-sake-of-which and when it is what
is for the sake of that.[333]) The actions of the other animals, on the other
hand, are fewer, and of the plants perhaps one small one.[334] For either

there is some one thing which they may attain, as there is for a human
being too, or the many things are a route toward the best one.³³⁵ One   10
thing, then, has and participates in the best, one reaches close to it by
means of few [steps], another by means of many, and another does not
even try, but it is sufficient for it to come close to the ultimate [end].³³⁶
For example, if health is the end, one thing, then, is always healthy,
another is slimming down [to be healthy], another running and slimming down, another does some other action for the sake of running,
so that its movements are more numerous; a distinct one, though, is   15
incapable of reaching being healthy, but only of running or slimming
down (and one or the other of these is the end for them). For on the
one hand it is best of all for each to attain the end; but on the other, if
this is not [possible], it would always be better to the degree that it got
closer to the best one.

And this is why the earth does not move at all, and things close
to it have few movements. For they do not reach the ultimate [end],   20
but as far as is possible attain the most divine starting-point.³³⁷ The
primary heaven, however, attains this directly by means of a single
movement.³³⁸ But the bodies intermediate between the first and the
last ones, though they do attain it, do so by means of more movements.

[*Resolution 1 of Puzzle 2*] As to the puzzle that in the primary spa-   25
tial movement, though it is one, a great number of stars is involved,
whereas each of the others has separately received its own movement, one might reasonably think this holds primarily because of one
thing. For one should understand that in the case of each one's life and
starting-point the primary one has a great superiority over the others, and this superiority would turn out to be proportional (*logos*).³³⁹   30
For the primary movement, though one, moves many divine bodies,
whereas the others, though many, each moves only one (for any one
of the planets spatially moves with several spatial movements). In this   293ᵃ1
way, then, nature both equalizes things and produces a certain order,
having given many bodies to the one spatial movement, and many spatial movements to the one body.³⁴⁰

[*Resolution 2 of Puzzle 2*] And, further, it is because of this that
the other spatial movements have one body, namely, that the spatial
movements before the final one, which has one star, move several   5
bodies. For the final sphere is carried fixed on many spheres, and
each sphere is a body. The work of this final sphere, then, would be
common [to all of them]. For while each sphere has a spatial movement that is by nature special to it, this spatial movement is, as it
were, added on, and the capacity of every limited body is related to a   10
limited one.³⁴¹

About the stars spatially moving with circular movement, it has been stated what they are like with respect to their substance and with respect to their shape, as also where their spatial movement and order are concerned.

II 13

It remains to speak about the earth, where it is situated, whether it is among things at rest or things moving, and about its shape.

[*Position*] About its position, then, not everyone has the same belief, but most people say that it is situated at the center (as do all those who say that the whole heaven is limited). But the Italian thinkers, the ones called Pythagoreans, say the contrary.[342] For they say that at the center there is fire, and that the earth, which is one of the stars, spatially moves in a circle around the center to produce night and day. Further, they establish another earth opposite this one, which they call by the name "anti-earth," not seeking their accounts and causes with an eye toward the things that appear to be so, but rather dragging the things that appear to be so toward certain of their accounts and beliefs, and trying to cosmeticize them to make them fit.[343]

Many others might believe along with them that one should not assign the region at the center to the earth, but their conviction is based not on looking at the things that appear to be so but rather on arguments.[344] For they think that it is fitting for the most estimable region to belong to the most estimable thing, that fire is more estimable than earth, the limit than the intermediate, and that the extremity and the center are limits. So analogizing on the basis of these considerations, they think that the earth is not situated at the center, but rather fire is.[345]

Further, the Pythagoreans, at any rate, also because it is most fitting that the most controlling [element] of the universe be safeguarded, and the center is like that, name the fire that occupies this region, "the guard of Zeus"—as if "center" were said unconditionally, and the center of its magnitude were also the center of the thing and of its nature![346] And yet, just as in the case of animals the center of the animal and of its body are not the same, one should rather suppose it to be this way too in the case of the whole heaven.[347] Due to this cause, then, there is no need for them to be disturbed about the universe, nor to introduce a safeguard at the center; instead they should seek that [other] center, what sort of thing and where it naturally is. For *that* center is a starting-point and is estimable, whereas the center of the place is more like an ending than a starting-point, since the center is what is determined, the limit what determines.[348] And what encompasses, that is, the limit, is more estimable than what is limited.³⁴⁹ For the second is matter, but the first is the substance of the composition.³⁵⁰

[*Movement*] About the place of the earth, then, some hold this belief,   15
and things are similar in the case of its immobility and movement. For not everyone conceives of them in the same way. Rather, those who say that it is not situated at the center, say that it moves in a circle around the center, and that not only the earth does so, but also the anti-earth, as we said previously.³⁵¹   20

Some people even believe that several bodies of this sort may spatially move around the center, invisible to us because of the interposition of the earth.³⁵² This, they say, is also why eclipses of the moon are more numerous than those of the sun. For each of the spatially moving bodies, and not only the earth, blocks it. For since the earth is not the   25
center, but is distant from it by a whole hemisphere, they think that even if we do not dwell at the center, there is nothing to prevent things from appearing in the same way as they would if the earth were at the center. For even as things stand nothing makes it clearly visible that we are at a distance of half a diameter from the center.

Some people also say that the earth, which is situated at the center,   30
winds—that is, moves—around the pole stretching through the universe, as is written in the *Timaeus*.³⁵³

[*Shape*] There is about as much dispute concerning its shape. Some believe that it is spherical, some that it is flat and drum-shaped.³⁵⁴ The latter produce as proof that, in setting and rising, the sun appears   294^{a}1
to make the part concealed by the earth a straight line rather than a curved one, whereas if indeed the earth were spherical, the line cutting it would have to be curved. But these people do not take into account the distance of the sun in relation to the earth and the magnitude of its circumference, which, on the apparently small circles [of the sun   5
on the horizon], appears straight from far away. They should not be unconvinced, then, because of this appearance, that the mass of the earth is circular. But they add something further and say that because of its being at rest it is necessary for it to have the shape it does.

[*Movement again*] And in fact, of course, about the movement and   10
immobility of the earth people have spoken in many ways. It is necessary, then, for a puzzle to strike everyone. For thought must be pretty anesthetized not to wonder how in the world a small piece of earth, raised up high and released, spatially moves and is unwilling to remain at rest, the larger always doing so faster, whereas if one were to raise the entire earth up high, it would not spatially move.³⁵⁵ But as things stand,   15
heavy as it is, it is at rest. Moreover, even if, when its parts are spatially moving, once removed the earth from below them before they

had fallen, they will spatially move downward when there is nothing resisting.

So it makes perfect sense that the puzzle became philosophical work for everyone.[356] But one might wonder why the resolutions of it do not seem more absurd [to people] than the puzzle. For because of the considerations we mentioned some, such as Xenophanes of Colophon, say that what is below the earth is unlimited, saying that it is rooted in the unlimited, in order not to have the work of seeking the cause.[357] That is also why Empedocles chastises them in the way he does, saying:

> If the depths of the earth and plentiful ether are unlimited,
> Like the words spoken pointlessly by the tongue of many
> Mouths are poured out, of those who have seen little of the universe.[358]

Some say, though, that the earth is situated on water. For this is the most ancient account that has come down to us, stated, they say, by Thales of Miletus, on the supposition that the earth remains at rest because it rises like a piece of wood, or something else of this sort (for in fact nothing of this sort is naturally such as to remain at rest on air, but on water)—as if the same argument did not apply to the earth and to the water supporting the earth. For water does not remain at rest when raised up high, unless it is on something.

Further, just as air is lighter than water, water is also lighter than earth. So how is it possible for a lighter thing to be situated below one that is heavier in nature?

Further, if indeed the whole earth naturally remains at rest on water, it is clear that each of its parts will too. As things stand, though, it is evident that this does not happen, but rather any random part spatially moves to the bottom, and the bigger one faster.

These people seem to inquire up to a certain point, but not as far as it is possible to take the puzzle. For it is customary for all of us to make our inquiry not with an eye to the thing at issue but with an eye to the person who says the contrary. For a person even inquires within himself up to the point at which he is no longer able to argue against himself. That is why a person who is going to inquire well must be capable of objecting by means of objections proper to the relevant genus, and this comes from having a theoretical grasp on all the differentiae.[359]

Anaximenes, Anaxagoras, and Democritus say that the cause of the earth's remaining at rest is its flatness.[360] For it does not cut the air below it but sits on it like a lid, which is just what bodies that are flat appear to do. For these bodies even have difficulty moving against winds because of the resistance. They say that because of its flatness the earth does the same thing in relation to the underlying air (which, not having enough room to change its place, is at rest because of the mass [of air] below it), just like the water in clepsydras.³⁶¹ And they state many proofs that air, when it is cut off and remains at rest, is capable of bearing great weight.

First, then, if the shape of the earth is not flat, it cannot be because of its flatness that it is at rest. And yet, from what they say, the cause of its immobility is not flatness, but rather magnitude. For because of a lack of space, the air, not having a way out, remains at rest because of its magnitude; and it is large in quantity because it is enclosed by the large magnitude of the earth. So, this would be the case even if the earth were spherical, but its magnitude were just as great. For according to their argument it will remain at rest.

In general, though, our dispute with those who speak in this way about the movement of the earth is not about parts, but about a certain whole and totality.³⁶² For one must determine at the start whether bodies have a certain movement by nature or none, and whether though by nature there is none, by force there is. But since determinations have been made previously about these matters as far as was in keeping with the capacity that was at our command, we must use them as things taken for granted.³⁶³

For if they have no movement by nature, nor will they have one by force; and if there is neither one by nature nor by force, there will be no movement at all. For about these matters it was determined previously that this result is necessary, and in addition that rest is not possible either.³⁶⁴ For just as movement belongs either by force or by nature, so too does rest.

But then if there *is* a certain movement in accord with nature, there could not be only forced spatial movement or forced rest. So if the earth now remains at rest by force, it also came together by being carried toward the center because of the vortex. For everyone says that this is the cause, on the basis of what happens in liquids or in the case of air.³⁶⁵ For in these greater or heavier things are always carried toward the center of the vortex. That is why, then, everyone who says that the heaven came to be says that the earth came together at the center; and, because it remains at rest there, they seek the cause of this. And some, speaking in this way, say that its flatness and magnitude is the cause, while others, like Empedocles, say that it is the spatial movement of the heaven which, rotating in a circle and spatially moving faster than the earth, prevents [the earth from moving], just like the water in ladles.³⁶⁶ For, when a [bronze] ladle spatially moves in a circle, the water is often below the bronze but nonetheless does not spatially move downward, though it is natural for it to spatially move so, due to the same cause. And yet if neither the vortex nor the flatness is doing the preventing, and instead the air [below] gives way, where will the earth move to?^{367} For it moved to the center by force, and remains at rest there by force. But it is necessary for it to have, at any rate, some spatial movement in accord with nature. Is this, then, upward, downward, or where? For it is necessary for it to have some sort of movement. But if it is no more downward than upward, and the air above does not prevent it spatially moving upward, nor would the air below prevent the earth from doing so downward. For it is necessary for the same things to be a cause of the same things for the same things.

Further, against Empedocles, one might also say the following. For when the elements had been disaggregated separately by strife, what cause was there of the earth's immobility?^{368} For of course he will not make the vortex the cause also at that time. But it is indeed absurd not to reflect on the following question: Previously the parts of the earth spatially moved to the center because of the vortex; but what is the cause due to which all things that have heaviness now move toward it? For the *vortex* is not near us.

Further, due to what cause does fire spatially move upward? For it is not because of the vortex. But if it naturally moves somewhere, it is clear that one must suppose that the earth does too.

Moreover, heavy and light are certainly not determined by the vortex either; instead, heavy and light things exist prior [to the vortex], one lot going to the center, the other lot rising to the surface because of the movement.^{369} Therefore, the one lot were heavy and the other light before the vortex came to be, but by what are they determined? And how is it natural for them to be spatially moved? And to where? For if the unlimited exists, it is impossible for there to be an up or down, and the heavy and light are determined by these.^{370}

Most people, then, spend their time on these causes. But there are some who say that the earth remains at rest because of the similarity, as among the ancient thinkers Anaximander does. For it is no more fitting for what is situated at the center and stands in a similar relation to the extremes to spatially move upward than downward or to the side; and it is impossible for it to make a movement in contrary directions at the same time. So of necessity it remains at rest.^{371}

This, though stated in a subtle way, is not stated in a true one.^{372} For according to this argument it is necessary for anything placed at the center to remain at rest, so that fire too will rest there (for what was mentioned is not a special attribute of earth).^{373} But this is not necessary. For it is not only evident that earth remains at rest at the center, but also that it spatially moves toward the center. For where any part [20] of it spatially moves to, there is where it is necessary for the whole of it to spatially move to as well; and where it spatially moves to in accord with nature, there is where it also remains at rest in accord with nature. Therefore, it does not [remain at rest] because of standing in a similar relation to the extremes (for this is common to all), whereas spatially moving toward the center is a special attribute of earth.

It is also absurd to inquire why earth remains at rest at the center, but [25] not to inquire why fire does so at the extremity. For if the extremity is by nature its place, it is clear that it is necessary for there also to be some place for earth by nature. But if this place [at the center] is not by nature its place, but instead it remains at rest because of the necessity of the similarity (as in the argument about the hair, that when stretched strongly [30] but similarly in every direction it will not break; or the one about the person who is similarly hungry and thirsty, and at an equal distance from food and drink—for he too [so the argument goes] is necessarily at rest), they must inquire about fire's immobility at the extremes.[374] [35]

A cause of wonder, too, is their inquiring about the immobility, but **296ª1** not inquiring about the spatial movement of these things, and due to what cause one spatially moves upward and the other toward the center, when nothing hinders them.

Moreover, what they do say is not even true. To be sure it *is* coincidentally true, in the sense that it is necessary that anything remain at rest at the center for which it is no more fitting to move here than [5] there. But on this argument at least [the earth] will not remain at rest, not—to be sure—as a whole, but having been dispersed. For the same argument will also apply to fire, since once placed there it must remain at rest in the same way as earth. For it will stand in a similar relation to any point of the extremities. But nonetheless it will spatially move [10] away from the center (as it evidently does spatially move) toward the extremity, if something does not prevent it; except, not as a whole toward one point (for it is only on the basis of the argument from similarity that it is necessary for this to happen), but rather a proportional part to a proportional part of the extremity—I mean, for example, a quarter of it toward a quarter of the encompassing [extremity] (for [15] no body is a point). And just as what is condensed can come together from a large to a smaller place, so what becomes rarer can do so from a smaller to a larger one.[375] So the earth would also move in this way from the center, even on the argument from similarity, if this were not [20] by nature the place of earth.

These, then, are pretty much all the suppositions about the shape of the earth, as well as about its place, immobility, and movement.

II 14

[*The immobility of the earth*] On our own behalf, though, let us first
say whether the earth has a movement or remains at rest. For, as
we said, some people make it one of the stars, whereas others say
that it winds—that is, moves—around the central pole.[376] That this
is impossible is clear if one takes as a starting-point that, if indeed
it spatially moves, whether it is outside the center or at the center,
it is necessary for it to be moved with this movement by force. For
the movement does not belong to the earth itself. For then each of
its parts would also have this spatial movement. But as things stand
they all spatially move in a straight line toward the center. That is
why [the proposed winding movement of it], being forced and contrary to nature, cannot be eternal. The order of the cosmos, however,
is eternal.

Further, all spatially moving bodies that spatially move in a circle appear to be left behind and to move with more than one spatial
movement, except for the primary one, so that it would be necessary
for the earth as well, whether it spatially moves around the center or
while situated at the center, to move with two spatial movements.[377]
But if this happens, it is necessary for there to be a passing and turning
of the fixed stars.[378] It is evident, however, that this does not occur, but
that instead the same stars always rise and set at the same places on
the earth.

Further, the spatial movement in accord with nature of the parts
and of the whole earth is toward the center of the universe. For it is
because of this, indeed, that as things stand the earth is situated at the
center. But since the center of both [the earth and the universe] is the
same, one might raise this puzzle: Toward which do things having
heaviness, in particular, the parts of the earth, spatially move in accord
with nature—is it because one is the center of the universe, or because
it is the center of the earth? It is necessary, surely, that it be toward that
of the universe, since light bodies, in particular, fire, in spatially moving in the contrary direction to heavy ones, spatially move toward the
extremity of the place that encompasses the center. It happens, however, that the center of the earth is the same as that of the universe. For
heavy bodies also spatially move toward the center of the earth, albeit
coincidentally, insofar as it has its center at the center of the universe.
A sign that they also spatially move toward the center of the earth is
that things having heaviness spatially moving toward it move not in
parallel but at similar angles, so that they spatially move toward one
center, which is also that of the earth.[379]

It is evident, therefore, that it is necessary for the earth to be at the center and immovable, both due to the causes mentioned and because things having heaviness that are thrown straight upward by force spatially move back again perpendicularly to the same point, even if the capacity involved throws them an unlimited distance.

That the earth, then, neither moves nor is situated outside the center, is evident from these considerations. In addition, the cause of the earth's immobility is clear from what has been said. For if it is naturally such as to spatially move by nature from anywhere toward the center, as is evident it is, and fire in turn from the center to the extremity, it is impossible for any part of it to spatially move from the center unless it is forced. For one [body] has one spatial movement; a simple one has a simple one, not contrary ones; and one from the center is contrary to one toward the center.[380] If, therefore, it is impossible for any part whatsoever to spatially move from the center, it is evident that it is yet more impossible for the whole to do so. For where the part is naturally such as to move to, is also where the whole is naturally such as to do so. So, if indeed it is impossible for it to move except because of a greater strength, it is necessary that it should remain at rest at the center.

Also testifying to these things is what is said by the mathematicians about astronomy. For the things that appear to be so, namely, the interchange of the configurations by which the order of the stars is determined, presuppose that the earth is situated at the center.

About the place of the earth, then, and the manner of its immobility and movement, let this much be said.

[*The shape of the earth*] As for its shape, it is necessary that it have a spherical shape. For each of its parts has heaviness up to the point at which [it is] near to the center, and when a smaller part is pushed by a greater one it cannot swell to form a wave, but rather the first is squeezed together by the second and combines with it, until it arrives at the center.[381] One should understand what is being said as if the earth comes to be in the way in which some of the physicists say it came to be.[382] Except that they give the force of the downward spatial movement as its cause. It is better, however, to set out what is true and say that this happens because what has heaviness spatially moves toward the center due to nature. When the mixture, then, was [merely] potential, the things that were disaggregated spatially moved from every direction toward the center in a similar way.[383] Whether, then, the parts were similarly divided at the extremes from which they were brought together toward the center, or were in another state, it will produce the same result. It is evident, then, that when bodies spatially move in a similar way from all directions toward a single center, the mass must

25

30

35
297^a1

5

10

15

20

become similar in every direction. For when an equal quantity is added in every direction, it is necessary for the extremity to be at an equal distance from the center; and this is the shape of a sphere. And it will make
25 no difference to the argument even if its parts did not travel together in a similar way from all directions toward the center. For it is necessary for a greater part always to push forward a smaller one that is in front of it up to the center, when both have balance-weight, and for a heavier one to push a less heavy one forward up to this.[384]

30 Indeed, the following puzzle that someone might raise has the same resolution as these [difficulties]: Since the earth is at the center and is spherical, if a heavy thing many times as heavy were added to one hemisphere, the center of the universe and of the earth will not be the same. So either the earth will not remain at rest at the center, or if indeed it does, it will *rest* even when it does not occupy the center, which is where it naturally moves to as things stand.

297^b1 Well then, this is what is puzzling. But it is not difficult to see [through] once we have tightened things up a little and determined the way in which we think of any magnitude whatsoever as moving toward the center, when it has heaviness. For it is clear that it does not do so up to the point at which its extremity makes contact with the center.
5 Instead, the greater body must exert mastery until it occupies the center with its center. For it retains its balance-weight up to this point.

There is no difference, therefore, between saying this of a clod, or of any random part, or of the whole of the earth. For the result was stated not because of smallness or magnitude, but with reference to everything that has balance-weight up to the center.
10 So whether it spatially moved from somewhere as a whole or in parts, it is necessary for it to move up to the point at which it occupies the center in a similar way in every direction, the smaller parts being counterbalanced by the larger ones by the forward push of its balance-weight.

If, then, the earth has come to be, it is necessary for it have come to be in this way, so that it is evident that its coming to be was spherical,
15 and, if it has not come to be but persists forever, remaining at rest, it is necessary for it to be in precisely the same way as the way it would first have come to be if it had come to be.

According to this argument, then, it is necessary for the earth's shape to be spherical, and because all things having heaviness spatially move at similar angles and not in parallel, and this is natural for [what spatially moves] toward what is by nature spherical. Either the earth
20 is spherical, then, or it is by nature, at any rate, spherical. One must, however, speak of each thing as being the sort of thing it tends to be,

and the sort it in fact is, by nature, and not the sort it is by force and contrary to nature.[385]

Further, [it is necessary for the earth's shape to be spherical] also because of what seems to be so according to perception. For otherwise lunar eclipses would not have sections of the sort they do. For, as things stand, in its monthly configurations the moon takes on all sorts of divisions (for it becomes straight, gibbous, and crescent), but during eclipses it always has a convex defining line, so that, if indeed it is eclipsed because of the interposition of the earth, the circumference of the earth, being spherical, would be the cause of the line's shape.

Further, because of the appearance of the stars, not only is it evident that the earth is round, but also that its magnitude is not great.[386] For when we change our position a little to the south or to the north the horizon clearly becomes visibly other than it was, so that the stars overhead change greatly, and the same ones do not appear to those who move to the north as to the south. For some stars are seen in Egypt and around Cyprus but are not seen in the regions to the north, and those stars always apparent in regions to the north set in the former regions. So not only is it clear from these things that the shape of the earth is round, but also that it is of a sphere that is not great in size. For otherwise it would not make it so quickly visible that it is so to those who change their position so little.

That is why those who suppose that the place around the Pillars of Hercules is connected to that around India, and in such a way that there is one sea, do not seem to suppose anything too unconvincing.[387] For they say, using elephants as their proof, that their genus is found in both extreme places, on the supposition that it is because of the connection between these extreme places that they share this feature with each other.

Also, the mathematicians who try to calculate the size of the earth's circumference say that it is about four-hundred-thousand stades.[388] On the basis of these proofs, it is necessary not only for the mass of the earth to be spherical, but also for it not to be great in relation to the magnitude of the other stars.

Book III

III 1

We have previously discussed the primary heaven and its parts, further, the stars spatially moving within it, of what they are composed and of what sort their nature is, and in addition [shown] that they are incapable of coming to be and incapable of passing away.[389]

Since of the things we say are by nature, some are substances, others works and affections of these—by substances I mean the simple bodies (for example, fire and earth and those co-ordinate with these), and whatever is composed of them (for example, the whole heaven and its parts), and, again, animals and plants and their parts; by affections and works, I mean the movements of these and of other [substances], that is, of whichever ones these, in accord with the capacity within them, are the cause; further, to their alterations and their transformations into each other)—it is evident that the study of nature is mostly concerned with bodies.[390] For all natural substances are either bodies or come to be along with bodies and magnitudes. This is clear from the definition of what sorts of things are by nature and from the theoretical knowledge of each of them.

Now, we have spoken about the first of the elements, about what sort its nature is, and [shown] that it is incapable of passing away and incapable of coming to be.[391] It remains to speak about the other two.[392] But at the same time it will turn out that speaking about them also involves having investigated coming to be and passing away. For either coming to be does not exist at all or exists only in these elements and the things composed of them. But perhaps this is what we must first get a theoretical grasp on, namely, whether it exists or not.

Those prior [to us] who philosophized about the truth, however, have disagreed both with the accounts at present being stated by ourselves and with each other.[393]

For some of them did away with coming to be and passing away altogether (for none of the beings, they say, either comes to be or passes away, but it only seems so to us)—for example, the followers of Melissus and Parmenides.[394] Of them, we must hold that, even if they speak correctly about other things, they do not do so *in a way appropriate to natural science*.[395] For the existence of certain beings that are incapable of coming to be and are wholly immovable is rather a matter for an investigation that is distinct from and prior to the natural scientific

one.[396] But because these thinkers assumed that there was no other   20
sort beyond the substance of perceptible beings, and were the first to
understand that there had to be certain natures of this [unchangea-
ble] sort if indeed there was going to be any knowledge or wisdom,
they transferred to perceptible beings the accounts applicable to those
natures.[397]

Others, as if on purpose, had the contrary belief. For some—
especially the followers of Hesiod, and next, of the others, the first   25
people who spoke about nature—say that none of the things at issue
is incapable of coming to be, but that all come to be, although some,
having come to be, remain there, incapable of passing away, whereas
others pass away.[398]

Others say that all things come to be and flow, none of them being
stable, save one thing only that persists, from whose natural changing   30
of shape all these things come. This is just what Heraclitus of Ephesus,
among many others, seems to wish to say.[399]

And there are also some who make all bodies capable of coming to
be, putting them together from and dissolving them into planes.[400]

About the others there will be an account on another occasion.[401]   299ᵃ1
But as for those who speak in this last way, that is, who compose all
bodies from planes, it is a superficial matter to see that the other things
they say are in conflict with mathematics.[402] And yet it is just either not
to alter mathematics or to alter it [only] by means of arguments that
are more convincing than its hypotheses.[403] It is clear, then, that on the   5
same account on which a solid is composed of planes, a plane is composed of lines, and these of points. But if so, it is not necessary for a
part of a line to be a line. These, though, are matters we have previously
investigated in the discussions concerning movement, [showing] that   10
there are no indivisible lengths.[404]

But where natural bodies are concerned we should on this occasion
also get a theoretical grasp on the impossible things that those who
produce indivisible lines result in saying. For although the resulting
impossibilities will follow for natural things as well, not all the ones
that apply to the latter will apply to the others, because the others,   15
the mathematical ones, are said of things on the basis of abstraction,
whereas the natural ones are said of things on the basis of an additional
posit.[405]

There are many affections that cannot belong to indivisible things
that necessarily belong to natural ones. For example, if there is an
indivisible one.[406] For in an indivisible one it is impossible for there
to be a divisible affection, and the divisible affections are all so in two
ways. For they are so either in species or coincidentally: in species, for   20

example, of color, white and black; coincidentally, if what it belongs to is divisible, so that the simple affections are all divisible in this way.[407] That is why one must investigate the impossibility in the case of this latter sort.

25   If it is impossible, then, when each of the two parts has no weight at all, for the two together to have weight, whereas the perceptible bodies, either all or some, have weight (for example, earth and water), as our opponents themselves would admit, and if a point has no weight at all, it is clear that neither do lines, and if they do not, then neither do planes, and so none of the bodies do either.

30   But then that a point cannot have weight is evident. For everything heavy can be heavier, and everything light lighter, than something
299^{b}1 else—though perhaps what is heavier or lighter is not necessarily heavy or light. Just as the great can be greater, though what is greater is not always great. For there are many things that are unconditionally small, but nonetheless are larger than other things.[408] If, then, something that, because it is heavy, would be heavier than something else, is necessar-
5 ily greater by weight than it, everything heavy would be divisible. But a point was assumed to be indivisible.[409]

Further, if what is heavy is a sort of dense, and what is light a sort of rare, and dense differs from rare in containing a greater quantity in an equal mass, then, if a point is heavy or light, it is also dense or rare. But
10 what is dense is divisible, whereas a point is indivisible.

And if it is necessary for everything heavy to be either soft or hard, it is easy to infer an impossibility from this. For a soft thing is what can be pressed into itself, whereas a hard one is what cannot be pressed in.[410] But what can be pressed in is divisible.

Moreover, what is composed of things that do not have weight will
15 not have weight. For in the case of how many will this result and in what way?[411] And how, without wishing to fabricate something, will they determine this? Also, if every weight greater than a weight is greater by a weight, it will follow that each of the parts that has no parts will have weight.[412] For if four points have weight, what is composed of a greater number of points has a weight greater than this weight. And if
20 it is necessary for that by which one weight is greater to be weight, just as that by which one white is more white is white, so that the greater will be heavier by one point, when the weight equal [to four points] has been subtracted, the result will be that the one point will also have weight.[413]

Further, if the planes can only be put together side-to-side, it is absurd. For just as there are two ways [we might think] to put lines
25 together, namely, end-to-end and one on top of the other, a plane

should be the same way. A [Platonic] line, though, *is* capable of being put together with a line by being put on top of it and not by being added to it [at its ends].⁴¹⁴ But then if indeed it is also possible for planes to be put together by being put one on top of the other, there will be some body that is neither an element nor composed of elements, consisting of planes put together in this way.   30

Further, if bodies are heavier due to the number of their constituent planes, as is declared in the *Timaeus*, it is clear that the line and the   **300ᵃ1** point will also have weight.⁴¹⁵ For they stand in a proportional relation to each other, as we also said previously.⁴¹⁶ If, on the other hand, they do not differ in this way but due to earth's being heavy and fire light, some planes will be heavy and others light. And what is more their   5 lines and points will be the same way. For the plane of earth will be heavier than the one of fire.

In general, the result is that either no magnitude at all, or magnitude can be done away with, if indeed as point stands in relation to line, line stands to plane, and it to body. For if all of them can be resolved into   10 each other, they will be resolved into the primary ones, so that it is possible for points alone to exist, but not body.

Besides this, if time stands similarly, it would be done away with at some time or could possibly be done away with. For the indivisible now is like a point on a line.⁴¹⁷

The same result follows for those who compose the heaven from numbers. For there are some thinkers, such as certain Pythagoreans,   15 who compose nature from numbers.⁴¹⁸ For it is evident that natural bodies have heaviness and lightness, whereas units can neither produce bodies by being put together nor have weight.⁴¹⁹

III 2

That it is necessary for some movement to belong by nature to all simple bodies is clear from the following. For since it is evident that they   20 move, it is necessary that they be moved by force, if they do not have a movement proper to them. But by force and contrary to nature are the same thing. But then if there is a movement [of them] contrary to nature, it is necessary for there also to be one in accord with nature, to which it is contrary.⁴²⁰ And if the contrary to nature is many, the in accord with nature is one. For each of them moves in accord with   25 nature in a simple way, whereas contrary to nature each has many movements.

Further, this is also clear from rest. For rest too is necessarily either by force or in accord with nature. And a thing remains at rest by force

where it spatially moves to by force, and remains at rest in accord with
nature where it spatially moves to in accord with nature. Since, then, it
is evident that something remains at rest at the center, if it does so in
accord with nature, it is clear that its spatial movement to there is also
in accord with nature, whereas if it remains at rest there by force, what
prevents it from spatially moving? If it is something at rest, we will
recycle the same argument. For it is necessary that either it is in accord
with nature that the first resting thing is at rest or it will go on without
limit, which is just impossible. On the other hand, if something moving is preventing it from spatially moving, as Empedocles says that the
earth rests because of the vortex, where could the earth spatially move
to, since to go on without limit is impossible?[421] For nothing impossible happens, and to traverse what is without limit is impossible. So
it is necessary for its spatial movement to stop somewhere, and there
it remains at rest, not by force but in accord with nature. But if there
is rest in accord with nature, there is also movement in accord with
nature, namely, the spatial movement to this place [of rest in accord
with nature].

That is why Leucippus and Democritus, who say that the primary bodies are always moving in the void, must say what sort of movement it is
and what movement of theirs is in accord with nature.[422] For if the elements are moved by each other by force, still it is necessary for each also to
have a movement in accord with nature against which it is forced.[423] Also
the primary mover must move not by force. For it will go on without limit,
if there is not some primary mover that moves in accord with nature, but
always a prior one that moves because it is moving by force.

The same difficulty necessarily results if, as is written in the *Timaeus*,
before the coming to be of the cosmos, the elements moved in a disorderly way.[424] For it is necessary for their movement to be either forced
or in accord with nature. But if they are moved in accord with nature,
it is necessary for there to be a cosmos—if one wishes to get a scientifically knowing theoretical grasp on the issue. For the primary mover
(which necessarily moves itself) moving in accord with nature, and
the ones (moving not by force) remaining at rest in their proper places,
produce the very order they have as things stand, the ones having
heaviness [moving] toward the center, and the ones having lightness
away from the center.[425] And this is the order that the cosmos has.

Further, one might ask whether it is not possible for some of the
things moving in a disorderly way to be so mixed together as to be
the ones from which bodies composed in accord with nature are composed (I mean, for example, bones and flesh), as Empedocles says happens under the reign of love.[426] For he says:

Many heads sprouted without necks.[427]

As for those who posit unlimitedly many things moving in unlimited [spatial movements], if their mover is one, it is necessary for them to be spatially moving with one spatial movement, with the result that they will not be moving in a disorderly way. On the other hand, if their movers are unlimitedly many, it is necessary for their spatial movements to be many as well. For if they are limitedly many, there will be some sort of order. For it is not by their spatially moving to the same place that disorder results. For even as things stand all things do not spatially move to the same place, but only those of the same kind (*suggenês*).

                                    301ᵃ1

Further, what is disorderly is nothing other than what is contrary to nature. For nature is the proper order of perceptible things. In any case, this very thing is absurd and impossible, namely, that what is unlimited has a disorderly movement. For the nature of things is that which most of them have for most of the time. The result, then, for these thinkers is the contrary, namely, that disorder is in accord with nature, while order and the cosmos are contrary to nature, even though nothing in accord with nature comes about by luck.[428] It seems, though, that Anaxagoras grasped at least this correctly, since he starts his cosmogony from unmoving things.[429] Others too try [elements that] are aggregating somehow and again moving and disaggregating. But to produce coming to be [of the cosmos] from things divided up and moving is not reasonable. That is why Empedocles omits it from what happens under the reign of love.[430] For he could not compose the heaven, establishing it from things separated, but made to aggregate because of love. For the cosmos is composed of elements that are disaggregated, so that it is necessary for it to have come to be from one aggregated thing.[431]

    5

    10

    15

That there is a natural movement for each of the [simple] bodies, with which it is moved neither by force nor contrary to nature, is evident from these considerations.

    20

On the other hand, that it is necessary for there to be some that have a balance-weight of heaviness and lightness is clear from the following.[432] For we say that it is necessary for them to move.[433] But if the moved thing will not have by nature a balance-weight, it is impossible for it to move either toward the center or away from the center.

    25

For let A be without heaviness, and B have heaviness, and let the one without heaviness spatially move a distance CD, and let B in an equal time spatially move a distance CE (for the one that has heaviness will move farther). If, then, the body that has heaviness is divided in the ratio CE to CD (for it is possible that this is the relation it stands in to one of its parts), if the whole spatially moves the whole of CE, the part

    30

must spatially move CD in an equal time. So what has no heaviness will spatially move the same distance as what has heaviness—which is just impossible. The same argument also applies to lightness.

301ᵇ1   Further, if there is to be a moving body that has neither lightness nor heaviness, it is necessary for it to be moved by force, and, since it is moving by force, for it to make an unlimited movement.[434] For since what moves a body is a capacity, and a smaller lighter body will be
5   moved farther by the same capacity, let A, the one without heaviness, be moved a distance CE, and B, the one with heaviness, be moved CD in an equal time. If, then, the body having weight is divided in the ratio CE to CD, the result will be that the part subtracted from the
10   body having heaviness is moved CE in equal time, since the whole was moved CD. For as the greater body is to the smaller, so will the speed of smaller be to the speed of the greater. Therefore, a body without weight and one having weight will spatially move an equal distance in the same time. But this is impossible. So, since the body without heavi-
15   ness will be moved a distance greater than any given distance, it would spatially move an unlimited one. It is evident, then, that it is necessary that every definite body have heaviness or lightness.[435]

Since nature is a starting-point of movement within the thing itself, a capacity is a starting-point of movement within another thing, or within the thing itself insofar as it is other, and all movement is either in accord with nature or by force, the one in accord with nature (for
20   example, that of a stone downward), will be made faster by force, whereas the one contrary to nature will be wholly due to it.[436] In either case, that of air is used like an instrument. For air is naturally both light and heavy. Insofar as it is light, it produces spatial movement upward, when it is pushed and gets a starting-point [of movement] from
25   a capacity, and again downward insofar as it is heavy. For, in either case, the capacity transmits it by, as it were, attaching [it to the air]. That is why what is moved by force continues to spatially move without the mover following along with it. For without a body of this sort there would be no movement by force. And it assists the movement in accord with nature of each thing in the same way.

That all [definite bodies] are either light or heavy, then, and how movements contrary to nature take place, is evident from these considerations.
30   That there is neither coming to be of everything nor of simply nothing, is clear from what was said previously.[437] For it is impossible for there to be a coming to be of every body, unless it is also possi-
302ᵃ1   ble for there to be a void that is separated.[438] For the place in which what is now coming into being will be when it has come to be, in it, it is necessary for there to be a void, since no body existed in it. For it

is possible for one body to come to be from another (for example, fire from air), but, in general, for it to do so from no preexisting other magnitude is impossible. But if the potential body is not actively some other body previously, there will be a void that is separated.[439]

III 3

It remains to say of what sorts of bodies there is coming to be and why. Since, then, in all cases knowledge is through what is primary, and primary among the constituents are the elements, we must investigate what sorts of the bodies in question are the elements, and why, and next after that what their number is and what their qualities are.[440]

This will be evident once we have set down what the nature of an element is. Let, then, an element of bodies be what other bodies are divided into, present in them either potentially or actively (for which of the two ways is still a matter for dispute), and is not itself divisible into things distinct in species.[441] Something like this is what everybody in any context wishes to mean by "element."

If, then, what was stated is an element, it is necessary for there to be some bodies of this elemental sort. For fire and earth are present potentially in flesh and wood and each thing of this sort. For it is evident that the latter are segregated out of the former. But neither flesh nor wood is present in fire either potentially or actively. For otherwise it would be segregated out. Similarly, even if there were only one thing of this sort, even then it would not be present in it.[442] For if there is going to be flesh, bone, or any of the others whatsoever, we must not just say that they are potentially present [in the element], but rather we must get a further theoretical grasp on what their mode of coming to be is.

Anaxagoras says things contrary to Empedocles about the elements. For Empedocles says that fire, earth, and the ones co-ordinate to these are elements of bodies and that everything is composed of these, whereas Anaxagoras says the contrary.[443] For he says that the homoeomerous things are the elements (I mean flesh, bone, and each of the others of that sort), and that air and fire are mixtures of these and of the other "seeds."[444] For each is composed of a mixum-gatherum of invisible homoeomerous things. That is why everything comes to be from these. For he calls fire and ether the same thing.[445]

But since every natural body has a proper movement, and some movements are simple, others mixed, and mixed ones are of mixed bodies, and simple ones of simple bodies, it is evident that there will be certain bodies that are simple.[446] For there are in fact simple movements. So it is clear that there are elements and why.

III 4

The next thing to investigate would be whether there are a limited
number of them or an unlimited, and if a limited one, how many they
are.

First, then, we must theoretically grasp that there are not, as some
people think, an unlimited number. And we shall begin with those
who make all the homoeomerous things elements, as Anaxagoras also
does.⁴⁴⁷ For none of those who think in this way correctly conceives
of an element. For we see many mixed bodies that are divisible into
homoeomerous parts—I mean, for example, flesh, bone, wood, and
stone. So, if indeed what is composite is not an element, not every
homoeomerous thing can be an element, but rather one that cannot be
divided into things distinct in species, as was said previously.⁴⁴⁸

Further, even if an element is conceived of in this way, it is not necessary to make an unlimited number. For one will achieve the same
results if one takes them to be limited in number. For one will produce
the same result, even if there are only two or three such things, as Empedocles tries to show.⁴⁴⁹ For since even on their view not everything is
produced from the homoeomerous things (for they do not produce
faces from faces, nor any other of the things that in accord with nature
have a certain shape), it is evident that it is much better to make the
starting-points limited in number, indeed as few as possible, consistent
at any rate with all the same things being shown to follow, just as the
mathematicians also demand. For they always take starting-points that
are limited in species or in number.

Further, if body is said to be distinct from body in accord with their
proper differentiae, and the differentiae of bodies are limited in number
(for they are differentiated by their perceptual qualities, and these are
limited in number; though this must be shown), it is evident that it is
necessary for the elements to be limited in number as well.⁴⁵⁰

But then what other people—for example, Leucippus and Democritus of Abdera—say does not have reasonable consequences either. For
they say that the primary things are unlimited in number and indivisible in magnitude, and that neither do many things come to be from
one nor one from many, but rather that it is by the interweaving—that
is, the combination—of the primary ones that all things will come to
be.⁴⁵¹ For in a certain way these thinkers too make all the beings be
numbers and composed of numbers.⁴⁵² For even if they do not show it
perspicuously, nonetheless this is what they wish to say.

Also, in addition to these considerations, since bodies differ in shape,
and the shapes are unlimited in number, they say that the simple bodies

are unlimited in number as well. But of what sort and what the shape is of each of the elements, they have not further determined at all, except they have assigned a spherical shape to fire.[453] On the other hand, air, water, and the others they determine by greatness and smallness, regarding these as a sort of a universal seedbed for all the elements.[454]

First of all, then, Leucippus and Democritus make the same error of not taking a limited number of starting-points, though it is possible to state the same results from them.

Further, if the differentiae of the shapes are not unlimited in number, it is clear that the elements will not be unlimited in number.

In addition to these considerations, it is necessary to be in conflict with the mathematical sciences in speaking of indivisible bodies and to do away with many reputable beliefs and things that appear to be so to perception, which have been spoken about previously in the [accounts] concerning time and movement.[455]

At the same time, though, it is even necessary for them to contradict themselves. For it is impossible, if the elements are indivisible, for greatness and smallness to differentiate air, earth, and water. For then they cannot come to be from each other. For the greatest bodies will always come to an end in being segregated out—which is the way they say water, air, and earth come to be from each other.[456]

Further, not even according to *their* supposition should one believe that the elements come to be unlimited, if indeed the [simple] bodies are differentiated by their shapes, and all shapes are composed of pyramids, rectilinear ones of rectilinear ones, and the sphere of its eight parts.[457] For it is necessary that there be certain starting-points of the shapes. So whether they are one, two, or many, the simple bodies will be the same in number.

Further, if for each of the elements there is a proper movement, and that of a simple body is simple, and the simple movements are not unlimited in number, because the simple spatial movements are not more than two and the places are not unlimited in number, the elements would not be unlimited in number either.

III 5

But since it is necessary for the elements to be limited in number, it remains to investigate whether there is more than one. For certain people suppose that there is only one, and some suppose that it is water, others air, others fire, and others something finer-grained than water and denser than air, which, being unlimited, they say encompasses all the heavens.[458]

Now those who make this one element water, air, or something
more fine-grained than water but denser than air, and have other
things come to be from these by rarefaction and condensation, all fail
to notice that they themselves are making something that is prior to
the element in question.[459] For coming to be from their elements is
composition, they say, and the one back into the elements, dissolution,
so that it is necessary for the finer-grained one to be prior in nature.[460]
Since, then, they say that of the bodies fire is the most fine-grained, fire
would be primary in nature. But [whether it is fire or not] makes no
difference. For it is necessary that it be one of the bodies other than the
one that is intermediate.

Further, having the other things generated by condensation and
rarefaction is no different from having them be so by fine-grainedness and density. For they wish the fine-grained to be rare, and the
coarse-grained to be condensed. But in turn fine-grainedness and
coarse-grainedness is the same as largeness and smallness. For what
has small parts is fine-grained and what has large parts is coarse-
grained. For what spreads itself out widely is fine-grained, and what is
composed of small parts is like that. So for these thinkers the result is
that it is by greatness and smallness that they distinguish the substance
of the others. But for those distinguishing things in this way the result
will be to say that all things are relatives, and that fire, water, and air
will not unconditionally be, but rather the same thing will be fire relative to one thing, but air relative to another.[461] This is just what results
too for those who say that there are several elements, saying that they
differ [only] in greatness and smallness. For since each is defined by
its quantity, their magnitudes will be in a certain ratio (*logos*) to each
other, so that it is necessary for the things that have this ratio to each
other to be air, fire, earth, or water, because of the ratio between smaller
magnitudes present in greater ones.

Those, on the other hand, who suppose fire to be the element avoid
this [difficulty] indeed, but for them other unreasonable consequences
necessarily result.

For some of them fasten a shape to fire, like those who make it
pyramidal, and of these, the more simple-minded ones say that it is
because the shape most capable of piercing is the pyramid, and the
body most capable of doing so fire; but the ones more subtle in argument put forward in addition that all bodies are composed of the most
fine-grained one and the solid figures of pyramids, so that, since fire is
the most fine-grained of the bodies, and the pyramid has the smallest
parts and is primary, and the primary figure belongs to the primary
body, fire would be pyramidal.[462]

Others show nothing by reasoning about the shape of fire, but only make this body the finest-grained one, and say that from it in composition the others come to be, as if they were growing together specks of dust.[463]

For both lots, however, the same difficulties result. For if they make the primary body indivisible, the arguments stated previously will come back again against their hypothesis.[464]

Further, it is not open to those who wish to get a theoretical grasp on things in a way appropriate to natural science to say this.[465] For if all bodies are comparable with respect to quantity, and the magnitudes of the homoeomerous ones stand in the same proportional relation to each other as their elements do (for example, as the magnitude of the totality of water is to that of the totality of air, so that of the element of the one is to that of the element of the other), and if there is more air than water, and, in general, more of a fine-grained one than of a coarse-grained one, it is evident that the element of water will also be smaller than that of air.[466] If, then, the smaller magnitude is contained in the greater one, the element of air would be divisible. And similarly for fire and, in general, for what is more fine-grained.

If, however, the primary body is divisible, then the result for those who assign a shape to fire is that a part of fire is not fire, because a pyramid is not composed of pyramids, and, further, that not every body will be either an element or composed of elements (for a part of fire will be neither fire nor any other element).[467] For those who differentiate by magnitude, on the other hand, the result is an element prior to their element, and this goes on without limit, if indeed every body is divisible, and the one with the smallest parts is their element.[468]

Further, for these too the result is one of saying that the same thing is fire in relation to one thing, air in relation to another, and, again, water and earth.

An error common to all who suppose a single element is to produce one natural movement only, the same for everything. For we see that every natural body has a starting-point of movement. If, then, all the bodies are one thing, the movement of all of them would be one. And with this one it is necessary for them, by just as much as they become bigger, to move more, just as fire by as much as it becomes bigger, spatially moves faster with the upward spatial movement that is its own. But the fact is many things spatially move *downward* faster [the bigger they become].

So, because of these considerations, and in addition to them, seeing that it has been determined previously that there are several natural movements, it is clear that it is impossible for there to be just one element.[469] And since there is neither an unlimited number nor just one, it is necessary for there to be several and limited in number.

III 6

First, though, we must investigate whether the elements are eternal or are coming to be and passing away.[470] For when this is shown it will also be evident both how many and of what sort they are.

25   Well, for them to be eternal is impossible. For we see fire, water, and each of the simple bodies dissolving. And it is necessary for their dissolution either to be unlimited or for it to come to a stop. Now if it is unlimited, the time of their dissolution will also be unlimited, and, again, that of their composition. For each part is dissolved and consti-

30   tuted in a distinct time. So the result will be that outside the one unlimited time there is another unlimited one, when that of composition is unlimited and, a further one, that of the dissolution prior to it. So that

305^{a}1   outside the unlimited one an unlimited one comes to be—which is just impossible.

On the other hand, if its dissolution will come to a stop somewhere, the body at which it stops will be either indivisible or, as Empedocles seems to wish to say, divisible though in fact never divided.[471]

Well, indivisible it will not be, because of the arguments stated previously.[472] But then neither is it divisible though in fact never

5   divided. For a smaller body is more easily destroyed than a larger one.[473] If indeed, then, a larger one is destroyed by this process of destruction, so that it is dissolved into smaller ones, it is reasonable that a smaller one will be yet more affected by it. But we see fire being destroyed in two ways. For it is destroyed by being extinguished by

10   its contrary, and also by itself, when it dies away. And the smaller is affected in this way by the larger, and the faster the smaller it is. So it is necessary for the elements of bodies to be capable of passing away and coming to be.

Since they are capable of coming to be, though, their coming to be will be either from an incorporeal thing or from a body, and, if from a

15   body, either from another body or from each other.

The account saying that the elements are generated from an incorporeal thing produces a separated void.[474] For everything that comes to be will have its coming to be either in something incorporeal or in one that has a body. And if it is one that has a body, there will be two bodies in the same place, the one that comes to be and also the preexisting one.[475] On the other hand, if it is incorporeal, it is necessary for there to be a definite

20   void. But that this is impossible was shown previously.[476]

But then neither can the elements come to be from some body. For the result will be that there is another body prior to the elements. But if this one has heaviness or lightness, it will be one of the elements; and if it has no balance-weight it will be immovable and mathematical, and, being such, will not be in a place.[477] For what it is at rest in, it is capable of moving in. And if by force, contrary to nature, and if not by force, in accord with nature. If, then, it is in a place, that is, somewhere, it will be one of the elements; whereas, if it is not in a place, nothing will be composed of it. For it is necessary for what comes to be and what it comes to be from to be together.[478]

Since the elements cannot come to be either from an incorporeal thing or from another body, it remains for them to come to be from each other.

III 7

Next in turn, then, we must investigate in what way it is they come to be from each other, whether as Empedocles and Democritus say, as those who dissolve them into planes do, or in some other way beyond these.[479]

Those who follow Empedocles and Democritus unwittingly do not produce coming to be of one thing from another, but only apparent coming to be. For they say that each one preexists and is segregated out, as if coming to be were from a vessel, and not from certain matter, and did not involve change.

Next, even if things were this way, the results would be no less unreasonable. For the same quantity does not seem to become heavier when compressed. But it is necessary for them to say this, if they claim that water is preexistent in air and is segregated out of it. For water, when it comes to be from air, is heavier [than the air].

Further, in the case of mixed bodies, it is not necessary, when one of the two components is segregated out, for it always to occupy a bigger place. However, when air comes to be from water it does take up a bigger place. For the finest-grained one comes to be in a bigger place.[480] This is evident too, indeed, in a case of transformation. For when a liquid becomes vaporized or pneumaticized the vessels encompassing the liquid masses break apart due to the lack of space [within them].[481] So if, in general, there is not a void and bodies cannot expand, as those who say these things claim, the impossibility [of this phenomenon] is evident.[482] On the other hand, if there is a void and expansion, it is unreasonable that of necessity what is segregated out always takes up a bigger place.

It is also necessary for the coming to be from each other to come
to a stop, if indeed in a limited quantity there is not present an unlimited number of limited quantities. For when water comes to be from
earth, a quantity is subtracted from the earth, if indeed coming to
be is by segregating out. And, in turn, when one is subtracted from
the remainder, it is the same way. If, then, this will go on forever, in
what is limited what is unlimited will be present. Since this is impossible, the generation of the elements from each other could not go on
forever.

That their change into each other, then, is not by segregating out,
has been recounted. It remains that they change into each other. And
this in two ways. For it is either by change of shape, as the same wax
can become either a sphere or a cube, or by dissolution into planes, as
some people say.[483]

If, then, it comes about by change of shape, saying that the [simple]
bodies are indivisible follows by necessity. For if they are divisible, a
part of fire will not be fire, nor a part of earth earth, because a part of
a pyramid is not in every case a pyramid, nor a part of a cube a cube.

On the other hand, if it comes about by the dissolution into planes,
first, it is absurd that not all the elements are generated from each
other, which is just what it is necessary for these people to say, and
do say. For it is not reasonable for one thing alone to be exempt from
transformation, neither does it appear to be in accord with perception,
but rather all alike appear to transform into each other. The result is
that people speaking about the things that appear to be so say things
that are not in agreement with the things that appear to be so. And the
cause of this is not correctly grasping the primary starting-points, but
instead wishing to lead everything back to certain previously determined beliefs. For presumably the starting-points of perceptible things
must be perceptible, of eternal ones eternal, of things capable of passing away things capable of passing away, and, in general, each must be
of the same genus (*homogenês*) as what falls under it. But out of love for
these beliefs of theirs they seem to do the same thing as those defending their theses in [dialectical] arguments.[484] For they submit to every
consequence on the supposition that they possess true starting-points,
as if starting-points must not sometimes be judged on the basis of what
follows from them, and most of all on the basis of their ends. And the
end in the case of productive science is the work, and in that of natural
science what appears to be so to perception has the controlling vote in
every case.[485]

The result for these thinkers is that earth is most of all an element,
and is alone incapable of passing away, if indeed the incapable of

dissolving is incapable of passing away and is an element. For earth alone is incapable of dissolving into another body.[486]

Moreover, in the case of those that do dissolve, the "dangling" of the triangles is not reasonable either. But this happens whenever one thing is transformed into another, because of the numerical inequality of the triangles that compose them.[487]

Further, it is necessary for those who state these views to make coming to be, be not from a body. For when something comes to be from planes, it will not come to be from a body.

In addition to these things it is necessary for them to say that not all body is divisible, yet this will conflict with the most exact sciences.[488] For these, the mathematical ones, suppose even an intelligible [body] to be divisible, whereas these thinkers, because of their wish to save their hypothesis, do not even admit that all perceptible [body] is divisible.[489] For it is necessary for those who produce a shape for each of the elements and define their substance by it to make these elements indivisible. For a pyramid or a sphere divided in a certain way will not leave a remainder that is a sphere or a pyramid. So a part of fire will not be fire, but rather there will be something prior to that element, because everything is either an element or composed of elements; or else not every body will be divisible.

III 8

In general, the attempt to assign a shape to the simple bodies is unreasonable, first, because the result will be that the whole will not be filled up.[490] For among plane figures three shapes seem to fill the [whole of] place, triangle, square, and hexagon, and among the solids two only, pyramid and cube.[491] But it is necessary to suppose more of these because they posit more [than two] elements.

Next, it is evident that all the simple bodies take their shape from the encompassing place, especially water and air. It is impossible, then, for the shape of the element to remain constant. For, if it did, the whole thing would not be on every side in contact with what encompasses it. But then if its shape will be changed, it will no longer be water, if indeed it was differentiated by shape. So it is evident that there are no definite shapes for these elements.

Indeed, it seems that nature itself indicates to us that this is in accord with reason (*logos*). For just as in other cases the underlying subject must be formless and shapeless (for in this condition it would be most capable of receiving shape, like the "all-receptive" written about in the *Timaeus*), in the same way too the elements must be considered as

20

25

30

306^b1

5

10

15

20   matter.[492] That is why indeed, being separate from their qualitative differences (*diaphora*), they are capable of changing into each other.

In addition to these considerations, how is it possible for flesh,
bone, or any other of the continuous bodies whatsoever to come to
be? For they cannot do so from the elements themselves, because what
is continuous does not come to be from what is composite, nor from
25   the composition of planes. For it is elements that would come to be
by composition and not the things composed of elements. So if one
wishes to argue in an exact way and not accept views of this on the
basis of a passing glance at the arguments, one will see that they do
away with the coming to be of the beings.

Moreover, the shapes attributed to bodies are discordant with the
30   very affections, capacities, and movements they especially looked
toward in assigning them as they do. For example, since fire is most
capable of movement, and also is capable of heating and of burning,
some people made it a sphere, others a pyramid.[493] For these are the
most capable of movement because they have minimal contact and are
the least stable, and are also most capable of heating and most capa-
307^{a}1   ble of burning, because the one is wholly angle, and the other has the
sharpest angles, and it is by their angles, they say, that they burn and
heat.

Now, in the first place, with reference to movement both lots are
in error. For even if these shapes are the most capable of movement,
5   yet they are not most capable of the movement of fire. For that of fire
is upward and rectilinear, whereas these shapes are most capable of
moving in a circle—so-called rolling. Next, if earth is a cube because it
is stable and remains at rest, but it remains at rest not in any random
place but in its own place, and spatially moves away from anywhere
10   else unless prevented, and fire and the others are the same way, it is
clear that fire too and each of the elements will be a sphere or pyramid
in an alien place, but in its proper one will be a cube.

Further, if fire heats and burns because of its angles, all the elements
will be capable of heating, though one perhaps more than another. For
15   all have angles—for example, the octahedron and the dodecahedron.
(For Democritus indeed even the sphere is a sort of angle, which cuts
because it is most capable of movement.[494]) So the elements will differ
[only] in the more and less. But it is evident that this is false.[495]

At the same time it will result that even mathematical bodies heat
20   and burn. For they too have angles and include indivisible spheres and
pyramids (anyhow if, as these thinkers say, there are in fact indivisible
magnitudes). For if one lot [of shapes] do and another lot do not, they

must state the difference, and not state it simply in the way they do state it.

Further, if what is burned becomes fire, and fire is a sphere or pyramid, it is necessary for what is burned to become spheres or pyramids. Now grant, as in accord with reason, that cutting and dividing are a result of these shapes. But that a pyramid of necessity produces pyramids or a sphere spheres is entirely nonrational, and is as if someone were to think a knife divides things into knives or a saw into saws.

Further, it is ridiculous to assign a shape to fire only with a view to dividing. For it seems more to aggregate and bring together than to disaggregate. For it disaggregates things of different kinds, but aggregates those of the same kind. And while the aggregating is intrinsic to it (for bringing together and uniting are characteristic of fire), the disaggregating is coincidental (for it is in aggregating what is of the same kind that it removes what is alien).[496] So that either they should have looked toward both when they assigned [it a shape] or, better, toward the aggregating.[497]

In addition to these considerations, since hot and cold are contrary in capacity, it is impossible to assign any shape to cold. For the shape assigned to it must be contrary to [the one assigned to hot], but no shape is contrary to a shape.[498] That is why all these thinkers omit this [, namely, assigning a shape to cold]. Yet it is fitting to have defined all by shape or none. Some, though, in having tried to say something about this capacity contradicted themselves. For what has large particles, they say, is cold, because it compresses and cannot pass through the ducts.[499] It is clear, therefore, that what is hot would be what does pass through. But something of that sort always has small particles. So the result is that hot and cold are determined by their largeness and smallness, and not by their shapes. Further, if the pyramids are unequal in size, the large ones would not be fire and neither would their shape be a cause of burning, but rather the contrary.

It is evident, then, from these considerations that the elements are not determined by their shapes. And since the most controlling differences (*diaphora*) characteristic of bodies are their affections, works, and capacities (for we say that each of the things that are by nature has works, affections, and capacities), we must speak about these first, in such a way that having got a theoretical grasp on them we would get hold of the differences between them.[500]

Book IV

IV 1

Concerning light and heavy, what each of them is and what their nature is, must be investigated, and due to what cause they have these capacities of theirs. For theoretical knowledge about these is proper to accounts dealing with movement. For we say that things are heavy or light in virtue of their being capable of being moved naturally in a certain way.[501] (To the activations of these, though, names are not assigned, unless it was thought that "balance-weight" is such.[502])

Because the work of natural science concerns movement, and these things have within them some spark (as it were) of movement, all thinkers make use of their capacities, but—except for a few—have not *defined* them.

Having first looked at what other people have said, then, and gone through the puzzles that it is necessary for this investigation to go through, let us then state the things that appear to us to be so about these matters.

Heavy and light, then, are said of things unconditionally and in relation to something else.[503] For of things having heaviness, we say that one is lighter, the other heavier—for example, bronze is heavier than wood. Now about the ones said unconditionally nothing has been said by our predecessors, though about those in relation to something else they did speak. For they do not say what heavy is and what light is, but only what heavier or lighter is in things that have heaviness. This will be more clear if we state it as follows. For some things are always naturally moved spatially away from the center, while others are so toward the center. Of these, the ones that spatially move away from the center, I say are moved upward, the ones toward the center downward.

For it is absurd to think that there is no up and down in the heaven, as some people claim. For there is no up and down, they say, if indeed it is similar in every direction, and from whatever point he traverses it a given person will come to his own antipodes.[504] For our part, we say that the extremity of the universe is up, both up as regards position and by nature primary.[505] And since the heaven has an extremity and a center, it is clear that it will also have an up and a down, as even ordinary people say, except not on adequate grounds.[506] The cause of this inadequacy is that they think that the heaven is not similar in every direction, but that the hemisphere above us is the only one, since if they supposed in addition that it was like this all around, with the center similarly related to all of it, they would say that the extremity is up, the center down.

We say, then, that the unconditionally light is what spatially moves upward, that is, toward the extremity, and the unconditionally heavy is what spatially moves toward the center. By contrast, we say that one thing is light or lighter in relation to something else, when of two bodies having heaviness and equal in mass, the other by nature spatially moves downward faster.

IV 2

Of those of our predecessors, then, who set out to investigate these things, pretty much the majority have spoken only about what is heavy and light in this relative way, in which of two things having heaviness, one is lighter than the other. And having proceeded in this way they think they have also made determinations about what is unconditionally heavy or light. But their argument does not apply to these. This will become more clear as we advance.

For some of them speak of lighter and heavier in the way one finds it written about in the *Timaeus*, where the heavier is what is composed of the greater number of the same sort of parts, the lighter what is composed of fewer, as in the case of lead a greater quantity of lead is heavier, and in the case of bronze a greater quantity of bronze.[507] And likewise for each of the other things that are the same in form. And in the same way, they say, lead is heavier than wood. For all bodies are composed of the same things and of one matter, though they do not seem to be.

Having made determinations in this way, then, they have said nothing about what is unconditionally light or heavy. For as things stand fire is always light and spatially moves upward, whereas earth and all earthy things spatially move toward the center, so that it is not because of the small number of the triangles of which, they say, each [body] is composed, that fire naturally moves upward. For otherwise a greater quantity would have spatially moved less and been heavier, being composed of a greater number of triangles. But as things stand it is evident that the contrary happens. For the greater the quantity of fire, the lighter it is and the faster it spatially moves upward. And from up to down a smaller quantity of fire is spatially moved faster, and a larger one more slowly.[508]

In addition to these considerations, since to be lighter is to have fewer of the homogeneous parts and to be heavier is to have more, and air, water, and fire are composed of the same triangles, though

differing in being less numerous and more numerous, due to which
some of these are lighter, others heavier, there will be some quantity of
air that will be heavier than water. But entirely the contrary happens.
For the larger the quantity of air the more it always spatially moves
upward, and any part of air whatsoever spatially moves upward out of
water.

This, then, is the way some people have made determinations about
light and heavy. Others, however, did not believe it sufficient to determine them in this way, but rather, even though they are of an older
generation than our contemporaries, they had a more novel understanding of the things now being discussed. For it is evident that certain
bodies, though their mass is smaller, are heavier than others. It is clear,
then, that it is not sufficient to say that bodies composed of an equal
number of primary things are equal in weight. For then they would be
equal in mass. While for those who say that planes are the primary and
indivisible things of which bodies having heaviness are composed, it is
absurd to say this, for those who say that they are solids it is more open
to say that the greater of them is the heavier. As for composites, since it
is evident indeed that not each of them has [heaviness] in this way, but
we see many heavier ones to be smaller in mass (for example, bronze
in comparison to wool), some people think up and state another cause.
For the void enclosed in the bodies lightens them, they say, sometime
making the larger ones lighter. For it is because of this too that the
greater mass is often composed of the same number of solid particles
[as the lesser] or even of fewer. And in general, in fact, in every case the
cause of being lighter is enclosing more void.

They speak, then, in this way. But it is necessary for those who make
their determinations in that way to add not only that the body contains
more void, but also less of what is solid. For if the proportion of solid
will exceed that of void, it will not be lighter.[509] For it is because of this
too, they say, that fire is lightest, namely, because it contains more void.
The result will be, then, that a large quantity of gold containing more
void will be lighter than a small quantity of fire, but for the fact that it
will also contain many times the amount of solid. So this must be said
[in addition].

Of those denying the existence of a void, some have determined
nothing about light and heavy—for example, Anaxagoras and Empedocles.[510] Others, however, having made determinations, while denying the existence of a void, said nothing about why there are bodies
that are unconditionally light or heavy, that is, why the one lot spatially
moves always upward and the other lot downward. And they made no
mention either about there being some bodies that are greater in mass

but lighter, nor is it clear, on the basis of what has been said, how what   25
they say will be in agreement with the things that seem to be so.

On the other hand, it is necessary for those who speak of the lightness of fire as being caused by its containing a larger quantity of void to
be subject to pretty much the same difficulties. For while it will contain
less solid and more void than other bodies, nonetheless there will be   30
some quantity of fire in which the solid and full part exceeds the solid
ones encompassed in some small quantity of earth. If they were to say
that there is also an excess of void, how will they determine what is
unconditionally heavy? Surely, either by its containing more solid or
less void. If, then, this is what they say, there will be some quantity of
earth so small that in it there will be less solid than in a large quantity   309^{b}1
of fire. Similarly, if they determine this by using the void, there will be a
body lighter than what is unconditionally light, which always spatially
moves upward though itself always spatially moving downward. But
this is impossible. For the unconditionally light is always lighter than
what has heaviness and moves downward, whereas what is lighter is   5
not always light, because, among the things that have heaviness, one is
said to be lighter than another—for example, water than earth.

Moreover, neither will having void stand in a proportional relation
to plenum be sufficient to resolve the puzzle now under discussion. For
speaking in this way will result in the same impossibility. For a larger   10
and a smaller quantity of fire will contain the same ratio (*logos*) of solid
to void.[511] But the larger quantity of fire spatially moves upward faster
than the smaller one, and, conversely, in the same way a larger quantity
of gold or of lead spatially moves downward faster than a smaller one.
Similarly too for each of the other things that have heaviness. But this
should not be the case, if indeed heavy and light are determined by this   15
[sort of proportional relation].

It is also absurd if it is because of a void that some things spatially
move upward, but the void itself does not move. But then if void naturally moves spatially upward, and plenum downward, and this is why
they are respectively the cause of these spatial movements in other
things, there is no need to investigate where composite bodies are concerned why some are light and others heavy, but rather to say where   20
these things themselves are concerned why one is light and the other
has heaviness, and, further, due to what cause do plenum and void not
stand apart from each other.[512]

It is also unreasonable to make a space for the void, as if the void
is not itself a sort of space. But it is necessary, if indeed the void is to   25
move, for there to be some place belonging to it, from which and to
which it changes.

In addition to these considerations, what is the cause of movement? For it is surely not voidness. For it is not void alone that is moved, but the solid as well.[513]

The results are the same if one were to determine things in another way, namely, by having smallness and largeness make one thing heav-
30   ier or lighter than another, or establishing them in some other way, whatever it might be, but only assigning the same matter to all, or if more than one, a pair of contraries only.

For if there is one matter, as there is for those who compose things from triangles, there will not be unconditional heaviness or lightness. On the other hand, if there are contrary ones, as there are for those with void and plenum, there will not be for the things intermediate
310^{a}1   between the unconditionally heavy and unconditionally light ones a cause due to which one is heavier or lighter than another or than the unconditional ones.[514]

To determine these by largeness and smallness seems more like a fab-rication than the previous ones; but because it can produce differences
5   (*diaphora*) between each of the four elements, it is better safeguarded against the foregoing puzzles. But making things have one nature, though differing in size, necessarily has the same result as for those who make them have one matter, namely, that nothing is unconditionally light or spatially moves upward, except by being passed by other things
10   or being squeezed out, and that many small things are heavier than a few large ones.[515] If this is going to be the case, however, the result will be that a large quantity of air or a large quantity of water will be heavier than a small quantity of water or earth. But this is impossible.

These, then, are the things said by others, and this the way they are
15   stated.

IV 3

Speaking for ourselves, though, our first task is one of making deter-minations about something that certain thinkers are most puzzled by, namely, why it is that some bodies always spatially move upward in accord with nature, others downward, and others both upward and downward, and, after this, about heavy and light and the coinciden-tal attributes pertaining to them, and due to what cause each comes about.[516]

20   About the spatial movement of each thing toward its own place, we must make the same supposition as about the other sorts of coming to be and of change. For there are three sorts of movement (with respect to size, with respect to form, and with respect to place), and in each

of these we see the change coming about from contraries to contra-   25
ries or to intermediates, and not the change from what is random to
what is random.⁵¹⁷ Similarly, neither is a random thing capable of moving a random thing. Instead, just as what is capable of being altered
and capable of being increased are distinct, so too are what is capable
of altering and what is capable of increasing. In the same way, then,
we must suppose about both what is capable of moving and of being
moved with respect to place that a random thing is not capable of mov-   30
ing or being moved by a random thing.

If, then, what is capable of moving upward or downward is what is
capable of making heavy or capable of making light, and what is moved
is what is potentially heavy or light, the spatial movement of each body
toward its own place is spatial movement toward its own form.⁵¹⁸ (This
is more how one should take what the ancients said, namely, that like   310ᵇ1
spatially moves to like.⁵¹⁹ For this does not result in every case. For if one
were to displace the earth to where the moon is now, each of its parts
would spatially move not toward it, but to just where it in fact is now.⁵²⁰
In general, then, when bodies that are similar and undifferentiated are   5
moved with the same movement this must result, namely, that the place
it is natural for any one part to spatially move toward is also the place it
is natural for all of it to move toward. But since place is the limit of what
encompasses, and the extremity and the center encompass all the things
moving upward and downward, it in a certain way becomes the form of
what is encompassed, it is to its like that a body moves when it moves to   10
its own place.⁵²¹ For the successive ones are like each other—for example, water is like air and air is like fire. And it is possible to reverse the
intermediate ones, but not the extremes—for example, air is like water,
water is like earth. For the relation of each higher body to the one falling
below it is that of form to matter.⁵²²)   15

Since [all that is so], to investigate why fire spatially moves upward
and earth downward is the same as investigating why what is capable of being made healthy, when moved and changed insofar as it is
capable of being made healthy, proceeds toward being healthy and not
toward whiteness.⁵²³ Likewise too for all the other things capable of
alteration. Whatever is capable of being increased, when it changes
insofar as it is capable of increase, proceeds not toward being healthy   20
but toward an increased size. And it is likewise too in the case of each
of them, one changes in quality, another in quantity, and, in place, light
ones [proceed] upward, heavy ones downward.

The one exception is that these seem to have a starting-point of
change within themselves (I mean the heavy and the light), whereas
the others do not, but rather an external one—for example, what is   25

capable of being made healthy and what is capable of being increased.
[*Objection*] And yet sometimes these too change of themselves, and on
a small movement coming about in what is external, the one proceeds
toward health, the other toward increase. [*Reply*] Yes, and since the
same thing that is capable of being made healthy is receptive of disease,
if it is moved insofar as it is capable of being made healthy, it moves
30 toward health, if it is moved insofar as it is [capable of being made]
diseased, toward disease.⁵²⁴ But the heavy and light, more than these,
appear to have within themselves the starting-point, because their
matter is closer to substance.⁵²⁵ A sign of this is that spatial movement
belongs to independent things, and in coming to be is the last of the
movements, so that this movement would be primary with respect to
311ᵃ1 substance.⁵²⁶ When, then, air comes to be from water and light from
heavy, it progresses upward. And at the same time it *is* light, and is
no longer becoming so, but in that place *is*.⁵²⁷ It is evident, then, that
being potentially, going toward actuality, it is progressing to that place,
5 quantity, and quality where the actualization of its quantity and quality
and place lie.⁵²⁸ And it is due to the same cause too that what already
exists and is earth or fire moves toward its own place if there is nothing impeding it. For nourishment too, when nothing prevents it, and
what is capable of being made healthy, insofar as nothing restrains it,
proceed immediately. But what causes the movement is what produces
10 it at the start, what removed the hindrance, or from which the thing
rebounded, as was said in our first accounts, in which we determined
that none of these things moves itself.⁵²⁹

The cause due to which each of the spatially moving bodies spatially
moves, and what moving to its own place is, has now been stated.

IV 4

We have now to speak about the differentiae and the coincidental attrib-
15 utes pertaining to these.⁵³⁰ First, then, let us take as determined, as evident to all, that the unconditionally heavy is what sinks below everything
else, and the unconditionally light, what rises above everything else. By
"unconditionally," I mean looking to the genus, and not to those things
to which both heavy and light belong.⁵³¹ For example, it is evident that
any random quantity of fire spatially moves upward, if no other random
20 thing prevents it, and one of earth does so downward. And in the same
way too a larger quantity does so faster.

But the things to which both belong are heavy and light in another
way. For they both sink below and rise above, as air and water do. For
neither of these is unconditionally light or heavy. For both are lighter

than earth (for any random part of either rises above it), but heavier   25
than fire (for any part whatsoever of these sinks below it), whereas in
relation to each, water is unconditionally heavy, air unconditionally
light. For air in whatever quantity rises above water, while water in
whatever quantity sinks below air.

But since of the other bodies, some have heaviness, others lightness,
it is clear that in every case the cause lies in the differentia of their   30
non-composite parts.[532] For some bodies will be light and others heavy
as they happen to have more of one and less of the other of these. So
it is about these that we must speak. For the other bodies follow along
with the primary ones. Which is just, as we said, what those thinkers
should have done who say that heaviness is due to the plenum and   35
lightness due to the void.[533]

The result, then, is that the same things do not seem to be heavy   311^{b}1
or light everywhere, because of the differentia of the primary parts. I
mean, for example, that in air a talent of wood is heavier than a mina
of lead, but in water it is lighter.[534] The cause is that all bodies have
heaviness except for fire, and lightness except for earth. Earth, then,   5
and whatever contains the most earth, necessarily has heaviness everywhere, water everywhere except in earth, air everywhere except in
water and in earth. For in their own space all have heaviness except fire,
even air. A sign of this is that an inflated wineskin weighs more than an
empty one. So that if something contains more air than earth or water,   10
it may be lighter than something else in water, but heavier in air. For it
does not rise above air, but it does rise to above water.

That there is an unconditionally light and an unconditionally heavy
is evident from the following. By "unconditionally light" I mean what
always spatially moves upward naturally, and by "unconditionally
heavy" what always does so downward, if nothing prevents it. For there   15
are bodies of both sorts, and it is not the case, as some people think,
that all bodies have heaviness.[535] For other people too think that there
is something heavy, that is, that always spatially moves toward the
center.[536] And in a similar way there is what is light. For we see, as was
said previously, that earthy bodies sink below everything else and spatially move toward the center.[537] But surely the center is definite.[538] If,   20
therefore, there is something that rises above everything else, as fire is
observed to spatially move upward even in air itself, the air remaining at rest, it is clear that it spatially moves toward the extremity.[539]
So it itself cannot have any heaviness. For if it did it would sink below
something. And if that were so, there would be something else that
spatially moves toward the extremity, and rises above all spatially mov-   25
ing things. But as things stand none appears to do so. Therefore, fire

has no heaviness at all, nor does earth have any lightness whatsoever, if indeed it sinks below all other things, and what sinks below spatially moves toward the center.

    Moreover, that there is a center that the spatial movement of bodies having heaviness is toward is clear from many considerations.

    First, no body can possibly go on spatially moving without limit. For just as nothing impossible can exist, in the same way neither can it come to be. And spatial movement is a process of coming to be from one place to another place.

    Next, fire spatially moving upward, and earth and everything having heaviness spatially moving downward, are observed to do so at similar angles.[540] So it is necessary for them to spatially move toward the center. (Whether the resulting movement is toward the center of the earth or toward that of the universe, since of these it is the same point, is for another account.[541]) But since what sinks below all bodies spatially moves toward the center, it is necessary for what rises above everything else to spatially move toward the extremity of the space in which their movement is produced. For the center is contrary to the extremity, and what is always sinking below is contrary to what is always rising above. That is why it is also reasonable that the light and the heavy are two things. For the places are also two: the center and the extremity.

    But there is also a place intermediate between these, which is said to be one relative to the other. For the intermediate is in a way extremity and center of both.[542] This is why there is also something else, namely, a heavy and light, such as water and air.

    And we say that what encompasses pertains to form, what is encompassed to matter.[543] And this distinction exists in every genus.[544] For in [the category] of quality as in of quantity, there is what is more the way form is, and what is more the way matter is.[545] And in the case of what has to do with place it is the same way: up pertains to what is defined, down pertains to matter.[546] So in the case of the matter itself for what is heavy and light, insofar as it is potentially of the one sort, it is matter for what is heavy, insofar as it is potentially of the other sort, matter for what is light. And it is the same matter, but its being is not the same [in the two cases], as in what is capable of being made diseased and what is capable of being made healthy.[547] For their being is not the same; which is why being diseased is not the same as being healthy either.

IV 5

What has the relevant sort of matter, then, is light and always [spatially moves] upward, and what has the contrary sort is heavy and always [does so] downward. And what has other sorts of matter than these, but ones having in relation to each other what these themselves have unconditionally, has both upward and downward spatial movements.^{548} That is why air and water each has both lightness and heaviness, water sinks below everything except earth, and earth rises above everything except fire.

But since there is only one body that rises above everything else and only one that sinks below everything else, it is necessary for there to be two others that both sink below some things and rise above others.

So it is also necessary for there to be just as many sorts of matter as of these bodies (namely, four), but in such a way that there is one matter common to all of them—especially if they come to be from each other—though its being is distinct.^{549} For there is nothing to prevent there being one or more intermediates between the contraries, as in the case of colors.^{550} For "intermediate" and "center" are said of things in many ways.^{551}

Each of the bodies having both heaviness and lightness, then, has heaviness in its own space (whereas earth has heaviness everywhere), but does not have lightness, except in those in which it rises.

That is also why if a supporting body is removed each spatially moves to the body next below it, air to the space of water, water to that of earth. But air will not spatially move upward into the space of fire, if the fire is done away with, except by force, just as water is drawn up when its surface becomes one [with that of air], and something draws it upward faster than the water's own spatial movement downward.^{552} Nor will water spatially move into the space of air, except in the way just now stated. Earth, on the other hand, is not thus affected, because its surface is not one [with that of water].^{553} That is why water is drawn up into a vessel heated by fire, whereas earth is not. And as earth does not spatially move upward, neither does fire move downward when the air supporting it is removed. For fire has no heaviness at all even in its own space, just as earth has no lightness. But the two other bodies spatially move downward when the supporting body is removed, because, while what is unconditionally heavy sinks below everything else, what is relatively heavy sinks as far as its own space or as the body in which it rises, because of the similarity of matter.^{554}

And that it is necessary to make differentia equal in number to bodies is clear. For if there is one sort of matter for all things (for example, void or plenum, or magnitude, or triangles), either all will spatially move upward or all downward, and the other spatial movement will not exist at all. So either nothing will be unconditionally light, if everything causes a balance to incline more downward due to the size

or number of its constituent bodies, or because there are plenums (we
see this, though, and it has been shown, that in the same way as there
is something that spatially moves always and everywhere downward,
there is something that does so always and everywhere upward); or, if
due to void or something of this sort, it does so always upward, nothing will do so always downward.[555] Also, there will of course be certain
intermediates that spatially move faster downward than earth does.
For in a large quantity of air there will be more triangles, or solids, or
small [particles].[556] But it is evident that not one part of air spatially
moves downward. It is likewise in the case of lightness too, if it is made
to depend on a greater quantity of the matter in question.

If on the other hand there are two sorts of matter, how will the
intermediates do the things air and water do? (For example, suppose
someone were to say that they are void and plenum. Fire, then, is void,
because it moves upward, whereas earth is a plenum, because it moves
downward. And air contains a preponderance of fire, water of earth.)
For there will then be a quantity of water containing more fire than a
small quantity of air does, and a large quantity of air containing more
earth than a small quantity of water does, so that some quantity of air
will have to spatially move downward faster than a small quantity of
water. But this never appears to happen anywhere.

It is necessary, therefore, that just as fire in fact moves upward,
because it contains something (for example, void), whereas the others do not, and earth moves downward, because it contains a plenum,
so air moves to its own [place] and above water, because it contains
something else, and water downward, because it contains something
else again.

But if air and water both contained one [matter], or two matters that
will both belong to each, there will be a certain quantity of each that
will make water exceed a small quantity of air in [its speed of] moving
upward, and air that of water in moving downward, as we have often said.

IV 6

Shapes are not a cause of unconditional spatial movement downward
or upward, but rather of making it faster or slower. And the causes due
to which they do so are not difficult to see. For what makes one puzzle
now is why a flat piece of iron or lead floats on water, whereas other
smaller and less heavy ones, if they are round or elongated—a needle,
for example—spatially move downward, and why it is that certain bodies float because of their smallness, as metal filings and other earthy
and dust-like particles do in air.

Where all three cases are concerned, to consider their cause to be as Democritus alleges is not correct. For he says that hot particles spatially moving upward from water hold up flat bodies that have heaviness, but let narrow ones fall through. For only a small number of these particles offer resistance to them. But this should happen more easily in air, an objection which he himself raises. But he resolves it in a weak way. For he says that "the surge" does not impel in [only] one direction, meaning by "the surge" the movement of the spatially moving bodies upward.[557]

But since some continuous bodies are more easily divided and other less, and since things capable of dividing them are the same way, some more capable, others less, it is this fact that we must consider to be the cause. Now what is easily bounded is easily divided, and more so what is more so; and air is more like this than water, water than earth. Also, the smaller the quantity in each genus, the more easily it is divided and dispersed.[558] But those having breadth remain in place because of covering so large a surface, and because the large quantity is less easily dispersed.[559] Those, on the other hand, that have contrary shapes, because of covering so small a surface, spatially move downward, because the division is easy. And this happens much more easily in air, insofar as it is more easily divided than water.

But since the heavy has a certain strength in accord with which it spatially moves downward, and continuous bodies have one for not being dispersed, these must be pitted against each other. For if the strength of the heavy one exceeds that in the continuous one for not being dispersed and divided, then it will force itself downward faster, whereas if it is weaker, it will float on the surface.

Concerning heaviness and lightness, then, and the coincidental attributes pertaining to these, let things be determined in this way.[560]

Notes

Book I

Note 1

It is evident that (*phainetai*): *Phainomena* are things that appear (often to perception) to be so, but that may or may not be so. The corresponding verb *phainesthai* ("appear"), when used with a participle, as it is here, endorses what appears to be so and is translated "it is evident that," "or it is seen to be that," or the like, and when used with an infinitive it neither endorses nor rejects what appears to be so and is translated "appears." When it occurs without a participle or an infinitive, it may either endorse or reject.

Scientific knowledge (*epistêmê*): (1) Aristotle usually divides sciences (*epistêmai*) into three kinds: theoretical (contemplative), practical (action-involving), and productive (crafts) (*Top.* VI 6 145^{a}15–16, *Met.* XI 7 1064^{a}16–19). But sometimes a more fine-grained classification is employed, in which theoretical sciences are divided into natural sciences (such as physics and biology) and strictly theoretical sciences (such as astronomy and theology) on the basis of the kinds of beings with which they deal (*Ph.* II 7 198^{a}21–^{b}4, *Met.* VI 1 1025^{b}18–1026^{a}32). The term *epistêmê* is sometimes reserved for the unconditional scientific knowledge provided exclusively by the strictly theoretical sciences (*NE* VI 3 1139^{b}31–34), but typically it is used in the looser sense, which encompasses the practical and productive sciences as well. To understand what a science—whether theoretical, productive, or practical—is like we must begin a few steps back.

(2) A statement (*logos apophantikos*) is the true (or false) predication of a single predicate term A of a single subject term B, either as an affirmation (*kataphasis*) (A belongs to B) or a denial (*apophasis*) (A does not belong to B) (*Int.* 5, 8). What makes a term a single subject term, however, is not that it is grammatically singular or serves as a grammatical subject but that it designates a substantial particular—a canonical example of which is a perceptible matter-form compound, such as Socrates. Similarly, what makes a term a predicate is that it designates a universal (man, pale)—something that can have many particular instances. When the role of predicate is restricted to universals, therefore, while that of subject is left open to both particulars and universals, it is more on ontological or metaphysical grounds than on what we would consider strictly logical ones. Subjects and predicates are thus ontological items, types of beings, rather than linguistic or conceptual ones, and logical principles, such as PNC, are very general ontological principles, truths about all beings as such, or qua beings. Particular affirmations (Socrates is a man) and general affirmations (Men are mortal) have the same

subject-predicate form, but when the subject is a universal, the affirmation may itself be either universal (All men are mortal) or particular (Some men are mortal)—that is to say, the predicate may be affirmed (denied) of the subject either universally (*katholou*) or in part (*kata meros*) or, if the quantifier is omitted (Men are mortal), indefinitely (*adioristôs*). General affirmations, as a result, which are the only ones of interest to science (*Met.* VII 15 1039ᵇ27–31), are of four types: A belongs to all B (**aAB**), A belongs to no B (**eAB**), A belongs to some B (**iAB**), A does not belong to all B (**oAB**).

(3) A *science* is a state of the soul that enables its possessor to give demonstrative explanations—where a demonstration (*apodeixis*) is a special sort of deduction (*sullogismos*) from scientific starting-points and a deduction is "an argument in which, certain things having been supposed, something different from those supposed things necessarily results because of their being so" (*APr.* I 2 24ᵇ18–20). The things supposed are the argument's premises; the necessitated result is its conclusion; all three are affirmations of one of the four types we looked at. In Aristotle's view, such deductions are *syllogisms* (*sullogismos*, again) consisting of a major premise, a minor premise, and a conclusion, where the premises have exactly one "middle" term in common, and the conclusion contains only the other two "extreme" terms. The conclusion's predicate term is the *major term*, contributed by the major premise; its subject is the *minor term*, contributed by the minor premise. The middle term must be either subject of both premises, predicate of both, or subject of one and predicate of the other. The resulting possible combinations of terms yield the so-called figures of the syllogism:

	First figure		Second figure		Third figure	
	Predicate	Subject	Predicate	Subject	Predicate	Subject
Premise	A	B	A	B	A	C
Premise	B	C	A	C	B	C
Conclusion	A	C	B	C	A	B

Systematic investigation of the possible combinations of premises in each of these figures results in the identification of the *moods* or modes that constitute valid deductions. In the first figure, these are as follows:

Form	Mnemonic	Proof
aAB, aBC ｜ aAC	Barbara	Perfect
eAB, aBC ｜ eAC	Celarent	Perfect
aAB, iBC ｜ iAC	Darii	Perfect
eAB, iBC ｜ oAC	Ferio	Perfect

A mood is perfect when there is a proof of its validity that is *direct*, in that it does not rely on the validity of any other mood. Only first figure syllogisms have perfect moods.

(4) Besides their logical interest as admitting of direct proof, perfect syllogisms in Barbara are also of particular importance to science. First, because "syllogisms that give the reason why, which hold either universally or for the most part, in most cases are carried out through this figure. That is why it is the most scientific of all; for getting a theoretical grasp on the reason why is most important for [scientific] knowledge" (*APo.* I 14 79ᵃ20–24). Second, "only through this figure can you hunt for scientific knowledge of something's essence" (79ᵃ24–25): essences hold universally, only perfect syllogisms in Barbara have universal conclusions, and definitions of essences, which are scientific starting-points, must hold universally.

(5) Specifically scientific starting-points are of just three types (*APo.* I 10 76ᵃ37–ᵇ22). Those *special* to a science are *definitions* (*Rh.* II 23 1398ᵃ15–27) of the real (as opposed to nominal) essences of the beings with which the science deals (II 3 90ᵇ24, II 10 93ᵇ29–94ᵃ19). Because these are definitions by genus and differentia (II 13 96ᵃ20–97ᵇ39), a single science must deal with a single genus (*APo.* I 7 75ᵇ10–11, I 23 84ᵃ17–18, 28 87ᵃ38–39). Other starting-points (so-called axioms) are common to all or many sciences (*APo.* I 2 72ᵃ14–24, I 32 88ᵃ36–ᵇ3). A third sort of starting-point posits the existence of the genus with which the science deals, but this may often be left implicit if the existence of the genus is clear (I 10 76ᵇ17–18). The source of these starting-points, in turn, is perception and experience, which lead by induction to a grasp by understanding of them: "From perception memory comes to be, and from many memories of the same thing, experience. For, then, memories that are many in number form one experience. And from experience, or from the whole universal that has come to rest in the soul (the one over and above the many, this being whatever is present as one and the same in all of them), comes a starting-point (*archê*) of craft knowledge and scientific knowledge—of craft knowledge if it concerns coming to be (*genesis*), of scientific knowledge if it concerns being" (*APo.* II 19 100ᵃ3–9).

(6) To constitute a *demonstration* (*apodeixis*) a deduction must be a valid syllogism in the mood Barbara, whose premises meet a number of conditions. First, they must be immediate or indemonstrable, and so must be reached through induction. Second, our confidence in them must be unsurpassed: "If we are to have scientific knowledge through demonstration, . . . we must know the starting-points [= definitions of essences] better and be better persuaded of them than of what is being shown but we must also not find anything more persuasive or better known among things opposed to the starting-points, from which a contrary mistaken conclusion may be deduced, since someone who has unconditional scientific knowledge must be incapable of being persuaded out of it" (*APo.* I 2 72ᵃ37–ᵇ4). Finally, they must be necessary (and so, of course, true) in a special sense: the predicates in them must belong to the subjects in every case, intrinsically, and universally (*APo.* I 4 73ᵃ24–27): (6a) *In every case:* A predicate A belongs to every subject B if and only if there is no B to which it fails to belong and no time at which it fails to belong to a B: "for example, if animal belongs to every man, then if it is true to say that this thing is a man, it is also true to say that it is an animal, and if the former is the case now, the latter is also the case now" (73ᵃ29–31). (6b) *Intrinsically:* A predicate A belongs intrinsically to a subject B just in case it is

related to B in one of four ways: (i) A is in the account or definition of what B is, or of B's substance, or essence (73^{a}34–37); (ii) B is a complex subject φB$_1$, where φ is an intrinsic coincident of B$_1$—for example, odd number or male or female animal (*Met.* XIII 3 1078^{a}5–11)—and A is in the definition of φB$_1$'s essence; (iii) A just is B's essence; (iv) A is not a part of B's essence or identical to it but stems causally from it, so that being B is an intrinsic cause of being A (73^{a}34–^{b}24). (6c) *Universally*: A predicate A belongs to a subject B universally just in case "it belongs to it in every case and intrinsically, that is, insofar as it is itself" (73^{b}26–27).

(7) Because intrinsic predicates stem in various ways from essences, the subjects to which they belong must have essences. In other words, they must be *intrinsic beings*, since—stemming as they do from essences—intrinsic predicates identify them or make them clear: "The things said to be intrinsically are the very ones signified by the figures of predication" (*Met.* V 7 1017^{a}22–23). These figures of predication are the so-called *categories*: "Anything that is predicated (*katêgoroumenon*) of something must either be . . . a definition . . . if it signifies the essence . . . or, if it does not, a special attribute (*idion*) . . . or one of the things in the definition, or not; and if it is one of the things in the definition, it must signify the genus or the differentiae, since the definition is composed of genus and differentia. If, however, it is not one of the things in the definition, it is clear that it must be a coincident; for a coincident was said to be that which belongs to a thing but that is neither a definition nor a genus nor a special attribute. Next we must distinguish the kinds (*genos*) of predication in which one will find the four mentioned above. These are ten in number: what it is, quantity, quality, relation, when, where, position, having, doing, and being affected. For the coincidents, the genus, the special attributes, and the definition will always be in one of these kinds of predication [or *categories*]" (*Top.* I 8–9 103^{b}7–25). For each of the intrinsic beings in these ten *categories* we can state what it is (*Met.* VII 4 1030^{a}17–24), even if strictly speaking only substances have definitions and essences (5 1031^{a}7–24). Specifying these beings is one of the tasks of *Categories*, where Aristotle explains how beings in categories other than that of substance are ontologically dependent on those in the category of substance. The list of categories itself, however, has a somewhat provisional status, as Aristotle's remark about the category of *having* indicates: "Some further ways of having might perhaps come to light, but we have made a pretty complete enumeration of those commonly spoken of" (*Cat.* 15 15^{b}30–32).

(8) What all four types of intrinsic beings have in common, what makes them worth the attention of someone inquiring into starting-points and causes, is that they are the ontological correlates or truth-makers for scientific theorems—the beings responsible for the necessary truth of those theorems. Moreover, they would seem to be the only sorts of being that can play this role, since they constitute an exhaustive catalogue of the necessary relations that can hold between a subject (A) and something (B) predicated of it: B is part of the essence of A; A is part of the essence of B; B is the essence of A; the essence of A (being A) is an intrinsic cause of (being) B.

Affections (*pathê*): What X *paschei* ("suffers," "undergoes") is what happens to him, so that he is passive with respect to it, as opposed to what he *poiei* ("does as an agent," "produces," "affects"). When Y does something to X, X is affected by it, so his *pathê* as a result are, in one sense, his affections and, in another, his passions or feelings. Here, as often elsewhere, however, a thing's *pathê*, while they include its affections, encompass its attributes more generally.

Substance (*ousias*): *Ousia* is a noun, perhaps formed from the present participle *ousa* of the verb *einai* ("to be"), though a quite different etymology is proposed by Collinge. "Substance" is the traditional translation. (1) The substance *of* something is its essence (I 9 278ᵃ3n), whereas (2) *a* substance, on the other hand, which is the sense relevant here, is something that has the fundamental sort of being possessed by an ultimate subject of predication—a *tode ti* ("this something")—which is not itself ever predicated of anything else (V 8 1017ᵇ23–26). It is usually but not always clear which of (1) or (2) is intended.

This sort of substance (*toiautês ousias*): "The science of nature is concerned with magnitudes, movement, and time" (*Ph.* III 4 202ᵇ30–31); "Natural science . . . is a science concerned with a particular genus of being (for it is concerned with the sort of substance in which the starting-point of movement and of rest is internal to itself)" (*Met.* VI 1 1025ᵇ18–21); "Substance seems to belong most evidently to bodies. That is why we say that animals and plants and their parts are substances, and also natural bodies, such as fire, water, earth, and each thing of this sort, as well as such things, whether all or some, as are parts of these or from which they are composed (for example, the heaven and its parts, stars and moon and sun)" (VII 2 1028ᵇ8–13).

Starting-points (*archas*): An *archê* ("starting-point," "first principle") is a primary cause: "This is what it is for something to be a starting-point, that it is itself the cause of many things, with nothing above it being a cause of it" (*GA* V 7 788ᵃ14–16).

Note 2

By nature (*phusei*): Things that are "by nature are the ones whose cause is within themselves and are orderly" (*Rh.* I 10 1369ᵃ35–ᵇ1), which cause is an internal starting-point of "movement and rest, whether in respect of place, growth and withering, or alteration" (*Ph.* II 1 192ᵇ13–15). And each such thing is a substance: "things that have a nature are those that have this sort of starting-point. And each of them is a substance. For a substance is a sort of underlying subject, and a nature is always in an underlying subject" (192ᵇ32–34). Examples are "animals and their parts, plants, and simple bodies—for example, earth, fire, air, and water" (192ᵇ9–11). Non-substantial phenomena, like the upward movement of fire, by contrast, though they occur by or in accord with nature, do not themselves have a nature: "And these things [that are by nature and have a nature] are also in accord with nature, as too is whatever belongs intrinsically to them, as spatial movement upward belongs to fire—for this neither is nor has a nature but is by nature and in accord with nature" (192ᵇ35–193ᵃ1). Compare *Cael.* III 1 298ᵃ27–ᵇ1.

When substantial things do have a nature, moreover, it derives not from their matter but from their distinctive manner of composition, or form: "That is why, as regards the things that are or come to be by nature, although that from which they naturally come to be or are is already present [namely, the matter], we still do not say that they have their nature if they do not have their form or shape" (*Met.* V 4 1015ª3–5). Thus, for example, a feline embryo has within it a starting-point that explains why it grows into a cat, why that cat moves and alters in the ways it does, and why it eventually decays and dies. A house or any other artifact, by contrast, has no such source within it; instead "the starting-point is in something else and external" (*Ph.* II 1 192ᵇ30–31), namely, the understanding of the crafts-man who produces it: "Nothing comes away from the carpenter to the matter of the timbers, nor is there any part of the craft of carpentry in the product, but the shape and the form are produced from the carpenter through the movement in the matter. And his soul, in which the form is and his scientific knowledge, moves his hands or some other part in a movement of a particular sort, different when the product is different, the same when it is the same, and the hands move the instru-ments, and the instruments move the matter" (*GA* I 22 730ᵇ11–19; also *Met.* VII 7 1032ª32–ᵇ10).

Of the things composed (*sunestôtôn***) by nature [1] some are bodies and magni-tudes, [2] some have body and magnitude, while [3] others are starting-points of things that have these (***tôn echontôn***):** The simple bodies, as well as things com-posed entirely of them are examples of [1]; animate beings, which have a soul as well as a body, are examples of [2]. Though [3] seems to refer to just the starting-points of things in [2], it is presumably intended to refer to those of the things in [1] as well, since that is what I 1 268ª3–4 more or less states. These include causes such as matter and form, however, which together compose matter-form (hylo-morphic) compounds, but do not seem to be composed, in the sense of being put together, whether by nature or by anything else. It may be, then, that Aristotle is using the verb *sunistanai* somewhat loosely, as he does in referring to the eternal and imperishable celestial objects: "Among the substances composed (*sunestasi*) by nature, some do not come to be or pass away throughout all eternity" (*PA* I 5 644ᵇ22–23). But most of these eternal substances are at least composed in the sense of being compounds. It seems better, therefore, to treat [3] as intended to be outside the scope of *sunestôtôn*. Things in [1] and [2] are composed by nature, but those in [3] are not.

Note 3

The continuous, accordingly, is what is divisible into things that are themselves always divisible: Compare: "Continuity is just a sort of contiguity. I mean that two things are continuous when the limits of each, by which they make contact and by which they are kept together, become one and the same, and—as the name signifies—contained in each other" (*Ph.* V 3 227ª10–12).

Note 4

A magnitude continuous in one dimension is a line, in two dimensions a plane, in three dimensions a body: "Of magnitudes those continuous in one dimension are lengths, in two, breadths, in three, depths. Of these, limited plurality is a num-ber, limited length a line, limited breadth a surface, limited depth a body" (*Met.*

V 13 1020^{a}11–14). Note that the definition of body focuses on aspects that bodies share with geometrical solids. But "the objects of mathematics are not substances more than bodies are" (XIII 2 1077^{b}12), whereas the bodies studied by natural science are substances (*Cael.* I 1 268^{a}3).

Note 5

The Pythagoreans in fact say [that] the All and all things are defined by [the number] three: "Among these thinkers and before them, the so-called Pythagoreans were the first to latch on to mathematics. They both advanced these inquiries and, having been brought up in mathematics, thought that its starting-points were the starting-points of all beings. Since [1] among these starting-points the numbers are by nature primary, and since [2] they seemed to get a theoretical grasp on many similarities to beings in the numbers, and to things that come to be, more so than in fire, earth, or water (for example, that such-and-such an attribute of numbers is justice, that such-and-such an attribute is soul and understanding, whereas another one is appropriate time, and—one might also say—each of the rest likewise), and, further, [3] seeing in harmonies attributes and ratios that are found in numbers—since, then, [2] the other things seemed to have been made like numbers in the whole of their nature, and [1] numbers were primary in the whole of nature, they took the elements of numbers to be the elements of all beings, and [3] the whole heaven to be harmony and number" (*Met.* I 5 985^{b}23–986^{a}3). See Archytas of Tarentum, F1 4–7 Huffman-2; also, *Cael.* III 1 300^{a}14–19n. After a survey of sources, Betegh, Pedriali, Pfeiffer concludes that "there is surprisingly little early evidence to support Aristotle's testimony according to which Pythagoreans connect three and all" (p. 57).

Defined (*hôristai*): See I 1 268^{b}8, and, for the sense in which they are defined, III 8 306^{b}9–15.

The All (*to pan*): In the *Metaphysics*, for example, *to pan* consistently refers not to the totality of things, but to the totality of the ones that make up the spatiotemporal universe. Thus at I 2 982^{b}17 *to pan* is something that comes to be; at 3 984^{a}2 it is *nature* as a whole; at 4 984^{b}26, 985^{a}25 it is something that comes to be and gets divided into the various elements by strife; at 5 986^{b}10–11, 17 and 8 988^{b}22 it is material and corporeal; at XI 10 1067^{a}3, 15, 16, 19, 22, *to pan* is again something that has material body.

Since end, middle, and starting-point have the number of the All: That is, constitute an ordered plurality—a whole—with a beginning, middle, and end.

Note 6

That is why, having taken these from nature (*phuseôs*), **as if it is one of its laws:** (1) Many of the things Aristotle means by *phusis* ("nature") are discussed in *Met.* V 4. But he uses the term more widely than that discussion suggests. In the "primary and full way" a being that is or does something by nature has a nature—an internal starting-point of movement and rest (1015^{a}13–15; *Cael.* III 2 301^{b}17–18). The world of nature, investigated by natural science, is a world of such beings, all of which have perceptible matter as a constituent (*Met.* VI 1 1025^{b}30–1026^{a}6).

This world is roughly speaking the sublunary one. Beyond it lies the world of the heavens studied by astronomy and theology (1026^{a}7–22), where beings either have no matter, or matter of a different sort (*Cael.* I 2 269^{b}2–6, 3 270^{b}19–25, *Mete.* I 3 339^{b}25–27). Although, strictly speaking, these beings do not have natures, since "nature is the proper order of perceptible things" (*Cael.* III 2 301^{a}5–6), Aristotle nonetheless speaks of them as if they do (III 1 298^{b}23). We use the term "nature" in a similar way when we speak of the nature of the numbers or the nature of fictional entities, not meaning to imply at all that these things are parts of the natural world (compare XIII 4 1078^{a}10). (2) Sometimes, instead of using *phusis* to refer to the, or a, *phusis of* X, Aristotle uses the term and its plural *phuseis* to mean something we translate as "a nature" (Greek has no indefinite article) or "natures." The thing or things referred to may or may not have natures in the strict sense; they are pretty much just entities of some sort. *Cael.* III 1 298^{b}23 is an example. (3) He also speaks of *phusis* or *hê phusis* in agentive terms—for example, when he says, as he frequently does, that nature does nothing pointlessly (for example, *Cael.* I 4 271^{a}33, *DA* II 5 415^{b}16–17, III 9 432^{b}21, 12 434^{a}31, *PA* I 1 641^{b}12–29) or that it does something correctly (*Cael.* I 3 269^{b}20), or for the best (II 5 288^{a}3). Just as when he speaks of "the nature of the All" (I 2 268^{b}11) or "the nature of the whole" (*Met.* XII 10 1075^{a}11) it is not entirely clear how exactly or how literally these words are to be taken. The same applies here to the "laws" of nature.

We make use of this number even in the worship of the gods: A number of cult actions in Greek religion had to be repeated three times. The first libation at a symposium or communal meal was to Olympian Zeus, the third to Zeus *Sôtêr* (Zeus the Savior), or Zeus *Teleios* (Zeus the Completer or Fulfiller)—notice *teleion* at I 1 268^{a}21. Thus Plato introduces his third proof of the superiority of justice to injustice with the words, "Now comes the third, which is dedicated in Olympic fashion to our savior, Olympian Zeus" (*Rep.* 583b). And in the *Laws*, he writes: "the god, as the ancient account also says, has the starting-point, end, and middle of all beings" (715e–716a). The scholiast on the latter text identifies the ancient account referred to with an Orphic text (Betegh, Col. 17.12, p. 37), also quoted in the pseudo-Aristotelian, *De Mundo*: "Zeus was born first, Zeus is last, ruler of the thunderbolt; / Zeus is the head, Zeus is the middle; from Zeus all things are made" (401^{a}28–29). Noticing other scholiasts, such as on Pindar, *Isthmian* 6.10a.18–20 and Plato, *Chrm.* 167a–b, Betegh, Pedriali, Pfeiffer comments: "these texts do not say that Zeus is *Teleios* in so far as he holds beginning, middle, and end, but in so far as the number three is *teleios* because it has the beginning, middle, and end. The completeness of Zeus is thus explained by the ancient commentators from the completeness of number three, in so far as the number three possesses beginning, middle, and end."

Note 7

And we assign labels (*prosêgorias*) too in this way. For we use "both" of two things and "both" of two people, but we do not use (*legomen*) "all," but rather three is the first number with reference to which we use the latter mode of address. And in these domains, as was said, we do so because of following the

lead of nature itself: The argument is not from religious and linguistic practices to claims about nature, but rather the reverse. These practices are explained (in part) by nature and its laws. It is a case of "the facts themselves" showing people what to do (*Met.* I 3 984ᵃ18–19).

Note 8

Since all things (*panta*), the All (*pan*), and the complete (*teleion*) do not differ from each other with respect to form (*idean*) but rather, if indeed they do differ, it is with respect to their matter and the things of which they are said: "Some things are one in number, others in form . . . : in number, those whose matter is one; in form (*eidos*), those whose account is one" (*Met.* V 6 1016ᵇ31–33). Thus the claim here is that if *panta* is said, or predicated, of x, *pan* of y, and *teleion* of z, then x, y, and z have the same account (definition), even if they differ in number or matter, so that x ≠ y ≠ z. *Idea*, which often refers to a Platonic, separable Form, is here a synonym of the more common *eidos*, which refers to form as Aristotle understands it. **Body alone among the magnitudes would be complete:** "A body is a sort of substance. For it already has completeness in a way. But how can lines be substances? Neither as a form or shape, like the soul (if indeed it is something of this sort), nor as matter is, like the body. For nothing is seen to be capable of being composed of lines or planes or points, though if these were some sort of material substance, things would have been seen to be capable of undergoing this" (*Met.* XIII 2 1077ᵃ31–36).
Complete (*teleion*): The adjective *teleios*, which derives from the noun *telos* ("end," "goal"), can also be translated as "perfect." See I 1 268ᵇ9n.

Note 9

[Body] alone is defined by [the number] three, and this is All: Because the All is composed primarily of bodies, as the only complete magnitudes (I 1 268ᵃ2, 22–23).

Note 10

Genus (*genos*): "Genus" (plural: "genera"), "differentia" (plural: "differentiae"), and "species" are the traditional Latinate translations of *genos*, *eidos*, and *diaphora*, and are best thought of as near transliterations, with no independent semantic content beyond that conveyed by Aristotle's uses of the terms, which are many and various. In his own philosophical lexicon, for example, we find the following entry on *genos*: "Something is said to be a *genos* if: [1] The coming to be of things with the same form (*eidos*) is continuous—for example, 'as long as the *genos* of human beings lasts' means 'as long as the coming to be of human beings is continuous.' [2] It is the first mover that brought things into existence. For it is in this way that some are said to be Hellenes by *genos* and others Ionians, because the former come from Hellen and the latter from Ion as their first begetter. And more so when from the male begetter than when from the matter, although the *genos* is also sometimes named from the female—for example, the descendants of Pyrrha. [3] Further, as the plane is said to be the *genos* of plane figures and solid of solids. For each of the figures is in the one case a plane of such-and-such a sort and in the other a solid of such-and-such a sort, this being the underlying subject for the differentiae. [4] Further, as the first constituent in accounts is said to be—the one said in the what-it-is. For this is the *genos*, whose differentiae the qualities are said to be" (*Met.* V 28 1024ᵃ29–ᵇ5). A *genos*, then, is [1–2] a race or bloodline and [3–4] the kind of thing—the genus—studied by a single science (see Introduction, pp. xxvii–xxviii). Similarly, he uses *eidos* to refer to the species of a genus, but also to form (as opposed to matter) and to a separate Platonic Form. By the same token *diaphorai* are sometimes, as presumably here, the differentiae that divide a genus into species, and so figure in their essential definitions: "species are composed of the genus and the differentiae" (*Met.* X 7 1057ᵇ7). But sometimes they are simply the different features that distinguish one kind of thing from another, without necessarily suggesting that the kinds are genera or species in the strict sense or that the differences are differentiae. To bring a semblance of order to all of this I have employed the traditional translation ("genus," "differentia," and "species"), adding the Greek term in parentheses when I deviated from it.

Surface (*epiphaneias*): Here, as often elsewhere, equivalent in meaning to *epipedon* ("plane").

Note 11

[1] It is not possible to transition to another genus of magnitude, as we pass to surface from length, and to body from surface. [2] For magnitude of this sort would no longer be complete. [3] For it is necessary that the passage come about in accord with a deficiency. [4] But what is complete cannot be defective. For it is (*estin*) **[complete] in all directions** (*pantê[i]*): *Pantê[i]*, as used at I 1 268ᵇ8–10, suggests that "complete" is the missing complement of *estin*. (Were *estin* existential, it would need no complement, but "is, or exists, in every direction," besides being hard to understand, has no clear basis in the discussion up to this point.) [2], which is the nerve of the argument, seems best understood as relying on the following principle: "the complete is prior to the incomplete, in nature, in account, and in time" (*Ph.* VIII 9 265ᵃ22–23; also *Cael.* I 2 269ᵃ19–20n). For A is prior in account to B if the account of A figures in the account of B, but not vice versa (*Met.* VII 1 1028ᵃ34–36). Thus what is complete (*teleion*) is prior in this way to what is incomplete, or not complete (*ateles*), because it is obvious that the latter is defined in terms of the former. (On the various meanings the *alpha* privative in Greek, as in *ateles*, see V 22 1022ᵇ32–1023ᵃ5). But this requires that only one kind (*genos*) of magnitude be involved, since otherwise the incomplete magnitude of (for example) a line would not have to be defined in terms of the (complete) magnitude of a body, since it could be defined in terms of some other kinds of complete magnitude altogether. [3] is now readily intelligible, since what makes (for example) a line incomplete is that it lacks (*alpha* privative) something of the same kind that body has. And that something is completeness in the dimension of depth.

Note 12

Account (*logos*): A *logos* in ordinary Greek is a word or organized string of words constituting an account, argument, explanation, definition, principle, reason, or piece of reasoning, discussion, conversation, or speech; what such words or their utterances mean, express, or refer to, such as, the ratio between quantities (*NE* V 3 1131ᵃ31–32); the capacity that enables someone to argue, give reasons, and so on (*Pol.* VII 13 1332ᵇ5). Aristotle also uses the word in a more technical sense: "A *logos* is a significant voiced sound some part of which is significant when separated—as an annunciation (*phasis*), not as an affirmation (*kataphasis*). I mean, for example, that human signifies something, but not that the thing is or is not (though it will be an affirmation or denial if something is added); the single syllables of human, by contrast, signify nothing" (*Int.* 4 16ᵇ26–31). "Account" and "argument" translate *logos*; in other cases *logos* is added in parentheses.

Note 13

Bodies, then, that are in the form of parts (*en moriou eidei sômatos*): Referred to as "the parts it [the All] possesses in virtue of its form" (I 2 268ᵇ13). These are the elements (earth, water, fire, air, ether), and the bodies (considered as such) composed of them. See I 2 268ᵇ26–27. Not considered as such, of course, many bodies or things that have them are defined by the natures internal to them, not by something outside.

Are each, according to this account, this sort [of complete]. For each has all the dimensions: That is, each of these of the All is complete only in the sense of having all three dimensions, in contrast with the All itself, which is complete, not only in this way, but in every way (I 1 268ᵇ8–10).

Note 14

[1] But each one is defined (*hôristai*) **by contact with what is neighboring** (*to plêsion*). **[2] That is why each of the bodies is in a way many. [3] The All of which these are parts, on the other hand, is necessarily complete, and, as its name signifies, in all ways, not in one way so and in another not:** Start with [3]. The ways in which something can be complete are the following: "What is said to be complete is, [C1] in one way, that outside which not even one part is to be found—for example, the complete time of each thing is the one outside which there is no time to be found that is part of that time. [C2] That which, as regards virtue or the good, cannot be surpassed relative to its kind (*genos*)—for example, a doctor is complete and a flute player is complete when they lack nothing as regards the form of their own proper virtue. (It is in this way, transferring the term to bad things, we speak of a complete scandalmonger and a complete thief—indeed we even say that they are good, for example, a good thief and a good scandalmonger.) Also, virtue is a sort of completion. For each thing is complete and every substance is complete when, as regards the form of its proper virtue, it lacks no part of its natural magnitude. [C3] Further, things that have attained their end, this being something excellent, are said to be complete. For things are complete in virtue of having attained their end. So, since the end is a last thing, we transfer the term to base things and say that a thing has been completely ruined and completely destroyed, when there is no deficiency in its destruction and badness but it has reached its last. This is why death, too, is by metaphorical transference said to be an end, because both are last things. And the end—that is, the for-the-sake-of-which—is a last thing" (*Met.* V 16 1021^{b}12–30). Now consider W, which is all the water there is. It has the three requisite dimensions, and so has attained the end of its genus (magnitude), and is complete in the sense of [C3]. But W is also in form, or essence, a part of the All. And what makes it a part and not—as in Thales' universe—the All itself, is [1]: it is defined (limited) by contact with what is neighboring (that is, by what surrounds it). Thus, unlike the All, it can be surpassed relative to its kind (*genos*), and so is not complete in the sense of [C2]. Moreover, W is a scattered object: different parts of it are defined by different neighboring, or surrounding, bodies. It is thus [2] in a way (coincidentally, not essentially) many, whereas the All, not being surrounded by anything, is (necessarily, essentially) one. See also III 8 306^{b}9–15.

Name (*tounoma*): An *onoma* is not always what we call a name, but a word more generally, or—when contrasted with a verb—a noun: "A noun or name is a composite significant voiced sound, without [a reference to] time, the parts of which are not intrinsically significant. . . . A verb is a composite significant voiced sound, involving [a reference to] time, the parts of which are not intrinsically significant" (*Po.* 20 1457^{a}10–15). A name, however, often signifies an account or (in some cases) a definition (*Met.* IV 7 1012^{a}22–24, VIII 6 1045^{a}26) of the form (VII 10 1035^{a}21) or essence (4 1029^{b}20) of the thing named.

Signifies (*sêmainei*): Aristotle uses the verb *sêmainein* and the cognate noun *sêmeion* to express (1) a relation between a linguistic element, such as a noun or name, and the thing it signifies, means, or denotes, but also, as here, (2) a relation between two nonlinguistic elements, as in, those spots are a sign of—are evidence of or an indicator of—measles. It is not always clear, therefore, whether quotation marks should or should not be supplied.

Note 15

The nature of the All: See I 1 268^{a}13n.

Mass (*ogkon*): An *ogkos* is generally a bulky body or mass.

Must be investigated later: At I 5–7.

Note 16

We shall speak about the parts of it with respect to form (*tôn kat' eidos autou moriôn*): That is, about the forms or kinds of the elements in the All. On form, see I 1 268^{a}21n.

Note 17

Intrinsically (*kath hauta*): A standard Aristotelian contrast is between what has an attribute B coincidentally or contingently (*kata sumbebêkos* or *per accidens* in Latin) and what has B intrinsically or non-contingently (*kath' hauto* or *per se*) (*Met.* V 18 1022^{a}24–36). The coincidental attributes of a thing hold of it by chance or luck and are of no scientific interest (VI 2 1026^{b}3–14), unless they happen to be among *ta kath hauta sumbebêkota*—the intrinsic coincidents or *per se* accidents—which are demonstrable from the definitions of the essences of the substances whose attributes they are (*APo.* I 7 75^{b}1, 22 83^{b}19, *Met.* V 30 1025^{a}30–32, XIII 3 1078^{a}5–9).

Note 18

Nature we say is the starting-point of movement for them: "Nature is a sort of starting-point and cause of moving and being at rest in that to which it belongs primarily, intrinsically, and not coincidentally" (*Ph.* I 2 192^{b}20–23).

Note 19

All movement with respect to place—which we call spatial movement—is either rectilinear or circular or a mixture of these: "Movement with respect to place has neither a common nor a special name, but we may call the common sort spatial movement, even though things are said to spatially move in the strict sense only when, without its being up to them to have stayed where they were, they change their place, as are things that do not move themselves with respect to place" (*Ph.* V 2 226^{a}32–^{b}1); "everything that is in spatial movement moves either in a circle, in a straight line, or in a mixture of the two" (VIII 8 261^{b}28–29).

Mixture (*miktê*): Aristotle often distinguishes a mere combination (*sunthesis*) or mechanical mixture from a chemical one (*mixis*), which involves the formation of a new homogeneous stuff with new emergent attributes: "mixture (*mixis*) is unification of the mixables, resulting from their alteration" (*GC* I 10 328^{b}22).

Note 20

For [rectilinear or circular] are the only simple movements: Why? Because "the movement follows along with the magnitude" (*Ph.* IV 11 219^{a}11–12).

Note 21

Cause (*aition*): One difference between *aition* (neuter), used here, and *aitia* (feminine), which is also often used, makes an *aitia* an explanatory argument (a type of deduction) that identifies causes, and an *aition* an item in the world that is causally efficacious. Aristotle does not seem to observe the distinction, though it is *aitia* that figures in his definitions of craft knowledge and scientific knowledge (*APo.* I 2 71^{b}9–12, II 11 94^{a}20–27). Both *aition* and *aitia* are translated as "cause." The four causes Aristotle recognizes (final, formal, material, efficient) are discussed in *Ph.* II 3.

Note 22

This seems to follow in accord with the account at the start: See I 1 268^{a}6–^{b}10.

Note 23

Fire and earth, the species of these: "For there is not only one species of fire. For glowing ember, flame, and light are distinct in species, though each of them is fire" (*Top.* V 5 134^{b}28–30). The species of earth are "sandy, stoney, earthy, black, white" (Simp. 16.19–20 = Hankinson, p. 35). Compare, "Salt water is heavy and sweet water is light" (*Pr.* XIII 20 933^{b}28–29).

And things of the same kind (*suggenê*) **as these:** See III 2 301^{a}3–4: "Even as things stand all things do not spatially move to the same place, but only those of the same kind (*suggenê*)."

The mastering component (*to epikratoun*): That is, the simple body that there is most of in the mixture. See I 2 269ᵃ29–30.

Note 24

By force (*bia[i]*) it is possible for it to be that of another, distinct body: "By force and contrary to nature are the same" (III 2 300ᵃ23); "what is forced [is] contrary to natural impulse" (*Met.* XII 7 1072ᵇ12; also V 5 1015ᵇ15).

Note 25

If one thing has one contrary: "It is evident that one thing cannot have more than one contrary (for there cannot be anything more extreme than the extreme and there cannot be more than two extremes of the same extension), and in general if contrariety is a difference, and a difference is between two things, then so too must be the complete difference" (*Met.* X 4 1055ᵃ19–25).

Note 26

If, then, fire or something else of this sort is the thing spatially moving in a circle, its spatial movement in accord with nature will be contrary to the circular. But one thing has one contrary, and up and down are contrary to each other: The argument is this: Suppose that the body B that is moving contrary to its nature in a circle is fire. Then the movement that is in accord with B's nature must be contrary to circular. But fire's natural movement is up (I 2 269ᵃ17), the contrary to up is down, and a thing has only one contrary. Therefore B is not fire. The same argument will show that B is not one of the other simple bodies, whether earth, water, or air.

Note 27

The complete is prior in nature to the incomplete, and the circle is one of the complete things, whereas no straight line is: "And it is clear that circular spatial movement is the primary sort of spatial movement. For every spatial movement, as we said earlier, is either circular, rectilinear, or a mixture of the two. And the first two must be prior to the last, since it is composed of them. And the circular is prior to the rectilinear, since it is simpler and more complete. For a straight line that is unlimited cannot be traversed, since such an unlimited line does not exist. And even if it did, nothing would traverse it, since the impossible does not happen, and it is impossible to traverse an unlimited line. But in the case of movement along a limited line, if it turns back, it is composed of two movements, while if it does not turn back, it is incomplete and capable of passing away. For the complete is prior to the incomplete, in nature, in account, and in time, and what is incapable of passing away to what is capable of passing away" (*Ph.* VIII 9 265ᵃ13–24).
Prior in nature: "Others, however, are said to be prior in nature and substance, when it is possible for them to be without other things, but not the others without them" (*Met.* V 11 1019ᵃ2–4).

Note 28

If indeed a movement that is prior is movement of a body that is prior in nature: This is the key move in the argument. Circular movements are prior in nature, because they are the movements of bodies that are prior in nature, so that the existence of other things (and their movements) depends on the prior one (and their movements).

Note 29

The spatial movement of mixed bodies, we have said, is in accord with the simple body that is the mastering one in the mixture: See I 2 269ª1–2.

Note 30

It is evident that there is some natural corporeal substance (*ousia sômatos*): See I 1 268ª3n.

Beyond the ones composed (*sustaseis*) **here:** "Composed" even in the case of the simple bodies, because these too are compounds of matter and form.

Here (*entautha*): That is, here where we are; in our world.

More divine (*theiotera*) **and prior to all these:** "If human beings are the best of the other animals, it makes no difference, since there exist other things that are far more divine in nature even than human beings—the most evident ones, certainly, being those from which the universe is composed" (*NE* VI 7 1141ª33–ᵇ2). These are divine, most pertinently, in being eternal (*Cael.* I 2 269ª8).

Note 31

The all-around spatial movement (*tên perix phoran*): See also II 4 287ᵇ19.

It would be a wondrous and altogether unreasonable (*alogos*) **thing for this movement alone to be continuous and eternal:** "Movements may be consecutive or successive in virtue of the time being continuous, but they can be continuous only in virtue of the movements themselves being so, and this is when extremities of both become one. That is why movement that is continuous and unconditionally one to be the same in species, must be of one thing, and in one time. In one time in order that there may be no intermediate interval of immobility. For during such an interval there must be rest, and a movement is many not one if it includes an intermediate interval of rest, so that if a movement is divided by a stop, it is neither one nor continuous, but is interrupted, if there is an intermediate interval of [rest] time. Of a movement that is not one in species (even if the time is not intermittent), although the time is one, the movement is distinct in species, [and so is not one]. For a movement that is one must be one in species, though it is not necessary for a movement that is one in species to be unconditionally one. What is it for a movement to be unconditionally one has now been stated" (*Ph.* V 4 228ª30–ᵇ11); "circular movement can be eternal, but none of the other sorts, whether of spatial movement or of any other sort whatsoever, can be so, since rest must occur, and if rest must, the movement must pass away" (VII 9 265ª25–27).

Since it is contrary to nature: And hence forced. See I 2 269ª7n.

Note 32

It is evident in other cases that the ones contrary to nature pass away fastest: See II 3 286ᵃ17–18.

Note 33

If indeed the thing spatially moving [in a circle] is fire, as some people say: See Thales DK A17a = TEGP 26; Anaximander DK A21 = TEGP 22, TEGP 29; Anaximenes DK A7, A12 = TEGP 12, 16; Heraclitus DK B30 = TEGP 47; Parmenides DK B12 = TEGP 26 F12; Anaxagoras DK A84 = TEGP 50; Plato, *Ti.* 40a, *Epin.* 982a–b.

Note 34

Having a nature that is more estimable (*timiôteran*) to the extent that it stands farther off from those here: The core sense of *timios* ("estimable") is captured in the remark that ordinary people "commonly say of those they find especially estimable and especially love that they 'come first'" (*Cat.* 12 14ᵇ5–7). Something is thus objectively *timios* when—like starting-points and causes—it "comes first by nature" (14ᵇ3–5). To say that something is estimable is thus to ascribe a distinct sort of goodness or value to it: "By what is estimable I mean such things as what is divine, what is superior (*beltion*) (for example, soul, understanding), what is more time-honored (*archaioteron*), what is a starting-point, and so on" (*MM* I 2 1183ᵇ21–23). Thus happiness, for example, is "something estimable and complete . . . since it is a starting-point . . . and the starting-point and the cause of goods is something we suppose to be estimable and divine" (*NE* I 12 1102ᵃ1–4).

Note 35

Later [we must set down what we mean by the light and the heavy] in a more exact one: See *Cael.* IV 1–4.

More exact (*akribesteron*): In his focal discussion of *akribeia*, Aristotle makes clear that a science's degree of it is measured along three different dimensions: "One science is more *akribês* than another, and prior to it, if [1] it is both of the facts and gives their explanation, and not of the facts separately from giving the scientific knowledge of their explanation; or if [2] it is not said of an underlying subject and the other is said of an underlying subject (as, for example, arithmetic is more *akribês* than harmonics); or if [3] it proceeds from fewer things and the other from some additional posit (as, for example, arithmetic is more *akribês* than geometry). By from an addition I mean, for example, that a unit is substance without position and a point is substance with position—the latter proceeds from an addition" (*APo.* I 27 87ᵃ31–37). The upshot is thus twofold. First, the most *akribês* version or formulation of a science is the most explanatory one—the one consisting of demonstrations from starting-points. Second, of two sciences, formulated in the most *akribês* way, one is more *akribês* than the other, if it demonstrates facts that the other deals with but does not demonstrate. Because a natural science has to posit sublunary matter in addition to such starting-points, the strictly theoretical sciences (theology, astronomy, and mathematics) are more *akribês* than any natural science. Hence it is among these that the most *akribês* one will be found. And it will be the one that explains what the others treat as a fact or undemonstrated posit.

The association of *akribeia* with demonstration from starting-points makes "exact" seem a good translation of it, as does its association with abstraction (mathematics) with what we think of as pure (solid geometry) as opposed to applied sciences (mechanics), and with the idea that the *akribeia* of a science or type of argument depends on its subject matter (*NE* I 3 1094^{b}24). As applied to craftsmen and their products, *akribês* comes closest to meaning "refinement" or "finish" or "sophistication." Applied to perceptual capacities, such as seeing or smelling (*DA* II 9 421^{a}10), it means "discriminating." Applied to virtue and nature, it may have more to do with accuracy—hitting a target (*NE* II 5 1106^{b}14–15)—as it may when applied to definitions (VIII 7 1159^{a}3) or distinctions (II 9 1107^{b}15–16) or units of measurement (*Met.* X 1 1053^{a}1). *Top.* II 4 111^{a}8–9 offers *saphês* ("perspicuous") as an equivalent.

When we investigate their substance: See I 1 268^{a}3n.

Note 36
The movement of each of the simple bodies is, as we saw, one movement: At I 2 269^{a}8–9.

Note 37
We posited that, of contrary movements, if one is contrary to nature for something, the other is in accord with nature: At I 2 269^{a}32–34.

Note 38
Since, however, the whole and the part—for example, all of earth and a small clod—spatially move in accord with nature to the same place, it follows, first, that it (*auto*) has neither lightness nor heaviness: The reference of *auto* is unclear. Most translators take it to refer to the body that spatially moves in a circle in accord with its nature, making this a further argument that it possesses neither heaviness nor lightness. DP takes it to refer to "the part," so that this would extend the first argument to the parts of that body. The importance of the extension emerges, for example, at IV 3 310^{b}2–7.

Note 39
Incapable of increase (*anauxes*): "Movement with respect to quantity, as regards its common feature, has no name, but with regard to each of its two varieties it is called increase and decrease—that to the complete magnitude being increase, that away from it being decrease" (*Ph.* V 2 226^{a}29–32). *Auxêsis kai phthisis*, increase and decrease, are often "growth and withering," especially when applied to living things.

Incapable of alteration (*analloiôton*): That is, qualitative change. See I 3 270^{a}27.

Everything that comes to be comes to be from its contrary: "A change from what is not an underlying subject to an underlying subject, the relation being that of contradiction, is a coming to be—an unconditional coming to be when the change is unconditional, in a particular respect when the change is in a particular respect. For example, a change from not pale to pale is a coming to be in this respect, pale, whereas a change from unconditionally not being to substance is unconditional coming to be, with respect to which we say that a thing comes to be unconditionally, not that it comes to be something. A change from an underlying subject to what is not an underlying subject is a passing away—an unconditional one when the change is from substance to not being, in a particular respect when the change is to the opposite contradictory, as was said in the case of coming to be" (*Ph.* V 1 225^{a}12–20). Compare *Met.* XII 1 1069^{b}2–7: "Now, perceptible substance is changeable. But if change is from opposites or from intermediates, and not from all opposites—since the voice is not white [but does not change to white]—but from the contrary one, there must be something underlying that changes to the contrary state, since the contraries do not change."

And from an underlying subject (*hupokeimenou*): "It is then evident that everything comes to be from both the underlying subject and the shape [or form]—if indeed there are causes and starting-points of the beings that are by nature, from which they primarily and not coincidentally are or have come to be the thing that each is said to be in accord with its substance. . . . It is clear, then, that whatever comes to be, comes to be from these things. The underlying subject, however, though one in number, is two in form. For on the one hand there is the human, the gold, and in general the countable matter, which is more of a this something, and it is not coincidentally that what comes to be comes to be from it; on the other hand there is the lack (that is, the opposite), which is coincident. And the form is one—for example, the order, the musicality, or anything else predicated in this way" (*Ph.* I 7 190^{b}17–29). In addition to being (1) what underlies or persists through every change whether in attributes (as a substantial subject) or in the coming to be or passing away (as matter), a *hupokeimenon* can be (2) a subject of predication, or (3) the subject-matter of a science or body of knowledge (*NE* I 3 1094^{b}12).

As was said in our first accounts: In *Ph.* I 7–9.

Note 40

Contrary spatial movements are of contraries: Aristotle rejects the view that substance (*Cat.* 5 3^{b}24–32) and quantity (6 5^{b}11–29) are contraries, and cites the fact that substance (which his predecessors failed to grasp) is not a contrary but an underlying subject of which contraries are predicated in rejecting the view that contraries are the starting-points of all things (*Met.* XIV 1 1087^{a}29–^{b}4; see also XII 10 1075^{a}28–34). Yet he himself accepts that "all things either are or are derived from contraries" (IV 2 1005^{a}3–4). It must be, then, that substances and quantities, though not contraries, are somehow derived from them: "Even if certain things do not have contraries, as substance seems not to have, still if they are derived from contraries, then, because knowledge of each of them depends on knowledge of the things from which it is derived, knowledge of these things would consist in knowledge of the contraries from which they are derived" (Alex. *In. Metaph.* 262.31–34 = Madigan, 41). This would explain why Aristotle includes substances in one of the two columns of opposites (*Met.* XII 7 1072ª30–31). His list of opposites is not restricted, however, to those recognized by his predecessors, since it includes (for example) actuality and potentiality (1072ª32). Hence he can reject the view that the traditional opposites are the ultimate starting-points while continuing to think that opposites of some sort have this status. This, presumably, is how we should object to Philoponus' objection (Wildberg, pp. 92–97) that the simple bodies, since they are substances (*Cael.* I 1 268ª3), are not contraries, so that the contrary-movements-are-of-contraries principle is inapplicable here. See also IV 4 312ª5–6.

Contraries (*enantiai*): "Said to be contraries are: Those things differing in genus that cannot belong to the same thing at the same time. The most different of the things in the same genus. The most different of the things in the same recipient. The most different of the things falling under the same capacity. The things whose difference is greatest either unconditionally or in genus or in species" (*Met.* V 10 1018ª25–31; also X 4 1055ᵇ13–17).

Note 41

Everything that increases, increases because of something of the same kind (*suggenous*) **being added to it and dissolving into its matter:** Secluding καὶ τὸ φθῖνον φθίνει ("and everything that decreases decreases") with Moraux. Compare: "It is impossible for there to be increase without previous alteration. For what increases is in one way increased by what is like itself, but in another way by what is unlike itself. For contrary is said to nourish contrary. But everything gets added by becoming like to like" (*Ph.* VIII 7 269ª29–32). Decrease, by contrast, requires the removal of matter: "again what decreases something decreases it when some part becomes detached from what is decreased" (VII 2 245ª13–14).

Matter (*hulên*): "Some matter is [1] perceptible, however, while [2] some is intelligible—perceptible matter being, for example, bronze, wood, and any matter that is movable, and intelligible matter being the sort that is in the perceptible things but not insofar as they are perceptible, such as the objects of mathematics" (*Met.* VII 10 1036ª9–12). Perceptible (as opposed to intelligible) matter comes in a variety of different sorts. [1a] Movable matter (*kinêtê hulê*), mentioned at 1036ª10, is the sort something needs if it is to be capable of moving from place to place. Hence it is also referred as *hulê topikê* (VIII 2 1042ᵇ6). [1b] Matter for alteration (*alloiôtê*) is the sort that things need if they are to change in quality (IX 8 1050ᵇ16–8). [1c] Then there is matter needed for movement with respect to magnitude, or increase and decrease (*auxêtê kai phthitê*) (*Ph.* VIII 7 260ª27). [1d] And finally the matter needed for coming to be and passing away (*gennêtê kai phthartê*), which is most of all and in the full sense matter (*GC* I 4 320^{a}2). Things that have [1a] but not [1d] include the various heavenly bodies (*Met.* IX 8 1050^{b}22–28, XII 2 1069^{b}24–26). *Hulê noêtê* is mentioned by name only in [2], at VII 11 1037^{a}5, and at VIII 6 1045^{a}33–35: "Some matter is intelligible, and some perceptible, and of the account always one part is the matter and the other the actuality [= the form]—for example, the circle is shape + plane (*ho kuklos schêma epipedon*)." But "the matter of the objects of mathematics (*hê tôn mathêmatikôn hulê*)" (XI 1 1059^{b}15–16) is fairly certainly a reference to the same sort of thing.

Note 42

But there is none from which this body has come to be: Coming to be requires matter as an underlying subject (I 3 269^{b}15n), since the body in circular movement does not come to be, it does not have such matter, and so has none to be added to in the way required for growth.

Note 43

Alteration is movement with respect to quality: "There is alteration (*alloiôsis*) when the underlying subject, which is perceptible, while remaining [the same], changes in its own affections, which are either contraries or intermediates" (*GC* I 4 319^{b}10–12); "There is alteration only in things that are said to be intrinsically affected by perceptibles" (*Ph.* VII 3 245^{b}4–5).

Quality (*poion*) **and qualitative states** (*hexeis*) **and dispositions** (*diatheseis*)—**for example, health and disease—do not come about without change with respect to the affections:** (1) Some qualities are states (*hexis*), such as the virtues and types of scientific knowledge, which are relatively permanent and difficult to change; dispositions (*diathesis*), such as being hot or ill, which are relatively impermanent and easy to change (*Cat.* 8 8^{b}26–9^{a}13). (2) Others are things that we are said to be in virtue of having a capacity, such as being a boxer, or incapacity, such as softness rather than hardness (9^{a}14–27). (3) Others are affective qualities and affections, such as sweetness, bitterness, sourness (9^{a}28–10^{a}10). (4) Others are figure (*schêma*) and the external shape or form (*morphê*) of a thing (10^{a}11–16). See also *Met.* V 14.

Affections (*pathê*): See I 1 268^{a}2n.

Note 44

Elements (*ta tôn stoicheiôn*): A *stoicheion* was originally one of a row (*stoichos*) of things and later a letter of the alphabet or an element of any complex whole (Plato, *Tht.* 201e). Aristotle uses it in these ways, and to refer to the five primary elemental bodies (earth, water, air, fire, and ether), from which all others are composed. See *Cael.* III 3 302^{a}15–19.

All natural bodies that change with respect to an affection we see are subject both to increase and decrease—for example, the bodies of animals and plants and their parts, and also those of the elements (*ta tôn stoicheiôn*): "Among the bodies or the elements (*ê tôn stoicheiôn*) fire alone is something that is nourished and grows (*auxomenon*). That is why we might suppose that in both plants and animals it is this that performs the function. But, though it is in a way a contributing cause, it is certainly not an unconditional cause. On the contrary, it is rather the soul that is this. For the growth of fire is unlimited, as long as there is fuel, but there is a limit and an account of size and growth for things that are put together by nature; and these are characteristic of soul but not of fire, and of the account rather than of the matter" (*DA* II 4 416ª10–18). In light of this text, we should not take ours to refer narrowly to natural growth but to increase generally. For a body of water, or of earth or air, can increase or decrease in size, by the relevant sort of addition or subtraction.

Note 45

The argument attests to the things that appear to be so, and the things that appear to be so attest to the argument: Aristotle often conjoins an appeal to perception (here, appearances) with an appeal to argument, or to things that are in accord with argument (*kata ton logon*) or in accord with reason (see I 5 272ª5–6, II 13 293ª29–30, 14 297ᵇ18–30, but also, among many other examples, *Ph.* VIII 8 262ª17–19, *Mete.* II 5 362ᵇ14–19, *PA* II 8 653ᵇ19–30, III 4 666ª13–18, *EE* I 6 1216ᵇ26–28, *Pol.* VII 4 1326ª27–28, 7 1328ª20–21). The argument in question, as here, typically appeals to general principles relevant to the subject matter under consideration, but seems seldom if ever to be a demonstration from the starting-points of a first-order science.

The things that appear to be so (*ta phainomena*): See I 1 268ª1n.

Note 46

Supposition (*hupolêpsin*): *Hupolêpsis* is like belief (*doxa*), but unlike scientific knowledge, in that it can be false as well as true (*NE* VI 3 1139ᵇ15–18). But whereas belief must be based on rational calculation (*DA* III 11 434ª5–11), supposition need not be.

Note 47

This result also follows sufficiently enough through perception, at any rate for (one might almost say) merely human conviction (*hôs ge pros anthrôpinên eipein pistin*): An *anthrôpos* in the most general sense is a human being of either sex. The associated adjective *anthrôpinos*, while it can certainly mean "human," often seems (as here) to mean something more like "*merely* human": "We should not, however, in accord with the makers of proverbs, 'think human things (*anthrôpina*), since you are human' or 'think mortal things, since you are mortal' but, rather, we should as far as possible immortalize, and do everything to live in accord with the element in us that is most excellent" (*NE* X 7 1177ᵇ31–33).

At any rate for (one might almost say) merely human conviction: Aristotle may be having a dig at Plato, who disparages astronomy based on perception, rather than on mathematics, at *Rep.* 528d–530b. The contrast between human conviction and some higher kind is returned to at II 5 287ᵇ33–34.

Note 48

According to the record people have handed down one to another: See II 12 292ª7–9.

The whole of the outermost heaven (*eschaton ouranon*): On the various senses of *ouranos*, see I 9 278ᵇ9–21. The outermost (or, looking inward, the first) heaven is the sphere of the fixed stars. See II 6 288ª14–17.

Or in the parts proper to it: The fixed stars and the constellations they form.

Proper (*oikeiôn*): *Oikeios* derives from *oikos* ("household"), so that what is *oikeios* to something belongs to it or is proper to it in the way that someone belongs to a family.

Note 49

One must acknowledge that the same beliefs return to us not once or twice but an unlimited number of times: "We say that the same beliefs come about in cycles among human beings, not once or twice or a few times, but an unlimited number of times" (*Mete.* I 3 339ᵇ27–29); "There is a tradition handed down from the ancients of the earliest times and bequeathed to posterity in the shape of a myth to the effect that the heavenly bodies are gods and that the divine encompasses the whole of nature. The rest of the tradition has been added later in a mythical way with a view to the persuasion of ordinary people and with a view to its use for legal purposes and for what is advantageous. For they say that these gods are human in form or like some of the other animals, and also other features similar that follow from or are similar to those just mentioned. But if we separate the first point from these additions and grasp it alone, namely, that they thought that the primary substances were gods, we would have to regard it as divinely (*theiôs*) said, and that while it is likely that each craft and each philosophy has often been developed as far as possible only to pass away again, these beliefs about the gods have survived like remnants until the present. In any case, the beliefs of our forefathers and of our earliest predecessors are to this extent alone illuminating to us" (*Met.* XII 8 1074ª38–ᵇ14); "We should take it, indeed, that pretty much everything else too has been discovered many times, or rather an unlimited number of times, in the long course of history. For our needs are likely to teach the necessities, and once they are present, the things that add refinement and abundance to life quite naturally develop" (*Pol.* VII 10 1329ᵇ25–30). The background explanation of this doctrine is presumably something like this: (1) the world and human beings have always existed (*Mete.* I 14 352ᵇ16–17, *DA* II 4 415ª25–ᵇ7, *GA* II 1 731ᵇ24–732ª3); (2) human beings are naturally adapted to form largely reliable beliefs about the world and what conduces to their welfare in it (*Met.* II 1 993ª30–ᵇ11, *Rh.* I 1 1355ª15–17).

Note 50

They gave the name *aithêr* ("ether") to the uppermost place: The place is the outermost or first heaven, which is eternally revolving. The same account, with minor variations, is given in *Mete.* I 3 339ᵇ19–30.

Positing a name for it from the fact that, throughout eternal time, it is running always (*thein aei*): "As for *aithêr*, I'd explain it as follows: it is right to call it *aithêr*, because it is always running and flowing (*aei thei rheôn*)" (Plato, *Crat.* 410b).

Note 51

Anaxagoras: See DK 59 = TEGP pp. 271–325.

Does not use this name correctly, since he uses "*aithêr*" in place of "fire": See DK B2 = TEGP F2, also *Cael.* III 3 302^{b}4, *Mete.* I 3 339^{b}22–25, II 9 369^{b}14–15. However, Anaxagoras is probably on better etymological grounds than Aristotle in connecting (if he did) *aithêr* to fire, since it seems in fact to derive from the verb *aithô* ("kindle," "light up"; passive: "burn"). See Chantraine, pp. 32–33.

Note 52

We say that the following are the only simple movements: circular and rectilinear, the latter having two parts, one away from the center, the other toward the center: See I 2 268^{b}14–26.

Note 53

We assume the straight line to be opposed above all to the circular. For concave and convex seem to be opposed not only to each other but also, when they are coupled and taken as put together, to the straight line: Start with two equal semicircles, S$_1$ and S$_2$. Nest S$_1$ inside S$_2$. Notice that the "concave" S$_1$ and the "convex" S$_2$, which seem to be opposed, have now been joined together: "The circle has its convexity and concavity in the same thing in a way" (*Ph.* IV 13 222^{b}2–3). But both clearly stand opposed to their common straight diameter. And that opposition remains when S$_1$ is flipped 180° along that diameter, so as to form the circumference of a circle with S$_2$.

Note 54

But rectilinear movements are opposed to each other because of their places. For up-down is at once a differentia of place and a contrariety: So if circular movement were to be contrary to rectilinear, it would have to be either upward or downward, depending on which rectilinear movement it was opposed to. But on the circumference of a circle, as Heraclitus already noticed, "a road up and down is one and the same" (DK B60 = TEGP 61 F38).

Differentia (*diaphora*): A *diaphora* is sometimes, as here, the differentia that divides a genus into species, and so defines each of its species: "species are composed of the genus and the differentiae" (*Met.* X 7 1057^{b}7). But sometimes it is simply one of the different features that distinguish one kind of thing from another, without necessarily suggesting that the kinds are genera or species in the strict sense or that the differences are differentiae.

Note 55

If someone supposes that the very same argument that applies to rectilinear applies also to spatial movement along a circumference (for example, that

spatial movement from A to B is contrary to that from B to A), it is [in fact] the rectilinear he is speaking of. For it is limited, whereas there would be an unlimited number of circular paths through the same points: Between two points, A and B, there are two opposed rectilinear movements, from A to B and from B to A. But for any circular movement from A to B there are an unlimited number of movements from B to A, corresponding to circles of different sizes that have A and B as points on their circumferences (Fig. 1). But one thing has only one contrary (I 2 269ᵃ10). Therefore circular movement from A to B is not contrary to that from B to A.

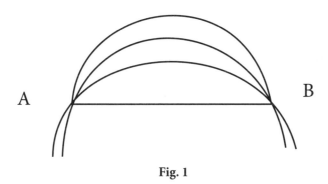

Fig. 1

Points (*sêmeia*): A *sêmeion* is usually a sign or indication, or a sort of rhetorical deduction (*Rh.* I 2 1357ᵃ33). But here, as at *APo.* I 10 76ᵇ5, *Top.* VI 4 141ᵇ12, and *Ph.* VI 9 240ᵇ3, it is a mathematical point, usually *stigmê* in Aristotle.

Note 56
It is the same too in the case of movement along one of the two semicircles—for example, from C to D and from D to C. For it (*hautê*) [the spatial movement] is the same as along the diameter, since we always suppose the distance between each pair of points to be a straight line:

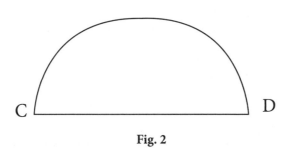

Fig. 2

"In the case of the semicircle drawn from C to D [Fig. 2], the movements from C to D along the circumference, if they are to be taken as contraries, will equally be so to that along the diameter. For if contrary movements are once again those from places that are farthest separated, and the greatest separation is a definite one, and we judge the definite separation as being the shortest of those having the same extremities, and this is a straight line, it is clear that the movements will take place as if along straight lines and on the same hypothesis, and the demonstration will hold no less if it takes place in the case of a single semicircle. And the case is the same here as it was there" (Simp. 147.28–148.7 = Hankinson, p. 96).

Note 57
Even if one constructed a circle and posited that . . . the spatial movement along semicircle G from E to F is contrary to that along semicircle H from F to E [Fig. 3], . . . it in no way follows that the spatial movements along the whole circle are contraries:

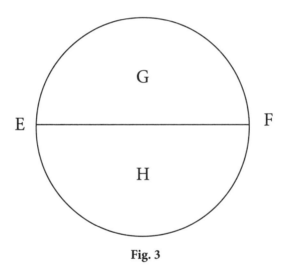

Fig. 3

When the semicircles G and H are separate, the spatial movement from E to F is distinct from the one from F to E, because they are to and from distinct places, and so are distinct for the same reason that the corresponding rectilinear ones would be. But when the semicircles are joined (Fig. 4), E and F are both starting point and end point of the same spatial movement.
{ . . . }: Lines I 4 271ª19–23 are transposed with Moraux to follow 271ª29.

Note 58
But then neither is spatial movement in a circle from A to B contrary to that from A to C [Fig. 4]. For the movement is from the same and to the same, but a contrary spatial movement was defined as from a contrary to a contrary:

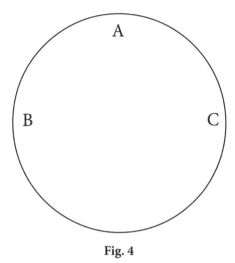

Fig. 4

Even though B and C have distinct labels, spatial movements in the same circle all have the same starting and ending points, and so cannot be contraries.

A contrary spatial movement was defined (*diôristhê*) **as from a contrary to a contrary:** The aorist *diôristhê*, if it refers to anything (Aristotle has not stated this definition in precisely these terms), must it seems refer to I 4 271ᵃ27–28. This favors the relocation of 271ᵃ19–23.

Note 59
If they were equal, there would be no movement of them, whereas if one of the movements did the mastering (*ekratei*), **the other would not exist:** That the "mastering" of one movement by another need not be, as here, absolute is especially clear in Aristotle's embryology, where actual movements in a male progenitor's semen, which transmit his form to the embryo, are changed in various ways by the potential movements in a female's menses, which provide the embryo's matter, ensuring that the offspring has traits stemming from both parents: "But it is necessary to grasp the universal assumptions. First, . . . that some movements are present potentially and others actively. But in addition two more: that what gets mastered (*kratoumenon*) departs from type, into the opposite; that what slackens passes into the movement that is next to it: slackening a little into a near movement; more, into one that is farther away; finally, [the movements] so run together that it [the fetus or child] does not resemble any of those that properly belong to it (*oikeiôn*) or of the same kind (*suggenôn*), rather all that is left is what is common, and it is [simply] human" (*GA* IV 3 768ᵇ5–12).

Note 60
We say that a shoe is pointless if it is not being worn (*mê estin hupodesis*): "Each piece of property has two uses, both of which are uses of it intrinsically, but not uses of it intrinsically in the same way. Instead, one properly belongs to the thing, while the other does not properly belong to it—for example, as regards a shoe, its use in wearing

it (*hupodesis*) and its use in exchange. For both are uses to which a shoe can be put. For someone who exchanges a shoe, in return for money or food, with someone who needs a shoe, is using the shoe insofar as it is a shoe. But this is not the use that properly belongs to it. For it does not come to exist for the sake of exchange" (*Pol.* I 9 1257ᵃ6–13).

Note 61

The god (*ho theos*) **and nature, however, make nothing pointlessly:** Aristotle recognizes the existence of a number of different divine beings or gods, among which he distinguishes a primary god, referred to as *ho theos* ("the god"), which is the one referred to as the immovable mover in *Ph.* VIII 10 and more fully discussed together with the other divine beings in *Met.* XII 7–10. The problem is that the primary god is exclusively a self-contemplating being (*Met.* VII 9 1074ᵇ34–35), not one that engages in any world-making. It is analogous to one that we meet in *NE* X, where we are told that "the gods exercise a sort of supervision over human affairs" (1179ᵃ24–25). For since the gods in question live exclusively contemplative lives (X 8 1178ᵇ8–23), whatever supervision they exercise must be of a somewhat special sort. Aristotle does not tell us what it is, but his identification of these gods with the heavenly spheres (*Met.* XII 8 1074ᵃ38–ᵇ14) suggests an answer. For the orderly revolutions of these spheres govern the seasons as well as the cycles of fertility and infertility of land and animals (*GA* IV 10 778ᵃ4–9). Hence they confer benefits on all beings, but especially on those wise people who, through astronomical contemplation of the heavens, learn about these cycles, and adjust their lives accordingly. A similar solution seems the most attractive option here, so that the reference of *ho theos* is indeed the primary god, but considered as the entire cosmic order he controls, "just as a city too or any other complex system, seems to be most of all its most controlling part" (*NE* IX 8 1168ᵇ31–32). See also I 1 268ᵃ13n.

Note 62

Most of the ancient philosophers thought [that there is an unlimited body]: See, for example, Anaximander DK A11, B2 = TEGP 10; Anaximenes DK A7 = TEGP 12; Anaxagoras B1, B2 = TEGP 11; Melissus DK B3; Democritus DK A37 = TEGP 12 F5.

Note 63

Getting a theoretical grasp (*theôrein*) **on the truth:** The verb *theasthai*, with which *theôria* is cognate, means to look at or gaze at. Thus *theôria* itself is sometimes what someone is doing in looking closely at something, or actively observing, studying, or contemplating it, and sometimes the capacity someone has to do these things (*Met.* IX 6 1048ᵃ34–35, 8 1045ᵃ36). When *theôria* is an exercise of understanding (*nous*), which is the element responsible for grasping scientific starting-points (*NE* VI 6 1141ᵃ7–8), such as (the definition of) right angle in the case of geometry, or (the definition of) happiness in the case of politics, it is translated as "contemplation," and the cognate verb *theôrein* as "contemplate." The corresponding capacity is translated as "theoretical knowledge," and what gives rise to it as "get a theoretical grasp on." So when we get a theoretical grasp on A, we acquire the theoretical scientific knowledge of A, which we exercise in contemplating A.

Note 64

If someone said there is a smallest magnitude, this person, by having introduced the smallest one, would have upset the greatest things in mathematics: "When Democritus and everyone else who made such suppositions had posited certain tiny things and smallest magnitudes as starting-points, because these, as starting-points, possessed the greatest capacity, when they made errors about them they upset the greatest truths about geometry, for example, that magnitudes are divisible without limit, which is why it is possible to bisect any given straight line" (Simp. 202.27–31 = Hankinson, pp. 18–19). But Aristotle may be thinking of Zeno's four puzzles, "two of which are based on the hypothesis of indivisible lines and magnitudes" (Heath-2, p. 163). See *Ph.* VI 9.

Note 65

The starting-point is greater in capacity than in magnitude, which is why what is small at the start becomes immensely great at the end: "The start is the most important part, as the saying goes" (*SE* 34 183^{b}22–23); "It seems indeed that the starting-point is more than half the whole and that many of the things we were inquiring about will at the same time become evident through it" (*NE* I 7 1098^{b}7–8); "the starting-point is said to be half the whole, so that even a small error in it is comparable to all the errors made at the later stages" (*Pol.* V 4 1303^{b}29–31).

Note 66

If the body moving spatially in a circle is unlimited, the radii produced from the center will be unlimited: The body moving spatially in a circle is the primary or outermost heaven (I 3 270^{b}15), or sphere of the fixed stars, so that the center referred to is that of the universe (and so of the earth).

Note 67

The interval (*diastêma*): A *diastêma* in music is an interval (*Pr.* XIX 47 922^{b}6) and in spatial magnitudes, a dimension (*Ph.* IV 1 209^{a}4). By extension, just as there are extreme and middle terms in a syllogism, so syllogisms themselves are *diastêmata* or intervals connecting the minor term to the major term (*APr.* I 25 42^{b}10) and premises are sub-intervals of those intervals, so that *protasis* ("premise," "proposition") and *diastêma* are equivalent (I 4 26^{b}1). Terms, as sub-intervals of those sub-intervals, are also *diastêmata*, so that the number of terms in a sequence of syllogisms is equal to the number of *diastêmata* in them (I 25 42^{b}1–26). Here the relevant *diastêma* is the ever larger one between the radii that enclose the volume of the segment (or cone, in the case of a sphere).

Note 68

It is not possible to traverse the unlimited: See *Ph.* VI 7.

Note 69

We see . . . and we have also determined by argument that movement in a circle belongs to a certain thing: At I 2 268^{b}14–269^{a}9. On "by argument," see I 3 270^{b}4n.

Note 70
Let, then, the line ACE be unlimited in one direction, E, and the line BB be unlimited in both:

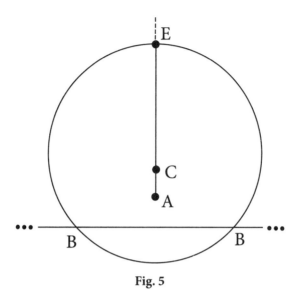

Fig. 5

Note 71
The cosmos (*kosmon*): Here, as at *NE* VI 7 1141^{b}1 and elsewhere, the cosmos is the primary (or outermost) heaven. But sometimes, as at *Cael.* I 10 280^{a}22, it is the cosmos as a whole.

Note 72
The discussions concerning movement (*tois peri kinêseôs*): *Ph.* V, VI, and VIII form a unified discussion, parts of which are often referred to as—or as included in—"our accounts concerning movement (*ta peri kinêseôs*)." *Ph.* VI is referred to in this way at VIII 8 263^{a}11–12, *APo.* II 12 95^{b}11, *Sens.* 6 445^{b}20, *Met.* IX 8 1049^{b}36; *Ph.* VIII here and at *GC* I 3 318^{a}3. Book VII interrupts this sequence, suggesting that it may have been incorporated into the *Physics* at a later date. See Ross, pp. 11–19 and, on VII 3, Maso, especially, pp. 131–136. See also *Cael.* I 7 274^{a}20–22.

Note 73
If it moves even the smallest distance, it is necessary for it to do so in an unlimited time: See I 5 272^{a}3–5.

Note 74
So it goes around any line within it—for example, AB: Either the chord AB or the corresponding arc.

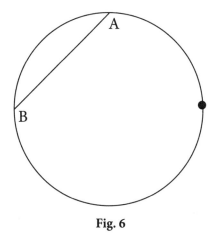

Fig. 6

Note 75

As a line, in that respect in which there is a limit (*peras*), **cannot possibly be unlimited:** For example, a line that has a limit in one direction may be unlimited in the other.

Note 76

If, then, neither a sphere nor a circle can be unlimited: Omitting μήτε τετράγωνον ("nor a square"), which Moraux, with some mss., secludes.

Note 77

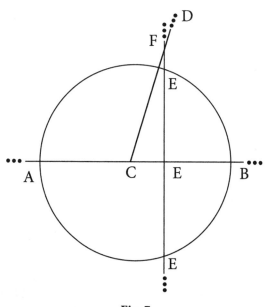

Fig. 7

Note 78

Let the heaven when remaining at rest be unlimited, and another heaven of equal magnitude be moving within it: Since H_r (the heaven at rest) and H_m (the heaven moving) are both unlimited, they cannot be spheres. Since no spheres are unlimited (I 5 272^b21–22), we should not think of H_m and H_r as one sphere nested inside the other, as Simplicius tells us Alexander thought, nor of H_r as a place (or space) and H_m as a sphere, whose boundary coincides with its boundary, as Simplicius himself thought (Simp. 215.3–10 = Hankinson, p. 32). Instead, Aristotle just seems to be assuming that one *unlimited* body can fit exactly inside another, with the one at rest being what the other is moving relative to.

Note 79

But this, we saw, is impossible: In *Ph.* VI 7.

Note 80

Conversely (*antestrammenôs*): The verb *antistrephein* (*antestrammenôs* is the correlative adverb) is used to signify: (1) a logical relation between propositions, so that, for example, the universal negative converts, because if no B is A, then no A is B (*APr.* I 2 25^a5–6) and so on; (2) a logical relation between terms (I 45 51^a4–5), equivalent to counterpredication, where B is counterpredicated of A if and only if A is predicated of B and B of A; (3) the substitution of one term for another, without logical convertibility (*APr.* II 15 64^a40); (4) the (valid) inference of (A admits of not being B) from (B admits of being A) (I 13 32^a30); (5) the substitution of the opposite of a premise for a premise (II 8 59^b4); (6) an argument in which from one premise in a syllogism, and the opposite of the conclusion, the opposite of the other premise is deduced (II 8–10, *Top.* VIII 14 163^a32–34). (6) is the sense relevant here. At *Top.* II 1 109^a10, and only there it seems, A and B convert if and only if (B *belongs* to A) $\supset$ (A *is* B).

Note 81

It cannot go farther than the center: If the body that by nature sinks were to move past the center, it would begin to move away from the center again (that is, upward), and would then have to do so contrary to its nature.

Note 82

If the places are definite, that is to say, limited, the bodies will also be limited: Since an unlimited body cannot be in a limited place.
Definite, that is to say (*kai*), **limited:** See I 5 272^b19.

Note 83

But that [unlimited movement] is impossible was shown previously: At I 5 272^a21–$^b17$ (= [3]).

Note 84

The middle (*to meson*) **is definite:** *To meson* is here the middle place that is between the up place and the down place. And since place is "the limit of what encompasses something at which it is in contact with what is encompassed" (*Ph.* IV 4 212ᵃ6–6a), the *place* that is the center of the universe is not a geometrical point but rather a sphere. Hence Aristotle describes it as "the one *around* the center" (*Cael.* I 8 277ᵇ15–16).

Note 85
[1] A body that is in it, or [2] that can come to be (*genesthai*) in it, is definite as well. Moreover, the bodies spatially moving upward or downward can come to be (*genesthai*) in it. For [3a] the one naturally moves away from the center, [3b] the other toward the center: The contrast between [1] and [2] is between [3b] bodies that are naturally at rest in the sphere around the center and [3a] bodies that come to be there (by force), though their natural movement is upward.

Note 86
Weight (*baros*): When *baros* is contrasted with *kouphos* or *kouphotês* ("light," "lightness") it is translated as "heavy" or "heaviness," but when, as here, it applies to whatever has either heaviness or lightness it is translated as weight. It helps to think of the contrast, as Aristotle does, in terms of tendencies to move to proper places. If something naturally tends to move down toward the center it has some degree of heaviness; if it tends to move upward, away from the center, it has some degree of lightness.

Note 87
GB: A limited subpart of the unlimited body greater than FB (previously, BF), which is unlimited.

Note 88
It makes no difference whether the weights are commensurable or incommensurable: That is, whether both are measurable without remainder by the same unit weight.

Note 89
If E, taken three times in measuring C, exceeds it: That is, $(3 \times E) > C$. Retaining τὸ E, which Moraux secludes.
Measuring (*metroun*): See II 4 287ᵃ25n.

Note 90
Three times the whole weight of the three magnitudes BD: BD serves as a unit E for measuring weight.
Will be greater than that of C. So that there will be the same impossibility: The impossibility being that the weight of a limited body is greater than that of an unlimited one. For $3 \times E$ (the measure of the weight of the limited body BD) $> C$ (the measure of the weight of the unlimited body AB).

Note 91
Demonstration (*apodeixin*): See I 1 268ᵃ1n(6).

Note 92
It is always possible to take bodies of equal weight to BD from the unlimited, subtracting or adding whatever one wishes: Adding a comma after τοῦ ἀπείρου with DP.

Note 93
Our discussions concerning the starting-points: In *Ph.* III 4–8. See I 5 272ᵃ30n.
There we previously determined in universal terms in what way the unlimited exists and in what way it does not exist: But note the following restriction on this claim: "Presumably this inquiry is universal: whether it is possible for there to be an unlimited present in mathematical objects as well [as in perceptibles] and in intelligible ones that have no magnitude. Our investigation, by contrast, concerns perceptibles and topics our methodical inquiry is concerned with: whether there is or is not present in *them* a body that is unlimited in extent" (*Ph.* III 5 204ᵃ34–ᵇ4).

Note 94
The universe (*to pan*): See I 1 268ᵃ11n.
After this we must investigate [whether the body of the universe is nonetheless enough for there to be several heavens]: In I 8–9.

Note 95
Someone might be puzzled (*aporêseien*): See I 10 279ᵇ8n.
The cosmos around us: See I 5 272ᵃ20n.

Note 96
Homoeomerous (*homoimeres*): Something is homoeomerous in the strict sense if its parts, however small, are of the same sort as the whole—as parts of water, however small, are (or were thought to be) water too (*PA* I 2 647ᵇ17–20).

Note 97
Our first assumptions: Those about simple movements, bodies, and places introduced in I 2–3. See I 7 274ᵇ11, 8 276ᵇ8.

Note 98
It is necessary for every natural body to have movement: Because a nature is an internal starting-point of movement and of rest. See I 1 268ᵃ3n.

Note 99
If the unlimited is to be composed of a limited number [of forms], it is necessary for each of the parts to be unlimited: Simplicius raises the following problem: "Why if the non-homoeomerous is composed of a limited number of forms,

is it necessary that *each* of the parts be limited? For it is possible that if one of the parts were unlimited, the whole would be unlimited" (Simp. 228.31–33 = Hankinson, p. 47). Aristotle does give an argument for this in *Ph.* III 5, to which Simplicius refers us: "[1] It will not be composite, if the elements are limited in multiplicity. For there must be more than one element, and the contrary element must always be equal, and no one of them can be unlimited. For however much one contrary in one body falls short in capacity of another in another (for example, suppose fire is limited and air is unlimited, and the capacity of a quantity of air is any multiple whatsoever of that of an equal quantity of fire, with the sole proviso that the multiple is some [finite] number), nonetheless it is evident that the unlimited body will overpower and destroy the limited one. But that each element should be unlimited is impossible. For a body is what has extension in all dimensions, and what is unlimited is what has unlimited extension, so that an unlimited body will be unlimitedly extended in all dimensions" (204^{b}11–22). But here Aristotle seems to rely on a different consideration (I 7 274^{b}8–9). Each of the simple bodies has weight (whether heaviness or lightness), earth having the most (heaviness and least lightness), fire the least (heaviness and most lightness). But it has been shown that weight (heaviness or lightness) cannot be unlimited, so each of the simple bodies must have a limited weight (heaviness or lightness), and so must be limited.

Note 100
It has been shown that neither heaviness nor lightness is unlimited: In I 6.

Note 101
Our first assumptions: See I 7 274^{a}34n.

Note 102
It is impossible for what cannot have come to be to be coming to be, alike in quality, quantity, and in place: The relevant sort of coming to be is movement, and "if the categories are distinguished as being substance, quality, place, time, relation, quantity, and affecting or being affected, it necessarily follows that there are three sorts of movement—that of a quality, that of a quantity, and that with respect to place" (*Ph.* V 5 225^{b}5–9).

Note 103
Even if they are dispersed, it might nonetheless still be thought possible for what is composed of all the particles [, for example,] of fire to be unlimited: Retaining πῦρ with Verdenius and the mss.; Moraux secludes. "[Aristotle] wished to add a third argument showing that it is impossible for each of the parts of the non-homoeomerous [supposedly unlimited body] to be unlimited from the fact that if each of them is everywhere it would allow no place for the remaining ones. He first shows this to be so even if one does not assume each to be one continuous unlimited, but rather composed of unlimited dispersed pieces, either [1] as Anaxagoras seemed to claim, with each form (*eidos*) an unlimited number of homoeomerous parts, or [2] as those who claim the cosmoses to be unlimited in number"

(Simp. 229.28–230.1 = Hankinson, pp. 48–49). [1] Anaxagoras DK B4 = TEGP 13 F4-5. [2] includes Leucippus, Democritus (DK 67A1 = TEGP 1, 68A40 =TEGP 53), and, though less certainly, Anaximander (DK 12A14 = TEGP 18, 12A17 = TEGP 41). See *Ph.* VIII 1 250^{b}18–19.

Note 104
Body, we saw, is what has extension in all ways: At I 1 268^{a}7.

Note 105
That the heaven is unlimited . . . has been shown to be impossible: In I 5.

Note 106
It will move either in accord with nature or by force: See I 2 269^{a}8–10.

Note 107
There will be another place of equal size toward which it will spatially move. But this is impossible: "Since if it were unlimited, it would already have occupied all of place prior to moving" (Simp. 231.12–13 = Hankinson, p. 50).

Note 108
It was assumed that the greater [causes an equal alteration] in a shorter time: This assumption has not been explicitly made before.

Note 109
Affecting and being affected do have [a limit]: "A change admits of being completed, and there is an end of change, and *it* we have shown to be indivisible because it is a limit" (*Ph.* VI 5 236^{a}11–13). See also *Cael.* I 8 277^{a}12–20.

Note 110
Whatever bodies are in a place, at any rate, are also perceptible: "It is natural indeed for everything that is perceptible to be somewhere, and there is a certain place for each, and the same place for a part of it and for the whole—for example, for the totality of earth and for a single clod, and for fire and a spark" (*Ph.* III 5 205^{a}10–12).

Note 111
There is no unlimited body outside the heaven; nor yet is there one that is so up to a certain point (*mechri tinos*): "Having shown that there is no unlimited body outside the cosmos, [Aristotle] then posits in addition that there is no limited one either (which he calls one 'up to a certain point'—for a body that extends 'up to a certain point' and not in every direction endlessly is limited). He now posits this as undemonstrated, completing the disjunctive proof as follows: if there is a body outside the heaven, it is either unlimited or limited; but it is neither unlimited nor limited; therefore there is not one" (Simp. 237.14–20 = Hankinson, p. 58). But

"(*sôma*) *mechri tinos* cannot have this meaning. The argument seems [rather] to be as follows: if an infinite body cannot be perceptible and if the sum of perceptible things is the universe, an infinite body, if anywhere, must be outside the universe, either completely or partly (*mechri tinos*). But anything outside the universe, even though it is only thought to be outside it, is thought to be in a place. Now, 'in a place' is equivalent to 'perceptible.' Consequently, the infinite cannot be anywhere" (Verdenius, p. 271). It is not clear which of these interpretations is correct. See also II 7 289ª19–21n.

Note 112

Intelligible (*noêton*): An intelligible object or content (*noêma*) is a universal form (*eidos*). Encoded in an appearance, it can be grasped by the understanding (*nous*) when it contemplates (*theôrein*) that appearance: "To the understanding (*dianoêtikê*) soul appearances (*phantasmata*) are like perceptual contents (*aisthêmata*). . . . The part that understands, then, understands the forms in the appearances (*eidê . . . en tois phantasmasi*)" (*DA* III 7 431ª14–ᵇ10). It differs from an appearance in being a propositional element—an element of something with a truth value: "when someone contemplates (*theôrê[i]*), he must at the same time contemplate an appearance (*phantasma*). . . . However, imagination (*phantasia*) is distinct from affirmation and denial, since truth and falsity involve a combination of intelligible objects (*noêmatôn*)" (8 432ª8–12).

If it is intelligible, it will be in a place: Aristotle imagines an objector (perhaps a Platonist) claiming that the body outside the heaven is intelligible, not perceptible. For when he describes Plato as separating (*chôrizein*) the Forms from perceptible particulars (*Met.* XIII 4 1078ᵇ30–34), the primary connotation is that of putting them in separate places (see *Cael.* I 9 278ª17n). But, on Aristotle's own view, intelligible things, as universals not perceptible particulars, cannot be in a place. For "place is special to particular things, which is why they are separable by place" (XIV 5 1092ª18–19).

Note 113

"Outside" and "inside" signify place: Compare I 9 279ª11–22, where a non-place "outside" the heaven is discussed.

Note 114

It is also possible to attack the issue in a more logico-linguistic way (*logikôteron*): (1) The adjective *logikos* is used to distinguish a set of propositions and problems from those belonging to natural science or ethics: "Propositions such as this are ethical—for example, whether one should obey our parents or the laws, if they disagree. *Logikos*, whether contraries belong to the same science or not. Natural scientific, whether the cosmos is eternal or not. And similarly for the problems" (*Top.* I 14 105ᵇ21–25). Since the question about a science of contraries is a philosophical one (*Met.* III 2 996ª18–21), *logikos* problems overlap with philosophical ones. At the same time, "if an argument depends on false but reputable beliefs, it is *logikos*" (*Top.* VIII 12 162ᵇ27), suggesting that *logikos* arguments overlap with dialectical ones, since both may rely on reputable beliefs (*endoxa*) or—more-or-less equivalently—on things said (*legomena*) about the topic (*Ph.* I 2 185ª2–3n). Indeed, the question about a science of contraries is itself identified as one for dialectic (*Met.* XIII 4 1078ᵇ25–27).

(2) When Plato, unlike previous thinkers, is accorded a share of dialectic it is due to his investigation of *logoi* or accounts (*Met.* I 6 987ᵇ31–33), which he almost always undertook through staged Socratic conversations, whose aim was to discover the correct definition (XIII 4 1078ᵇ23–25) of what something essentially or intrinsically is, or is itself-by-itself (*auto kath' hauto*)—the "itself" in the name of a Form probably stems from its being the ontological correlate of such a definition (III 2 997ᵇ8–9). One core meaning of *logikos*, in fact, relates it to conversation and speaking, while another relates it to reason—the *logikai aretai* are the virtues of reason or thought (*NE* II 8 1108ᵇ9–10). When we ask *logikôs* (adverb) why it is that these bricks and stones are a house, what we are asking for is a formal cause or an essence (*Met.* VII 17 1041ª26–28), which is presumably why a deduction of the essence is a *logikos sullogismos* (*APo.* II 8 93ª15).

(3) When dialecticians are contrasted with natural scientists it is on the grounds that "the scientist gives the matter, whereas the dialectician gives the form and the account" (*DA* I 1 403ᵇ1–2)—again associating dialectic with proceeding *logikôs*. The dialectician proceeds *logikôs*, the natural scientist *phusikôs*—looking to matter but also to form, when the relevant essence requires it (*Met.* VI 1 1026ª5–6). So to proceed in a strictly *logikôs* way, when there is empirical evidence bearing on the subject, is bad scientific practice: "It seems that the knowledge of the what-it-is is not only useful for getting a theoretical grasp on the causes of the coincidents connected to the essences [= intrinsic coincidents] . . . but also, conversely, knowing these coincidents contributes in great part to knowing the what-it-is. For when we can give an account of the way either all or most of these coincidents appear to be, we will then be able to speak best about the essence. For the starting-point of all demonstration is [the definition of] the what-it-is, so that insofar as definitions do not lead us to know the coincidents, or fail even to facilitate a likely conjecture about [how to demonstrate] them, it is clear that they have all been stated in a dialectical and empty way" (*DA* I 1 402ᵇ16–403ª2). This is presumably the relevant contrast in our text: the previous arguments have been more *phusikôs*, because focused on natural things, this one is more *logikôs*, because it is more general in its application.

(4) Before we start defining essences *logikôs*, then, we should have intimate knowledge of the empirical data that they are supposed to explain: "What causes our inability to take a comprehensive view of the agreed-upon facts is lack of experience. That is why those who dwell in more intimate association with the facts of nature are better able to lay down starting-points that can bring together a good many of these, whereas those whom many arguments have made unobservant of the facts come too readily to their conclusions after looking at only a few facts" (*GC* I 2 316ª5–10). Thus a frequent criticism of Plato and the Platonists is that in proceeding *logikôs* they leave the earth and the world of facts too far behind and proceed at too abstract and general a level (*Met.* I 2 987ᵇ29–988ª7, XII 1 1069ª26–28).

(5) When the perceptual data are scarce, however, it is still possible to make some scientific headway. Astronomy is a case in point. Our theoretical knowledge of the heavenly bodies is relatively slight, "since as regards both those things on the basis of which one would investigate them and those things about them that we long to know, the perceptual appearances are altogether few" (*PA* I 5 644^{b}25–28). There are many puzzles in astronomy, therefore, about which we can do little but conjecture, since "where things not apparent to perception are concerned, we think we have adequately shown our case to be in accord with reason if we have brought things back to what is possible, given the available appearances" (*Mete.* I 7 344^{a}5–7). To become a "little less puzzled" in areas like these is—until further perceptual data become available—the most we can hope for (*Cael.* II 12 291^{b}24–28).

The argument here seems to be *logikôteron*, however, largely because it relies on the meaning of the terms involved, "unlimited," "circle," "spatial movement."

Note 115
The unlimited, when homoeomerous, cannot move in a circle: "'When homoeomerous' is added not because the non-homoeomerous and composite ones that revolve do not move around a center (for everything that moves in a circle moves around a center), but because the argument is now concerned with simple bodies. 'When homoeomerous' is added in place of 'simple,' since he produces the demonstration in this case, because in the case of composite ones too natural movement comes about in accord with whichever of the simple bodies is the mastering one in it" (Alex. 239.3–8 = Hankinson, pp. 59–60).

Note 116
Another just as large (that is, unlimited) place that it will spatially move toward: That is, just as large as the place it moves from.
There would need to be another just as large (that is, unlimited) place that it will spatially move toward in accord with nature, and a distinct one, just as large, that it will move toward contrary to nature: "But it is impossible for there to be two unlimited places . . . if indeed the unlimited is everywhere" (Alex. 239.14–15 = Hankinson, p. 60).

Note 117
There is an argument in the discussions concerning movement that nothing limited has unlimited capacity and nothing unlimited has limited capacity: See *Ph.* VIII 10 266^{a}24–^{b}27.
The discussions concerning movement: See I 5 272^{a}30n.

Note 118
If, then, what can be moved in accord with nature can also be moved contrary to nature, there will be two unlimited things, the one that is a mover in this way and the one that is a moved: Suppose an unlimited body U$_b$ is moving in accord with nature in movement M$_1$ (in a circle, for example). Then there is a movement M$_2$ (upward, for example) that is contrary to nature for U. So there must be an

unlimited mover U_m with the unlimited strength or capacity needed to move U_b in M_2. Therefore, there are two unlimited things the moved U_b and the mover U_m. But this is impossible.

Note 119

If it moves itself, it will be animate: Though even animals do not strictly speaking move themselves: "That a moving thing is moved by something is most evident in the case of things that are moved contrary to nature, since they are clearly moved by something else. After things that are moved contrary to nature the next most evident case is that of things that by nature move themselves—for example, animals. For what is unclear in this case is not whether they are moved by something, but rather how we are to distinguish in them the mover from the moved. For just as in ships and things not composed by nature, so too in animals, the mover and the moved seem to be distinct, and it is in this way that the whole thing moves itself" (*Ph.* VIII 4 254^{b}24–33).

Note 120

If its mover is something else, there will be two unlimited things, the mover and the moved, differing in shape (*morphê*) and capacity: *Morphê* is often, as here, equivalent in meaning to *eidos*—"form." And the form is a limit: "there is a limit and an account of size and growth for things that are put together by nature; and these are characteristic of soul . . . and of the account rather than of the matter" (*DA* II 12 416^{a}16–18). Moreover, "the substance of each thing and the essence of each [is a limit] (for this is the limit of knowledge, and if of knowledge, of its object too)" (*Met.* V 17 1022^{a}8–10). But if the series is not itself to go on without limit, the (new) mover must be an animate self-mover, and so must differ in form and in capacity from the (un-self-moving) unlimited thing it moves. *Morphê* and *dunamis* appear in close association again at *Pol.* VII 1 1323^{b}33–36a): "the courage, justice, practical wisdom, and temperance of a city have the same *dunamis* and *morphê* as those in which each human being who is said to be courageous, just, practically-wise, and temperate should share."

Capacity (*dunamis*): The term *dunamis* (plural: *dunameis*) is used by Aristotle to capture two different but related things. (1) As in ordinary Greek, it signifies a power or capacity something has, especially to cause movement in something else (productive *dunamis*) or to be caused to move by something else (passive *dunamis*). (2) It signifies a way of being, namely, potential (*dunamei*) being as opposed to actual (*entelecheia[i]*) or active (*energeia[i]*) being. See also *Met.* V 12.

Note 121

Leucippus and Democritus: See DK 67–68 = TEGP pp. 516–685.

Void (*kenon*): See I 9 279^{a}13.

Note 122

The particles are determined by their shapes: "Democritus for his part seems to think that there were three differentiae. For he thinks that the underlying body and the matter are one and the same, but it is differentiated either by rhythm (that is, shape), or by turning (that is, position), or by contact (that is, order). It is evident, however, that there are many differentiae" (*Met.* VIII 2 1042ᵇ11–15).

Note 123

Where a single clod of earth spatially moves to, the totality of earth does as well: "It is natural indeed for everything that is perceptible to be somewhere, and there is a certain place for each, and the same place for a part of it and for the whole—for example, for the totality of earth and for a single clod, and for fire and a spark" (*Ph.* III 5 205ᵃ10–13).

Note 124

None of these bodies will be unconditionally light, if all have heaviness, whereas if all have lightness, none will be heavy: Which is contrary to the way things seem to be, but also contrary to argument. See III 2 301ᵃ22–ᵇ17, IV 2 308ᵇ28–309ᵇ27.

Note 125

Induction (*epagôgês*): See Introduction, pp. xli–xlii, I 1 268ᵃ1n(5).

Note 126

We said that [why there cannot be several heavens] must be investigated: At I 7 274ᵃ24–28.

In case someone thinks that it has not been shown universally about all bodies that it is impossible for any of them at all to exist outside the cosmos, but that the argument applies only to those with no definite position: The argument referred to is that of I 7 275ᵇ5–11: "[1] Moreover, whatever bodies are in a place, at any rate, are also perceptible. [2] Therefore, there is no unlimited body outside the heaven. Nor yet is there one up to a certain magnitude. Therefore, there is no body at all outside the heaven. [3] For if it is intelligible, it will be in a place. For 'outside' and 'inside' signify place. So it will be perceptible. But nothing perceptible is not in a place." The potential objector worries, then, that in [1] and [3], "place" means "definite place" (that is, the spatial envelope of a definite body). But, for example, the Platonic Forms (intelligible objects) might be thought to be "outside" the heaven, without being in some definite place. See 275ᵇ10n. "I think he speaks of things with no definite position in contrast with those that contribute to the disposition of the cosmos" (Simp. 247.12–13 = Hankinson, p. 69).

Note 127

Here: See I 2 269ᵃ31n.

Note 128

But the spatial movement that is in accord with nature is a single one: Reading μία δ' with Verdenius, p. 272 and DP for Moraux μία γὰρ ("for the spatial movement that is in accord with nature is a single one").

Note 129
It is necessary for all the cosmoses, being admittedly (*ge*) similar in nature, to be composed of the same bodies: For the admission, see I 6 275ᵇ32–276ᵃ1.

Note 130
The ones intermediate between them: Namely, air and water.

Note 131
If these are homonyms and are not said of things there in accord with the same form (*idean*) as of those among us, then the universe too would be said to be a cosmos homonymously: "Things are said to be *homonymous* when they have only a name in common, but the account of the substance [= essence, form] that corresponds to the name is distinct—for example, both a human and a picture are animals. These have only a name in common and the account of the essence corresponding to the name is distinct. For if we are to say what-it-is for each of them to be an animal, we will give a special account to each" (*Cat.* 1 1ᵃ1–6). Notice that it is things, not names that are homonymous.

Note 132
Undifferentiated (*adiaphoron*): "A thing is said to be one in another way when its underlying subject is undifferentiated in form, and it is undifferentiated when its form is perceptually indivisible" (*Met.* V 6 1216ᵃ17–19).

Note 133
Proofs (*tekmêriois*): "Of signs (*sêmeiôn*), some are related as particular to universal, others as universal to particular. Of these, a necessary sign is a proof (*tekmêrion*), while that which is not necessary has no distinguishing name. Now I call necessary those from which a deduction comes about. . . . An example of signs related as particular to universal is if someone were to say that since Socrates is wise and just it is a sign that the wise are just. This is indeed a sign, but it is refutable, even if true of the case mentioned, since it is non-deductive. But if someone were to say that there is a sign that someone is ill, since he has a fever, or that a woman has given birth, because she has milk, it is a necessary one. And among signs, this is just what only a proof is. For only it, if true, is irrefutable. An example of signs related as universal to particular is if someone were to say that there is a sign that a person is feverish, since he is breathing rapidly. This too is refutable, even if true [of the person in question]. For it is possible to breathe rapidly and not be feverish" (*Rh.* I 2 1357ᵇ1–20).

Note 134
All change is limited: "No change, though, is unlimited. For every change, whether between contradictories or between contraries, is from something to something. So in changes with respect to contradiction, the affirmation or the denial is the limit—for example, in coming to be it is being, in passing away it is not being. And in those between contraries it is the contraries that are the limit. For these

are the extremities of the change, and so of all alteration (for alteration is always based on certain contraries). It is likewise with increase and decrease. For the limit of increase is the complete magnitude that is in accord with the nature proper to what is increasing, while the limit of decrease is the complete departure from this. Spatial movement on the other hand is not limited in this way, since it is not always between contraries. But since what has an incapacity to be cut . . . does not admit of *being* cut, and in general what has an incapacity to come to be does not admit of *coming* to be, and what has an incapacity to change does not admit of *changing* to what it has an incapacity to change to. If, then, what is in spatial movement is changing to something, it will have the capacity to have changed to it. So its movement is not unlimited, nor will it be in spatial movement over an unlimited distance, since it cannot traverse it" (*Ph.* VI 10 241ª26–ᵇ11).

Note 135
What becomes healthy [does not change to] some random destination, nor to whichever one the mover wishes: What becomes healthy must change precisely to being healthy (otherwise healthy would not be what it was becoming), and this is so even if the mover (that is, the doctor) is trying (ineptly or criminally) to make him something other than healthy.

Note 136
Even spatial movement in a circle has in a way (*pôs*) opposite points: The reason it has them only in a way is this: "A circular movement . . . will be one and continuous. For nothing impossible follows. For what is moving from A will at the same time be moving to A with the same proposed end (since what it will arrive at is what it is moving to), but without having contrary or opposite movements at the same time. For not every movement to A is contrary or opposite to a movement from A, but rather they are contrary only if they are along a straight line (for it has contraries with respect to place, such as the extremities of a diameter, since they are furthest apart), and opposite if they are along the same line. So there is nothing to prevent the movement from being continuous and without temporal intermission. For circular movement is movement from a point to itself, whereas movement along a straight line is from a point to another" (*Ph.* VIII 8 264ᵇ9–19). **So even for these (*toutois*) the movement is in a certain way toward opposite and limited points:** *Toutois* refers to things that spatially move in a circle, the pertinent ones being the celestial bodies.

Note 137
Proof: See I 8 277ª11n.

Note 138
For just as a thing that is lower than another because of its speed is fast because of its heaviness, so if the increase in heaviness were unlimited, the increase in speed would be unlimited as well: Rejecting with Verdenius p. 273, the addition of εἰ. Simp. 264.2–6 (= Hankinson, p. 86) explains: "For just as something that is

spatially moving below something else, that is, that takes the lead and spatially moves downward faster because of its greater speed, is faster by the addition of heaviness, similarly too in the case of the very same thing, if the increment is unlimited, so will be the increment in speed."

Note 139

But then neither could they be moved upward and downward by something else, nor by force or by squeezing out (*ekthlipsei*), **as some people say:** "For [Democritus] the shapes and atoms are unlimited and those that are spherical he says are fire and soul—which are like the so-called motes in the air that appear in the sunbeams that come through our windows. The aggregate of such seeds, he says (and likewise Leucippus), are the elements of the whole of nature, while those of them that are spherical are the soul, because being of such a shape they are especially capable of moving through everything and—being themselves moving—of moving the rest, on the supposition that the soul is what imparts movement to animals. That is why, too, they make breathing the defining mark of being alive. For when the surrounding air compresses their bodies it squeezes out (*ekthlibontos*) those atomic shapes which, because they are never at rest themselves, impart movement to animals. Then aid comes from outside by the entry of other similar atoms in breathing. For these prevent the squeezing out of those that are already inside, helping to counteract what is doing the compressing and solidifying. And life continues just so long as they are capable of doing this" (*DA* I 2 404^{a}1–16). *Mete.* II 9 369^{a}23–24 uses squeezing out the pit of a fruit as an illustration.

Note 140

The arguments from primary philosophy: Developed in *Met.* XII 6–10, especially 8 1074^{a}31–38: "It is evident that there is but one heaven. For if there are many, as there are many humans, the starting-point for each will be one in form but in number many. But all things that are many in number have matter, for one and the same account applies to many, for example, humans, whereas Socrates is one. But the primary essence does not have matter, since it is an actuality. The primary immovable mover, therefore, is one both in account and in number. And so, therefore, is what is moved always and continuously. Therefore, there is only one heaven."
Primary philosophy: Aristotle sometimes applies the term *philosophia* (or sometimes just *sophia*) to any science aiming at truth rather than action (*Met.* II 1 993^{b}19–21). In this sense of the term, all the broadly theoretical sciences count as branches of philosophy, and *philosophia* is more or less equivalent in meaning to *epistêmê* in its most exact sense. *Philosophia* also has a narrower sense, however, in which it applies exclusively to sciences providing knowledge of starting-points (XI 1 1059^{a}18, *NE* VI 7 1141^{a}16–18). In addition to these, Aristotle occasionally mentions practical philosophies, such as "the philosophy of human affairs" (*NE* X 9 1181^{b}15). It is among these that his own ethical writings belong (*Pol.* III 12 1282^{b}18–23). It is the narrower sense, explained in the following text, that is pertinent here: "That natural science is a theoretical science, then, is evident from

these considerations. Mathematics too is a theoretical one, but whether its objects are immovable and separable is not now clear; however, it is clear that *some* parts of mathematics get a theoretical grasp on their objects insofar as they are immovable and insofar as they are separable. But if there is something that is eternal and immovable and separable, it is evident that knowledge of it belongs to a theoretical science—not, however, to *natural* science (for natural science is concerned with certain moveable things) nor to mathematics, but to something prior to both. For natural science is concerned with things that are inseparable but not immovable, while certain parts of mathematics are concerned with things that are immovable and not separable but as in matter. The primary science, by contrast, is concerned with things that are both separable and immovable. Now all causes are necessarily eternal, and these most of all. For they are the causes of the divine beings that are perceptible. There must, then, be three theoretical philosophies, mathematical, natural, and theological, since it is quite clear that if the divine belongs anywhere, it belongs in a nature of this sort. And of these, the most estimable must be concerned with the most estimable genus. Thus, the theoretical are the more choiceworthy of the various sciences, and this of the theoretical. . . . If, then, there is no other substance beyond those composed by nature, natural science will be the primary science. But if there is some immovable substance, this [that is, theological philosophy] will be prior and will be primary philosophy" (*Met.* VI 1 1026ᵃ6–30). Primary philosophy, then, is the science of being qua being developed in the *Metaphysics*.

And from movement in a circle: That only movement in a circle can be eternal is argued in *Ph.* VIII 8, but no argument exists connecting this to the uniqueness of the heaven, though argument [3] (I 8 276ᵇ26–277ᵃ12) shows how one might be constructed.

Note 141

Since there are three corporeal elements, the places of the elements will also be three, one around the center for the body that sinks, another for the body that spatially moves in a circle, which is the extremity, and a third intermediate between them for the middle body: Aristotle has so far distinguished only three proper places: up, down, and center. So he has made correlative room for only three bodily elements: the one that sinks (earth); the one that moves in a circle (ether); and what he here refers to simply as "the middle body," whose place must be intermediate between the other two. Later, as he says at I 8 277ᵇ23–24, this place will be differentiated into a place for water (above earth) and for fire (above water). But for present purposes these differentiations are unneeded.

Corporeal (*sômatikôn*) **elements:** Contrasted with incorporeal ones at *Ph.* IV 1 209ᵃ14–15.

Note 142

What the differentiae of this place are, we shall say later: At IV 4.

The differentiae (*diaphorai*): *Diaphorai* are sometimes, as here, the differentiae that divide a genus into species, and so figure in their essential definitions: "species are composed of the genus and the differentiae" (*Met.* X 7 1057ᵇ7). But some-times they are simply the different features that distinguish one kind of thing from another, without necessarily suggesting that the kinds are genera or species in the strict sense or that the differences are differentiae. The Greek term is added in parentheses for clarity when needed.

Note 143
That the heaven is not only unique: Reading οὐ μόνον εἷς ἐστίν οὐρανός with Allan and Guthrie for Moraux οὐ μόνον εἷς ἐστίν.
But that there cannot come to be more, and, further, that it is eternal, being incapable of coming to be and of passing away, we should now state: See I 10–12.
Going through the puzzles (*diaporêsantes*): See Introduction, pp. xxix–l, I 7 274ᵇ26n.

Note 144
In stating the essence (*to ti ên einai*) **for sphere or for circle we do not mention bronze or gold in the account, on the supposition that these are not [parts] of its substance** (*ousias*): (1) The substance *of* something (I 1 268ᵃ3n) is *to ti ên einai*—literally: "the what-it-was-to-be"—of it, a phrase of Aristotle's coinage, of which "essence," from the Latin verb *esse* ("to be") is the standard translation. The imperfect tense *ên* ("was") may—as in the Latin phrase *quod erat demonstrandum* ("which was to be proved")—stem from an original context (such as a Socratic conversation) in which someone is asked to say or define what X is, and concludes by giving his answer in the imperfect tense to signal that he is giving the answer that was asked for (*ên* at *Met.* VII 4 1030ᵃ1 may be a case in point). Apart from that it seems to have no special significance, so we could equally well translate *to ti ên einai* as "the what-it-*is*-to-be."

Note 145
If only one circle were grasped: A form (shape) is a universal (*Met.* VII 11 1036ᵃ28), which is reached by induction from particulars (I 1 268ᵃ1n(5)). If the inductive basis consists of just one particular, the universal may be difficult to distinguish from it, nonetheless the being for (essence of) the particular is distinct from that of the universal: "In the case of things that evidently come to be in different kinds (*eidos*) [of materials], as circle does in bronze and stone and wood, it seems clear that these, for example, the bronze or the wood, in no way belong to the substance of the circle, because of being separate from them. But in the case of things that are not seen being separate, nothing prevents the situation from being similar, just as if all the circles were seen to be of bronze. For nonetheless the bronze would still not belong to the form, but it would be difficult to subtract it in thought" (1036ᵃ31–ᵇ3).

Note 146
The being for circle (*to kuklô[i]*) **will be no less distinct from the being for this circle:** The being for (*einai* + dative) A = what A is intrinsically = the essence of A (*Met.* VII 4 1029ᵇ13–1030ᵇ13).

Note 147

If there are Forms, as some say, it is necessary for this to result—and no less so if nothing of this sort is separable: "Having been from his youth familiar first with Cratylus and the Heraclitean beliefs that all perceptibles are always flowing, and that there is no scientific knowledge concerning them, these views he [Plato] also held later. The work Socrates did, on the other hand, was concerned with ethical issues, not at all with nature as a whole. In these, however, he was inquiring into what is universal and was the first to fix his thought on definitions. Plato, accepting him [as a teacher], took it that this fixing is done concerning other things and not the perceptible ones, since it is impossible for there to be a common definition of any perceptibles, as *they* at any rate are always changing. He, then, called beings of this other sort "Ideas," and the perceptible ones are beyond these and are all called after these. For the many things that have the same name as the Forms are [what they are] through participation in them" (*Met.* I 6 987ᵃ32–ᵇ10); "There are two things that may be fairly ascribed to Socrates—inductive arguments and universal definition, both of which are concerned with a starting-point of scientific knowledge. However, whereas Socrates did not make the universals separable nor the definitions, the others did separate them, and these were the sorts of beings they called Ideas, so that it followed for them, pretty much by the same argument, that there are Ideas of all things that are spoken of universally" (XIII 4 1078ᵇ27–34). Thus what must result is that there are or can be many particular participants in the same universal Platonic Form or Idea, even if it is not separable from particulars in the way Plato, but not Socrates, claimed.

Separable (*chôriston*): Verbals ending in -*ton*—of which *chôriston* is an example—sometimes have the meaning of a perfect passive participle ("separated") and sometimes express possibility ("separable"). When *chôriston* is applied to substances "separable" often seems to better capture its sense, especially that of its negative (see *Met.* VII 1 1028ᵃ23–24). For things, such as the form and matter of a matter-form compound, are not just separated, in that they are always found together (11 1036ᵇ3–4)—they cannot be separated. Moreover, things that are separable, such as the understanding and the other parts of the soul, do not become actually separated until, for example, death: "this [productive] understanding is separable (*chôristos*), impassive, and unmixed, being in substance an activity, [that is,] not sometimes understanding and at other times not. But, when separated (*chôristheis*), this alone is just what it is" (*DA* III 5 430ᵃ17–23). Just what the separability of substance amounts to is another matter.

(1) Walking and being healthy are characterized as "incapable of being separated," on the grounds that there is some particular substantial underlying subject of which they are predicated (*Met.* VII 1 1028ᵃ20–31). Often, separability is associated with being such a subject: "The underlying subject is prior, which is why the substance is prior" (V 11 1019ᵃ5–6); "If we do not posit substances to be separated, and in the way in which particular things are said to be separated, we will do away with the sort of substance we wish to maintain" (XIII 10 1086ᵇ16–19). Similarly, not being separable is associated with being predicated of such a subject. Being predicated of a substance—being an attribute—seems, then, to be a sufficient

condition of not being separable. Moreover, not being separable seems itself to be a sufficient condition of being ontologically dependent: (1a) "All the other things are either said of the primary substances as subjects or in them as subjects. So if the primary substances were not, it would be impossible for any of the other things to be" (*Cat.* 5 2ᵇ3–6).

(2) Couched in terms of priority, what is attributed to primary substances in (1a) is *substantial* priority, or priority in nature, which Aristotle defines in two ways: (2a) "[Things are said to be prior in nature and substance, when it is possible for them to be (*einai*) without other things, but not the others without them" (*Met.* V 11 1019ᵃ3–4); (2b) "Those things are prior in substance [to others] which, when separated, surpass [them] in being (*tô[i] einai huperballei*)" (XIII 2 1077ᵇ2–3). Moreover, in a text apparently expressing an idea similar to (2b), the form of a matter-form compound is said to be "prior to the matter and more (*mallon*) of a being" (VII 3 1029ᵃ5–6). Since existence, like identity, does not come in degrees, the use of the verb *huperballein* and the adverb *mallon* makes it difficult to understand *einai* ("being," "to be") as having an exclusively existential sense (*Ph.* I 2 185ᵃ22n). At the same time, *einai* does seem to have some existential import, as it surely does in (2c): "if everyone were well, health would be (*estai* = exist) but not sickness, and if everything were white, whiteness would be (*estai*) but not blackness" (*Cat.* 11 14ᵃ7–10). It seems reasonable, therefore, to think that to be is to be a being of some sort, and that to be a being entails existing. To be a being, however, is to be either a coincidental being (the pale human) or an intrinsic being, something with an essence (the human). To be an intrinsic being, in turn, is to be either an intrinsic coincident (185ᵇ1n), a matter-form compound, or simply a substantial form (*Met.* VI 1 1025ᵇ28–1026ᵃ15). As identical to its tightly unified essence (VII 12 1037ᵇ10–27), a substantial form, is an intrinsic being of the highest order— a primary substance (11 1037ᵃ33–ᵇ4). A matter-form compound, by contrast, since it is never identical to its essence (1037ᵇ4–7), is an intrinsic being of a lower order (XII 7 1072ᵃ30–32), since it is always a complex thing—a this in this (VII 5 1030ᵇ18)—whose essence is complex in a structurally parallel way (10 1035ᵇ27–30). Similarly, an intrinsically coincidental being, while it follows from an essence, is still a complex of two intrinsic beings, one a substance with an essence, the other an attribute. For X to be more of a being than Y, or to exceed Y in being, we might reasonably conclude is for it to be closer to a substantial form on this scale. It is, as we might put it, for X to be more intrinsic a being than Y. Degrees of being are degrees of intrinsicality, then, not degrees of existence.

(3) Attributes depend for their existence on substance, but not on that of some particular substance, any substance that has them will do: white exists if something is white, but the something does not have to be Bucephalus. Hence the parallel claim about substances should not be that a substance can exist without any attributes, suggesting that substances are bare particulars, but that substances in general can exist whether or not attributes do. On an *ante rem* (or Platonist) theory attributes can exist uninstantiated by particulars. On an *in re* theory, like Aristotle's, they cannot. That is the message of (2c). Hence the ontological dependence of attributes—and the cognate ontological independence of substances—must be

formulated differently by these theories. It seems, then, that if *in re* attributes were ontologically independent of substances, it could only be because *they were instantiated by something else*, since they cannot exist uninstantiated by particulars of some sort. This is the way we see Aristotle thinking in the following text: "Heat and straightness [and whiteness] can be present in every part of a thing, but it is impossible for all of it to be hot, white, or straight [and nothing else]. For then the attributes would be separated" (*Long.* 3 465ᵇ12–14). Whiteness would be separate from substance, notice, not if it existed entirely uninstantiated, but if it were instantiated by a being that was wholly and exclusively white. Such a being is obviously not an Aristotelian substance, but something more like the Platonic Form of whiteness, which does seem to be white and nothing else (Plato, *Phd.* 78d5–7). Aristotelian substances can exist, then, whether or not their attributes exist by being instantiated by something else. Attributes, on the other hand, cannot exist unless they are instantiated by Aristotelian substances, since such substances are (in Aristotle's view) the only ultimate subjects of predication. The separability of substance from attributes, on this way of looking at it, is entirely of a piece with their inseparability from it.

(4) The verb *chôrizein* derives from *chôra* ("place"), and means "to separate, part, sever, or divide" things by causing them (roughly speaking) to be in separate (or disjoint) places (*Met.* III 2 998ª17–19, XI 12 1068ᵇ26–27). Thus when Aristotle describes Plato as separating the Forms from perceptible particulars (XIII 4 1078ᵇ30–34), a view he adverts to in our text, the primary connotation is that of putting them in separate places: perceptible particulars are "here (*entautha*)," Forms are "over there (*kakei*)" (I 9 990ᵇ34–991ª1). For a Form is "a particular, they say, and separable" (VII 15 1040ª8–9) and "place is special to particular things, which is why they are separable by place" (XIV 5 1092ª18–19). Moreover, the fundamental objection Aristotle makes to such separable Forms is that they are an incoherent mixture of universals and of the particulars needed for their instantiation and existence: "They say that there is man-itself and horse-itself and health-itself, and nothing else—like those who introduce gods, but say that they are human in form. For those people were making the gods nothing but eternal human beings, and these are making the Forms nothing but eternal perceptibles" (III 2 997ᵇ9–12); "They at the same time make the Ideas universal and contrariwise treat them as separable and as particulars . . . that this is not possible is a puzzle that has been gone through before" (XIII 9 1086ª32–35; III 6 1003ª5–17). We might expect, therefore, as (4) implies, that the separability Aristotle accords to his own substances, but denies to attributes, would be the separability he denies to Platonic Forms: attributes are in substances around here not in substances (= Forms) that are elsewhere.

(5) Though separability is often characterized in terms of existential independence, in some cases this seems not to be required: "Of things that reciprocate as to implication of being (*einai*), that which is in some way the cause of the other's being might perfectly sensibly be called prior in nature. And that there are some such cases is clear. For there being a human reciprocates as to implication of being with the true statement about it: if there is a human, the statement whereby we say

that there is a human is true, and reciprocally—since if the statement whereby we say there is a human is true, there is a human. And whereas the true statement is in no way the cause of the thing's being, the thing does seem in some way to be the cause of the statement's being true. For it is because of the thing's being or not being that the statement is called true or false" (*Cat.* 12 14ᵇ11–22). What lies at the bottom of separability, then, seems rather to be a sort of ontological independence that is causal or explanatory in nature. In any case, this is clearly what we find in the following texts: "This [vegetative soul] can be separated from the others, but the others cannot be separated from it, in the case of the mortal ones. This is evident in the case of plants, since they have no other capacity of soul" (*DA* II 2 413ᵃ31–ᵇ1; also I 1 403ᵃ10–16, ᵇ17–19); "Bodily parts . . . cannot even exist when they are separated. For it is not a finger in any and every state that is the finger of an animal, rather, a dead finger is only homonymously a finger" (*Met.* VII 10 1035ᵇ23–25). For what makes perceptual soul inseparable from nutritive soul, or a finger inseparable from an animal, are the causal relations that make the former dependent on the latter. Again, this makes the separability accorded to substances, but denied to attributes, the same as the separability denied to Platonic Forms. For the latter too were intended to play an explanatory role: "the Forms are the causes of the what-it-is of other things, as *the one* is of the Forms" (I 6 988ᵃ10–11).

(6) The separability of substance and the inseparability of attributes, while obviously essential to the account of both, is a special case of a more general phenomenon. For substance as form is not just separable from attributes but from matter as well. But if this is the sort of separability characterized in (1)–(6), it must be antisymmetrical, so that form can exist apart from matter but not matter apart from form. In the case of the forms of form-matter compounds, whether their matter is perceptible or intelligible, this is clearly not the case: like snub, but unlike concavity, they cannot exist apart from matter (*Met.* VI 1 1025ᵇ28–1026ᵃ15). But in the case of other forms, those that are like concavity, it is possible (1026ᵃ15–16, XII 6 1071ᵇ20). These are the primary intelligible substances, on which all others— including matter-form compounds—causally depend for their existence (IX 8 1050ᵇ19) and order (XI 2 1060ᵃ26–27). Matter, by contrast, cannot exist apart from form of some sort (XIV 2 1089ᵇ27–28), since without form it is not intrinsically anything at all (VII 3 1029ᵃ20–21).

(7) In (1) separability is tied to being a particular subject of predication, and so seems to be somehow logical or logico-linguistic in nature. (6), on the other hand, seems to tell a different sort of story, in which separability has more to do with causation and explanation than with logic. To bring the two together we need only reflect that Aristotle's logic is primarily a logic of science, and that whenever we have a subject-predicate proposition there is always a question as to why the predicate holds of the subject. The target of scientific explanation, indeed, is always just that: Why does predicate P hold of subject S (*Met.* VII 17 1041ᵃ10–11)? If P holds of S coincidentally, or by luck or chance, science has nothing to say about it (VI 2 1026ᵇ3–5). There is no explanation. But if P is an intrinsic coincident of S, or if P is part of S's essence, or is S's essence, science does have something to say about it (see *Cael.* I 1 268ᵃ1n [6–8]). What this implies is that the primary

explanatory entities cannot themselves have a subject-predicate structure (*Met.* IX 10 1051ª34–ᵇ5). They cannot be expressed as one thing said of another—they are not thises-in-thises. Instead, in comparison to things with such a structure, they are simple—forms, not form-matter compounds. The problem is—and it is one of the deepest—is how separable forms, which, like all forms, are universals (VII 11 1036ª28–29), can indeed be primary subjects and this somethings—separable "in the way in which *particular things* are said to be separated." For Aristotle's answer, see XIII 10 1087ª10–25.

Nothing of this sort: That is, no universal.

Note 148

Flesh is matter for aquilinity: That is, flesh is the hypothetically necessary matter for acquilinity—the only matter in which it can be realized—in the way that iron is for a saw: "Why is a saw such as it is? So that *this* may be, and for the sake of *this*. But in fact it is impossible that this thing that the saw is for the sake of should come to be unless it is made of iron. It is necessary, therefore, for it to be made of iron, if there is to be a saw with its function. The necessity, then, is hypothetical, but not [necessary] as an end. For the necessity lies in the matter, whereas the for-the-sake-of-which lies in the account" (*Ph.* II 9 200ª10–15). Notice "proper matter" at I 9 279ª8.

Aquilinity (*grupotēs*): "But we must not neglect to consider the *way* the essence or its account is, because, without this, inquiry produces no result. Of things defined, however, that is, of the 'whats' that things are, some are the way the snub is, others the way the concave is. And these differ because the snub is grasped in combination with the matter (for the snub is a concave *nose*), whereas the concavity is without perceptible matter. If, then, all natural things are said the way the snub is (for example, nose, eye, face, flesh, bone, and, in general, animal, and leaf, root, bark, and, in general, plant—for the account of none of these is without [reference to] movement, but always includes matter), the way we must inquire into and define the what-it-is in the case of natural things is clear, as is why it belongs to the natural scientist to get a theoretical grasp even on some of the soul, that is, on as much of it as is not without matter" (*Met.* VI 1 1025ᵇ28–1026ª6). Here aquilinity substitutes for the more common snubness to make the same point.

Note 149

Let us first state what we say it is to be a heaven and in how many ways, in order that what we are inquiring into will become clearer to us: "If we know in how many ways something is said of things, we shall not be trapped by a paralogism ourselves, but rather will know if the questioner should fail to produce his argument related to the same thing [as we asked about]" (*Top.* I 18 108ª26–29).

Note 150

It has been shown that the one that spatially moves in a circle cannot change its own place: In I 2–3.

Note 151
But there is, we saw, no other body beyond these: In I 2–3.

Note 152
Its matter is natural perceptible body: See I 9 278^{b}22–23.

Note 153
Complete: See I 1 268^{b}9n.

Note 154
In every place (*topos*) body can exist: Place is defined at *Cael.* III 3 310^{b}7–8.
Void (*kenon*), they say, is that in which body does not exist, but in which it can:
"Void must, if it exists, be place lacking body, and it has been stated in what way
place exists and in what way it does not, it is evident that a void does not exist as
a place lacking body, whether separated or un-separated" (*Ph.* IV 7 214^{a}16–19).
Time is a number of movement: "Time is the measure of movement" (*Ph.* IV 12
221^{b}7); "time is a number of movement" (221^{b}11).

Note 155
It has been shown that outside the heaven there neither is nor can be body: At
I 9 278^{b}21–279^{a}9.

Note 156
**Things that are [outside the heaven] are naturally such as not to be in place, nor
does time age them, nor is there any change for any of the things that are stationed above the outermost spatial movement, instead, unalterable and unaffectable, having the best and most self-sufficient life, they are attaining their
end throughout all eternity:** (1) One of the things so stationed is the primary
god, an intelligible substance, a divine self-understanding, that is at once an "active
understanding [that] is active understanding of active understanding" (*Met.* XII 9
1074^{b}34–35), and the unmoved mover of the primary or outermost heaven, and
so of all else:

> This, therefore, is the sort of starting-point on which the heaven and
> nature depend. And its pastime is like the best that we can have—and
> have for a short time (for it is always in that state [of activity], whereas
> we cannot be)—since its activity is also pleasure. . . . Active under-
> standing, though, is intrinsically of what is intrinsically best, and the
> sort that is to the highest degree best is of what is to the highest degree
> best. . . . If, then, that good state [of activity], which we are sometimes
> in, the [primary] god is always in, that is a wonderful thing, and if to
> a higher degree, that is yet more wonderful. But that is his state. And
> life too certainly belongs to him. For the activity of understanding is
> life, and he is that activity; and his intrinsic activity is life that is best

and eternal. We say, indeed, that the god is a living being who is eternal and best, so that living and a continuous and everlasting eternity belong to the god, since this is the god. (*Met.* 7 1072^{b}13–30)

(2) In *Met.* XII 8, however, Aristotle raises the question of "whether we should posit one substance of this sort or several, and, if several, how many" (1073^{a}14–15). He argues:

Since what is moved must be moved by something, and the prime mover must be intrinsically immovable, and eternal movement must be caused by something eternal, and a single movement by a single thing, and since we see that beyond the simple spatial movement of the universe, which we say the primary and immovable substance causes, there are other spatial movements—of the planets—that are eternal (for the body with a circular movement is eternal and un-resting, as has been shown in our works on natural science), each of *these* spatial movements must be caused by a substance that is both intrinsically immovable and eternal. For the nature of the stars is eternal, because it is a certain sort of substance, and the mover is eternal and prior to the moved, and what is prior to a substance must be a substance. It is evident, accordingly, that there must be this number of substances that are in their nature eternal and intrinsically immovable, and without magnitude (due to the cause mentioned earlier). (1073^{a}26–^{b}1)

He concludes:

Since the spheres in which the planets themselves are carried along are eight [for Jupiter and Saturn] and twenty-five [for the others], and of these, only those in which the lowest one is carried along does not need to be counteracted, the spheres that counteract those of the first [or outermost] two planets will be six, and those counteracting the spheres of the next four will be sixteen. The number, then, of all the spheres, both moving and counteracting, will be fifty-five. And if we do not add to the moon and the sun the movements we mentioned, all the spheres will be forty-seven in number. (1074^{a}6–12)

(The mss. have forty-seven, but the correct number is forty-nine = fifty-five minus six.) Thus, including the primary god, there are at least fifty things that are "stationed above the outermost spatial movement."

Most self-sufficient (*autarkestatên*): "We posit that what is self-sufficient is what, on its own, makes a life choiceworthy and lacking in nothing, and this, we think, is what happiness is like" (*NE* I 7 1097^{b}14–16).

They are attaining their end (*diatelei*): The verb *diatelein* means "persist," "remain," as at I 10 279^{b}15, but also "accomplish," and "bring to an end." Here the idea is that the beings outside the heaven are always happy—always achieving the happiness that is the most complete and most self-sufficient end.

Note 157

The philosophical works in circulation (*ekukliois*): The reference, apparently, is to works written by Aristotle himself, or by someone else, and "in circulation" (*NE* I 5 1096ª3) outside the Lyceum. Whatever the precise reference here, it must be to accounts with which the audience of *De Caelo* were familiar. *Exôterikoi logoi* ("external accounts"), which seem to be the same sort of things, are also mentioned at *Ph.* IV 10 217ᵇ30, *Met.* XIII 1 1076ª28–29, *NE* I 13 1102ª26, VI 4 1140ª2, *EE* I 8 1217ᵇ20, II 1 1218ᵇ32, *Pol.* III 6 1278ᵇ30, VII 1 1323ª21, "the common accounts" at *DA* I 4 407ᵇ29.

Philosophical works (*philosophêmasi*): A *philosophêma* at *Top.* VIII 11 162ª15 is a "philosophical demonstration"; at *Cael.* I 9 294ª20 it is a philosophical work focused on a puzzle.

Note 158

Neither is there anything else greater that will move it (for then that thing would be more divine): "Issues concerning the [divine] understanding involve certain puzzles. . . . For if on the one hand it understands nothing, where is its dignity? It would be just like someone asleep. And if on the other hand it does understand something, but this other thing controls it (since what it is, its substance, is not active understanding, but a capacity), it would not be the best substance. For it is because of actively understanding that esteem belongs to it. . . . It is itself, therefore, that it understands, if indeed it is the most excellent thing, and the active understanding is active understanding of active understanding" (*Met.* XII 9 1074ᵇ15–35).

Greater (*kreittôn*): *Kreittôn*, comes from *kratus* ("strong"), but is also used as the comparative of *agathos* ("good"). Thus, at *NE* X 7 1177ᵇ34–1178ª2, the activity of the *kratiston* (superlative of *kratus*) divine element (1177ᵇ28) in us (= the understanding) is that of the element that exceeds everything "in capacity and esteem (*dunamei kai timiotêti*)." *Kreittôn*, therefore, should be understood both as greater in capacity and greater in esteem—on which, see I 2 269ᵇ16n.

Nor does it lack any of the noble things (*kalôn*) **proper to it:** The adjective *kalos* is often a term of vague or general commendation ("fine," "beautiful," "good"), with different connotations in different contexts: "The contrary of *to kalon* when applied to an animal is *to aischron* ["ugly in appearance"], but when applied to a house it is *to mochthêron* ["wretched"], and so *kalon* is homonymous" (*Top.* I 15 106ª20–22). (Similarly, the adverb *kalôs* often means something like "well," or "correct.")

Even in the general sense, however, *kalos* has a distinctive evaluative coloration suggestive of "order (*taxis*), proportion (*summetria*), and definiteness (*hôrismenon*)" (*Met.* XIII 3 1078ª36–ᵇ1), making a term with aesthetic connotation, such as "beauty," seem a good equivalent: to bear the stamp of happiness one must have *kallos* as opposed to being "very ugly (*panaischês*)" (*NE* I 8 1099ᵇ3–4; also *Pol.* V 9

1309^{b}23–25). Moreover, just as a thing need not have a purpose in order to be beautiful, a *kalon* thing can be contrasted with a purposeful one: a great-souled person is one "whose possessions are more *kalon* and purposeless (*akarpa*) than purposeful and beneficial" (*NE* IV 3 1125^{a}11–12). At the same time, it seems wrong to associate *kalon* with beauty in general, since to be *kalon* a thing has to be on a certain scale: "greatness of soul requires magnitude, just as *to kallos* ('nobility of appearance') requires a large body, whereas small people are elegant and well proportioned but not *kaloi*" (1123^{b}6–8); "any *kalon* object . . . made up of parts must not only have them properly ordered but also have a magnitude which is not random, since what is *kalon* consists in magnitude and order (*taxis*)" (*Po.* 7 1450^{b}34–37; also *Pol.* VII 4 1326^{a}33–34). It is this requirement that makes "nobility" in its more aesthetic sense, or "noble beauty," a closer equivalent than "beauty."

In ethical or political contexts, the canonical application of *kalon* is to ends that are intrinsically choiceworthy and intrinsically commendable or praiseworthy (*epaineton*): "Of all goods, the ends are those choiceworthy for their own sake. Of these, in turn, the *kalon* ones are all those praiseworthy because of themselves" (*EE* VIII 3 1248^{b}18–20; also *NE* I 13 1103^{a}9–10). It is because ethically *kalon* actions are intrinsically choiceworthy ends, indeed, that a good person can do virtuous actions because of themselves (*NE* II 4 1105^{a}32) *and* for the sake of what is *kalon* (III 7 1115^{b}12–13). What makes such actions choiceworthy (VI 1 1138^{a}18–20) and praiseworthy (II 6 1106^{b}24–27), however, is that they exhibit the sort of order (X 9 1180^{a}14–18), proportionality (II 2 1104^{a}18), and definiteness (II 6 1106^{b}29–30, IX 9 1170^{a}19–24) that consists in lying in a mean (*meson*) between two extremes. This brings us full circle, connecting what is ethically *kalon* to what is aesthetically noble, lending the former too an aesthetic tinge.

Finally, what is ethically *kalon* includes an element of self-sacrifice that recommends "nobility," in its more ethical sense, as a good equivalent for it as well: "It is true of an excellent person too that he does many actions for the sake of his friends and his fatherland, even dying for them if need be. For he will give up wealth, honors, and fought-about goods generally, in keeping for himself what is *kalon*" (*NE* IX 8 1169^{a}18–22). One reason people praise a *kalon* agent, indeed, is that his actions benefit them: "The greatest virtues must be those that are most useful to others, and because of this, just people and courageous ones are honored most of all; for courage is useful to others in war, justice both in war and peace" (*Rh.* I 9 1366^{b}3–7). But since what is *kalon* is a greater good than those an excellent person gives up or confers on others, there is also a strong element of self-interest in what he does: "The greater good, then, he allocates to himself" (*NE* IX 8 1169^{a}28–29). An excellent person does *kalon* actions for their own sake, not for an ulterior motive, because it is only as done in that way that they constitute the doing well in action (*eupraxia*) that just *is* happiness.

Note 159

Suppositions: See I 3 270^{b}6n.

Incapable of coming to be or capable of coming to be, and incapable of passing away or capable of passing away: These notions are explained in I 11 280^{b}6–281^{a}1.

Note 160

Demonstrations: See I 1 268ᵃ1n(6).

Puzzles (*aporiai*): "A dialectical problem is a speculation, directed either to choice and avoidance or to truth and knowledge (either by itself or when working together with something else of this sort), about which [1] people believe nothing either way, or [2] ordinary people believe in a contrary way to the wise, or [3] the wise to ordinary people, or [4] each of them to themselves. . . . Problems also exist [5] where there are contrary deductions (for there is a puzzle as to whether it is so or not so, because there are persuasive arguments concerning both sides), as well as [6] those we have no arguments about, because they are so large, thinking it difficult to give the why of them (for example, whether the cosmos is eternal or not). For one could also inquire into things of that sort" (*Top.* I 11 104ᵇ1–17). Thus a problem is [5] a *puzzle* just in case there are strong arguments on one side of it and strong arguments on the other: "A certain sophistical argument constitutes a puzzle. For because they wish to refute in a way that is *paradoxos* in order to be clever when they engage in ordinary discussions, the resulting deduction turns into a puzzle. For thought is tied up when it does not wish to stand still, because what has been concluded is not pleasing but cannot move forward, because of its inability to refute the argument" (*NE* VII 2 1146ᵃ21–27).

Note 161

What we are about to say will also be more convincing to people who have previously heard the pleas of the arguments disputing them: "When a reasonable explanation is given of why an untrue view appears true, this makes us more convinced of the true view" (*NE* VII 14 1154ᵃ24–25); "refutations of those who dispute them are demonstrations of the contrary arguments" (*EE* I 3 1215ᵃ6–7).

Note 162

Arbitrators (*diaitêtas*): "Everywhere, though, an arbitrator (*diatêtês*) is most trusted, and the middling person is an arbitrator" (*Pol.* IV 12 1297ᵃ5–6); "When people are involved in dispute they have recourse to a judge. Going to a judge, however, is going to justice. For the judge wishes to be, as it were, animate justice. Also, they seek a judge as an intermediary—in fact, some people call judges 'mediators,' on the supposition that those who can hit the mean are the ones who will hit the just. Therefore the just is a mean in some way, if indeed the judge is also one" (*NE* V 6 1132ᵃ19–24).

Note 163

Everyone says, then, that it has come to be: Some theists think of the world not just as created, but as created out of nothing (*ex nihilo*). But that is not what is at issue here. Instead, for a cosmos to come to be is for some preexisting things to come to be arranged (*kosmein*) in a certain way. The cosmic arrangement then is something predicated, therefore, of these things, or this matter. See I 12 281ᵃ29n.

Some say that having come to be it is eternal: See I 10 280ᵃ30–32.

Others say that it is capable of passing away: For example, (perhaps) Anaximander DK A10 = TEGP 19: "the unlimited contained the whole cause of the coming to be and passing away of the universe (*tou pantos*), from which he says the heavens are separated and, universally, all the cosmoses, which are unlimited." Also, Leucippus and Democritus DK 67A1 = TEGP 47 F13, 68A40 = TEGP 53.

Still others say that it is alternately sometimes in the one state and other times in the other (passing away): Retaining φθειρόμενον with Verdenius p. 273 and DP; Moraux secludes.

And it continues being like this always: So that it is always such that it is at times coming to be and at other times passing away.

As Empedocles of Acragas and Heraclitus of Ephesus say: On Empedocles, see DK 31 = TEGP pp. 326–433, *Cael.* III 2 301ᵃ15–16n; on Heraclitus, DK 22 = TEGP pp. 135–200, in particular B30 = TEGP 47 F29: "This cosmos, the same of all, no human being nor no god has made, but it always was and is and will be, fire ever living, kindling in measures and in measures going out."

Note 164

The aid with which some of those who say that the cosmos came to be but is incapable of passing away attempt to support their case is not a true one: Isnardi prints *Cael.* I 10 279ᵇ32–280ᵃ10 as F73 of Xenocrates of Colophon. Compare: *APr.* I 41 49ᵇ33–50ᵃ4: "We must not think that something absurd results from the setting out (*to ektithesthai*). For we make no use of the existence of the this something (*to tode ti*), but rather do just as the geometer does when he says that this line here (*tênde*) is a foot long, straight, and without breadth, when it is not, but does not use these things as something from which to deduce. . . . We use setting out just as we use perception, speaking to the student (*pros ton mantha-nonta legontes*); for we do not use it on the supposition that it is not possible to give a demonstration without these things, as it would be with the premises of a deductive argument."

Note 165

Just as if one thought that a man coming to be from a boy or a boy from a man is at one time passing away and at another is in being: "If the cosmos is all the matter that is endowed with form and put in order, and if even when they say it has passed away it has form . . . , in describing this as the passing away of the cosmos, they are saying something of the same sort as if someone were to think that a man who comes to be from a boy and a boy from a man passed away at one time and exists at another, since it is in this way that the cosmos remains as a cosmos through the changes" (Simp. 307.20–25 = Hankinson, p. 19).

Note 166

They assign to each of the two dispositions [of the elements] a contrary cause: As Empedocles makes love the cause of composition and its contrary, strife, the cause of dissolution. See I 10 279ᵇ16n.

Note 167

Dispositions: See I 3 270ᵃ28n.

Note 168

It is impossible that, having come to be, it passed away as a whole, without making a return, since it is one: Because the cosmos (heaven) is one, that is, a unique particular, it cannot cease to exist and later exist again: "For it is not the case that Socrates, once having passed away, comes to be Socrates once again" (Simp. 309.28 = Hankinson, p. 21).

Note 169

[a] Before it came to be, the composition before it always existed, and, [b] not having come to be, cannot (we say) change: [b] means, "and not having come to be up to the moment of its supposed beginning." See I 10 279^{b}21–24 (= [2]).

Note 170

If there are an unlimited number [of cosmoses], however, this is more possible: "Alexander [of Aphrodisias] states the cause: 'For,' he says, 'it is not into the matter of the cosmos that there is dissolution and passing away for it, which matter has the capacity to become a cosmos, but into another cosmos, and since there are an unlimited number of them surrounding each other, it is not necessary for there to be again a recurrence of the same one'" (Simp. 310.4–9 = Hankinson, p. 22). See I 10 279^{b}24–31 (= [3]).

This is more possible: Presumably, because what passes away as a whole is an arrangement of cosmoses (atoms), not a substance (a matter-form compound), and what comes to be, as Alexander has it, is another arrangement, not the same unique particular again.

Note 171

Whether even this is impossible or possible will be clear from later considerations: It is unclear to what Aristotle is referring.

Note 172

There are some people to whom it seems possible both for something that is incapable of coming to be to pass away, and for something that has come to be to persist, incapable of passing away, as in the *Timaeus*. For there he says that while the heaven came to be, nonetheless it will always be for the remainder of time: Plato, of course, is the unmentioned author of the *Timaeus*. But the "he" may not be Plato, but rather Timaeus, as at *DA* I 3 406^{b}26. But whatever about that, when the Demiurge addresses the gods, he does seem to state the view Aristotle assigns to the work: "Gods, works divine whose maker and father I am, whatever has come to be by my hands cannot be dissolved without my consent. Now while it is true that everything that is put together can be dissolved, still only someone evil would consent to the dissolution of what has been beautifully fitted together and is in good condition. That is why you, as creatures that have come to be, are neither completely immortal nor completely exempt from dissolution. Still, you will not be dissolved nor will death be your lot, since you have received the guarantee of my will" (*Ti.* 41a–b). The question of whether this is indeed Plato's view, or a useful fiction is a vexed one, despite the fact that Aristotle quite clearly takes it literally. That point aside, it is noteworthy that impossibility of the cosmos (or the gods) passing away is not absolute and metaphysical, but mediated by Demiurgic will.

Note 173

We have spoken about the heaven only in natural scientific terms (*phusikôs*)**, but when we have investigated everything in universal ones:** The universal does not, of course, exclude the natural scientific, but rather includes it and more besides. See I 7 274^{a}19–24n and, on *phusikôs*, I 7 275^{b}12n(3). Notice also, *logos katholou* at I 12 282^{a}14 and the return to the contrast at 273^{b}17–18.

Note 174

But first of all we must distinguish the ways in which we say things are incapable of coming to be, capable of coming to be, capable of passing away, and incapable of passing away: *Aphtharton* ("incapable of coming to be"), like other verbals ending in *-ton,* sometimes (1) has the meaning of a perfect passive participle ("did not/had not come to be") (see I 11 280^{b}9–11 (= [1b])) and sometimes (2) express possibility ("incapable of coming to be"). Generally here (2) is the intended meaning, and I have translated accordingly, noting clear exceptions when necessary. It is important to bear in mind, however, that even when possibility is involved it comes in different grades. See, for example, 280^{b}12–14 (= [1c–ii]).

Note 175

Thought (*dianoian*): *Dianoia* is often contrasted with the body (*Pol.* II 9 1270^{b}40, VII 16 1335^{b}16), making "mind" seem a natural translation of it. But unlike the mind, which includes perception, imagination, belief, knowledge, desire, virtues of character, and other such things, *dianoia* is contrasted with each of these. It is not perception, because all animals have that, whereas "the majority of animals do not have *dianoia*" (*DA* I 5 410^{b}24). It is not imagination, because, as we might put it, *dianoia* is propositional, or operates on things that can be true or false, asserted or denied (*Pol.* II 11 1273^{a}22), whereas imagination is a representational state that is more like perception, more "imagistic." Thus "what assertion and denial are in the case of thought, that, in the case of desire, is precisely what pursuit and avoidance are" (*NE* VI 2 1139^{a}21–22). Unlike belief and knowledge, however, "thought is in fact not yet assertion" (VI 9 1142^{b}12–13), making it natural to think of it, or some of it anyway, as the process of reasoning that can culminate in a belief or an asserted proposition (*Pol.* IV 15 1299^{a}30 and V 8 1307^{b}35 are nice examples). And this is further evidenced by the fact that the virtues of thought, which are theoretical wisdom and practical wisdom (*NE* I 13 1103^{a}4–6), are (respectively) those of the scientific sub-part and the rationally calculative sub-part, of the part of the soul that has reason (VI 1 1139^{a}5–12). At the same time, the fact that scientific knowledge includes both demonstrative reasoning and a grasp of scientific starting-points by the understanding, implies that not all thinking need be in any sense inferential, since understanding is non-inferential—a grasping of something rather than something process-like (*Pol.* VII 13 1325^{b}20 is a good example).

Thought will be indefinite if one uses what is divided in many ways as undivided: "When it is unclear in how many ways something is said of things, it is possible that the answerer and the questioner are not directing their thought to the same thing. But when it has been made evident in how many ways it is said of things, and to which of them the answerer is directing his thought in positing it, the questioner would appear ridiculous, if he did not make his argument about this" (*Top.* I 18 108ᵃ22–26).

Note 176
It is unclear with reference to which nature (*phusin*) what is said applies to it: See I 1 268ᵃ3n(2).

Note 177
[1a] Something is said in one way to be incapable of coming to be if it is now but previously was not, without any coming to be or change: "Let it be granted, then, if you wish, that in the case of certain things it is possible for them at times to be and at times not to be without any process of coming to be or passing away (for perhaps it is necessary, if something without parts at one time is and another time is not, that anything of that sort should, without undergoing any process of change, at one time be and another time not be)" (*Ph.* VIII 6 258ᵇ16–20).

As is the case, some people say: It is unclear to whom Aristotle is referring—Zeno, the Atomists, and the Platonist have all been suggested as likely candidates. But the views themselves are ones Aristotle himself accepts. Indeed, in addition to being in contact and being in movement, he thinks that nows (*Met.* III 5 1002ᵇ6–7), points (VIII 5 1044ᵇ22), and essences or forms (3 1043ᵇ14–18) are like this, as are the various activities or actualities, such as hearing or perceiving (*Sens.* 6 446ᵇ2–4).

With being in contact: "When bodies make contact or are divided, at one time (when they make contact) there immediately comes to be one surface, whereas at another time (when they are divided) there immediately come to be two, so that when they are put together one surface does not exist, but has passed away, whereas when they are divided, surfaces exist that did not exist earlier (for it certainly is not that an indivisible point has been divided into two)" (*Met.* III 5 1002ᵃ34–ᵇ4). See I 11 280ᵇ27.

And being in movement: "There is no movement [and so no process of coming to be] of movement nor coming to be of coming to be, nor in general change of change. For, in the first place, there are just two ways in which there might be movement of movement: [1] As an underlying subject (for example, as a human is in movement because he changes from pale to dark), so that in this way the movement too might be heated or cooled, change its place, increase or decrease. But this is impossible (for a change is not a sort of underlying subject). Or [2] some other underlying subject might change from one change to some other species [of change], like a human does from sick to healthy. But this is not possible either, except coincidentally. For this movement is a change from one species to another. (Coming to be and passing way are also like that, except that they are to things opposed in one way, whereas the other—movement—is to things opposed in another way.) Hence a thing changes at the same time from health to sickness, and from this change itself to another. It is clear, then, that when it has become sick, it will have changed to whatever the other sort of change may be (since it may remain at rest), and furthermore never to some random sort. And this new change will be from something to something else, so that this will in fact be the opposite change: becoming healthy. But [we will respond], this is by coincidence, as there is change from recollecting to forgetting, because what these belong to changes, now to scientific knowledge, now to health. Further, it will go on without limit, if there is to be change of a change and coming to be of a coming to be" (*Ph.* V 2 225^{b}14–35).

Note 178
Something is said to be incapable (*adunaton*) [of this] in two ways: because of its not being true that it could come to be; or because of its not doing so easily, quickly, or well: "The states in virtue of which something is wholly unaffectable or unchangeable or not easily moved for the worse are said to be capacities (*dunameis*). For things get broken and crushed and bent and in general pass away not by being capable but by being not capable and deficient in something. And they are unaffectable in these ways if they are scarcely or slightly affected because of a capacity they have and by being capable and being in some state" (*Met.* V 12 1019^{a}26–32).

Note 179
Or what is capable of passing away is [4b] what is, but is capable of not being, or what will not be at some time but now is: This reference to capable of passing away in the midst of a discussion of incapable of passing away may be out of place, as Moraux suggests (pp. 158–159), but whatever about that, [4b] is equally applicable to incapable of passing away. For what is incapable of passing away, in the sense simply of not yet having passed away, is something capable of not being, in the sense that it will not be at some time but now is.

Note 180
Most strictly speaking (*malista kuriôs*): See II 13 293^{b}2n.

Note 181
Capable (*dunaton*) and incapable (*adunaton*): "What is said to be capable is in one way what has a starting-point of movement or change. . . . And in another way if something else has a capacity of this sort with regard to it. And in another way if it has the capacity to change into something, whether for the worse or the better. . . . And in another way, if neither another thing nor the thing itself insofar as it is other has a capacity or a starting-point that is destructive of it. Further, all of these are said to be capable of something either merely because the thing might happen to come about or not to come about, or because it might do so *well*. . . . Incapacity is lack of capacity, that is, lack of the sort of starting-point that has been described, either generally or by what naturally should have it, or even by what at the time should naturally already have it. For a boy, a man, and a

eunuch would not in the same way be said to be incapable of begetting children. Further, to each of the two sorts of capacity there is an opposite incapacity—both to what can merely produce movement and to what can produce movement well. Some things, then, are also said to be incapable in virtue of this sort of incapacity, whereas others are in another way both capable and incapable, namely [possible and impossible], where an impossible thing is that of which the contrary is of necessity true. For example, it is impossible for the diagonal to be commensurable, because something like that is a falsehood whose contrary is not only true but also necessary. Hence that it is commensurable is not only false but of necessity false. . . . The contrary of this, the possible, is found whenever it is not necessary that the contrary is false. . . . In one way, then, the possible, as was said, signifies what is not of necessity false; in another what is true; and in another what admits of being true" (*Met.* V 12 1019ᵃ33–ᵇ33).

Note 182

The commensurable diameter: "What is said to be false in one way is what is false as a thing . . . because it is not combined or cannot be combined—as is said, for example, of the diagonal's being commensurable with the side or of you being seated, since of these the former is always false and the latter sometimes false" (*Met.* V 29 1024ᵇ17–21).

Note 183

Lifting one hundred talents or walking one hundred stades: A talent ≈ 57 pounds; a stade ≈ .09 miles.

Note 184

[1] Some things (*enia*) are capable of being (*einai*) and of not being (*mê*): We think of the word "being" as having four different senses or meanings: (1) Existential "is"—where to say that something "is" means that it "exists." This is the sense captured by the existential quantifier. (2) "Is" of identity—where to say that A "is" B means that A "is identical to" B, or A "is one and the same thing as" B. (3) "Is" of predication—where to say that A "is" B means that "B belongs to A." (4) Veridical "is"—where to say that something "is" means that it "is the case" or "is true." In his account of being in *Met.* V 7, Aristotle mentions a sort of being that corresponds to (2) at 1017ᵃ8–30 and to (4) at ᵃ30–35, and in V 9 and X 3 1054ᵃ32–ᵇ3 he has much to say about identity and sameness, including that "everything that is a being is either distinct or the same" (1054ᵇ25). (1), however, is absent from his discussion, although potential and actual being (V 7 1017ᵃ35–ᵇ9) surely bears on it, and it does seem to play some role in explaining what the separability distinctive of substance consists in (V 11 1019ᵃ1–4, *Cael.* I 9 278ᵃ17n). One reason for this is that a demonstrative science posits the existence of the genus it investigates, and proceeds to investigate it (*APo.* I 10 76ᵇ11–22), so that existence itself escapes the focus of the science—even of the science of being qua being. (This does not mean, however, that there may not be puzzles to solve before the existence of the posited genus can be taken as established—*Met.* VI 1 1026ᵃ23–32 is a case in point.) A second reason, though, is that until the discovery of quantifiers it was difficult to say very much about existence as such.

[2] It is necessary that there be some greatest time determined both for their being and for their not being, I mean, during which the thing at issue is capable of being and of not being, with [3] respect to any category: (i) Start with [3] and notice that it shows that the sense of "being" employed in [1] is (3) predicative being, so that the claim is that some things are capable of being F and of not being F—where F is drawn from one of the categories. See I 1 268ª1n(7).

(ii) Notice, second, the difference between [2a] being for a maximum time capable of being F and of not being F, and [2b] being capable of being F for a maximal time and of not being F for a maximal time. That [2b] is the intended sense is clear from I 12 282ᵇ12–14: "For each is capable of being and of not being for a definite time (I mean each of being for a quantity of time and of not being [for a quantity of time])."

(iii) Notice, third, that Aristotle is not claiming that if something is capable of being F and of not being F, then there is some time at which it must be F and some time at which it must be not F. He is explicit that a thing can be capable of something that it never at any time actually does: "this cloak is capable of being cut up, but it will not be cut up but will wear out first" (*Int.* 19 19ª12–14). His thought is rather that if something is capable of being F and of not being F, there must be a time at which *it is possible* for it to be F and a time at which *it is possible* for it to be not F—which is just what is ruled out in the case of an eternally existing being, since there cannot be two eternities, one in which it is F and another in which it is not F. That there be a *greatest* time in which a thing that is capable of being F can actually be F is probably a consequence of the idea that beings have definite lifetimes. See I 9 279ª23–25.

(iv) Notice, finally, that [1] is not true of finitely existing beings. For if, for example, the greatest time determined for their being alive is some finite time, then there is no greatest one fixed for their being not alive, since that time is unlimited.

The net result of (i)–(iv) is that *enia* in [1] must be taken to refer to the eternally existing things whose ordering results in a cosmos. See I 10 279ª12–17n. and Judson, especially, pp. 225–228.

Note 185

If there will not be a certain quantity [of time], but always a longer one than any proposed and none than which it is shorter: See I 10 283ª7–10.

Note 186

Impossible (*adunaton*) and false do not signify the same thing: The sense of *adunaton*, previously better captured by "incapable," is now, as on other occasions, better captured by "impossible." See I 11 281ª2n.

Note 187

It is impossible for a triangle to contain two right angles: That is, to have its interior angles equal to two right angles.

If these things hold: For a deduction is "an argument in which, *certain things having been supposed*, something different from those supposed things necessarily results because of their being so" (*APr.* I 2 24^{b}18–20).

Note 188
Actively (*kat' energeian*): The term *energeia* is an Aristotelian coinage, which I have translated as "activation," when it is being predicated of something, and as "activity," when it is not. The dative or adverbial form *energeia[i]* is translated as "active" or "actively," in order to signal its relation to *energeia*. The etymology of the coinage is unclear, but Aristotle is explicit that it has been extended from movement to other things (*Met.* IX 1 1046^{a}1–2, 3 1047^{a}30–32), and that it is related to another term with an *erg-* root, namely, *ergon*: "The *ergon* ('function,' 'work') is the *telos* ('end'), and the *energeia* is the *ergon*, and that is why the name *energeia* is said [of things] with reference to the *ergon* and extends to the *entelecheian* ('actuality')" (8 1050^{a}21–23). *Entelecheia* (for example, *Cael.* I 12 283^{a}26), which is mostly used as a synonym of *energeia*, but with a slightly different connotation, is also an Aristotelian coinage: *energeia* is action, activity, and movement oriented; *entelecheia*—as the *tel-* suggests—is end or *telos* or completion (*enteles*) oriented (*Met.* V 16 1021^{b}24–30). The dative or adverbial form *entelecheia[i]* is translated as "actual" or "actually." The *energeia of* is translated as "the activation of" and *entelecheia of* as "the actualization of." Putting all this together: the activation or actualization of X is an activity, which is X active or actual, which is X achieving its end, which—since "the for-the-sake-of-which is the function" (III 2 996^{b}7)—is X fulfilling its function, and being actively or actually X, and so being complete.

Note 189
[1] If for an unlimited time something is capable of passing away, it would have the capacity for not being. If, then, it has it for an unlimited time, let what it is capable of doing be realized. [2] At the same time, therefore, it will actively be and not be at the same time. [3] A falsehood would result, then, because a falsehood was assumed. But if what was assumed was not impossible, the result would not actually be impossible. Therefore everything that always is is unconditionally incapable of passing away: At [1] Aristotle appeals to the following principle: "A given thing is capable if nothing impossible follows from the assumption that the activity it is said to have the capacity for belongs to it. I mean, for example, if a thing is capable of sitting and it is possible for it to sit, if sitting should belong to it, there will be nothing impossible occurring" (*Met.* IX 3 1047^{a}24–26). But [2] does not seem to follow from it. For what is shown is [4] it is impossible that (if X always is, X passes away), not [5] if X always is, it is impossible that (X pass away). For it seems that X could just happen never to pass away, though it could: "this cloak is capable of being cut up, but it will not be cut up but will wear out first" (*Int.* 19 19^{a}12–14). Since the move from [4] (the necessity of the consequence) to [5] (the necessity of the consequent) is a trivially invalid one, it seems unlikely that Aristotle would have made it. So the question is, can the move

be defended on the basis of things that he holds? Suppose, then, that X is capable of passing away but for an unlimited past time has not in fact done so? Now ask, why has it not passed away given that it could? (A question Aristotle raises explicitly at *Cael.* I 12 283ª11–14.) Suppose C is the cause of its not having passed away. Then it is the possibility of C's ceasing to play that role that also explains why X is capable of passing away: C could stop operating. Now the question recurs: if C can stop operating, why for an unlimited time has it not stopped? And so on, for any other causes that may be appealed to. The invariant continued being of X for an unlimited time, then, as opposed to that of the cloak, whose limited temporal extent makes its not being cut up simply a matter of chance or luck, seems to be the nub of the matter. But of things that are matters of chance or luck, things that are coincidental, there is no scientific explanation: "that there is no scientific knowledge of the coincidental is evident. For all scientific knowledge is either of what always is or of what for the most part is" (*Met.* VI 2 1027ª19–21; compare *Cael.* I 12 283ª29–283ᵇ2). Why think, though, that things that hold always or for the most part have a cause for science to discover? One ground might lie in some sort of *principle of sufficient reason*. If this is based on an induction from the success of sciences (including productive and practical ones) in discovering such causes, Aristotle's commitment to it is manifest in his very characterization of scientific knowledge as either of what always is or of what for the most part is (for more details, see I 1 268ª1n). But the sort of a priori basis for it that one associates with the rationalist tradition in philosophy seems entirely absent from his thought. Look back now at X. If X's being as it is is part of its essence, or follows from its essence, there is a cause of it in that very fact. But if C is the cause, we will need to keep going until once again we reach a necessity based in an essence. And in it we have a basis for the otherwise unjustified move from [4] to [5]. But what this means is that we must take the possibilities and impossibilities in [1–3] not as merely logical or mathematical, but as natural scientific or metaphysical— based in the nature of being itself. For a different route to the same conclusion, see Judson, pp. 235–241.

Note 190

If it is impossible for the prior one to hold, it is also impossible for the posterior one to hold: See I 2 269ª19n.

Notes 191

Let A and B be incapable of belonging to the same thing, and let A or C and B or D belong to everything: A = what is always capable of being = what always is; B (its contrary) = what is always capable of not being = what always is not; C (its contradictory) = what is not always capable of being; D (contradictory of B) = what is not always capable of not being. See Fig. 8 in the text.

Note 192

It will at the same time be capable of always being and capable of not always being; but that this is impossible was shown previously: At I 12 281ᵇ20–25.

Note 193
If it is incapable of coming to be, it has been established that it is incapable of passing away: At I 12 281^{b}25–33.

Note 194
If it is incapable of passing away, it has been established that it is incapable of coming to be: At I 12 281^{b}33–282^{a}1.

Note 195
There is no time in the direction of either limit: Either toward the past or toward the future.

Note 196
As for F [capable of coming to be] and H [capable of passing away], it has been shown that they follow along with each other: The reference is probably to I 12 281^{b}18–25 but could be to 282^{a}4–14 (= part of [*Argument 2*]).

Note 197
(And an unlimited one [simply] because of this, namely, because [1] the unlimited is in a way (*pôs*) definite, being what nothing is greater than): Moraux marks a lacuna in the text prior to what, with DP, I treat as a parenthetical comment, making the lacuna unnecessary. The point of the comment becomes clearer if we link it to the following text: "the unlimited is the contrary of what people say it is. For it is not [2] what nothing is outside of, but rather [3] what something is always outside of, that is unlimited" (*Ph.* III 6 207^{a}1–3). Thus what [1] excludes is [2], which is something actually unlimited, and what it allows is [3]. For if [3] something is always outside X, then [1] nothing is greater than X. But both [3] and [1] are consistent with the universe being the sort of—*in that sense* unlimited— whole that Aristotle thinks it to be: "What has nothing outside is complete and whole. For this is how we define what is whole, namely, as that from which nothing is absent—for example, a whole human being or a whole box. And just as with the particular case, so too with what is whole in the strict sense: it is what nothing is outside of. But what something is absent from and outside of is not an 'all' [that is, a universe] whatever may be absent. Whole and complete are either entirely the same or very close in nature. Nothing is complete (*teleion*) that has no end (*telos*), and the end is a limit" (207^{a}8–15).

Note 198
What is unlimited in some way (*pê[i]*), then, is neither unlimited nor definite: The meaning is illuminated by the following text: "'This belongs to that' and 'this is true of that' must be taken in as many ways as those in which predicates have been divided [= categories], and these either in some way (*pê[i]*) or unconditionally (*haplôs*), and, further, either as simple or composite; and similarly too with not belonging" (*APr.* I 37 49^{a}6–9). So our contrast is first between what is unlimited in sense [1] or [3] (previous note) and what is unconditionally (= actually or actively)

156

unlimited, that is sense [2], and second between what is unlimited in sense [1] or [3] and what is definite. For what is unlimited in these senses is only *in a way* definite.

Note 199
Therefore, it will at the same time have a capacity for not being and for being: Reading ἄρ' ἕξει with ms. E, Verdenius, pp. 275–276, and DP for Moraux γὰρ ἕξει.

Note 200
For an unlimited time it will have a capacity for not being and for being; but it has been shown that this is impossible: At I 12 181ᵇ20–25.

Note 201
Activation (*energeias*): See I 12 281ᵇ22n.
Even when it had not come to be (*agenêton*) **and was not—the unlimited time in which it is capable of coming to be:** Reading καὶ ὄν ἀγένητον ἦν καὶ μὴ ὄν, τὸν ἄπειρον χρόνον γίγνεσθαι δυνάμενον with Verdenius, p. 276 and DP for Moraux καὶ ὄν ἀγένητον ἦν καὶ μὴ ὄν [τὸν ἄπειρον χρόνον], γίγνεσθαι δὲ δυνάμενον. All the mss. have τὸν ἄπειρον χρόνον, but some omit δὲ. Here *agenêton* must be translated as a perfect passive participle, not as "incapable of coming to be." See I 11 280ᵇ1–2n.

Note 202
It is also evident in another way that [that the unlimited is incapable of passing away, because it is evident that] it is impossible for what is capable of passing away not to have passed away at some time: The additional clause is needed because it has not yet been shown that it is impossible for what is capable of passing away not to have passed away at some time. See Verdenius, p. 276.

Note 203
It will always be at the same time both capable of passing away and not actually (*entelecheia[i]*) **passed away:** See I 12 281ᵇ22n.

Note 204
Nothing can be by chance either incapable of passing away or incapable of coming to be: See I 12 281ᵃ20–25n.
Chance (*automaton*): Things that come about by chance (*to automaton*) are the ones "whose cause is indefinite and that come about not for the sake of something, and neither always nor for the most part nor in an orderly way" (*Rh.* I 10 1369ᵃ32–34). Living things that come to be by chance are the so-called *spontaneously generated* ones. For the contrast with luck, see the next note.

Note 205
By luck (*apo tuchês*): What happens by luck (*tuchê*) in the broad sense is what happens coincidentally or contingently (*APo.* I 30 87ᵇ19–22), so that luck in that

sense is pretty much the same as chance. But in a narrower sense, which is contrasted with chance, what happens by luck is what has a coincidental final cause: "Luck is a coincidental cause in things that come about in accord with deliberate choice for the sake of an end" (*Met.* XI 8 1065ª30–31). Thus if a tree's being by the back door is the sort of thing that might be an outcome of deliberative thought, it is a candidate final cause of action—an end we aim at (*Ph.* II 5 197ª5–14, 6 197ᵇ20– 22). If wish, which is the desire involved in deliberation and deliberate choice, is what causes it to be there, the tree's being by the back door has a genuine final cause. If not, its being there has a coincidental final cause. Unlike chance, then, which applies quite generally to whatever results from coincidental efficient causes, narrow luck applies only to what could come about because of action and deliberate choice. Hence it is the sphere relevant to action: "Luck and the results of luck are found in things that are capable of being lucky, and, in general, of action. That is why indeed luck is concerned with things doable in action" (197ᵇ1–2). The sphere of narrow luck is also that of the practical and productive sciences (*Rh.* I 5 1362ª2).

For the most part (*hôs epi to polu*): "The contrary of what is *hôs epi to polu* is always said to be something that rarely occurs" (*Top.* II 6 112ᵇ10–11); "When something comes about always or *hôs epi to polu*, it does not do so coincidentally or by luck, but in what is natural it always does so in this way provided there is no impediment" (*Ph.* II 8 199ᵇ24–26); "What is either universally or *hôs epi to polu* so is in accord with nature" (*PA* III 2 663ᵇ28–29). *Hôs epi to polu* is not equivalent in meaning, however, to the quantifier "most," since "*hôs d' epi to polu* all (*pantes*) crabs have the right claw bigger and stronger than the left" (*HA* IV 3 527ᵇ6–7). Instead, it seems to be a special type or grade of modality that is in between contingency and unconditional necessity: "from *this* of necessity *this* ('from this' either unconditionally or *hôs epi to polu*)" (*Ph.* II 7 198ᵇ5–6).

Note 206

And the matter is the cause of their being and not being: "Nature tends to measure comings to be and endings by the number of these revolutions [of the sun and moon], but cannot bring this about in an exact way because of the indefiniteness of matter, and because many starting-points exist that impede coming to be and passing away from being in accord with nature, and often cause things to happen contrary to nature" (*GA* IV 10 778ª4–9; also *Met.* VI 2 1027ª13–15). Since the "indefiniteness of matter" seems to be a standing condition, while the "many starting-points . . . which impede" are not, we should presumably divide things up as follows. The indefiniteness of matter explains why what is by nature holds *hôs epi to polu*, and so has contraries that are rarely true, while impediments explain why what otherwise would occur rarely may occur quite often. All human beings are two-footed, and this would remain true even if some freak accident or genetic disorder resulted in all or most human beings having only one leg. Nonetheless, it would still hold *hôs epi to polu*, since even under normal conditions a human offspring may be born with only one leg, simply due to facts about his father's seed (form) and his mother's menses (matter).

Note 207

[1] **Therefore it is necessarily by nature that things of this sort are at some times and not at others. [2] And in things of this sort [that is, that are for an unlimited time, whether unconditionally or from a certain point] the same capacity is for what is contradictory, and the matter is the cause of their being and not being. [3] So it is necessary for opposites to belong actively too at the same time:** Reading καὶ ἅμα in [3] with Verdenius, p. 277 for Moraux ἅμα. Leggatt transposes these sentences to follow I 12 233ᵇ22 at the end of the chapter, but the argument seems to require that they be read here. [1] is established by appeal to the claim that what holds always or for the most part cannot hold by luck or chance (that is coincidentally) and so must hold by nature. And it entails [2] and [3]: "But as nature remains the same, so too the capacity remains the same, as does the underlying subject, since it has the same capacity, and does not lose it in changing into the contraries, if indeed the matter is eternal. Since, then, both the nature and the matter remain the same, the same capacity must always be. For prior to its becoming fire or one of the other elements, the matter had the capacity for becoming these things, and having become them it has not lost these capacities, but remains having the same ones. For the same matter has the capacity both for being this something and for not being it (for this is what it is to be matter for it) and it cannot pass away. For what could it pass away into? If, then, something capable of coming to be, prior to its coming to be, has the capacity for not being this very thing it will become, it will remain having the same capacity after it has come to be. If, then, the cosmos is supposed to have come to be but be incapable of passing away, then after it has come to be it will have the capacity for not being. For there was a time when it was not [and so had the capacity not to be]. If, then, it is supposed to be incapable of passing away, and will be for the remainder of eternity, actively having the capacity for not being, then whenever we suppose that what it is capable of is realized, it will at the same time both actively be and not be. So that opposites will belong to the same thing at the same time, which is impossible and follows from an impossibility" (Simp. 354.23–355.9 = Hankinson, pp. 73–74).

Opposites (*antikeimena*): "One thing is said to be opposed to another in four ways: as relatives, as contraries, as lacking and having, and as affirmation and denial" (*Cat.* 10 11ᵇ17–19); "The sorts of opposition are contradiction, lack, contrariety, and relatives, and of these the primary sort is contradiction" (*Met.* X 5 1055ᵃ38–ᵇ1).

Note 208

Moreover, it is not true to say of anything now that it *is* last year, or of something last year that it *is* now: "Having shown that for anyone who says that something that comes to be can be incapable of passing away it follows that it has the capacity for opposites to belong to it at the same time, Aristotle goes on to resolve the following objection which could be brought against the argument. What is capable of coming to be but incapable of passing away has the capacity for not being in respect of the past, if indeed previously it is not but later it is, and for being in the future, if indeed it is assumed to be incapable of passing away. Therefore, it will not have the capacity for being and not being at the same time, so that it will not actively have opposites [true of it] at the same time. He resolves this objection by saying that every capacity is either in respect of the present or in respect of the future. For we say that things are capable in the strict sense if they are not yet but can come to be, differentiating them in this way from things that belong in that they will be but are not yet. If, then, it is not true 'to say of anything now that it *is* last year' . . ., since it is not true now to say that last year *is*, it will not be true to say of any of the things that were last year that they *are* now. . . . If, then, this is true, it is impossible for what *is not* at some time later to be eternal, that is, for something that has come to be to become incapable of passing away for the remainder of time. For since it *is not* previously but later *is*, it will have the capacity for not being even when it has come to be, although not for not-being-at-that-time, when it has already come to be. For it belongs actively at the time it *is*. It is necessary, then, for a thing of this sort to have had this capacity a year ago, that is, in time past" (Simp. 355.18–356.6 = Hankinson, pp. 74–75).

Note 209
Alterable: See I 3 270^{a}27n.

BOOK II

Note 210
The cause of the start of the others: That is, of the others that in fact have a start and a cessation. For the details, see *GC* I 10, *GA* IV 10.
Receives their cessation: "Because the passing away of one thing is the coming to be of another" (Simp. 372.19 = Mueller, p. 16).

Note 211
It is unlabored, because it needs no additional necessary force which restrains it, preventing it from spatially moving in another way that is natural to it: "The sun, the stars, and the whole heaven are always active, and there is no fear that they may sometime stand still, which is what those concerned with nature fear, nor do they get tired doing this. For movement is not for them connected with a capacity for the contradictory, as it is for things that can pass away, so that the continuity of the movement is laborious, since the substance that is matter and potentiality, and not activity, is what causes this" (*Met.* IX 8 1050^{b}22–28). See also *MA* 3 699^{a}27–30.

Note 212
The best disposition: See I 9 279^{a}18–22 and, on disposition, I 3 270^{a}28n.

Note 213
Atlas: See Hesiod, *Theogony*, 517. "What hinders a thing from moving or acting in accord with its own impulse is said to hold it—for example, the pillars hold the

weight lying on them, and, as the poets say, 'Atlas holds up the heaven,' on the supposition that it would fall to the earth otherwise, as some of the physicists also say" (*Met.* V 23 1023ª17–21).

Note 214

Balance-weight (*rhopê*): "We see that the things that have a greater balance-weight (*rhopên*) of heaviness or lightness, other things being equal, spatially move across equal distances faster, and in accord with the ratio that their magnitudes bear to each other" (*Ph.* IV 8 216ª13–16). A's heaviness is its non-comparative tendency to move downward; its lightness, its non-comparative tendency to move upward: "By unconditionally light, then, we mean that which spatially moves upward or to the extremity, and by unconditionally heavy that which spatially moves downward or to the center. By light in relation to something else, or lighter, we mean that, of two bodies possessed of weight and of equal volume, the lighter one is the one that is exceeded by the other in the speed of its by nature downward movement" (*Cael.* IV 1 308ª29–33). A's balance-weight is its weight or lightness in comparison to B's, when A is in one pan of a (fair) balance or weighing-scale and B is in the other. If the A-pan moves downward, A has a greater balance-weight of heaviness than B, and a smaller balance-weight of lightness.

Because of its whirling's having a spatial movement that is faster than its own balance-weight: See II 13 295ª14–ᵇ9.
As Empedocles says: At DK B35 = TEGP 51 F28.

Note 215

Blessedly happy (*makarian*): *Makarios* is often a synonym for *eudaimôn* ("happy"), but sometimes, as here, with the implication of being extremely happy (*NE* I 10 1101ª7) or in a condition like that of the gods (X 8 1178ᵇ25–32).

Note 216

It necessarily, with respect to its movement, involves force: Reading κατὰ τὴν κίνησιν with Verdenius, p. 277 (followed by DP) for Moraux καὶ τὴν κίνησιν.
The primary body: That is, the heaven.
Unleisured (*ascholon*): Aristotle's way of thinking about leisure (*scholê*) overlaps with ours but differs from it in important ways. We think of leisure time as time off from work in which we can do as we choose. Aristotle agrees that leisure time and work time are distinct (*Pol.* I 8 1256ª31–35), but thinks that activities that are entirely leisured must be choiceworthy solely because of themselves. Among these he includes such scientific activities as the exercise of theoretical wisdom or mathematical knowledge, which we might think of as work. In these, he thinks, complete happiness consists (*NE* X 7 1177ᵇ19–26). Entirely unleisured activities, he thinks, are choiceworthy solely because of some additional end, such as producing or providing the necessities of life (X 6 1176ᵇ2–3)—included among these are the canonical productive crafts (*Met.* IX 6 1048ᵇ18–35). Activities which are choiceworthy in part because of themselves, and in part because of an additional end, include activities in accord with practical wisdom and the virtues of character. These too

constitute happiness, but of a less than complete or secondary sort (*NE* X 7 1177^{b}4–18, 8 1178^{a}9–22). Most people would include amusing pastimes as leisured activities par excellence (X 6 1176^{b}6–17), but Aristotle does not agree: "Happiness is not found in amusement, since it would be absurd indeed for the end to be amusement, and our life's labors and sufferings to be for the sake of amusement. For we choose almost everything, except happiness, for the sake of something else, since it is the [unconditional] end. To work hard and toil [just] for the sake of amusement, however, appears a silly and entirely childish thing to do. Rather 'play to be serious,' as Anacharsis puts it, seems to have it right. For amusement is a form of relaxation, and it is because we cannot toil continuously that we need relaxation. Relaxation, then, is not an end, since it occurs for the sake of activity [in accord with virtue]" (X 6 1176^{b}27–1177^{a}1). Nonetheless, because humans do have to engage in unleisured practical and productive activities, a good political constitution "should permit amusement, but be careful to use it at the correct time, dispensing it as a medicine for the ills of unleisure" (*Pol.* VIII 3 1337^{b}35–42; also VIII 5 1339^{b}31–42).

Deprived of all thought-involving ease (*rhastônês emphronos*): The adjective *emphrôn* is rare in Aristotle, occurring just four times. Its sense here is best captured by its use at *Rh.* I 4 1359^{b}5–8, where the craft of rhetoric is contrasted with "a more thought-involving (*emphronesteras*) and more truth-focused one." This pegs the latter as, in particular, theoretical or contemplative thinking: "Of theoretical science the end is truth, whereas of practical science it is work (since, whenever practical people investigate the how of things, what they get a theoretical grasp on is the cause not intrinsically but in relation to something and now)" (*Met.* II 1 993^{b}20–23). Thus what the soul in question is deprived of in particular is the leisure that would enable it to engage in the contemplation in which true happiness resides.

Sleep (*hupnon*): "Sleep is not every incapacity of the perceptual part, but rather this affection arises from the evaporation that attends eating food. For that which is vaporized must be driven on to a given point and then must turn back and change just like the tide in a narrow strait. And in every animal the hot is made by nature to move upward, but when it has reached the upper parts, it turns back, and moves downward in a mass. That is why sleepiness mostly occurs after eating food, for, then, a large watery and earthy mass is carried upward. When this comes to a stop, therefore, it weighs down and makes drowsy; but when it has actually sunk downward, and by its return has driven back the hot, then sleepiness comes on and the animal falls asleep" (*Somn.* 3 456^{b}17–28)

Note 217

Ixion: A Thessalian king who attempted to rape Hera, the wife of Zeus; Zeus punished him by chaining him to a fiery wheel on which he was condemned to revolve forever.

Note 218

If, then, as we said, it is possible to speak in the way we have about the primary spatial movement: At II 1 284^{a}2–11. The primary spatial movement is the circular movement of the (primary or outermost) heaven.

This is the only way to provide harmonious accounts that are in agreement with the prophecy (*tê[i] manteia[i]*) **about the god** (*peri ton theon*): The noun *manteia* occurs three times in Aristotle: here, at *HA* VIII 18 601^{b}2 (referring to a text of Hesiod), and in F10 (= Sextus Empiricus, *adversus mathematicos* IX.20–23 = Barnes, pp. 2391–2392). The last, which is alone salient, is as follows:

> Aristotle used to say that a conception (*ennoian*) of the gods came about in human beings from two starting-points: from experiences in the soul and from astronomical phenomena (*meteôrôn*). From experiences in the soul because of its ecstatic experiences and prophetic powers (*manteias*) in dreams. For, he says, when the soul comes to be by itself in sleep, it then assumes its proper nature and prophesizes (*promanteutai*) and foretells the future. And this is the sort of condition it is in when it is separated from the body at death. At any rate he accepts even the poet Homer as having observed this. For he has represented Patroclus, at the moment of his death, as foretelling the doing away with Hector, and Hector as foretelling the end of Achilles. It is from such things, he says, that human beings suspect (*huponoêsan*) there to be something divine (*ti theon*), something intrinsically (*kath' heauto*) like the soul, and of all things most capable of scientific knowledge (*epistêmonikôtaton*). And from astronomical phenomena too: seeing by day the revolution of the sun and by night the well-ordered movement of the other stars, they came to think that there was some divine thing (*tina theon*) that is the cause of such movement and good order.

One possibility, then, is that *tê[i] manteia[i] peri ton theon* is referring to (1) prophetic experience of the sort that human beings allegedly have in sleep. Another possibility is (2) that floated by Simplicius: "Only if we say that [the heaven's] activity is not forced but in accord with nature can we provide indisputably harmonious accounts. He calls this common conception (*koinên ennoian*) we have of the freedom from labor and blessed happiness of the divine an oracle because it inheres more strongly than what is demonstrated and is most steadfast and unchangeable. And the oracles that are in accord with divine knowledge are of this sort, beyond all demonstration and of unchangeable convincingness" (Simp. 382.26–32 = Mueller, p. 28). A third option takes the reference to be to (3) the view of the ancients described at II 1 284^{a}11–18, which is essentially that mentioned by Alexander. But it is not merely a "common conception," or "the inspired guesses of common sense" (Stocks). Instead, stemming as it does from myths and so on, it has a genuinely inspirational character of the sort Sextus attests to. See *Met.* XII 8 1074^{a}38–^{b}14 (noting *theiôs* at 1074^{b}9). But then these myths, however inspired they may seem to us, are at the same time the decayed remnants of past scientific theories every bit as sophisticated as our own—see I 3 270^{b}20n in which the *Met.* XII 8 passage is quoted. Notice the reference to prophets at II 2 285^{a}3–4.

All of which brings us to the question of why we have (a) *peri* + the accusative *ton theon*, rather than (b) *peri* + genitive *tou theou* (a question perceptively raised by Bos, pp. 169–171). With the genitive *peri* means "about" in the sense of "concerning" or "dealing with," so that *tê[i] manteia[i] peri ton theon* is the prophecy dealing with the god. But this faces a problem: *manteia* is about the future. Hence the Platonic definition of *manteia* as "scientific knowledge foreshowing an action without a demonstrative argument" (*Def.* 414b) and the joke at *Rh.* III 17 1418ª23–24 that the past is "scientifically knowable—'even to prophets (*mantesin*),' as Epimenides the Cretan said." *Peri* + the accusative, on the other hand, gives "around" a spatial sense of "around and about," or "surrounding," so that *tê[i] manteia[i] peri ton theon* refers to prophetic activity around (and so dependent on) the god, with no implication as to content, and so no requirement of futurity.

Next step: At *NE* X 8 1179ª24–30 Aristotle writes: "if the gods exercise a sort of supervision over human affairs, as indeed they seem to, it would also be quite reasonable both that they should enjoy what is best and most akin to themselves (and this would be understanding) and that they should reward those who most like and honor it for supervising what they themselves love and for acting correctly and nobly. But that all these attributes belong most of all to a wise person is quite clear. Therefore, he is most beloved by the gods." At the same time, however, he is explicit that the gods in question live exclusively contemplative lives (X 8 1178ᵇ8–23), so that whatever supervision they exercise over human affairs must be of a somewhat special sort. Aristotle does not tell us what it is, but his identification of these gods with the heavenly spheres (*Met.* XII 8 1074ª38–ᵇ14) suggests an answer. For the orderly revolutions of these spheres govern the seasons as well as the cycles of fertility and infertility of land and animals (*GA* IV 10 778ª4–9). Hence they confer benefits on all beings, but especially on those wise people who, through astronomical contemplation of the heavens, learn about these cycles, and adjust their lives accordingly. We might think of the case of Thales who "apprehended from his astronomy that a good olive harvest was coming" (*Pol.* I 11 1259ª10–11).

Putting everything together, then, we should take *tê[i] manteia[i] peri ton theon* as referring to prophetic activity based on scientific knowledge of the movements of the primary heaven and other celestial phenomena, whose order and unforced movement is dependent on the soul (Aristotle's primary god) that is the basis in fact of the myth of Atlas.

The god: That is, the one responsible for the primary spatial movement of the (primary or outermost) heaven. See I 4 271ª33n.

Note 219

Those called Pythagoreans (for this account is theirs): See II 2 285ª11–14, ª25–27, ᵇ25–27, and Huffman-1, pp. 222–226.

Note 220

Our works on the movement of animals: In particular, *Progression of Animals* (*IA*) 4–5.

Note 221

While in plants only up and down belong: See II 2 284ᵇ27–29n.

Note 222
It is reasonable that the first one, as we said, that belongs in animals belongs in it too: At II 2 284^{b}11–14.

Note 223
Growth, though, starts from the up, movement with respect to place from the right, and perception from the front: In the case of all sublunary living things, up and down are not just spatially or relationally distinguished but functionally and absolutely so: "the part from which the distribution of nourishment and growth derives in each living thing is up and the last part toward which this travels is down—the one is a sort of starting-point, the other a limit; and up is a starting-point" (*IA* 2 705^{a}32–^{b}2). That is why a plant, whose roots are down below, not as in animals up above, is a sort of upside-down animal: "Up and down are not the same for all things as they are for the universe, but as the head is of animals, so the roots are of plants—if we are to speak of instrumental parts as distinct or the same by appeal to their functions" (*DA* II 4 416^{a}2–5; see also *PA* IV 10 686^{a}25–687^{a}2). Similarly, in animals the front is a starting-point, because it is what perception is directed toward (*IA* 4 705^{b}10–13). Even in earthworms, where right and left are more difficult to distinguish perceptually, the functional difference between them still exists: "the starting-point of the movement is the same in all animals and by nature has its position in the same place; and it is from the right that the starting-point of movement derives" (5 706^{a}10–13). Thus human beings put their left foot forward, unless they accidentally do the opposite, since "they are moved not by the foot they put in front, but by the one with which they step off" (706^{a}8–9).

Note 224
We speak of them either with reference to our own right, as prophets do: "We say that a bird that is on our right is a bird from the right and call it a right [= good] omen (*sumbolon*) in this way" (Simp. 383.38–284.2 = Mueller, p. 30).
What has its position in the contrary way, speaking of right with reference to our left, and left with reference to our right: "As in the case of mirrors where right is what is on our left and left what is on our right" (Simp. 384.4–6 = Mueller, p. 30).
{, and of back with reference to our front}: Secluded by M.

Note 225
That is why one might wonder at the Pythagoreans because they said that only two of these, right and left, are starting-points, but omitted the four remaining starting-points: "The Pythagoreans, having put all the oppositions (*antitheseis*) into two columns, a better and a worse, or good and bad, . . . they took each of their ten oppositions as also making evident all the oppositions akin to it. And of the spatial relations (*topikôn*) they took right and left, because these at the same time indicate good and bad (at any rate we speak of a right nature or a right luck, meaning a good nature or good luck, and we mean the contrary by left). . . . It was reasonable, then, for them to use right and left to indicate the other spatial

oppositions. For they called right, up, and front good, and left, down, and back bad" (Simp. 386.9–22 = Mueller, p. 33). Pythagorean columns of ten contraries appears at *Met.* I 5 983ᵃ23–26.

No less controlling: See II 13 293ᵇ2n.

Note 226

Some of these differ in capacity only, others in their shapes as well: "For example, right or left hands or feet, which do not differ from each other in their shapes, differ only in capacity, the right hand being more vigorous than the left, whereas the left foot is more suitable for standing still, the right for starting to move off . . . but head is differentiated from feet, branches from roots, and, in general, up from down and front from back not only in capacity but also in shape" (Simp. 384.30–385.2 = Mueller, p. 31).

Shapes (*schêmasi*): Figure (*schêma*) = external form/shape (*morphê*) of a thing (*Cat.* 8 10ᵃ11–16).

Note 227

Up would be prior to right in coming to be: Not mentioned explicitly in *Cat.* 12 or *Met.* V 11, where priority and posteriority are focally discussed, but treated as a sort of priority in time at *Met.* IX 8 1049ᵇ17–29.

Things are said to be prior in many ways: "One thing is said to be prior to another in four ways. [1] First, and most strictly, with respect to time, as when one thing is said to be older or more ancient than another. . . . [2] Second, what does not reciprocate as to the following along of existence—for example, one is prior to two (for the existence of two follows along at once with the existence of one, whereas the existence of one does not necessitate the existence of two). . . . [3] A thing is said to be prior with respect to some order, as with sciences and speeches. For in the demonstrative sciences there is a prior and posterior in order (for the elements are prior to the constructions (*diagrammatôn*), and in the case of grammar, the letters are prior to the syllables); and in the case of speeches it is likewise (for the introduction is prior in order to the narration). [4] Further, in addition to the ones just mentioned, what is better and more estimable seems to be prior. . . . The fourth way is of course pretty much the most distant of the ways" (*Cat.* 12 14ᵃ26–ᵇ8). In *Met.* V 11, Aristotle mentions: priority in the sense of being closer to a starting-point (which includes [1]), priority in knowledge (= [3] which includes priority in account), in nature and substance (= [2]; on which see *Cael.* I 2 269ᵃ19n). On [4], see I 2 269ᵇ16n.

Note 228

They thought that the starting-points belong alike in all things: Whereas right and left do not belong, for example, in plants (II 2 285ᵃ18–19) in the same way as in inanimate things (285ᵃ1–3).

Note 229

We have determined previously that capacities of this sort belong in things that have a starting-point of movement: In *IA* 4–5. See II 2 284ᵇ25–30n.

The heaven is animate, that is (*kai*), has a starting-point of movement: Since the heaven has not previously been characterized as animate, *kai* should be treated as epexegetic, so that the heaven's possession of a soul amounts here simply to its having a starting-point of movement, although there will later turn out to be more to it than that. See II 12 292ª18–21.

Note 230

Only in these hemispheres do we see a difference, because of their poles not moving: The poles of these two hemispheres are stationary, and so we can designate one of them up, the other down. But we cannot make a similar demarcation of the left and right hemisphere, even though it is clear that movement comes from the right. The daily rotation of the fixed stars is from the east, so that has to be the right as far as this movement is concerned. Nevertheless, it is not possible on the basis of this to designate an eastern and a western hemisphere in the heaven, because any celestial hemisphere will partake in the daily motion of the fixed stars. This, however means that—with the exception of poles, and the axis of the northern and southern celestial hemispheres—the poles and the axis of any other pair of hemispheres we would demarcate in the sky would also take part in the daily celestial revolution. Accordingly, in the case of a putative pair of eastern and western hemispheres, they would just exchange their places in half a day.

Note 231

The sides (*plagia*) in the cosmos ... what is beside the poles (*to para tous polous*): The regions of the cosmos lying outside the poles, or at an angle to the north-south axis.

Note 232

Revolves to the right (*epi dexia*): Think of passing a wine bottle to the person sitting on your right at a circular dinner table (as in Plato, *Smp.* 177d, 249b–c, 223c). The bottle will travel counterclockwise. See Braunlich.

Note 233

If it is the apparent one, the movement will be to the left, which is just what we say it is not: And "we" say it is not on the basis of an argument likes this: (1) the right is a starting-point of movement in the sublunary animals that are available to us for close empirical study; (2) the heaven has a starting-point of movement and is to that extent animate; (3) it is reasonable to extend our empirically well-based knowledge of sublunary animals to celestial animals about which we have less empirical evidence and less ability to acquire more; (4) therefore it is reasonable to think that the movement of the heaven will be from the right, and since it is observed to be circular, toward the right. We see (3) at work in the following well-known text: "Among the substances formed by nature, some [such as the heavenly bodies] never for all eternity either come to be or pass away, while others share in coming to be and passing away. Yet, as it happens, our theoretical knowledge (*theôria*) of the former, though they are estimable and divine, is slighter, since as regards both those things on the basis of which one would investigate them and those things about them that we long to know, the perceptual appearances are altogether few. Where the plants and animals that pass away are concerned, however, we are much better off as regards knowledge, because we live among them. For anyone willing to take sufficient trouble can grasp a lot about each genus of them. Each type of theoretical knowledge has its attractions. For even if our contact with eternal things is but slight, all the same, because of its esteem, this knowledge is a greater pleasure than our knowledge of everything around us, just as even a chance, brief glimpse of those we love is a greater pleasure than the most exact view of other things, however many or great they are. On the other hand, because we know more of them and know them more fully, our scientific knowledge of things that pass away exceeds that of the others. Further, because they are nearer to us and because their nature is more akin to ours, they provide their own compensations in comparison with the philosophy concerned with divine things. . . . For even in the theoretical knowledge of animals that are disagreeable to perception, the nature that crafted them likewise provides extraordinary pleasures to those who can know their causes and are by nature philosophers . . . that is why we should not be childishly disgusted at the investigation of the less estimable animals, since in all natural things there is something wondrous" (PA I 5 644^{b}22–645^{a}17; see also Cael. II 3 286^{a}3–7). We should not think, therefore, that Aristotle has abandoned his empiricism in arguing as he does here. Instead, he uses (as he thinks) empirically well-established theories, by a sort of inference to the best explanation, to account for phenomena where adequate empirical evidence is slight—always aware that later evidence may require him to go back to the drawing board. See II 4 287^{b}29–288^{a}2n.

Note 234
The people who dwell there are in the upper hemisphere and near the right-side things: Contrast Mete. II 5 362^{a}33–34.

Note 235
The people there [in the other hemisphere] down and in the left one: Aristotle himself does not explicitly acknowledge the existence of such inhabitants, though he does acknowledge the existence of the lower hemisphere: "There must be a place related to the other pole as the one we dwell in is related to our pole" (Mete. II 5 362^{b}30–32).

Note 236
Their coincidental attributes (tôn sumbebêkotôn): A standard Aristotelian contrast is between (1a) what has an attribute B coincidentally (kata sumbebêkos or per accidens in Latin) and (2) what has B intrinsically (kath' hauto or per se) (Met. V 18 1022^{a}24–36). Included in (1), however, are the so-called per se accidents, the kath' hauta sumbebêkota, which are attributes that belong to a subject intrinsically and thus demonstrably, but are not part of its ousia, or essence (APo. I 7 75^{b}1, 22 83^{b}19, Met. V 30 1025^{a}30–32, XIII 3 1078^{a}5–9). They are contrasted with (1b) the non-intrinsic coincidents which belong to a subject contingently, and so non-demonstrably.

Note 237

Each thing of which there is a function (*ergon*) is for the sake of the function:
A function is (1) an activity that is the use or actualization of a state, capacity,
or disposition; (2) a work or product that is the further result of such an activity
(*NE* I 1 1094ª5–6). It is intimately related, as we see here, to its possessor's end or
final cause: "The function is the end, and the activity is the function" (*Met.* VIII 8
1050ª21–22). Moreover, a thing's good or doing well "seems to lie in its function"
(*NE* I 7 1097ᵇ26–27). But this holds only when the thing itself is not already something bad (*Met.* VIII 9 1051ª15–16). Finally, a thing's function is intimately related
to its nature, form, and essence. For a thing's nature is "its for-the-sake-of-which"
(*Ph.* II 2 194ª27–28), its form is more its nature than its matter (1 193ᵇ6–7), and
its essence and form are the same (VII 7 1032ᵇ1–2). Hence "all things are defined
by their function" (*Mete.* IV 12 390ª10), with the result that if something cannot
function, it has no more than a name in common with its functional self (*Met.*
VII 10 1035ᵇ14–25, *Pol.* I 2 1253ª20–25, *PA* I 1 640ᵇ33–641ª6). Functions are thus
attributed to a wide variety of things, whether living or non-living. These include
plants (*GA* I 23 731ª24–26) and animals generally (*NE* X 5 1176ª3–5), parts of
their bodies and souls (*PA* II 7 652ᵇ6–14, IV 10 686ª26–29), instruments or tools of
various sorts (*EE* VII 10 1242ª15–19), crafts, sciences (II 1 1219ª17), philosophies
(*Met.* VII 11 1037ª15) and their practitioners (*NE* VI 7 1141ᵇ10), cities (*Pol.* VII 4
1326ª13–14), and nature itself (I 10 1258ª35).

Note 238

The activity of a god is immortality, and this is eternal living: Since the activity
in question must, for the previous sentence (II 3 286ª8–9) to be relevant to it, be
the activation of a function, it follows that gods too have functions. On activity,
see I 12 281ᵇ22n.

Note 239

It is necessary that eternal movement belongs to the god: Reading (1) θεῷ ("god")
with Moraux and most mss.; other mss. (followed by Guthrie and Leggatt) read (2)
θείῳ ("divine"). The problem with (1) is that it seems to conflict with the fact that
(3) Aristotle's (primary) god—a wholly intelligible self-contemplator—is "immovable and eternal" (*Ph.* VIII 6 259ᵇ32–33; also *Met.* VII 6 1071ᵇ4–5, 7 1072ª25–26,
and *Cael.* I 4 271ª33n). (a) One way to remove the supposed conflict is to suppose
that (1) belongs to an earlier phase in Aristotle's thought in which "the unmoved
mover was not yet a part of [his] theology" (Guthrie, p. 149). But another is available that is more attractive, since it involves no otherwise unsupported appeals to
chronology. (b) The primary heaven (or outermost sphere of the fixed stars) is a
corporeal (though ethereal) sphere which, as animate, has a soul of its own (*Met.*
XII 8), which soul, in the case of the primary heaven, is the immovable wholly
intelligible self-contemplator that is the (primary) god. But just as "human" can
refer to the animate body, the compound of body and soul, or to the understanding, which is the divine element in the human soul (see, I 3 270ᵇ11n), so *theos*
("god") can refer either to the animate sphere or to the immovable understanding

that moves it. We see this clearly in Plato: "Because we have not seen a god or adequately grasped one with our understanding," he says, "we imagine a kind of immortal living creature that has both a soul and a body, combined for all time" (*Phdr.* 246c–d). But really it is the souls of these immortal creatures that are alone gods: "Consider the stars and the moon, the years, months, and all the seasons: what other account can we give except this same one? Since a soul or souls are evidently the causes of all these things, and good souls possessed of every virtue, we shall declare these souls to be gods" (*Lg.* 899b). The next sentence in our text (II 3 286ª10–12) involves essentially the same ambiguity (see next note). So "the god" in our text should therefore be taken to refer to the animate sphere, whose movement is quite consistent with the immovability of the understanding (which *is* the god) that moves it.

Note 240

The heaven [1] is such (*toioutos*) (for [2] it is a certain divine body), because of this [3] it has a circular body: *Toioutos* in [1] is probably best understood as referring to the previous sentence (II 3 286ª10) and so as meaning "such as to have eternal movement belonging to it." [2] is, then, not a gloss to be secluded (as Elders, p. 192 n2, followed by DP, p. 430 n1, thinks), but as genuinely explanatory. For knowing that the god (286ª10) *is* an unmoved mover (previous note), Aristotle knows he must explain how eternal movement can belong to it. Answer: considered as an animate sphere it is "a certain divine body," which is divine for just the reason that a human being's body is human, and as such can (coincidentally) move (see *DA* I 3). [3] then draws the appropriate conclusion: as a human being is an animate body and so has a body, so the god, as an animate sphere, has a spherical body. But the god that has it—the being that is alone strictly speaking the god (previous note)—is the immovable self-contemplator, already in the picture in *Ph.* VIII and properly discussed in *Met.* XII 7–10.

Note 241

At the center (*epi tou mesou*): Compare the characterization of the proper place of earth as "the one *around* the center" (*Cael.* I 8 277ᵇ15–16).

Note 242

No part of it can remain at rest either in general or at the center: For its movement in accord with nature is eternal circular movement, so that remaining at rest anywhere would be contrary to nature for it, and so could not be eternal.

Note 243

Nothing contrary to nature is eternal: See I 2 269ᵇ6–10.

Note 244

What is contrary to nature is posterior to what is in accord with nature: See II 2 285ª21n.

What is contrary to nature is a sort of departure (*ekstasis tis*) **from what is in accord with nature:** Compare: "Virtue is a sort of completion (for when each thing acquires its own virtue, at that point it is said to be complete, since then it is most of all in accord with its nature, just as a circle is complete when it has most of all become a circle and when it is best) and vice the passing away and departure of this completion" (*Ph.* VII 3 246ª13–17). In a related sense mad people are said to be *ekstatikoi* ("beside themselves," as we might say) (*Po.* 17 1455ª32–33). And, in another related sense, the verb *exetazein* often simply means "examine" or "audit" political officials (for example, *Pol.* II 9 1271ᵇ14), because what stands (*stasis*) outside (*ek*) is an unbiased or independent judge: "dialectic, . . . because of its capacity to stand outside and examine (*exetastikê*), provides a route toward the starting-points of all methodological inquiries" (*Top.* I 2 101ᵇ2–4).

Note 245
Later this will be shown about [earth that it rests at the center]: At II 14.

Note 246
By nature . . . has some nature: On the difference, see I 1 268ª3n.

Note 247
The matter of contraries is the same: Contraries differ maximally in the same genus (*Met.* X 4 1055ª27–28); a genus is in relevant ways like matter (VII 12 1038ª6–8); therefore, "all contrary things have matter" (XII 10 1075ᵇ22). And because one contrary (the negative one) is a lack of the other (the negative one), the matter must be the same.
Positive (*kataphasis*): "Affirmation" and "denial" are *kataphasis* (or *phasis*) and *apophasis*. If X affirms that A is B and Y denies that A is B (by affirming A is not B), then what Y affirms is the contradictory (*antiphasis*) of what A affirms. But just as *antiphasis* is better translated as "negative," so, as here, *kataphasis* is better translated as "positive."
Lack (*sterêsis*): "[1] Something is said to lack something in one way if it does not have one of the attributes that something or other naturally has, even if this thing itself does not naturally have it—for example, a plant is said to lack eyes. [2] In another way if what it or its genus naturally has, it itself does not have—for example, a human who is blind and a mole lack sight in different ways, the one in contrast to its genus, the other intrinsically. [3] Further, if it does not have what it is natural for it to have when it is natural for it to have it. For blindness is a sort of lack, but a being is not blind at any and every age, but only if it does not have sight when it is natural for it to have it. Similarly, if it does not have sight in that in which, and in virtue of which, and in relation to which, and in the way in which, is natural. [4] Further, a thing forcefully taken away is said to be lacked" (*Met.* V 22 1022ᵇ22–32).
The positive is prior to the lack: In particular, it is prior in account (see, II 2 285ª21n), because "the same account makes clear both the positive thing and its lack, except not in the same way—that is, in a way it is of both, but in a way it is rather of the positive thing" (*Met.* IX 2 1046ᵇ8–9).

Note 248
The bodies intermediate between them: That is, water and air. See I 8 277^b13–17n.

Note 249
Each element has a contrariety in relation to each: Since fire is hot and dry; earth, cold and dry; air, hot and wet; water, cold and wet (*GC* II 3 330^a30–$^b7$).
Let this too be assumed for now; later we must try to show it: See IV 4 and *GC* II 3–4.

Note 250
Contraries are affected by, and affect, each other, and are destructive of each other: "It is impossible for the same thing to be hot and cold, wet and dry" (*GC* II 3 330^a31–33), and if elements are adjacent, so that like earth and water, they share a differentia, transformation (destruction of one by the other) occurs when one of the differentia masters its contrary (4 331^a27–30).

Note 251
Further, it is not reasonable for something moveable, whose movement in accord with nature does not admit of being eternal, to be eternal. But of these there is [such] movement. That it is, therefore, necessary for there to be coming to be is clear from these considerations: The movements in accord with nature of earth, water, air, and fire are rectilinear; no rectilinear movement can be eternal (see *Ph.* VII 7 261^a31–$^b26$); therefore earth cannot be in eternal movement in accord with nature; therefore, it cannot have the capacity for eternal movement in accord with nature—capacities must admit of activation (see *Cael.* I 12 281^b20–25n); but having that capacity is part of the form or essence of earth (see *Ph.* VIII 4 255^b13–22); therefore not to have it is to pass away (V 1 225^a17–20); but there must always be earth; therefore earth cannot (all) pass away; therefore, earth must not just pass away, it must also come to be.

Note 252
For with respect to the spatial movement of the whole, the elements of the bodies necessarily relate to each other in the same way. We shall speak more perspicuously about this in what follows: The reference is probably to the following account in *GC* II 10: "Since we have posited and shown that things are subject to continuous coming to be and passing away, and since we say that spatial movement is the cause of coming to be, it is evident that if the spatial movement is one, it will not be possible for both processes to occur, because they are contraries. For what is the same, and remains in the same state, by its nature produces the same thing, so that either coming to be or passing away will always occur. And so the spatial movements must be more than one and must be contraries, either because of the direction of their movement or because of its irregularity, since contraries have contraries as their causes. That is why it is not the sun's primary spatial movement that is the cause of coming to be and passing away, but that in the inclined circle. For in this there is both continuity and being moved in two movements. For

if coming to be and passing away are always to be continuous there must on the one hand be something that is being moved, so that these changes do not fail, and on the other hand two movements, in order that not only one of the two processes will occur. The spatial movement of the whole [that is, the primary heaven—the ethereal sphere of the fixed stars], then, is the cause of the continuity, whereas the inclination is the cause of the approach and retreat. For this results in its becoming further away at one time and closer at another, and since the distance is unequal the movement will be irregular. So, if it causes coming to be by approaching and being close, this same thing causes passing away by retreating and becoming further away; and if it causes coming to be by repeatedly approaching, it also causes passing away by repeatedly retreating. For contraries have contraries as their causes, and passing away and coming to be in accord with nature occur in equal periods of time. That is why the times—that is, the lives—of each [sort of] thing has a number that determines it" (336ª23–ᵇ12). But see also *Met.* XII 7 1072ª9–18: "If, then, there is a constant cycle, something [A] must always remain, acting in the same way. And if there is to be coming to be and passing away, there must be something else [B] that is always acting now in one way now in another. This [B] must, therefore, act in one way intrinsically and in another in virtue of something else—either of a third thing [C], therefore, or of the first [A]. It must, then, be in virtue of this one [A]. For otherwise this [A] again causes the movement of that one [C] and of the other one [B]. Accordingly, it is better to say 'the first' [A]. For it was the cause of things always occurring in the same way, and something else the cause of their occurring in another way, and of their always occurring in another way clearly both are the cause. This, therefore, is the way the movements actually take place."

More perspicuously (*saphesteron*): *Saphêneia* is associated with explanation, which is ultimately from starting-points: "Beginning with things that are truly stated but not perspicuously, we proceed to make them perspicuous as well. . . . That is why even politicians should not regard as peripheral to their work the sort of theoretical knowledge that makes evident (*phaneron*) not only the fact that but also the explanation why" (*EE* I 6 1216ᵇ32–39).

Note 253

It is necessary for the heaven to have a spherical shape. For this most properly belongs to its substance: Substance = essence. See I 1 268ª3n.
And is by nature primary: See II 4 286ᵇ16–18n.

Note 254

In each genus (*genei*): "Something is said to be a *genos* if: [1] The coming to be of things with the same form (*eidos*) is continuous—for example, 'as long as the *genos* of humans lasts' means 'as long as the coming to be of humans is continuous.' [2] It is the first mover that brought things into existence. For it is in this way that some are said to be Hellenes by *genos* and others Ionians, because the former come from Hellen and the latter from Ion as their first begetter. And more so when from the male begetter than when from the matter, although the *genos* is also sometimes named from the female—for example, the descendants of Pyrrha. [3] Further, as the plane is said to be the *genos* of plane figures and solid of solids. For each of the figures is in the one case a plane of such-and-such a sort and in the other a solid of such-and-such a sort, this being the underlying subject for the differentiae. [4] Further, as the first constituent in accounts is said to be—the one said in the what-it-is. For this is the *genos*, whose differentiae the qualities are said to be" (*Met.* V 28 1024^{a}29–^{b}5). Aristotle uses *genos*, then, to refer to [1–2] a race or bloodline and [3–4] to a genuine genus, which is studied by a single science. Similarly, he uses *eidos* to refer to the species of a genus, but also to form (as opposed to matter) and to a separate Platonic Form. But he also uses both terms in a more general sense to mean "kind." Transliterations are added for precision when needed.

Since in each genus, the one is prior by nature to the many, and the simple to the compound: Reading πρότερον τῇ φύσει with DP, Guthrie, Leggatt, Stocks, Verdenius, and some mss.; others, read by Allan and Moraux, seclude τῇ φύσει. In any case, the priority of one to many and simple to compound is clearly priority in nature: the one can exist without the many, but not vice versa, and likewise for simple and compound. See I 2 269^{a}19n.

Note 255

If indeed the complete is that outside which no part of it can possibly be found, as it was previously defined: The reference seems to be to the following definition: "what has nothing outside is complete and whole. For this is how we define what is whole, namely, as that from which nothing is absent—for example, a whole human being or a whole box" (*Ph.* III 6 207^{a}8–10). See also I 1 268^{b}9n.

It is always possible to add to the straight line, but never to that of the circle: "The straight line" and "the circle" can be (1) generic noun phrases ("the tiger is a carnivore") or (2) singular terms ("the tiger in that cage is a carnivore"). (1) is about universals; (2) about a particular: "The human and the horse, though, and things that are in this way set over the particulars, that is, [taken] universally, are not substance but rather a compound of a sort, [consisting] of this account and this matter taken universally. As a particular, though, Socrates is already composed of the ultimate matter, and similarly in the other cases" (*Met.* VII 10 1035^{b}27–31). Here (1) is clearly the relevant sense. The idea is not that one can always add something to a straight line, even one with definite endpoints, since that is obviously false, but rather that there is nothing in the universal definition (essence, substance) of a straight line to preclude one adding to it, since the definition, as applying to lines of arbitrary length, is (as we would say) a topologically *open* set of points. In the case of the (universal) circle, the definition itself precludes doing this, since the circle (like a definite particular straight line) is a *closed* set.

Note 256

The complete is prior to the incomplete: See I 2 269^{a}19n.

Note 257
Even those who divide bodies into plane figures and generate them from plane figures apparently testify to this: See Plato, *Ti.* 53c–56c (Appendix).

Note 258
The division into plane figures is not [1] as someone cutting something into parts would divide the whole, rather it is divided [2] as someone would who was dividing into things that are distinct in form (*eidei*): In [1] solids are divided into other solids (material chunks of the whole); in [2] solids are divided into planes, which differ in form from the whole.

Note 259
It is also most reasonable for those who assign [the shapes] a numerical order: It is unclear to whom Aristotle is referring.
To do so by assigning one to the circle, two to the triangle (since it has [interior angles equal to] two right angles): The idea seems to be one of assigning numbers to shapes on the basis of the number of their interior right angles. The circle has none, and so comes first; the next shape (the triangle) has two, and so comes second; the square (rectangle) has four, and so comes third; and so on.

Note 260
But if one is assigned to the triangle, the circle will no longer be a shape: Because there will be nowhere for something with no interior right angles to appear in the order.

Note 261
The primary shape belongs to the primary body: The body is a substance; the shape is an attribute; substances are prior to attributes, since they, as alone separable (see I 9 278ª17n), are primary in every way; so bodies are prior to shapes; bodies are primary in turn, if other bodies depend for their existence on them; so for a shape to be primary it must belong to a primary body, since otherwise it could exist (in a secondary body) while the primary body did not exist.

Note 262
So all of them would be spherical: Reading ὥστε σφαιροειδὴς ἂν εἴη πάντα with DP for Moraux and mss. ὥστε σφαιροειδὴς ἂν εἴη πᾶσα ("so it would be entirely spherical").

Note 263
It has been shown that there is neither void nor place outside the outermost revolution: At I 9 279ª11–18.

Note 264
If it is rectilinear: That is, a polyhedron.

Note 265

The spatial movement of the heavens is the measure (*metron*) of movements . . . and what is least in each thing is its measure: "A measure is that by which quantity is known, and a quantity insofar as it is a quantity is known either by a one [or a unit] or by a number, and all number by a one, so that all quantity insofar as it is quantity is known by the one, and what quantities are primarily known by, this is itself one. That is why the one is the starting-point of number insofar as it is number. And, by extension from this, so too in the other genera what is said to be a measure is the primary thing by which each is known, and the measure of each thing is a one [or a unit], in length, in breadth, in depth, in weight, in speed. . . . In all these, then, the measure and starting-point is something that is one and indivisible, since even in lines we use the one-foot line as indivisible. For everywhere people seek as a measure something that is one and indivisible. And this is the simple in either quality or quantity. Now, where it seems impossible to take away or add, this measure is exact, which is why that of number is most exact—for people posit the unit as in every way indivisible. And in the other cases they imitate this sort of measure. For in the case of a stade [two-hundred yards], a talent [six thousand drachmas], or anything comparably large, some addition or subtraction might more readily escape notice than in the case of something smaller. So the first [or primary] thing from which, as far as perception goes, that cannot happen, this is what everyone makes a measure, whether of liquids or of solids, weight or magnitude, and they think they know the quantity when they know it by means of this measure. Indeed, people think they know movement too by the movement that is simple and fastest, since this takes the least time. That is why in astronomy a one [or unit] of this sort is a starting-point and measure (for they posit the movement of the heaven to be uniform and fastest, and judge the others relative to it). And in music, it is the quarter-tone (because it is the smallest interval), and in speech the phonetic element" (*Met.* X 1 1052^{b}20–1053^{a}13); "But since there are spatial movements and, among them, circular movement, and each thing is counted by some one thing of the same kind (*genos*), units by a unit, horses by a horse, and in the same way times by some definite time, and since, as we said, time is measured by movement as well as movement by time (and this is so because the quantity of the movement and the time is measured by the movement defined by the time)—if, then, what is first is the measure of all things of the same kind (*genos*), regular circular spatial movement is most of all a measure, because the number of it is most knowable" (*Ph.* IV 14 223^{b}12–20).
Regular (*homalês*): See II 6 288^{a}13n.

Note 266

The line of the circle is the least line from a point to itself: Reading ἀπὸ τοῦ αὐτὸ ἐπὶ τὸ αὐτὸ with Simp. 412.11 (also 413.10, 14–15) and DP for Moraux ἀφ' αὐτοῦ ἐφ' αὐτὸ ("from and to the same point"). "The least extension from a point to itself, that is, the least of the extensions circumscribing and defining one of the shapes, is the circular in the case of plane figures and the spherical in the case of solids. Why this is so was certainly shown to hold generally even before Aristotle ([which he knew] if indeed he has made use of it as something that has been shown), both by Archimedes and by Zenodorus, namely, that of isoperimetric shapes the most spacious is the circle among plane figures and the sphere among solids. What Aristotle says . . . follows from this" (Alex. 412.13–18). On Archimedes, see Heath-1 vol. II, pp. 17–109, and, on Zenodorus, pp. 207–213.

Note 267
If water surrounds earth, air water, and fire air, the upper bodies will also be in the same ratio (*logos*): For an explanation of why logos is used and why it means ratio here, see II 4 287^{b}20–21.

Note 268
Let, then, the lines AB and AC be drawn from the center, and let them be joined by the line BC:

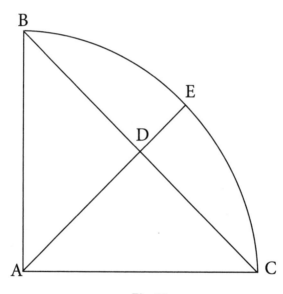

Fig. 11

Note 269
For then it will rest: Because it is in its proper place, surrounding earth (II 4 287^{a}32).

Note 270
Exactness: See I 3 269^{b}21n.

Note 271
The all-around body (*perix sômatos*): See also I 2 269^{b}7.

Note 272

As water is to earth, so it always is too with the more distant of the co-ordinate ones (*sustoichôn*): A *sustoichia* is a column, like the two columns in which the Pythagoreans arranged their basic starting-points (see II 2 285ª10–13n). Co-ordinate (*sustoichos*) things are thus items in the same column—here the column of Aristotle's own elements. Earth is closest to the center, water next closest. The more distant ones are air and fire (II 4 287ª32–34).

Note 273

There are two ways of moving in a circle: Clockwise and counterclockwise.
For example, from A to B and from A to C; that these movements are not contraries has been said previously: At I 4 271ª19–22. See Fig. 4 in the associated note.

Note 274

It is necessary for this either to be a starting-point or that there be a starting-point of it: That is, the directionality of the heaven's rotation is either a starting-point, and so not open to demonstration, or something that can be demonstrated from a starting-point. See I 1 268ª1n(5–6).

Note 275

To try to prove (*apophainesthai*) **all things, omitting nothing, in the same way as one does certain things:** On the translation of Ἴσως . . . καὶ, see Verdenius, p. 278 (followed by DP). Compare: "Now some people do demand that we demonstrate even this [the principle of non-contradiction], but this is due to lack of educatedness. For it is lack of educatedness not to know what things we should look for a demonstration of and what things we should not. For it is in general impossible to demonstrate everything (for it would go on without limit, so that even then there would be no demonstration). But if there are things we should not look for a demonstration of, these people would not be able say what starting-point they think has more of a claim to be such" (*Met.* IV 4 1006ª5–11).

Note 276

One must look to see . . . in what way they have hold of their conviction, whether in a merely human way or something stronger: See I 3 270ᵇ11–13n.

Note 277

When someone hits on necessities that are more exact, then one must show gratitude to the discoverers, for now, though, we must state what appears to be so: Compare: "Now that the spatial movements are more numerous than the bodies that are moved is evident to those with even a moderate grasp of the subject, since each of the planets has more than one spatial movement. But as to how many these are, we now—to give some notion of it—state what some of the mathematicians say, so that there be some definite number for our thought to grasp. For the rest, though, we must partly inquire for ourselves, partly learn from other inquirers, and if something contrary to what is now being said appears correct to those who are busying themselves with these issues, we should be amicable to both sides, but follow the more exact ones" (*Met.* XII 8 1073^{b}8–17). On mathematical astronomers and reliance on their works, see *Cael.* II 10, and, on exactness, I 3 269^{b}21n.

Note 278

If nature always produces the best of the things that are possible: See I 1 268^{a}13n.

And if, just as in the case of rectilinear spatial movements, that toward the upper place is more estimable (for the upper place is more divine than the lower): See I 2 269^{a}30–32n, II 1 284^{a}11–13, and on esteem, I 2 269^{b}16n.

And in the same way too forward spatial movement is more estimable than backward: See II 2 284^{b}28n.

And if indeed [the heaven] has a right and a left: Reading ἔχει δέ with Verdenius, p. 278, DP and some mss. for Moraux ἔχει.

As was said previously: At II 2 285^{a}31.

It has a priority and a posteriority: That is, a front (that it faces and moves in the direction it faces) and a back.

Note 279

Regular (*homalês*) and not irregular (*anômalos*): "A movement is said to be one . . . [also] when it is regular. For an irregular movement seems in a way not to be one, while a regular one does seem so, as a rectilinear one does. For an irregular one is divisible. The difference, though, would seem to be one of the more and less. In the case of every sort of movement, however, it may proceed regularly or not. For a thing may alter in a regular way, and move spatially in a regular path (for example, in a circle or in a straight line), and it is the same with regard to increase and decrease. And irregularity is sometimes a differentiation (*diaphora*) in the path of the movement (for a movement cannot be regular if its path is an irregular magnitude—for example, a broken line, a spiral, or any other magnitude that is not such that any random part fits on to any other random part). Sometimes, though, it lies neither in the place nor in the time nor in that to which, but in the manner, since sometimes the movement is differentiated by fastness and slowness. For if its speed remains the same, it is regular, but if it does not, it is irregular. . . . Irregular movement, then, while it is one in virtue of being continuous, is less so, just as is the case with spatial movement in a broken line. And what is less so always involves an admixture of the contrary. But if every movement that is one admits of being both regular and irregular, movements that are contiguous but not the same in species cannot be one and continuous. For how could a movement composed of an alteration and a spatial movement be regular? For if a movement is to be regular it must fit together" (*Ph.* V 4 228^{b}15–229^{a}6).

Note 280

In the lower [places] several spatial movements have already come together into one: See II 12 292^{b}4–11.

Note 281

Perhaps for things spatially moving in accord with nature it is at the point to which they move, for those that move contrary to nature it is at the one from which they move, and for projectiles at the mid-point: The thought, apparently, is that projectiles, as having a mixture of movement in accord with nature and movement contrary to nature, have a top-speed that is itself in a mean between their top-speeds. For similar reasoning, see IV 5 312^{a}28–31.

Note 282

In time it is eternal and in length joined in one (*sunêgmenê*) and unbroken: "It is not possible for a thing to move continuously in a semicircle or in any other arc. For it would of necessity make the same movement repeatedly and change to contrary changes. For the starting-point and limit are not united, whereas in circular movement they are, and it alone is complete" (*Ph.* VIII 8 264^{b}24–28).

Note 283

It is necessary for irregularity of movement to come about either because of the mover, because of the thing moved, or because of both: "[Aristotle] seems to have omitted another cause of irregularity in a movement, namely, difference in the medium through which the movement occurs. . . . For if the medium is fine-grained, the movement through it is faster, but if it is denser, the movement is slower. However, since the heavenly body is continuous with itself and has nothing outside it, it has nothing as a medium" (Simp. 426.32–427.3 = Mueller, p. 80).

Note 284

It has been shown that the thing moved is primary, simple, incapable of coming to be, and wholly unchangeable: See I 2–3.

Note 285

Since, then, the thing moved, which is a body, does not change, neither will its mover, which is incorporeal, change: See II 1 284^{a}27–^{b}5n.

Note 286

Incapacity (*adunamia*) is contrary to nature: See I 11 281^{a}2n.

Note 287

[1] The incapacities in animals are all contrary to nature—for example, old age and wasting away: [2] "All passing away that is in accord with nature is a road to decay—for example old age and withering" (*Mete.* IV 1 379^{a}4–5); "Old age is a natural (*phusikên*) disease" (*GA* V 784^{b}33–34). The apparent conflict between [1] and [2], noted by DP, p. 435 n6), is removed if we consider the difference between nature considered as (a) form and (b) as form + matter: "If it belongs to the same science to know the form and, up to a point, the matter (for example, it belongs to the doctor to know health, and also bile and phlegm, in which health resides, and to the builder to know the form of a house, and also the matter, that it is bricks and beams, and similarly in the case of the others), then it belongs to the natural scientist to know both natures" (*Ph.* II 2 194ª22–27). For [1] is consistent with [2] when nature is understood as (a) in [1] and (b) in [2]. For what causes an animal to age and wither away naturally is not its form, but the matter in which its form is realized, which, precisely because it is not in its proper place or places (*Cael.* II 6 288ᵇ16–18), has a built-in tendency to resist form and finally overcome it, resulting in death. It is (partly) for this reason, indeed, that the heaven, because it is eternal, must be composed of something other than earth, water, fire, and air, namely, ether or primary body.

Note 288

The primary things (*tois prôtois*): The primary things (*ta prôta*) in the wholly unconditional sense are the primary substances (*Met.* XI 1 1059ª33–34), and of these, the most primary is the one that is simple and an activity (XII 7 1072ª31–32). Consequently, it has no matter (or no reference to matter) in its essence (6 1071ᵇ19–21, 8 1074ª35–36). Unlike the essences of matter-form compounds, therefore, which have a structure like that of the compounds themselves (VII 11 1037ª9–10), its essence is not a compound of this form in this matter, both taken universally (5 1030ᵇ14–20). Equivalently, in its essence the activation or form is not predicated or said of anything else, in the way that it is predicated or said of the matter in matter-form compounds (VIII 2 1043ª5–6), and so in their similarly structured essences. That is why it is said or expressed "*not* by way of saying one thing of another" (VII 4 1030ª10–11; see also IX 10 1051ᵇ17–1052ª4). It is for this reason, too, that the primary things are what the most exact science—theoretical wisdom—is concerned with (I 2 982ª25–26n). For as the starting-points of unconditional demonstrations (V 5 1015ᵇ8–9), they are the primary starting-points and causes (I 2 982ᵇ1–4), so that "if they were not, nothing would be" (IX 8 1050ᵇ19). See also *GC* II 9 335ª29 "eternal and primary things."

The primary things . . . are . . . in their proper space (*tê[i] oikeia[i] chôra[i]*): *Chôra* ("space," "region") is usually equivalent in meaning to *topos* ("place") (*Ph.* IV 1 208ᵇ7, 209ª8). Place, however, is "the limit of what encompasses something at which it is in contact with what is encompassed" (4 212ª5–6a), which seems to entail that the primary heaven cannot be in a place, proper or otherwise, since there is nothing outside it to encompass it (*Cael.* I 9 278ᵇ11–18). One way to resolve this apparent inconsistency, which Aristotle seems unaware of, or untroubled by if he is aware of it, is to speak in the counterfactual way that he does when he says of the primary heaven that "even if it never began moving, nonetheless it is necessary for it to have a starting-point from which it would have begun if it had begun moving, and, if it were to come to a stop, from which it would start moving again"

(II 2 285^{b}6–8). For then we can say that *if there were* something encompassing the heaven, then the heaven would be in its proper place. Alternatively, and without resorting to the counterfactual, we can say that "the limit of a natural body," in contrast with the abstract limit studied by mathematicians (*Ph.* II 193^{b}31–32), is located, like the skin, where the body it defines is located.

Note 289
Nothing appears to be contrary to nature for an unlimited time (and incapacity is contrary to nature), nor contrary to nature and in accord with nature for an equal time, nor, in general, capable and incapable for an equal time: It is important to recall the unlimited past not just of the heaven itself, but also of observation of it. See I 3 270^{b}16–25.

Note 290
It is necessary, if the movement decelerates, that it do so for an unlimited time: What is unreasonable is incapacity followed by capacity (II 6 288^{b}22–23), or deceleration followed by acceleration (288^{b}20–22), so if there is incapacity/deceleration, it must last for an unlimited time.

Note 291
All movement, we say, is from something to something, that is, definite: For example, I 8 277^{a}14–20.

Note 292
This, though, is entirely unreasonable and like a fabrication: "By 'fabricated' I mean 'forced to fit with a hypothesis'" (*Met.* XIII 7 1082^{b}3–4).

Note 293
Further, if such were the case, it is also more reasonable that it not go unnoticed. For things put next to each other are easier to perceive: Another place where it is important to recall the unlimited past not just of the heaven itself, but also of observation of it. See II 6 288^{b}23–26.

Note 294
We said that there is something that is of a nature to spatially move in a circle: See I 2–3.

Note 295
Those who declare that the stars are fiery do so because they say that the upper body is fire: See I 2 269^{b}10–11n.

Note 296
The heat and light from the stars come about when air is chafed by their spatial movement: The implication in our text that there is air in contact with the

sphere of the stars (which include the sun and moon) is explicitly embraced in II 9: "if indeed the bodies of the stars are moving either in a quantity of air or of fire spread through the universe, *as everyone says*" (291ª18–20). But it is also suggested by the following text: "We say that [1] what is upper (*to anô*) as far as the moon (*mechri selênês*) is [2] a body distinct from air or fire, but varying in purity and freedom from admixture, and admitting of difference (*diaphoras echein*), especially [3] toward its limit on the side of the air, and the cosmos surrounding the earth" (*Mete.* I 3 340ᵇ6–10). For since [2] refers to ether (primary body) and attributes variation to it, especially as it gets closer to (roughly) the earth and its atmosphere, [1] must refer to the upper region of the cosmos *down* as far as the moon (see Wilson, especially pp. 42–48; and for a forceful argument that [1] refers to the region *up* as far as the moon, Baksa). The fieriness of the lunar region is evidenced by the following texts: "The outermost part of what is called 'the air' has the capacity of fire" (8 345ᵇ33–34); "the air . . . is composed of . . . vapor, which is wet and cold, . . . and smoke, which is hot and dry" (II 4 360ª21–25); "The fourth genus [of animals] must not be sought in these places [land, water, air], although there certainly wants (*bouletai*) to be one corresponding to fire in the order. For it is counted as the fourth of the [simple] bodies. But fire always appears to have a shape [= form] that is not special to it, on the contrary, it is always in another of the bodies. For what is on fire appears to be either air, smoke, or earth. Instead, this fourth genus must be sought on the moon. For it appears to participate in [the body] at the fourth remove [= fire]" (*GA* III 11 761ᵇ15–22). No parallel explanation of the light from the stars is given, but one is easily provided by appeal to the account of light in *DA* II 12: "It is not insofar as something is water or insofar as it is air that it is visible, but because there is a certain nature in it that is the same in both of them and in the [eternal] body above [= ether]. And light is the activity of this, of the transparent insofar as it is transparent. But whatever this is present in, so potentially is darkness. For light is a sort of color of the transparent, when it is made actually transparent by fire or something of that sort, such as the body above. For one and the same [affection] also belongs to it" (418ᵇ7–13). Thus as the air mixed in with the ether explains, via friction, the heat from the stars, so the ether mixed in with the air explains their light.

Note 297

These missiles themselves, then, are heated up because of their spatial movement in air, which becomes fire because of a blow struck by the movement: "We see that movement is capable of disaggregating (*diakrinein*) and igniting air, so that even things in spatial movement often appear to melt. The sun's spatial movement, then, is sufficient by itself to produce warmth and provide heat. For to do so it must be fast and not too far away. Now, the spatial movement of the [fixed] stars, though fast, is far off, while that of the moon, though close by, is slow. But that of the sun has enough of both characteristics. That more heat should be generated when the sun itself is there is reasonable, if we take the similarity from what comes about where we are. For here too it is the air that is closest to what is spatially moving by force that becomes most hot. And this happens quite reasonably. For the movement of a solid object disaggregates it most. This, then, is one cause due to which heat reaches this place here. Another is that the fire encompassing the air is often dispersed by the [sun's] movement and by force carried downward" (*Mete.* I 3 341ª17–31).

Note 298

The whole heaven: That is the sphere to which the relevant stars are fixed and by which they are carried in circular orbits. For the details see *Met.* XII 8—the pertinent sections are quoted in I 9 279ª18–22n(2).

Note 299

The speeds of the stars and of their circles: See previous note.

Note 300

Luck is not found in things that are by nature, and what holds by luck is not what holds everywhere and in all cases: See, on nature, I 12 283ª33n, and, on luck, I 1 268ª13n.

Note 301

The outer stars: The ones "that are further from the poles [of the cosmos]" (Simp. 448.28 = Mueller, p. 105), and so closest to its equator.

Note 302

It is not reasonable either that [2] both move or [3] that the star alone does: Reading τὸ ἄστρον μόνον with Allan, Guthrie, and some mss. for Moraux and other mss. τὸ ἕτερον μόνον.

Note 303

As in the case of other things the greater body carries out its own proper spatial movement faster, so it is too in the case of circular bodies: So that things in the superlunary region obey the same laws of motion as those "other things" that are in the sublunary one.

Note 304

Of arcs cut off by lines from the center, that of the greater circle is greater, so that it is reasonable for the greater circle [and the smaller one] to rotate in an equal time: Alexander of Aphrodisias raises the following problem for this claim: "It is true in the case of circles in the fixed sphere that a greater circle is restored [to the same place] in an equal time as a smaller one, but it is not true in the case of the planetary spheres, either with respect to their own proper movement [from west to east] (since they are restored [to the same place] in a different time) or with respect to their movement together with the universe (since each is left behind by that movement to the extent that in its own movement it moves in a reverse direction to that of the universe). That is why the stars in the planetary spheres appear not to be restored [to the same place] at the same time as the fixed stars they happen to be in conjunction with, but they are left behind" (Simp. 150.15–24 = Mueller, p. 107).

Note 305

Because it has been shown that the whole is continuous: The reference is presumably to II 4 287ª2–11 (= [*Argument 1*]), 287ª30–ᵇ14 (= [*Argument 4*]).

The result is that the heaven is not dispersed: For a different argument for a related conclusion, see *Met.* XII 10.

Note 306

The stars are spherical, as others too say, and for us it is consistent to say, generating them as we do from that body [namely, ether]: See II 4.

Rolling (*kulisis*) **and rotation** (*dinêsis*): "Rotation occurs when a sphere turns around its own axis in the same place; rolling when it [also] changes place" (Simp. 452.18–19 = Mueller, p. 110).

Note 307

The sun seems to [rotate] . . . not because of itself [rotating], but because of the distance from our [1] sight (*opseôs*). **For [2] sight** (*opsis*), **when extended a great distance, wobbles** (*helissetai*) **because of its weakness. This is also the very cause, perhaps, of the stars appearing to twinkle, and of the planets' not appearing to twinkle. For the planets are close by, so that [3] sight** (*opsis*) **reaches them while it is strong, but when it reaches the fixed stars, it shakes because it is stretched out too far:** *Opsis* (*opseôs* is the genitive) must surely have the same meaning in [1–3], and it must be something that [3] extends from the eye to the visual object and that progressively weakens as it gets farther from the eye [1, 3], and that becomes increasing subject to perturbation as it weakens. Now, one possibility (embraced, for example, by Stocks) is that Aristotle, at this stage in his thought, accepted Plato's theory of vision, in which an *opsis* is a "ray of sight" (*Ti.* 67d–e) emitted from the eye as a sort of light (45d–e). But already in the *Topics*, Aristotle rejects such a view: "we see by taking something in, not sending something out (for it is this way too in the case of the other perceptual capacities, since we hear by taking something in, not sending something out, taste in the same way, and similarly too in the case of the others)" (*Top.* I 14 105ᵇ7–10). Moreover, when *opsis* occurs again at *Cael.* II 11 291ᵇ19, it certainly cannot refer to rays of any sort. But consider how naturally even we talk of sight as penetrative—a gaze is penetrating, we say, and the fog too dense for our sight to penetrate. What we should infer, then, from this natural way of talking is that speaking of an *opsis* as wobbling is a sort of convenient metonymy. What is actually distorted and weakened when too far stretched out is the light reflected from (or in the case of the sun, for example, emitted by) the object, the sight of which, as a result, wobbles, shakes, and is dim (an *opsis* can also be a visual impression or image, as at Plato, *Tht.* 193c). Aristotle also talks in this way *GA* V I 781ª3–12: "It makes no difference whether we say, as some do, that seeing is due to the *opsis* [= ray of sight] going out from the eye (for if there is nothing projecting over the eyes, it is necessary for the *opsis* to be dispersed, for less of it to fall on the things being seen, and for the ones far away to be seen less well) or that seeing is due to the movement coming from the things being seen. For it is necessary for the *opsis* to resemble the movement. Things far away, then, would be seen best if there were a sort of continuous tube straight from the organ of sight to the thing being seen. For then the movement from visible objects would not be dispersed; otherwise, the farther the tube extends, the more exact it is necessary for the seeing of faraway things to be."

Note 308

Instrument (*organon*): An *organon* is often what we would naturally call an "organ," but just as often it refers to some part of an animal, such as a foot, that we would not call one, or to a craftsman's tools, making "instrument" a preferable translation in many cases.
Nature does nothing by luck: See, on nature, I 12 283ᵃ33n, and, on luck, I 1 268ᵃ13n.
Estimable: See I 2 269ᵇ16n.

Note 309

The sphere is the shape best adapted for movement within itself: That is, for movement with the place defined by its own surface boundary. See II 4 287ᵃ15–19.

Note 310

It has nothing appended (*apêrtêmenon*) **or projecting** (*proechon*), **as in a rectilinear figure** (*to euthugrammon*), **but stands farthest apart from the shape of bodies capable of perambulation:** The verb *apartan* means "detach," "separate," and also "hang loose," so that the participle used here applies to appendages, such as limbs, that are somewhat separate from the main body or trunk. *To euthugrammon* is the figure (a polyhedron) referred to as such at II 4 287ᵃ16. The projections or appendages are presumably the angles or edges of its faces, which are imagined as sticking out from the inscribed sphere.
Capable of perambulation (*poreutikon*): Or so-called "progressive movement," as in the treatise, *The Progression of Animals*.

Note 311

The stars: Reading τὰ δ᾽ἄστρα with DP and some mss. for Moraux τὰ δ᾽ἄλλα [ἄστρα].

Note 312

Though stated in an extraordinarily subtle way (*kompsôs*): See II 13 295ᵇ16n.
By those who express it: Identified at II 9 291ᵃ8 as Pythagoreans, particularly (perhaps) Archytas of Tarentum (see F1 Huffman-2 and pp. 131–132).

Note 313

These things, then, as was said earlier, are harmoniously and musically stated: See II 9 290ᵇ14.

Note 314

They do try to resolve [the puzzle] about its cause: Reading περὶ οὗ λύειν ἐγχειροῦσι τὴν αἰτίαν with Verdenius, p. 279, DP, and the mss. for Moraux περὶ οὗ λέγειν ἐγχειροῦσι τὴν αἰτίαν ("they do try to state the cause concerning it").

Note 315

Proof: See I 8 277ᵃ11n.

Note 316

When [something] is in, and continuous with, something spatially moving and does not produce a blow, it cannot produce a sound: "When a sound actively comes about, however, it is always of something, in relation to something, and in something. For a blow is what produces it" (*DA* II 8 419ᵇ9–11).

Note 317

If indeed the bodies of the stars are moving either in a quantity of air or of fire spread through the universe, as everyone says, it is necessary for them to produce a sound of enormous magnitude: Notice that Aristotle does not argue that the stars cannot produce sound because there is not air or fire where they are. Instead, he argues that they cannot make one because they, though not the spheres in which they are carried, are not moving at all in the way that produces blows and sounds. For the importance of this, see II 7 289ᵃ19–21n. The friction that the spheres cause by rubbing against the air (like a ship gliding silently through water) is presumably not sufficiently percussive to produce sound.

Note 318

The way in which each is positioned: Reading ἕκαστα κεῖται with Guthrie, DP, and one mss. for Moraux, Allan, and most mss. ἕκαστα κινεῖται ("the way in which each moves").

Some being prior and some posterior, that is, how they are related to each other with respect to their distances: "It is necessary for those who discuss heavenly things also to discuss the order with respect to position (*thesin*) of the spheres and the stars and to say which ones are prior, that is, more proximate to the fixed stars, and which are posterior, that is, closer to the earth" (Simp. 470.29–31 = Mueller, p. 11).

On the basis of astronomical accounts: Those developed by "the mathematicians" referred to at II 10 291ᵃ9–10, and named in *Met.* XII 8 as Eudoxus of Cnidus, an important mathematician, astronomer, and philosopher (c. 390–c. 340 BC) who developed the general theory of proportion for incommensurable as well as commensurable magnitudes, and Callippus of Cyzicus (fl. c. 330 BC), who studied with Eudoxus, and is said to have stayed with Aristotle in Athens. Aristotle's discussion of the number of celestial spheres in *Met.* XII 8 draws on Eudoxus' system, and also on Callippus' additions to Eudoxus' system of homocentric spheres. See also I 9 279ᵃ18–22n and II 4 287ᵇ34–288ᵃ2n.

Note 319

The closest is most of all controlled (*krateitai*) **by the primary locomotion, the farthest away least of all, because of its distance:** "What then? Do the spheres closer to the fixed sphere move more slowly because they are forced to by that sphere? And yet if it is by force, they also move in a completely unnatural way. So both of their movements, that from the east in which they are carried around by the fixed sphere and their own movement from the west, would be forced and contrary to nature" (Simp. 472.4–7 = Mueller, p. 12). How should this puzzle be resolved? The answer lies in the verb *kratein*, or—better—in the sort of control it refers to, whether as a sort of direct efficient causal influence, or in some other way.

Although, as entirely contemplative, Aristotle's primary god (the unmoved mover) issues no prescriptions he is analogized to prescriptive rulers, such as the general of an army and the ruler of a city (*Met.* XII 10 1075^{a}11–25, 1075^{b}37–1076^{a}4). Similarly, our own understanding (*nous*), though its purview is restricted to cognizing the starting-points of the sciences (*Cael.* I 1 268^{a}1n(5)) is characterized as the constituent in the soul that has "most control (*kuriôtatô[i]*)" (*NE* IX 8 1168^{b}30; at 1168^{b}35 *kratein* is used) and the one a virtuous person "obeys in everything" (1168^{b}31). In the following text the analogous roles of the two are explicitly described: "It is clear, then, that just as in the universe [the starting-point of movement] is god, so it is [in the soul] too. For the divine thing in us [= the understanding] in a way moves everything. Of reason (*logos*), however, the starting-point is not reason, but something superior. But what besides god is superior even to scientific knowledge and understanding? For virtue is an instrument of understanding" (*EE* VIII 2 1248^{a}25–29).

Holding these thoughts, let us next move to *Met.* XII 8 and to the argument given there for the uniqueness of the heaven:

> It is evident that there is but one heaven. For if there are many, as there are many humans, the starting-point for each will be one in form but in number many. But all things that are many in number have matter, for one and the same account applies to many, for example, humans, whereas Socrates is one. But the primary essence does not have matter, since it is an actuality. The primary immovable mover, therefore, is one both in account and in number. And so, therefore, is what is moved always and continuously. Therefore, there is only one heaven. (1074^{a}31–38)

The argument is difficult because it moves from the immateriality of an immovable mover to its uniqueness, via the claim that (1) "all things that are many in number have matter" (1074^{a}33–34; also VII 8 1034^{a}5–8). But (1) seems flatly inconsistent with the conclusion just reached in XII 8 to the effect that (2) there are forty-seven (or forty-nine) immovable movers, all of which are substances, and none of which has matter (6 1071^{b}20–21). We should bear in mind, however, that all the immovable movers except the primary one are inside the sphere of the primary heaven (*Cael.* I 9 279^{a}11–28), and so are in space and time in a way that the prime mover alone is not. This suggests or implies that even if these other immovable movers are in some way immaterial they nonetheless have a close enough association with the superlunary material element ether constituting their spheres to account for their multiplicity. The fact that these spheres, as celestial animals, are analogous in structure to ourselves helps us to make some sense of what this association might be.

The soul of the primary heaven needs to have both an understanding and wish, which is "always found in the rationally calculative part" of the soul (*Top.* IV 5 126^{a}13), if it is to be moved by the prime mover as the object of its wish (*Met.* XII 7 1072^{a}26–27). The primary mover, by contrast, just is an understanding (9 1074^{b}34–35), and so has no wish. Understanding differs from the rationally calculative part, however, in that it alone is separate from the matter-form compound, and thus from the soul regarded as the form of the body. That is why it alone of the parts of the soul is immortal (3 1070^{a}23–26). To say that the primary mover has no matter, then, is literally true; to say that the other immovable movers do not is an overstatement, since they essentially have a rationally calculative part, and it does have matter, just as anger and snubness do (*DA* I 5 403^{a}24–^{b}18). But it is not merely an overstatement. For in characterizing the relationship between us and our understanding Aristotle tells us that "just as a city too or any other complex system, seems to be most of all) its most controlling part [= the understanding)], so also does a human being" (*NE* IX 8 1168^{b}31–32; see also *Cael.* I 3 270^{b}11n). So just as we *are* our understandings because we are *most of all* these, the same we may suppose is surely true of the non-primary immovable movers. They are not without matter. That is true. But they are most of all something without matter. And the reason they are, since it applies to all complex systems, must be a general teleological one: a complex system is most of all that element for the sake of which all its movements and actions occur. That, in fact, is just what Aristotle has shown to be true of the celestial spheres (*Met.* X 8 1074^{a}17–31).

Putting all this together, then, in a way that more-or-less just elaborates on what we find in *Cael.* II 12 292^{a}14–293^{a}11, what we should say is this: The control exerted by the primary heaven (the outermost sphere) is probably best understood not as direct efficient causal influence, of a roughly mechanical sort, but as an indirect sort, mediated by the desires of the immaterial movers of the spheres, the strength of which is proportional to their distance from the happy state that only the mover of the outermost sphere fully attains. Thus even though the movements of these spheres are influenced by the primary locomotion, the fact that the influence is mediated by their own desires, which are reflective of their very positions in the celestial order, insures that they are no more forced or contrary to nature than the reproductive activities of the sublunary animals: "The most natural function in those living things that are complete and not disabled or spontaneously generated, to produce another like itself—an animal producing an animal, a plant a plant—in order that they may partake in the eternal and divine insofar as they can. For all desire that, and it is for the sake of it that they do whatever they do by nature. (The for-the-sake-of-which, though, is twofold—the purpose for which and the beneficiary for whom.) Since, then, they cannot share in what is eternal and divine by continuous existence, because nothing that admits of passing away can persist as the same and numerically one, they share in them insofar as each can, some more and some less. And what persists is not the thing itself but something like itself, not one in number but one in form" (*DA* II 4 415^{a}26–^{b}7). Human beings are no different in this regard: "Those who cannot be without each other necessarily form a couple, as female and male do for the sake of generating offspring (they do not do so because they deliberately choose to, but, like other animals and plants, because the urge to leave behind something of the same kind as themselves is natural)" (*Pol.* I 2 1252^{a}26–30).

Note 320
Since it has been shown that they are not naturally such as to move because of themselves: See II 8.
Nature produces nothing unreasonably or pointlessly: See I 1 268^{a}13n.

Note 321
Waxing and waning (*auxanomenê kai phthinousa*): Usually, increasing and decreasing.

Note 322
And, again (*palin*), **[it is shown] through astronomy that eclipses of the sun would not be crescent-shaped:** It is unclear by whom this was shown, but *palin* may refer us back to II 10 291^{a}32 (see associated note).

Note 323
There are two puzzles (*aporiain*): See I 7 279^{b}8n.
About which we must try to state what appears to be so (*to phainomenon*): See *NE* VII 1 1145^{b}2–7 (Introduction p. xlix) and, on *phainomena*, I 1 268^{a}1n.
Thinking such audaciousness (*prothumia*) **to be reverence** (*aidous*) **rather than rashness** (*thrasous*): *Prothumia* occurred previously at II 5 287^{b}31; *aidôs*: "shame" in *NE*; but here "reverence," "awe," "respect" is the meaning; *thrasos*: "the one who is excessive in his confidence is rash, and the one who is excessively fearful and deficient in confidence is cowardly" (*NE* II 7 1107^{b}2–4).
If someone, because of his thirst for philosophy: "The mathematical science that is most akin to philosophy [is] astronomy" (*Met.* XII 8 1073^{b}4–5). See also, *Cael.* I 8 277^{a}10n.
Is content to become a little more puzzle-free (*euporias*) **concerning the things about which we have the greatest puzzlement** (*aporias*): See Introduction, pp. xxxvii–l.

Note 324
Wandering stars (*planômenôn astrôn*): That is, planets.
The sun and the moon move with fewer movements than some of the wandering stars: In *Met.* XII 8, three versions of the theory of homocentric spheres are considered: Eudoxus', Callippus', and Aristotle's own theory. In Eudoxus' theory,

the sun and the moon have 3 movements each, the other planets 4 each. So they have fewer movements than *all* of the planets. In Callippus' theory the sun and the moon have 5 movements each, as do Venus, Mercury, and Mars, while Jupiter and Saturn have 4. So in his theory they have fewer movements than none of the planets. In Aristotle's view, however, "if all the spheres combined are to account for the appearances, then for each of the planets there must be other spheres, but one fewer, which counteract the former, and in each case restore to the same position the first [or outermost] sphere of the star that is placed beneath the star in question. For only in this way is it possible for all the combined spheres to produce the spatial movements of the planets" (*Met.* XII 8 1073^{b}36–1074^{a}5). Starting with the primary or outermost heaven, then, we have on his theory a series of concentric spheres encircling the earth. The sphere of the moon is the innermost celestial sphere, so that below it there is no other. Suppose, then, that A (outermost), B, C, D (innermost) are the four spheres to which, according to Eudoxus and Callippus, Saturn is affixed. Inside sphere D, Aristotle inserts a first reactive sphere D*, which rotates on the poles of D and at the same speed, but in the opposite direction. The rotations of D and D* cancel each other, so that any point on D* will move as if rigidly connected to C. Inside D*, in turn, is placed a second reactive sphere C*, which is related to C as D* is to D, so that any point of C* will move as if rigidly connected to B. Finally, inside C* is placed B*, with the result that any point on B* will move as if rigidly connected to A. But A, as the outermost sphere of Saturn, has the movement of the fixed stars, hence B* will also have that movement. As a result the spheres of Jupiter, which are inside those of Saturn, can move inside B* as if Saturn's spheres did not exist and as if B* were the sphere of the fixed stars. Thus the moon moves with 5 movements (+ none counteracting) the sun with 5 (+ 4 counteracting); Jupiter and Saturn 4 (+ 3 counteracting) each, Mercury, Venus, and Mars with 5 (+ 4 counteracting) each. So here too the sun and the moon fewer movements than none of the planets. It may be, then, that what we have in *Cael.* II 12 is not Aristotle's "mature" theory, assuming that is what we have in *Met.* XII 8, but an earlier version of it. See Easterling, pp. 138–141. Alternatively, the reference may be a weaker than justified ("some of the wandering stars" rather than "all of the wandering stars") characterization of Eudoxus' theory.

Note 325

We have seen the moon, when half-full, move under the star of Ares [Mars], which was occulted by the dark half of the moon, and come out on its light and bright side: Dating the sighting (according to Longrigg, p. 174) to May 4 357 BC between 7:49 and 8:00 pm, Athens mean time. This, however, is subject to a "clock error" of about 1,000 seconds. See Bodnár, especially p. 244.

Note 326

Comprehension (*sunesis*): In one sense *sunesis* is concerned exclusively with practical matters: "What is *sunesis* and with what is it concerned? *Sunesis* operates in the same areas as practical wisdom also does—that concerned with matters of action. For someone is said to have *sunesis* because of his capacity for deliberation, that is (*kai*), in that he judges and sees things correctly; but the judgment is about small matters and in small areas. *Sunesis* is a part of practical wisdom, then, and being a *sunetos* is part of being a practically wise man, since to separate the *sunetos* from the practically wise is impossible" (*MM* I 34 1197^{b}11–17; compare *NE* VI 10 1042^{b}34–1043^{a}8). Here, however, it has the rather different sense in which it involves knowledge of causes and is not exclusively practical: "We regard knowledge and comprehension as characteristic of craft rather than of experience, and take it that craftsmen are wiser than experienced people, on the supposition that in every case wisdom follows along rather with knowledge than with experience. This is because craftsmen know the cause (*aitian*), whereas experienced people do not. For experienced people know the that but do not know the why, whereas craftsmen know the why, that is, the cause" (*Met.* I 1 981^{a}24–30).

Note 327

Action (*praxeôs*): The noun *praxis* (plural: *praxeis*; verb: *prattein*) is used in a broad sense to refer to any intentional action, including one performed by a child or wild beast (*NE* III 1 1111^{a}25–26, 2 1111^{b}8–9), and in a narrower one to refer exclusively to what results from deliberation (*bouleusis*) and deliberate choice (*prohairesis*), of which neither beasts nor children are capable (I 9 1099^{b}32–1100^{a}5, *EE* II 8 1224^{a}28–29). Both senses are involved in our text, as the reference to the praxis of animals and plants at II 12 292^{b}1–2 makes clear.

A *praxis* in this second sense is usually contrasted with a *poiêsis* ("production"), and what distinguishes the two is that the latter is always performed for the sake of some further end, whereas a *praxis* can be its own end: "Thought by itself, however, moves nothing. But the one that is for the sake of something and practical does. Indeed, it even rules productive thought. For every producer produces for the sake of something, and what is unconditionally an end (as opposed to in relation to something and for something else) is not what is producible but what is doable in action. For doing well in action (*eupraxia*) [= *eudaimonia* or happiness] is the end, and the desire is for it" (*NE* VI 2 1139^{a}35–^{b}4).

Thus the distinction between a *praxis* and a *poiêsis* is a special case of a more general distinction Aristotle draws between an *energeia* ("activity") (*Cael.* I 12 281^{b}22n) and a *kinêsis* ("movement"; plural: *kinêseis*): "Since, though, of the actions that have a limit none is an end, but all are in relation to an end (for example, making thin), and since the things themselves, when one is making them thin, are in movement in this way, [namely,] that what the movement is for the sake of does not yet belong to them, these [movements] are not cases of action, at least not of complete action, since none is an end. But the sort in which the end belongs *is* an action. For example, at the same time one is seeing [a thing] and has seen [it], is thinking and has thought, is understanding [something] and has understood [it], whereas it is not the case that [at the same time] one is learning [something] and has learned [it], nor that one is being made healthy and has been made healthy. Someone who is living well, however, at the same time has lived well, and is happy and has been happy [at the same time]. If this were not so, these would have to come to an end at some time, as when one is making [something] thin.

But as things stand it is not so, but one is living and has lived. Of these, then, one sort should be called movements and the other activities. For every movement is incomplete, for example, making thin, learning, walking, building. These are movements and are certainly incomplete. For it is not the case that at the same time one is walking and has taken a walk, nor that one is building [something] and has built [it], or is coming to be [something] and has come to be [it], or is being moved [in some way] and has been moved [in that way], but they are different, as are one's moving and having moved [something]. By contrast one has seen and is seeing the same thing at the same time, or is understanding and has understood. The latter sort, then, I call an activity, the former a movement" (*Met.* IX 6 1048^{b}18–35). Expressed linguistically, the contrast is one of aspect rather than tense. Roughly speaking, a verb whose present tense has imperfective meaning designates a *kinêsis*, while one whose present tense has perfective meaning designates an *energeia*. The distinction itself is ontological, however, not linguistic: *energeiai* and *kinêseis* are types of beings, not types of verbs. A *poiêsis* or *kinêsis* is something that takes time to complete and, like the time it takes, is infinitely divisible (*Ph.* III 7 207^{b}21–25, *Met.* V 13 1020^{a}26–32). It has a definite termination point or limit, before which it is incomplete and after which it cannot continue (*NE* X 4 1174^{a}21–23). A *praxis*, by contrast, does not take time to complete, and so does not really occur "in time" (*Ph.* VIII 8 262^{b}20–21) but is temporally point-like (*NE* X 4 1174^{b}12–13). Having no definite termination, while it may stop, it need never finish (*Met.* IX 6 1048^{b}25–27).

Life (*zôês*): Two Greek words correspond to the English word "life": *zôê*, used here, and *bios*. *Zôê* refers to the sorts of life processes and activities studied by biologists, zoologists, psychologists, and so on, such as growth, reproduction, perception, and understanding. *Bios* refers to the sort of life a natural historian or biographer might investigate—the life of the otter, the life of Pericles—and so to a span of time throughout which someone possesses *zôê* at least as a capacity (*NE* I 13 1102^{b}5–7). Thus, in the conclusion of the famous function argument, we are reminded that a certain *zôê* will not be happiness for a human being unless it occurs "in a complete *bios*" (I 7 1098^{a}18–20). And so it is *zôê* that the primary god enjoys (see next note).

Note 328

In this way what happens will not seem at all contrary to reason: Compare: "We consider that we have adequately demonstrated in accord with reason (*logos*) things unapparent to perception if we have led things back to what is possible" (*Mete.* I 7 344^{a}5–7).

Note 329

It seems that the good (*to eu*) **belongs without action** (*aneu praxeôs*) **to what is in the best state** (*arista echonti*): What is being described, as the following text shows, is the primary god (the immovable mover of the primary heaven): "What is receptive of the intelligible object and of the substance is the understanding, and it is active when it possesses it, so that this rather than that seems to be the divine thing that understanding possesses, and contemplation seems to be most pleasant and best. If, then, that good state (*eu echei*) [of activity], which we are sometimes in, the [primary] god is always in, that is a wonderful thing, and if to a higher degree, that is yet more wonderful. But that is his state. And life (*zôê*) too certainly belongs to him. For the activity of understanding is life, and he is that activity; and his intrinsic activity is life that is best (*aristê*) and eternal. We say, indeed, that the god is a living being who is eternal and best, so that living and a continuous and everlasting eternity belong to the god, since this is the god" (*Met.* XII 1072^{b}22–30). What is puzzling about the description is that it characterizes the primary god as possessing the good "without action" while at the same time identifying him with contemplative activity, which is itself a sort of action. We find the same puzzle in *NE* X 8: "Everything to do with actions is petty and unworthy of gods. Nonetheless, everyone supposes them to be living, at least, and hence in activity, since surely they are not sleeping like Endymion. If, then, living has doing actions taken away from it and still more so producing, what is left except contemplating? So the activity of a god, superior as it is in blessedness, will be contemplative. And so the activity of humans, then, that is most akin to this will most bear the stamp of happiness" (1178^{b}17–23).

To resolve the puzzle our first port of call must be another puzzling text: "the [primary] god always enjoys a single simple pleasure. For there is not only an activity of moving but also an activity of immobility (*akinêsias*), and pleasure is found more in rest than in movement" (*NE* VII 13 1154^{b}26–28). Now "in the case of what movement belongs to, immobility is rest" (*Ph.* III 2 202^{a}5), but to the primary god, as we see, movement does not belong, so its immobility is not simply rest or lack of movement. Thus step one in the resolution of our puzzle is that god's immobility is not simply one of rest. That opens up the requisite possibility that it involves something else.

Second step: The paradigm cases of *actions*, as we understand them, are temporally extended bodily movements appropriately related to (perhaps by being caused by) beliefs, desires, and intentions. Hence "action" is clearly a somewhat misleading translation of *praxis* (on which, see *Cael.* II 12 292^{a}21n). Nonetheless, there is one type of action that *praxeis* seem to resemble quite closely, namely, so-called *basic actions*—actions we do directly without having to do anything else. This is especially true, if, as Aristotle himself seems to believe, these are thought to be *internal* mental acts of some: "we say that in the most controlling sense the ones who above all do actions, even in the case of external actions, are the ones who by means of their thoughts are their architectonic craftsmen" (*Pol.* VII 3 1325^{b}21–23). Like *praxeis*, in any case, these sorts of mental acts are not bodily movements and do not seem to take time to perform. Moreover, just as we do not perform basic actions by doing something else first, the same seems true of *praxeis*, so that a human being, for example, "is a starting-point and begetter of *praxeis* just as he is of children" (*NE* III 5 1113^{b}18–19; also VI 2 1139^{b}5). So what we should say, then, is that the good belongs without *external* action to what is in the best state. But that, of course, is quite consistent with its not doing so without internal actions, such as the contemplative ones in which the primary god's life exclusively consists.

Third step: Some actions are done both for their own sake and for the sake of other things, which may themselves be actions: "The activity of the practical virtues occurs in politics or in warfare, and the actions concerned with these seem to be unleisured and those in warfare completely so (for no one chooses to wage war for the sake of waging war, or to foment war either, since someone would seem completely bloodthirsty, if he made enemies of his friends in order to bring about battles and killings). But the activity of a politician too is unleisured and beyond political activity itself he tries to get positions of power and honors or, at any rate, happiness for himself and his fellow citizens—this being different from the exercise of politics and something we clearly seek on the supposition of its being different" (*NE* X 7 1177^{b}6–15). Other actions or activities, by contrast, are done solely for their own sake, and these (or this) are the ones in which happiness consists: "It is not necessary, as some suppose, for an action-involving (*praktikon*) life to be lived in relation to other people, nor are those thoughts alone action-involving that arise for the sake of the consequences of doing an action, rather, much more so are the acts of contemplation and thought that are their own ends and are engaged in for their own sake. For doing well in action is the end, and so action of a sort is the end too" (*Pol.* VII 3 1325^{b}17–21). In *Cael.* itself, Aristotle will shortly rely on this very point (II 12 292^{b}4–7).

Putting the three steps together, the entire solution to our puzzle is now before us: the good belongs without any action *that is either an external action or not exclusively an end* to what is in the best state.

Now, when a group of dramatic actions have a plot-structure (*mythos*) of the sort a good tragedy possesses, Aristotle says that they constitute a single action that is "one, whole, and complete" (*Po.* 23 1459^{a}19). By being enactments of the real-life equivalent of the relevant sort of plot or plan, therefore, the same should also be true of a group of non-dramatic actions. As a group of actors can set out to perform *Oedipus Tyrannus*, so a single agent can set out to enact a unified plan of action, which involves doing many different things in some sort of sequence. The complex action that fits this plan may be what constitutes his acting well—his *eupraxia*, his *eudaimonia*.

To understand why the agent is doing any of the things specified by the plan, we will typically need to see it in relation to the plan as a whole. For many of these, taken individually, might not be ends or goods choiceworthy for their own sakes: some might be otherwise valueless means to ends, some might be productions of needed equipment, some might be actions whose status as being intrinsically choiceworthy (because constitutive of *eupraxia*) nonetheless depends on their role in the plan. As parts of the whole complex action they help constitute, however, all *are* intrinsically choiceworthy, since the complex action is itself so. Hence the unified plan itself might be likened to the form of health in the soul of the doctor, which dictates the bodily movements that constitute, for example, producing the uniform state in a tense muscle, which is the relevant defining-mark of health (*Met.* VII 7 1032^{b}6–10). The actualization of the plan, the setting of it in motion, is an action, as is the carrying out of the subsequent steps. In performing each of them, the agent is achieving the goal of acting well. For acting well, since it is not an external end, is not something attained only when the plan is fully executed, as health is produced only when the muscles relax and the patient becomes healthy. At the same time, it does not seem to be an entirely internal end, either, since the plan may fail to be completely carried out.

We set the associated plan in motion, which is a basic action, but whether we will succeed in carrying it out fully is in part a matter of luck. If we fail through no fault of our own, we have in one way done what is required of us—we have tried, we have done all that we could do. In another way, though, we have failed, and may now have something more to do, such as try again, or make amends of some sort. The possibility of failure of this sort taints complex actions with unleisure, since it means there are usually obstacles or resistances to overcome in order to carry them out. Many—perhaps most—actions are surely complex. They would be unleisured, therefore, and subject to a sort of incompleteness, even if they had no additional external ends. We might think of a political constitution as a plan for a very complex action, with the citizens, who act in obedience to its laws and so on, as its executors or agents. Similarly, a household, which is part of a city with such a constitution, is also such an executor (*Pol.* I 13 1260^{b}8–20), and its "constitution"—its operating instructions—is itself a plan of action, which the members of the household put into effect by doing what it prescribes. Thus even when what it prescribes is a production, rather than an action proper, that production too becomes part of the complex action that is the household in activity.

In *Met.* XII 10 this way of looking at actions attains truly cosmic application, as it does in *Cael.* II 12 as well, when the universe itself is analogized first to a household and then to a political constitution: "All things are jointly organized in a way, although not in the same way—even swimming creatures, flying creatures, and plants. And the organization is not such that one thing has no relation to another but rather there is a relation. For all things are jointly organized in relation to one thing—but it is as in a household, where the free people least of all do things at random, but all or most of the things they do are organized, while the slaves and beasts can do a little for the common thing, but mostly do things at random. For this is the sort of starting-point that the nature is of each of them. I mean, for example, that all must at least come to be segregated [into their elements]; and similarly there are other things which they all share for [the good of] the whole" (1075^{a}16–25); "Beings, however, do not wish to be badly governed: 'To have many rulers is not good; let there be one ruler'" (1076^{a}3–4).

Note 330

While to another again this good would not yet belong no matter how much exertion he undergoes, but rather a distinct one: Namely, the next best thing. See II 12 292^{b}17–19.

Note 331

To make ten-thousand Chian throws at knucklebones (*astragalous*) is inconceivable: An *astragalos* is an ancient form of die made from the knucklebone of a sheep (Google "astragalus" for images). To have the bones land in a Chian configuration would evidently be like landing ten-thousand double sixes in throwing dice. On some of the difficulties involved in developing a more precise understanding of what is being described, see Mueller, p. 103 n75.

Note 332

It is easy to succeed at one stage or two: Reading ἑνὶ καὶ δυσὶ as *lectio difficilior* with Verdenius for Moraux ἑνὶ ἢ δυσὶ, but understanding (and translating) καὶ as equivalent in meaning to ἤ.

Note 333

What is in the best state, by contrast, has no need of action, since it is itself the for-the-sake-of which: "For it is not in this way that the god is in a good state [of activity], instead, he is better than to understand something else beyond himself. And the cause of this is that for us the good is in accord with something else, whereas for *that being* he himself is the good of himself" (*EE* VII 12 1245ᵇ16–19). The divine understanding, the primary god, attains the good by understanding himself: "It is itself, therefore, that it understands, if indeed it is the most excellent thing, and the active understanding is active understanding of active understanding" (*Met.* XII 9 1074ᵇ33–35). We, on the other hand, attain it, not by reflexive self-understanding, but by understanding him.

Action, though, is always in two [varieties], namely, when it is the for-the-sake-of-which and when it is what is for the sake of that: See II 12 292ᵃ22–23n.

Note 334

The actions of the other animals, on the other hand, are fewer, and of the plants perhaps one small one: "The substance of plants is no other function or action (*praxis*) than the generation of seed" (*GA* I 23 731ᵃ25–26). See also *DA* II 4 415ᵃ26–ᵇ7, quoted in *Cael.* II 10 291ᵇ6–10n.

Note 335

Either [1] there is some one thing which they may attain, as there is for a human being too, or [2] the many things are a route toward the best one: [1] is an action that, as the best and ultimate end, is the ultimate for the sake of which; [2] are the many actions that are a means to [1].

Note 336

[1] One thing, then, has and participates in the best, [2] one reaches close (*eggus*) to it by means of few [steps], [3] another by means of many, and [4] another does not even try, but it is sufficient for it to come close (*eggus*) to the ultimate [end]: Reading τὸ δ' ἀφικνεῖται ἐγγὺς δι' ὀλίγων in [2] with all the mss. Moraux secludes ἐγγὺς, which DP retain but do not translate; Stocks, followed by Allan and Guthrie, reads εὐθὺς ("immediately"). To defend the mss. reading, we need to proceed in stages.

(a) Only the primary god attains (indeed is) the best good (the best sort of happiness) in the best way (no movement) and to the fullest degree: "If, then, that good state [of activity], which we are sometimes in, the [primary] god is always in, that is a wonderful thing, and if to a higher degree, that is yet more wonderful. But that is his state" (*Met.* XII 7 1072^{b}24–26).

(b) The various heavenly spheres come close to achieving it to degrees determined by their distance from it (*Cael.* II 10 291^{a}6–10n), and in ways that deviate from the best one by the number of movements involved, which nonetheless remain few in comparison to those of human beings (*Cael.* II 12 292^{b}3). Still, they are eternally in this state, whereas human beings are only in it sometimes—though there is also a second-best sort of happiness (or an approximation to the best sort) that they attain when they are active in accord, not with the theoretical wisdom (*sophia*) that makes contemplation excellent, but with practical wisdom and the virtues of character: "Happiest, but in a secondary way, is the life in accord with the other virtue, since the activities in accord with it are human. For just actions, brave actions, and other actions that we do in accord with the virtues, we do in relation to each other in contracts, catering to needs, and in every sort of action and in feelings as well, by keeping closely to what is appropriate to each person. And all of these are evidently human. Indeed, some of them even seem to arise from the body, and virtue of character seems in many ways to be intimately attached to feelings" (*NE* X 8 1178^{a}9–16).

(c) Other animals are excluded from contemplation altogether, since their souls lack the divine element—*nous* or understanding (*PA* II 10 656^{a}7–8, *NE* X 8 1178^{b}24–25)—that is needed for it, as for the grasp of any scientific starting-points (*Cael.* I 1 268^{a}1n(5)), and have at best analogues of the various virtues: "The majority of other animals, indeed, possess traces of the sorts of characteristics having to do with the soul that are more clearly differentiated in the case of human beings. For tameness and wildness, gentleness and roughness, courage and cowardice, fearfulness and boldness, spiritedness and mischievousness are present in many of them together with a semblance, where thought is concerned, of comprehension. . . . For some of these characteristics differ by the more-and-the-less from the human, as the human does from the majority of animals (for certain characteristics of this sort are present to a greater degree in the human case, certain others to a greater degree in other animals), whereas others differ by analogy: for certain animals possess some other natural capacities that correspond and are akin to craft knowledge, theoretical wisdom, and comprehension" (*HA* VII 1 588^{a}18–31; also I 1 488^{b}15, IX 5 611^{a}15–16, 10 614^{b}18, *PA* II 2 648^{a}5–8, 4 650^{b}18–27, *GA* III 2 753^{a}10–17, *Met.* I 1 980^{b}22–25). Plants seem yet more distant, possessed as they are of only nutritive soul, and so having "no share in human virtue" (*NE* I 13 1102^{b}12). They participate in the immortality of the best simply in producing seed (*GA* I 23 731^{a}25–26, *DA* II 4 415^{a}26–^{b}7).

First, then, we have an end or goal G—the best or ultimate good (happiness)—that can be attained to different degrees: perfectly by the one being in (a), namely, the primary god; less perfectly by the beings in (b); and not at all by those in (c). Second, we have a measure in terms of number of actions or steps needed (i) to attain an end X, which may be G (a–b), or may not (c)—a number which may be zero, one, or more than one. In the illustration in the text, G is health and X is running or slimming down (II 12 292^{b}13–17). It is this that the different roles of *eggus* in [2] and [4] is intended to express. In [2] we have beings that are trying to attain G and are coming, to different degrees, close to doing so; in [4] we have beings that are trying to attain not G but rather X, and so are content with coming as close to G as they can. In [2], then, *eggus* marks failure, whereas in [4] it marks a success, so that both should be read.

Note 337

The most divine starting-point: "That the for-the-sake-of-which does exist among the immovable things is made clear by a distinction. For the for-the-sake-of-which is both the one *for whom* and *that toward which*, and of these the latter is among the immovable things and the former is not. And it produces movement insofar as it is loved, whereas it is by being moved that the other things move. . . . This, therefore, is the sort of starting-point on which the heaven and nature depend" (*Met.* XII 7 1072^{b}1–14). See also, II 10 291^{a}6–10n.

Note 338

The primary heaven, however, attains this directly by means of a single movement: "This" refers not to the ultimate end (which only the primary god attains) but rather to getting as close to it as possible. See II 12 292^{b}10–13n.

Note 339

In the case of each one's life and starting-point: "The soul is as it were a starting-point of living things" (*DA* I 1 402^{a}6–7).

Note 340

Nature both equalizes things and produces a certain order: I 1 268^{a}13n.

Note 341

While each sphere has a spatial movement that is by nature special to it, this spatial movement is, as it were, added on: "Since, then, each sphere is a body, and in the case of outermost sphere in each system, which moves with the fixed sphere, there is added to its own movement the fact that it also causes all the other spheres it contains to move in common with the same movement with which it moves" (Simp. 492.28–493.1 = Mueller, p. 32).
Special (*idios*): See II 13 295^{b}19n.
The capacity of every limited body is related to a limited one: See I 7 274^{b}33–275^{b}4, and for a discussion relevant to the sort of capacity involved, and why it does not involve any contrary to nature or forced movements, II 10 291^{a}6–10n.

Note 342

The Italian thinkers, the ones called Pythagoreans, say the contrary: In particular, Philolaus of Croton, DK A16–17 = TEGP 27–28, Huffman-1, pp. 231–261.

Note 343

They establish another earth opposite this one, which they call by the name "anti-earth," not seeking their accounts and causes with an eye toward the things that appear to be so, but rather dragging the things that appear to be so toward certain of their accounts and beliefs, and trying to cosmeticize them to make them fit: "And whenever they found consistencies and harmonies in the numbers with the attributes and parts of the heaven and with the whole arrangement of the cosmos, they collected these together and fitted them into their scheme. And if there was something missing, they added it eagerly, in order to make their work a connected whole. I mean, for example, that since the number ten seems to be complete and to encompass the whole nature of the numbers, they say that the bodies that move through the heaven are ten, but because those that are visible are only nine they make anti-earth the tenth" (*Met.* I 5 986ª3–12).
Cosmeticize them to make them fit (*sunkosmein*): The verb *sunkosmein* occurs only here in Aristotle and is otherwise rare. The slight overtranslation is intended to capture the apparent pun on *kosmein*. See I 12 279ᵇ12–17n.

Note 344

Many others might believe along with them that one should not assign the region at the center to the earth, but their conviction is based not on looking at the things that appear to be so but rather on arguments: The many others, here distinguished from the Pythagoreans, may be Platonists (see Leggatt, p. 254). In any case, Aristotle often criticizes Platonists for being too fond of argument and too neglectful of the perceptual evidence. See I 7 275ᵇ12n(4).

Note 345

Analogizing (*analogizomenoi*) **on the basis of these considerations:** *Analogizesthai* means "calculate" or "reckon up," as it does at II 14 298ª16, but here it seems to have the negative connotations that "analogizing" attempts to covey.

Note 346

The Pythagoreans, at any rate . . . name the fire that occupies this region, "the guard of Zeus": Again the reference seems to be (or to include) Philolaus. See DK A16 = TEGP 27.
The most controlling [element] (*to kuriôtaton*) **of the universe:** What is *kurios* is what has executive power or authority or the power to compel, so that a general is *kurios* over his army (*NE* III 8 1116ª29–ᵇ2) and a political ruler is *kurios* over a city and its inhabitants. Since what is *kurios* in a sphere determines or partly determines what happens within it, it is one of the most estimable or important elements in the sphere, so that what is inferior or less important than something not *kurios* there (VI 12 1143ᵇ33–35, 13 1145ª6–7). The *kurios* meaning of a term is thus its "prevailing" meaning (*Rh.* III 2 1405ª1–2). When Aristotle contrasts natural virtue of character with the *kurios* variety (*NE* VI 13 1144ᵇ1–32), the control exerted by the latter seems to be teleological: the natural variety is a sort of virtue because it is an early stage in the development of mature virtue. Hence *kuria aretê*

is "full virtue" or virtue in the strict sense of the term. It is in this sense, which is the one relevant here, that the life of those who are active and awake is a more *kurios* life—life in a fuller or stricter sense—than that of the inactive or asleep (I 7 1098^{a}5–8). *Kuriôs* and *haplôs* ("unconditionally") are often used interchangeably, for example, *Cat.* 13 14^{b}24, as are *kuriôs* and *kath' hauta* ("intrinsically"), for example, *Cat.* 6 5^{b}8.

Unconditionally (*haplôs*): The adjective *haplous* means "simple" or "single-fold." The adverb *haplôs* thus points in two somewhat opposed directions. (1) To speak *haplôs* sometimes means, as here, to put things simply or in general terms, so that qualifications and conditions will need to be added later. (2) Sometimes to be F *haplôs* means to be F unconditionally, or in a way that allows for no ifs, ands, or buts (*Top.* II 11 115^{b}29–35). In this sense, things that are F *haplôs* are F in the strictest, most absolute, and most unqualified way (*Met.* V 5 1015^{b}11–12).

As if "center" were said unconditionally: When in fact qualifications are needed. For what is at the center of things (that is, at the important place), need not be at the geometrical center. Hence "center" is said of things in many ways. See IV 5 312^{b}2.

Note 347

In the case of animals the center of the animal and of its body are not the same: The center of the animal is the heart, which is "situated in a region suitable for a starting-point (*archikên*). For it is *near the center*, more above than below, and more in front than behind. For nature puts the more estimable things in the more estimable regions, when nothing more important prevents it" (*PA* III 4 665^{b}18–21).

Note 348

The center of the place is more like an ending than a starting-point, since the center is what is determined, the limit what determines: Where the center of a place (or region) is depends on its boundaries or limits, so they are starting-points relative to it, not it relative to them.

Note 349

What encompasses, that is, the limit, is more estimable than what is limited: See I 2 269^{b}16n.

Note 350

The second is matter, but the first is the substance of the composition: The composition (*sustasis*) is the matter-form compound; the substance or essence (I 1 268^{a}3n) of which is the limit, in the sense of form: "What is said to be a limit is . . . the form, whatever it may be, of a spatial magnitude or of what has spatial magnitude" (*Met.* V 22 1022^{a}4–6). Thus "as the matter and the unlimited are what are encompassed and inside, the form is what encompasses" (*Ph.* III 7 207^{a}35–^{b}1). See also I 3 270^{a}24n.

Note 351
[The anti-earth] moves in a circle around the center . . . as we said previously: At II 13 293ª24.

Note 352
Some people even believe that several bodies of this sort may spatially move around the center, invisible to us because of the interposition of the earth: A view of this sort is attributed to Anaxagoras by Hippolytus. See DK A42 = TEGP 38, especially (6), (10). But Aristotle seems to have Pythagoreans in mind: "Alexander says that it is possible that it is to be understood that certain Pythagoreans have this belief" (Simp. 515.25–26 = Mueller, p. 55).

Note 353
The earth, which is situated at the center, winds—that is, moves (*kai kineisthai*)—around the pole stretching through the universe, as is written in the *Timaeus*: What is written in the *Timaeus* is this: "Earth he [the Demiurge] devised to be our nurturer, and, because it [1a] winds (*illomenên*) or [2a] is packed around (*eillomenên*) the axis stretching through the universe, also to be the maker and guardian of day and night" (40b8–c2). If we read [1a], we have a moving earth at the center; if we read [2a], we do not. A parallel ambiguity is found in the mss. of our text between [1b] *illesthai*, which Moraux, followed by DP, reads, and [2] *eileisthai*. But if with the majority of mss., we also read *kai kineisthai*, we may conclude that Aristotle at any rate read [1a], adding considerable weight to that reading. OCT reads [1a]; the Budé reads [1b]. Aristotle discusses this view at II 14 296ª26–ᵇ25.

Note 354
Some believe that the [earth] [1] is spherical, [2] some that it is flat and [3] drum-shaped: [1] Pythagoreans and Parmenides (DK A44 = TEGP 40); Plato (*Ti.* 33b); Aristotle (*Cael.* II 14). [2] Anaximenes, Anaxagoras, Democritus (*Cael.* II 13 294ᵇ13–14n); [3] Leucippus (DK A26 =TEGP 72).

Note 355
Thought (*dianoias*): See I 10 280ᵇ3n.
Must be pretty anesthetized (*alupoteras*): Literally, "feeling no pain."

Note 356
Philosophical work (*philosophêma*): Notice "a puzzle for political philosophy" at *Pol.* III 12 1282ᵇ22–23. See also *Cael.* I 9 279ª30n.

Note 357
Some, such as Xenophanes of Colophon, say that what is below the earth is unlimited, saying that it is rooted in the unlimited: See DK B28 = TEGP 52 F30.

Note 358
That is also why Empedocles chastises them in the way he does, saying ... : DK
B39 = TEGP 68 F40.

Note 359
A person who is going to inquire well must be capable of objecting by means
of objections proper to the relevant genus, and this comes from having a theo-
retical grasp on all the differentiae: "The instruments through which we shall
become well equipped with deductions [to use against an opponent or ourselves]
are four: [1] one is getting hold of premises; [2] the second is being able to distinguish in how many ways something is said of things; [3] the third is finding differentiae; and [4] the fourth is the investigation of similarity" (*Top.* I 13 105ᵃ21–25).
Top. I 16, 18 deal with [3]. Differentiae are important largely because definitions of
essences, which are scientific starting-points, are by genus and differentia. See I 1
268ᵃ1n(5) and, on differentiae, I 4 271ᵃ5n.

Note 360
Anaximenes, Anaxagoras, and Democritus say that the cause of the earth's
remaining at rest is its flatness: Anaximenes DK A7 = TEGP 12 (4); Anaxagoras
DK A1 = TEGP 37, TEGP 40 = Martianus Capella 6.590, 592; Democritus DK
A94 = TEGP 73.

Note 361
Is at rest because of the mass [of air] below it: Reading ἀθρόῳ τῷ with Allan and
Verdenius for Moraux ἀθρόως [τῷ] ("is at rest in a mass below it").
Just like the water in clepsydras: A clepsydra is a water clock in which time is
measured by water dripping slowly from a small opening at the bottom when
the top is opened. But when water is instead allowed to enter and then the top is
closed, it also functioned as a pipette or syphon, which is how it is functioning
here. Invert the pipette and the water rests on the trapped air. See *Ph.* IV 6 213ᵃ26,
Pr. XVI 8.

Note 362
Our dispute with those who speak in this way about the movement of the
earth is not about parts, but about a certain whole and totality: The dispute
is not about "the earth itself, which is a part of the universe, but about the
whole constitution of natural bodies. For it is necessary that what holds of other
things, holds also for the earth. One must determine at the start, then, whether
bodies by nature have a movement or have none" (Simp. 526.11–15 = Mueller,
p. 68).

Note 363
Determinations have been made previously about these matters: In I 2 (also
Ph. V 6).

Note 364
About these matters it was determined previously that this result is necessary, and in addition that rest is not possible either: Again the reference is to I 2, but see also I 8 276^{a}22–26.

Note 365
Everyone says that [the vortex] is the cause, on the basis of what happens in liquids or in the case of air: See Empedocles (see II 13 295^{a}17n); Anaxagoras DK B12 = TEGP 31 F15; Leucippus DK A1 = TEGP 47; Democritus DK B167 = TEGP 50 F14; Diogenes of Apollonia DK A1 = TEGP 1.

Note 366
Others, like Empedocles, say that it is the spatial movement of the heaven which, rotating in a circle and spatially moving faster than the earth, prevents [the earth from moving], just like the water in ladles: See DK B35 = TEGP 51 F28 = Simp. 529.1–15. See also *Cael.* III 2 300^{b}2–3, Plato, *Phd.* 99b6–7.
Just like the water in ladles: When the ladle is swung in a circle fast enough, the water stays in it even when it is upside down.

Note 367
The air [below] gives way: Reading ὑπελθόντος with Verdenius, DP, and the better mss. for Moraux ὑπείκοντος.

Note 368
When the elements had been disaggregated separately by strife, what cause was there of the earth's immobility: See DK B17 = TEGP 41 F20, B21 = TEGP 45 F22, B35 = TEGP 51 F28, B122 = TEGP 183 F129, B115 = TEGP 25 F8, and I 10 279^{b}16n.

Note 369
The other lot rising to the surface because of the movement: Reading κίνησιν with Moraux and the mss. DP read δίνησιν ("because of the vortex"), which is given the annotation *fortasse scribendum* by Moraux. But heavy things and light things exist *prior* to the vortex, and so will move downward or upward (respectively) prior to its action.

Note 370
It is impossible for there to be an up or down, and the heavy and light are determined by these: "And yet this is what is being inquired into, namely, why it is that the light and the heavy do move to their own place. And the cause is that it is natural for them to be somewhere, and this is the being for the light and the heavy, the one being determined by up and the other by down" (*Ph.* VIII 4 255^{b}13–17).

Note 371
There are some who say that the earth remains at rest because of the similarity (*homoiotêta*), **as among the ancient thinkers Anaximander does. For it is no more fitting for what is situated at the center and stands in a similar relation** (*homoiôs . . . echon*) **to the extremes to spatially move upward than downward or to the side; and it is impossible for it to make a movement in contrary directions at the same time. So of necessity it remains at rest:** = DK A26 = TEGP 21, DK A11 = TEGP 19. "Well then, he [Socrates] said, the first thing of which I am convinced is that if the earth is a sphere in the middle of the heavens, it has no need of air or any other such necessity to prevent it from falling. The similarity (*homoiotêta*) of the heaven itself on all sides and the earth's own equilibrium (*isorrapia*) are sufficient to hold it, for if a thing in equilibrium is placed at the center of something similar throughout (*homoiou*), it will not be able to incline more in any direction than any other but standing is a similar relation [to all] (*homoiôs d'echon*) remains in place without inclining" (*Phd.* 108e–109a). Simplicius comments: "Plato is also of this belief. . . . But Aristotle, finding that it was assumed earlier by Anaximander, thinks it more gracious to refute him than to argue against Plato" (Simp. 531.34–532.4 = Mueller, p. 75). Notice the close verbal parallels between the *Phaedo* passage and our own text, suggesting that Aristotle may indeed have had Plato in mind. But be that as it may, the principle involved in the argument, whether attributed to Plato or to Anaximander, seems to be some version of the Principle of Sufficient Reason (on which, see https://plato.stanford.edu/entries/sufficient-reason/).

Note 372
This, though stated in a subtle way (*kompsôs*), **is not stated in a true one:** Compare I 9 290^{b}14–15, and (bearing on the issues in the previous note): "All the Socratic accounts [that is, all or most of Plato's works] are extraordinary, *kompson*, innovative, and exhibit a spirit of inquiry, but it is presumably difficult to do everything well" (*Pol.* II 6 1265^{a}10–13).

Note 373
What was mentioned: Namely, being at the center and standing in a similar relation to the extremes (II 13 295^{b}13–14).
Is not a special attribute of earth: "A special attribute (*idion*) is one that does not reveal the essence of a thing yet belongs to that thing alone and is predicated convertibly of it. Thus it is a special attribute of a human to be receptive of grammar, since if someone is human he is receptive of grammar, and if he is receptive of grammar he is human" (*Top.* I 5 102^{a}18–22).

Note 374
The one about the person who is similarly hungry and thirsty, and at an equal distance from food and drink—for he too [so the argument goes] is necessarily at rest: An anticipation of the puzzle that we know as Buridan's Ass.

Note 375

Condensed (*puknoumenon*) . . . **rarer** (*manoteron*): "The starting-point of all affections is condensation and rarefaction (*puknôsis kai manôsis*). For heavy and light, soft and hard, hot and cold, seem to be sorts of density or rarity. And condensation and rarefaction are aggregation and disaggregation, in virtue of which substances are said to come to be and pass away" (*Ph.* VIII 7 260^{b}7–12).

Note 376

As we said, some people make it one of the stars, whereas others say that it winds—that is, moves—around the central pole: At II 13 293^{a}17–^{b}32.

Note 377

Except for the primary one: That of the primary heaven.

Note 378

It is necessary for there to be a passing and turning of the fixed stars: "The planets (including the sun and the moon) undergo a movement along the ecliptic as well as a sidereal movement along with the fixed stars. If one notes the position at which a planet rises on the horizon, then at its next rising it will be seen to be at a point either a little north or a little south of its previous position. In this way, the planet may be seen to 'pass' along the horizon (hence Aristotle's talk of 'passing'). By charting the daily risings of the planet, one will see that it appears more and more northward or southward on the horizon until it reaches a northernmost or southernmost point from which, in subsequent risings, it 'turns' back in the other direction—hence the 'turnings' mentioned" (Leggatt, p. 264, 296^{b}4n).

Note 379

Things having heaviness spatially moving toward it move not in parallel but at similar angles, so that they spatially move toward one center, which is also that of the earth: "If they fell in parallel, they would not both converge to the same center point" (Simp. 538.19–20 = Mueller, p. 83). See also II 14 297^{b}17–23. How did Aristotle know this? Eratosthenes of Cyrene (297–195 BC) discovered it empirically by observing that the sun shone directly down a well at high noon on the day of the summer solstice in one place and cast a shadow on the side of another at a distant place directly south of the first. So it is at least possible that Aristotle knew it in the same way. Eratosthenes went on to measure the angle of the shadow to the Earth, and used it to calculate the circumference of the Earth. Compare II 14 297^{b}30–298^{a}9.

Note 380

One [body] has one spatial movement; a simple one has a simple one: See I 2 268^{b}14–269^{a}9.

Note 381

[1] Each of its parts has heaviness up to the point at which [it is] near to (*pros*) **the center, and [2] when a smaller part is pushed by a greater one it cannot**

swell to form a wave (*kumainein*), **but rather the first is squeezed together** (*sumpezesthai*) **by the second and combines** (*sugchôrein*) **with it, until it arrives at the center:** Imagine all the parts of earth spatially moving, as by nature they will if unimpeded, down to C, the center of the universe. [2] describes what will happen when a larger part P_1 and a smaller one P_s arrive at C: P_s will be squeezed by P_1 and—rather than swelling or bulging out from P_1—will combine with it to form a large sphere S, with no bulges (or waves) on its surface. [1] tells us that each of the parts has heaviness, and so moves toward the center of the universe, until it coalesces with S_s around that center.

Note 382

Physicists (*phusiologôn*): The *phusiologoi* were thinkers who tried to give a general account of reality that, among other things, made no reference to incorporeal beings: "They posit the elements of bodies alone, but [1] not of the incorporeal things, although incorporeal ones are also beings. And when they try to state the causes of coming to be and passing away and to give a physical account of all things, [2] they do away with the cause of movement" (*Met.* I 8 988^{b}24–26). See also *Cael.* III 1 298^{b}29 for the corresponding verb.

Note 383

When the mixture, then, was [merely] potential: That is, when disaggregation or segregation had already begun: "So not only is it coincidentally possible for something to come to be from what is not, but in fact for all things to come to be from what is—from what is *potentially*, however, but from what *actually* is not. And this is 'the one' of Anaxagoras (for this is better than 'all things were together'), and the 'mixture' of Empedocles and Anaximander, and what Democritus says, namely, 'all things were together'—potentially, yes, but not actively" (*Met.* XII 1069^{b}18–23).
The things that were disaggregated moved spatially from every direction toward the center in a similar way: "Others say that the contrarieties are present in the one and are segregated out of it—for example, Anaximander speaks like this, as do those, such as Empedocles and Anaxagoras, who say that the beings are one and many. For they too segregate out the others from the mixture. They differ from each other, however, in that Empedocles posits a cycle of mixings and segregations, whereas Anaxagoras posits just one, and Anaxagoras posits an unlimited number both of homoeomerous things and of contraries, whereas Empedocles posits the so-called elements only" (*Ph.* I 4 187^{a}20–26). On Empedocles, see II 13 295^{a}31n. On Anaxagoras on the mixture, see DK B1–2 = TEGP 11 = Simp. 608.21–23, 155.31–156.1.

Note 384
Balance-weight: See II 1 284^{a}25n.

Note 385
The sort it in fact is: Reading ὃ ὑπάρχειν with DP and some mss. for Moraux and other mss. ὑπάρχειν.

Note 386
The earth is round (*peripherês*): The adjective *peripherês* has a variety of meanings: "curved," "rounded," "circular," "spherical." Here, as with our word "round," it means "spherical."

Note 387
Pillars of Hercules: The Straits of Gibraltar.

Note 388
The mathematicians: Perhaps Archytas or Eudoxus. See also II 11 291^{b}17–23n.
Who try to calculate the size of the earth's circumference say that it is about four-hundred-thousand stades: The precise length of a stade is unknown, but if we assume a stade of approximately .09 of a mile, then 400,000 stades is roughly 36,000 miles. The actual circumference is approximately 25,000 miles.

BOOK III

Note 389
We have previously discussed the primary heaven and its parts, further, the stars spatially moving within it (*en autô[i]*): The primary heaven is the outermost sphere of the fixed stars (II 6 288^{a}15); since the stars spatially moving within it cannot be the ones fixed on it, which do not move because of themselves, the parts referred to must be the other celestial spheres nested within the outermost one.
Of what they are composed: See II 7 239^{a}11–19n.
They are incapable of coming to be and incapable of passing away: See II 6.

Note 390
Of the things we say are by nature: See I 1 268^{a}13n.
Some are substances: See I 1 268^{a}3n.
By substances I mean the simple bodies (for example, fire and earth and those co-ordinate with these), and whatever is composed of them (for example, the whole heaven and its parts), and, again, animals and plants and their parts: Compare: "Now substance seems to belong most evidently to bodies. That is why we say that animals and plants and their parts are substances, and also natural bodies, such as fire, water, earth, and each thing of this sort, together with all their parts and all things composed from some or all of them (for example, the heaven and its parts, stars and moon and sun), but whether these alone are substances, or others as well, or some of these and some others as well, or none of these but some others, is something that must be investigated" (*Met.* VII 2 1028^{b}8–15).
The whole heaven and its parts: The fact that the heaven and its parts are substances (I 2 269^{a}30–32, *Met.* XII 8 1073^{a}14) has bearing on the interpretation of the phrase "the nature of the whole" (*Met.* XII 10 1075^{a}11), since if the heaven is a substance—indeed an animate substance (*Cael.* II 2 285^{a}29)—it must have a

nature (form, essence) and soul of its own that is beyond those of the substances that constitute it. This has important consequences, obviously, for the interpretation of Aristotle's entire philosophy of nature, not to say his entire philosophy *tout court*. (Think of the importance of the world soul in Plato's *Timaeus*.) However, if some or all of the parts of the heaven are of the same kind as the whole, *Met*. VII 13 1039ᵃ3–4 seems to tell us that the whole cannot be a substance and its parts substances as well: "it is impossible for a substance to be composed of substances that are actually present in it." But this doctrine seems intended to apply only to primary substances, which are not matter-form compounds like the heavens, but pure actualities, like the primary god (see *Cael*. I 4 271ᵃ33n). In any case, since the claim of the heaven to be not just an "agreed upon" substance (*Met*. VIII 1 1042ᵃ10–11) but a *correctly* agreed upon one seems never to be revoked or explicitly undercut, there is at a minimum a puzzle as to how to make the doctrine consistent with it.

Others works (*erga*) and affections (*pathê*) of these: Here *ergon* (plural: *erga*) is co-ordinate with *pathê*, and means "works," "doings," rather than functions, in the strict sense. See II 3 285ᵇ8n, and, on affections, I 1 268ᵃ2n.

Fire and earth and those co-ordinate (*sustoicha*) with these: See II 4 287ᵇ21n.

Note 391

The first of the elements: Namely, primary body (II 1 284ᵃ30), ether (I 3 270ᵇ22).

Is incapable of passing away and incapable of coming to be: See I 3.

Note 392

It remains to speak about the other two: That is, earth and fire, between which water and air are intermediate. See I 8 276ᵇ1, 277ᵇ13–14n.

Note 393

Those prior [to us] who philosophized about the truth (*philosophêsantes peri alêtheias*): That is, the sort of truth about the nature of things and about starting-points that philosophy seeks (*Met*. I 7 988ᵃ19–20, II 1 993ᵃ30–ᵇ2, ᵇ17, 20). Compare: "those prior to us who undertook the investigation of beings and philosophized about the truth (*philosophêsantes peri alêtheias*)" (I 3 983ᵇ1–3).

Note 394

The followers of Melissus and Parmenides: See III 1 298ᵇ21–25n.

Melissus [of Samos] and Parmenides [of Elea] See DK 28 = TEGP pp. 203–244. See DK 30 = TEGP pp. 462–485. Aristotle discusses their views in *Ph*. I 2.

Note 395

Of them, we must hold that, even if they speak correctly about other things, they do not do so *in a way appropriate to natural science* (*phusikôs*): Because they deny one of the starting-points of natural science: "As for ourselves, we must assume that the things that are by nature are in movement, either all of them or some of them. And this is clear from induction. At the same time, we should not resolve every [contentious argument] at hand, but those that involve false demonstration from the starting-points, and not those that do not. . . . Nevertheless, although they [Melissus and Parmenides] are concerned with nature, but the puzzles they speak about are not natural scientific ones, perhaps it would be good to discuss them briefly, since the investigation involves philosophy" (*Ph.* I 2 185ᵃ12–20).

Note 396
The existence of certain beings that are incapable of coming to be and are wholly immovable is rather a matter for an investigation that is distinct from and prior to the natural scientific one: Namely, primary philosophy. See I 8 277ᵃ10n.

Note 397
Because these thinkers assumed that there was no other sort beyond the substance of perceptible beings, and were the first to understand that there had to be certain natures of this [unchangeable] sort if indeed there was going to be any knowledge or wisdom, they transferred to perceptible beings the accounts applicable to those natures: This suggests that the followers of Parmenides and Melissus referred to (III 1 298ᵇ17) are or include Platonists: "Those who accept the Forms speak correctly in one way, namely, in separating them (if indeed the Forms are substances), but in another way not correctly. . . . And the cause of this is that they do not have [an account] to give of the substances that are of this sort—the imperishable ones that are beyond the particular perceptible ones. So they make them the same in kind (*eidos*) as perishable things (for these are the ones we do know), man-itself and horse-itself, adding to the perceptible ones the word 'itself'" (*Met.* VII 16 1040ᵇ27–34); "They thought that the particulars in the realm of perceptible things were flowing and that none of them remains the same, but that the universal was both beyond these and something distinct from them. . . . For without universals it is not possible to get scientific knowledge" (XIII 9 1086ᵃ37–ᵇ6).

Certain natures (*phuseis*): On this rather unfortunate use of the term *phusis*, see I 1 268ᵃ13n.

Knowledge (*gnôsis*): There may be little difference between *gnôsis* and *epistêmê* (verb, *epistasthai*), as III 3 302ᵃ11–14 shows. Nonetheless, *epistêmê* is usually applied only to demonstrative sciences, crafts, or other bodies of systematic knowledge, so that *epistêmê* is specifically scientific knowledge. *Gnôsis* is weaker and is used for perceptual knowledge and knowledge by acquaintance—something familiar is *gnôrimos*. If X knows that p, it follows that p is true and that X is justified in believing it. Similar entailments hold in the cases of *epistasthai* and *eidenai* (used in the opening sentence) but may not hold in that of *gignôskein*.

Wisdom (*phronêsis*): *Phronêsis* (verb *phronein*) is used: (1) in a broad sense to refer to thought or (roughly speaking) intelligence of any sort (as at *Met.* IV 5 1009ᵇ13, 30); (2) in a narrower sense to refer to the distinctively practical wisdom discussed in *NE* VI 5; and (3) as equivalent in meaning to *sophia* or theoretical wisdom (XIII 4 1078ᵇ15, and throughout *Protr.*), which is its sense here. (2), in its fullest form, and (3) are distinctively human possessions. But Aristotle does some-times attribute a weaker form (*HA* VII 1 588ª18–31) of (1) to non-human animals, such as deer, hare, cranes, bees, and ants (I 2 488ᵇ15, IX 5 611ª15–16, IX 10 614ᵇ18, *PA* II 2 648ª5–8, 4 650ᵇ18–27, *GA* III 2 753ª10–17).

Note 398
The followers of Hesiod: "The followers of Hesiod and all the theologians thought only of what was persuasive to themselves, but had contempt for people like us. For they made the starting-points to be gods and what is born from gods, and say that those who did not taste nectar or ambrosia became mortal, clearly using terms familiar to themselves. Although about the very *ingestion* of these causes they have spoken over our heads. For if it is for the sake of pleasure that the gods touch these, then nectar and ambrosia are in no way the causes of their being; but if these *are* the causes of their being, how could the gods be eternal, since they need nourish-ment?" (*Met.* III 4 1000ª9–18).
Hesiod: Hesiod was one of the oldest known Greek poets (c. 700 BC), author of the *Theogony, Works and Days*, and the *Catalogue of Women*. His works, like those of Homer, played a substantial role in Greek education.
The first people who spoke about nature (*phusiologêsantes*): The characterization of the *phusiologountes* at *Met.* I 8 988ᵇ27 suggests that they are the same as the physicists (*phusiologoi*), on whom, see II 14 297ª13n.

Note 399
Others say that all things come to be and flow, none of them being stable, save one thing only that persists, from whose natural changing of shape all these things come. This is just what Heraclitus of Ephesus, among many oth-ers, seems to wish to say: For Heraclitus, the one persisting thing is fire (see I 10 279ᵇ16n); for Thales, "the one who started this sort of philosophy, . . . it is water" (*Met.* I 3 983ᵇ20–21); "Anaximenes and Diogenes posit air as prior to water and as more than anything else the starting-point of the simple bodies" (984ª5–7); for Anaximander it is the unlimited, see DK A11, B2 = TEGP 10.
Natural changing of shape (*metaschêmatizesthai*): See III 7 305ᵇ29–30.

Note 400
And there are also some who make all bodies capable of coming to be, put-ting them together from and dissolving them into planes: See Plato, *Ti.* 53a–57d (Appendix).

Note 401
About the others there will be an account on another occasion: There is some further discussion in III 5, and, of course, in *Ph.* and *Met.*

Note 402
The other things they say are in conflict with mathematics: The reference (as *LI* 969ᵇ26–31 suggests) is probably to the Platonic rejection of geometrical points:

"In fact, Plato used even to contest this kind (*genos*) [that is, points] as being a geometrical dogma. Instead, he called it 'starting-point of line,' and often posited that it consisted of indivisible lines" (*Met.* I 9 992ᵃ20–22). Though the rejection is otherwise unattested, *GC* I 2 316ᵃ11–12 mentions those who argue in a logico-linguistic (*logikôs*) way (*Cael.* I 7 275ᵇ12n) that there must be indivisible magnitudes, "because otherwise [the Form of] the triangle will be more than one." The author of *LI* gives the argument: "If there is an Idea of line, and if the first of the things called by the same name, then, since the parts are prior to the whole, line-itself must be indivisible (*adiairetos*). And in the same way so must the [Idea of] the square, the triangle, the other [Ideas of] figures, and in general plane-itself and body-itself, since otherwise there will be things prior to each of them" (968ᵃ9–14). But indivisible lines conflict with a starting-point of mathematics that quantities are divisible without limit. In this regard positing them is quite different from raising puzzles or paralogisms proper to mathematics, because based on its starting-points. Hippocrates' argument for squaring the circle by means of lunes, for example, is a geometrical paralogism, because it "proceeds from starting-points proper to geometry" and "cannot be adapted to any subject except geometry" (*SE* 11 172ᵃ4–5), whereas someone who gives Antiphon's argument for squaring the circle, which assumes that a circle is a polygon with a large but finite number of sides, has produced a sophistical refutation, since his argument is not proper to geometry but "*koinos* (common)" (172ᵃ8–9). Dealing with him, as a result, is a job for dialecticians: "It is dialecticians who get a theoretical grasp on a refutation that depends on common beliefs, that is to say, that do not belong to any [specialized] craft" (9 170ᵃ38–39).

Note 403
It is just either not to alter mathematics or to alter it [only] by means of arguments that are more convincing than its hypotheses (*hupotheseôn*): The hypotheses of a science such as mathematics are its fundamental—typically unargued for—starting points: "hypotheses are the starting-points of demonstrations" (*Met.* V 1 1013ᵃ16).

Note 404
In the discussions concerning movement: See I 5 272ᵃ30n.

Note 405
The others, the mathematical ones, are said of things on the basis of abstraction (*ex aphaireseôs*): "The mathematician produces his theoretical knowledge about things that result from abstraction, for he gets his theoretical grasp on them having first stripped away all the perceptible attributes (for example, weight and lightness, hardness and its contrary, and further, also heat and cold, and the other perceptible contrarieties), and leaves behind only the quantitative and the continuous (sometimes in one, sometimes in two, sometimes in three dimensions) and the attributes of things insofar as they are quantitative and continuous, and does not get a theoretical grasp on any other aspect of them, but investigates the relative positions of some and what belongs to them, and the commensurabilities and incommensurabilities of others, and the ratios of others still" (*Met.* XI 3 1061ᵃ28–ᵇ2).

The natural ones are said of things on the basis of an additional posit (*ek pros-theseseôs*): "One science is more exact than another, and prior to it, if . . . it proceeds from fewer things and the other from some additional posit (as, for example, arithmetic is more exact than geometry). By from an addition I mean, for example, that a unit is substance without position and a point is substance with position—the latter proceeds from an addition" (*APo.* I 27 87ᵃ31–37). In the case of natural bodies, the additional posit is perceptual matter.

Note 406

For example, if there is an indivisible *one*: Reading οἷον εἴ τί ἐστιν ἀδιαίρετον with DP and the mss. Moraux and Allan seclude; Stocks reads διαιρετόν ("if there is a divisible one").

Note 407

[Divisible] in species, for example, of color, white and black: The other colors are mixtures of black and white in some ratio or other: "It is possible that white and black should be so juxtaposed that each is invisible because it is very small, but that what is composed of both is visible. This can appear neither as white nor as black. But since it must have some color, and cannot have either of these, it must be some kind of mixture—that is, some other species of color. Such then is a possible way of supposing there to be a plurality of colors beyond white and black, but which are a plurality because of the ratio [of white to black in them]; for these may be juxtaposed in the ratio 3 : 2 or 3 : 4, or in ratios expressible by other numbers, or they may be in no numerically expressible ratio, but in some incommensurable relation of excess or deficiency" (*Sens.* 3 439ᵇ19–30).

Note 408

There are many things that are unconditionally small, but nonetheless are larger than other things: Consider the following argument: "It is impossible for an animal or a plant to be of any size whatsoever, in the direction of greatness and of smallness, [so] it is evident that none of its parts can be either. For if it could, so similarly could the whole. But flesh and bone and things of that sort are parts of an animal" (*Ph.* I 4 187ᵇ16–19). Therefore, "if every body from which something is subtracted must become smaller, and if flesh is definite in quantity, both in greatness and in smallness, it is evident that from the smallest possible quantity of flesh no body can be segregated out. For otherwise there will be a quantity of it smaller than the smallest possible one" (187ᵇ35–188ᵃ2). But two smallest quantities of flesh, which as such are unconditionally small, need not be the same in amount, so long as the amount they differ by is not an amount of flesh. On unconditional lightness and heaviness, see *Cael.* IV 1 308ᵃ7–33, 4 311ᵃ16–29.

Note 409

A point (*stigmê*) **was assumed to be indivisible:** "What is divisible in quantity in one dimension is a *line*, in two a *plane*, in all—that is, in three—a *body*. And, reversing the order, what is divisible in two dimensions is a plane, in one dimension a line, and what is in no dimension divisible in quantity is a point or unit, what lacks position being a unit and what has position a point" (*Met.* V 6 1016^{b}26–31).

Note 410

A soft thing is what can be pressed into itself, whereas a hard one is what cannot be pressed in: "Hard is that whose surface cannot be pressed into itself; soft is that whose surface can be pressed in, but not by being replaced. For water is not soft, since its surface is not pressed downward by pressure exerted on it, but replaced" (*Mete.* IV 4 382^{a}11–14).

Note 411

In the case of how many points will this result and in what way?: Reading καὶ πῶς with ms. E^5 and DP for Moraux and mss. καὶ ἐπὶ ποίων ("and of what sort"). This seems required by III 1 299^{b}23–31.

Note 412

Each of the parts that has no parts will have weight: Reading ἕκαστον τῶν ἀμερῶν with Allan, DP, and one mss. for Moraux and other mss. ἕκαστον τῶν ἀβαρῶν.

Note 413

If it is necessary for that by which one weight is greater to be weight, just as that by which one white is more white is white: Reading ᾧ δὲ βαρέος . . . ᾧ λευκοῦ with Allan, Guthrie, and DP for Moraux and the mss. τὸ δὲ βαρέος . . . τὸ λευκοῦ. **So that the greater will be heavier by one point, when the weight equal [to four points] has been subtracted, the result will be that the one point will also have weight:** Reading ὥστε τὸ μεῖζον μιᾷ στιγμῇ βαρύτερον ἔσται ἀφαιρεθέντος τοῦ ἴσου, ὥστε καὶ ἡ μία στιγμὴ βάρος ἕξει with Guthrie, Longo, Verdenius, p. 282, and the mss. for Moraux ἔσται τὸ μεῖζον μιᾷ στιγμῇ βαρύτερον, ὥστε, ἀφαιρεθέντος τοῦ ἴσου, [ὥστε] καὶ ἡ μία στιγμὴ βάρος ἕξει.

Note 414

For just as there are two ways [we might think] to put lines together, namely, [1] end-to-end and [2] one on top of the other, a plane should be the same way. [3] A [Platonic] line, though, *is* capable of being put together with a line by being put on top of it and not by being added to it [at its ends]: Aristotle's thought seems to go like this: We might think we can add lines in way [1] *and* in way [2]. But in fact, since (Aristotelian or geometric) lines, as divisible in only one dimension (III 1 299^{b}6–7n), have length but no breadth, they cannot be added in way [2]. But [3] a Platonic line can be added in way [2], since it is something physical, and so must, it seems, have some breadth in addition to its length. Stacked Platonic planes, then, will apparently be solids, though not ones that Plato acknowledges. Hence the absurdity that Aristotle is exploring.

Note 415

If bodies are heavier due to the number of their constituent planes, as is declared in the *Timaeus*: See Plato, *Ti.* 56b (Appendix).

Note 416

It is clear that the line and the point will also have weight. For they stand in a proportional relation to each other, as we also said previously: See III 1 299^{b}18–21.

Note 417

The indivisible now is like a point on a line: Aristotle discusses the now (or temporal instant) in *Ph.* IV 10–11. Just as a line is not composed of dimensionless points, since no number of things without length can compose something that has length, so time is not composed of nows.

Note 418

There are some thinkers, such as certain Pythagoreans, who compose nature from numbers: "The Pythagorean version . . . has difficulties special to itself . . . [since] for bodies to be composed of numbers, and for this number to be mathematical, is impossible. For it is not true to say that there are indivisible spatial magnitudes, but even if it were true that they were fully this way, units at least have no magnitude—and how can a magnitude be composed of things that are indivisible? Moreover, arithmetical number, at any rate, is composed of units, whereas these thinkers say that beings are numbers—at any rate, they apply their speculations to bodies on the supposition that the latter beings are composed of numbers" (*Met.* XIII 8 1083^{b}8–19). See also I 1 268^{a}10–13n.

Note 419

Units (*monadas*): Units are discussed in *Met.* XIII 6–8.

Note 420

If there is a movement [of them] contrary to nature, it is necessary for there also to be one in accord with nature, to which it is contrary: See I 2 269^{a}9–12, II 3 286^{a}18–20.

Note 421

As Empedocles says that the earth rests because of the vortex: See II 13 295^{a}7–^{b}9.

Note 422

[1] Leucippus and Democritus, who say that the primary bodies are always moving in the void, [2] must say what sort of movement it is and what movement of theirs is in accord with nature: [1] "Leucippus, however, and his associate Democritus say that plenum and void are the elements, calling the one 'being,' and the other 'not being,' and, of these, plenum or solid is being, while void is not being (that is why they also say that being no more *is* than not being, because body no more *is* than void), and that these, as matter, are the causes of beings. And just as those who make the underlying substance one generate the other things by means of its attributes, positing rare and dense as starting-points of these attributes, in the same way, these people too say that the differentiae are the causes of the other things. And these differentiae, they say, are three—shape, order, and position. For they say that being is differentiated by 'rhythm', 'contact', and 'turning' alone. And of these rhythm is shape, contact is order, and turning is position. For A differs from N in shape, AN from NA in order, and Z from N in position. But the question of movement—where it comes from and in what way it belongs to beings—these people, in a quite similar way to the others, carelessly neglected" (*Met.* I 4 985^{b}4–20 = DK 67A6 = TEGP 10 F 4). [2] "Some thinkers, such as Leucippus and Plato, posit eternal activity, since they say that there is always movement. But why and what it is they do not say, nor, if the movement is this way or that, what the cause is. For nothing is moved at random, but there must always be some particular sort present—just as, as things stand, a thing moves in one way by nature and in another by force or as a result of understanding or of something else. Further, what sort of movement is primary? This makes an enormous difference. But again in the case of Plato, at any rate, it is not possible even to state what he sometimes thinks the starting-point is, namely, what moves itself, since the soul is later than and coeval with the heaven, according to his account" (*Met.* XII 6 1071^{b}32–1072^{a}3).

Note 423

If the elements are moved by each other by force, still it is necessary for each also to have a movement in accord with nature against which it is forced: See III 2 300^{a}22–25n.

Note 424

As is written in the *Timaeus,* before the coming to be of the cosmos, the elements moved in a disorderly way: "The god wanted everything to be good and nothing to be bad so far as that was possible, and so he took over all that was visible—not at rest but in discordant and disorderly movement—and brought it from a state of disorder to one of order, because he believed that order was in every way better than disorder" (Plato, *Ti.* 30a). See also 52d–53b (Appendix), and *Cael.* III 2 300^{b}8–11n.

Note 425

The primary mover (which necessarily moves itself): Reading ἑαυτὸ with Moraux, Verdenius p. 282, and the mss. for Simp. 584.29–585.1, Allan, Kouremenos, Longo, Stocks, αὐτό. See, for the supporting argument, *Cael.* III 2 300^{b}13–14. Aristotle is not committing himself to a primary mover that is a self-mover, but is arguing on the supposition, shared by Leucippus, Democritus, and Plato, that the primary bodies or elements are always moving.

Note 426

As Empedocles says happens under the reign of love: See I 10 279^{b}16n.

Note 427
Many heads sprouted without necks: DK 57 = TEGP 118 F71.

Note 428
Nothing in accord with nature comes about by luck: See I 12 283ᵃ33n.

Note 429
Anaxagoras grasped at least this correctly, since he starts his cosmogony from unmoving things: See DK B12–13 = TEGP 30–31 F14–15, which imply that things were unmoving before the (divine) understanding started them moving. What Anaxagoras gets right, however, is what this in turn implies, namely, that things were not all moving in a disorderly way prior to the production of cosmic order. He was not right in thinking that there was a (unlimited) time before that when they were at rest: "For things to be at rest for an unlimited time, then in movement at some time, and no difference at all to cause this happening now rather than earlier, and with no order of any sort involved either, is no longer a work of nature. For what holds by nature is either simple, and not sometimes one way and sometimes another (for example, fire spatially moves upward by nature, and not sometimes up and sometimes not), or it involves some ratio, if it is not simple" (*Ph.* VIII 1 252ᵃ14–19).

Note 430
Others too try [elements that] are aggregating somehow and again moving and disaggregating: "It is better to say with Empedocles, or anyone else who may have spoken as he does, that the universe is alternately at rest and in movement again [than that things were at rest for an unlimited time before being caused to move]. For such a state of affairs already involves some sort of order. But even someone who says this should not only state it but also say what the cause of it is—and he should neither merely posit something or assume an un-argued axiom, but should produce either an induction or a demonstration. For the things assumed by Empedocles are not themselves causes of this alternation, nor was it the being for love or for strife to cause it, but for the one to aggregate and for the other to disaggregate. And if he is going to go on to determine the details of their alternation, he must say under what conditions it happens, just as he says that there is something that causes *human beings* to aggregate, namely, love, and that enemies flee each other. For he assumes that this also holds in the whole cosmos, because it is apparently so in some cases. And that love and strife rule for equal periods of time also requires some argument" (*Ph.* VIII 1 252ᵃ19–32).

Note 431
For the cosmos is composed of elements that are disaggregated, so that it is necessary for it to have come to be from one aggregated thing: Compare: "Love often disaggregates things for him, while strife aggregates them. For whenever the universe is divided up into its elements because of strife, the fire is aggregated into one, and so is each of the other elements, and whenever things come together into

one again under the influence of love, it is necessary that the parts from each get disaggregated again" (*Met.* I 4 985ᵃ24–29).

Note 432
Balance-weight: See II 1 284ᵃ25n.

Note 433
We say that it is necessary for them to move: See III 1 300ᵃ20–21.

Note 434
If there is to be a moving body that has neither lightness nor heaviness, it is necessary for it to be moved by force, and, since it is moving by force, for it to make an unlimited movement: Because the moving body has no weight (no heaviness or lightness), there is nothing within it to cause it to rest when it reaches its proper place. So, once set in movement, it will keep moving forever.

Note 435
It is necessary that every definite (*diôrismenon*) body have heaviness or lightness: *Diôrismenon* could also be taken with "weight or lightness": "It is necessary that every body have a definite weight or lightness." But it should not be. For since there is no unlimited heaviness or lightness, the point is to distinguish definite particular bodies from the body of the universe, which has neither heaviness nor lightness. See Moraux p. 163.

Note 436
Nature is a starting-point of movement within the thing itself: "Nature is a sort of starting-point and cause of moving and being at rest in that to which it belongs primarily, intrinsically, and not coincidentally. (I say 'not coincidentally' because, for example, someone who is a doctor might come to be a cause of health to himself. Nonetheless, it is not insofar as he is made healthy that he possesses the craft of medicine, but rather being a doctor and being made healthy are coincident in the same person. That is why they are separated from each other.)" (*Ph.* II 1 192ᵇ21–27).
Capacity is a starting-point of movement within another thing, or within the thing itself insofar as it is other: "Something is said to be a capacity when it is a starting-point of movement or change either in another thing or in a thing insofar as it is other—for example, the craft of building is a capacity that is not a component of the thing being built, whereas the craft of making healthy, which is a capacity, might be a component of the thing being made healthy, but not of it insofar as it is being made healthy" (*Met.* V 12 1019ᵃ15–18).

Note 437
There is neither coming to be (*genesis*) of everything nor of simply (*haplôs*) nothing: *Haplôs* could also be taken with *genesis*, as it is by Guthrie and Stocks: "There is neither simple (or unconditional) coming to be of everything nor of

nothing." But unconditional coming to be plays no part in the preceding argument. See Verdenius, pp. 282–283, followed by DP.
Is clear from what was said previously: See III 1 298^{b}14–24.

Note 438

It is impossible for there to be a coming to be of every body, unless it is also possible for there to be a void that is separated: A separated void is one "actively existing" (*Ph.* IV 6 231^{a}32–33) without a body in it; an un-separated one is one that has a body in it, but could not have one in it, and so exists potentially. The impossibility of a separated void is argued for in *Ph.* IV 6–9. See also, *Cael.* III 6 305^{a}14–22, and on separation, I 9 278^{a}17n.

Note 439

If what is potentially a body is not actively some other body previously, there will be a void that is separated: See, on potentially, I 7 275^{b}29n, and, on actively, I 12 281^{b}22n.

Note 440

The bodies in question: The ones of which there is coming to be.

Note 441

Let, then, an element of bodies be what other bodies are divided into, present in them either potentially or actively (for which of the two ways is still a matter for dispute), and is not itself divisible into things distinct in species: Compare: "Similarly those who speak of the elements of bodies mean the ultimate things into which bodies are divided, while they are no longer divided into other things differing in form; and whether the things of this sort are one or more than one, they call these elements" (*Met.* V 3 1014^{a}31–35).
Which is present in them either potentially or actively: See, on potentially, I 7 275^{b}29n, and, on actively, I 12 281^{b}22n.

Note 442

Even if there were only one thing of this sort, even then it would not be present in it: That is, even if there were only one non-elemental thing (for example, flesh), it would not be present in an elemental one (for example, fire) (see DP, p. 446 n3). Less plausibly: Even if there were only one elemental thing, the non-elemental things would not be present in it (Moraux, Guthrie, Kouremenos).

Note 443

Empedocles says that fire, earth, and the ones co-ordinate to these are elements of bodies and that everything is composed of these: "Empedocles, then, going beyond his predecessors, was the first to introduce the dividing of this cause, not making the starting-point of the movement one thing, but distinct and contrary ones. Further, he was the first to say that the kinds (*eidos*) of matter, the so-called elements, were four. Yet he does not *use* four but treats them as two only, fire by itself, on the one hand, and its opposites—earth, air, and water—taken as one nature, on the other (as we may gather from studying his verses)" (*Met.* I 4 985ᵃ29–ᵇ3). See DK B62 = TEGP 125 F76.

The ones co-ordinate to these: See II 4 287ᵇ21n.

Note 444

Anaxagoras says the contrary. For he says that the homoeomerous things are the elements (I mean flesh, bone, and each of the others of that sort), and that air and fire are mixtures of these and of the other "seeds": See DK B2–4 = TEGP 11–13 F1–5, also *Cael.* III 4 303ᵃ14–16n.

Homoeomerous things: See I 7 274ᵃ31n.

Note 445

For Anaxagoras calls fire and ether the same thing: I 3 270ᵇ24–25n. Ether, as eternal (on Aristotle's view), could not as such come to be. But for Anaxagoras, it is fire, and so it could come to be. Hence the reminder here. See Verdenius, p. 283.

Note 446

Some movements are simple, others mixed: See I 2 268ᵇ17–19.

Note 447

Those who make all the homoeomerous things elements, as Anaxagoras also does: See III 3 302ᵃ30–ᵇ2n.

Note 448

One that cannot be divided into things distinct in species, as was said previously: At III 3 302ᵃ18.

Note 449

One will produce the same result, even if there are only two or three such things, as Empedocles tries to show: See III 3 302ᵃ28–31n.

Note 450

Differentiae: 4 271ᵃ5n.

They are differentiated by their perceptual qualities, and these are limited in number; but this must be shown: "Since, then, we are inquiring after the starting-points of perceptible body, and it is tangible, and the tangible is that of which the perception is touch, it is evident that not all the contrarieties produce species and starting-points of body, but only those in accord with touch. For bodies are differentiated in accord with a contrariety, that is, in accord with a tangible contrariety. That is why neither whiteness and blackness, sweetness and bitterness, nor likewise any of the perceptible contraries other [than the tangible ones] produces an element. . . . Of the tangible ones themselves, then, it must be determined which are the primary differentiae and contrarieties. And the contrarieties that are in accord with touch are the following ones: hot cold, dry wet, heavy light, hard soft, viscous brittle, rough smooth, coarse-grained fine-grained. . . . [And] all these other differentiae can be led back to the four primary ones [hot, cold, dry, wet], whereas these cannot further be led back to a smaller number. . . . So it is necessary for there to be these four" (*GC* II 1 2 329ᵇ7–330ᵃ29). See also *Sens.* 6 445ᵇ23–446ᵃ20.

Note 451

They say that the primary things are unlimited in number and indivisible in magnitude, [and] that it is by the interweaving—that is, the combination—of the primary ones that all things will come to be: "They said that the starting-points were unlimited in number, believing them to be atomic—that is, indivisible— and unaffectable because they were compact and had no share of void. For they said that division came about in accord with the presence of void in bodies, whereas the atoms existed separated from each other in the unlimited void and, being different in shape, size, orientation, and order, were spatially moving in the void. When they encounter each other they collide, and some rebound, to wherever they happen to, whereas some become entangled (*periplekesthai*) with each other in accord with a symmetry in shape, size, orientation, and order, and combine and in this way accomplish the coming to be of composite things" (Simp. 242.18–26 = DK67 A 14 = TEGP 23).

Neither do many things come to be from one nor one from many: "Being in the strict sense (*kuriôs*) is completely a plenum. But such being is not one, but unlimited in number and indivisible because of the smallness of the masses. And these things spatially move in the void (for there is a void), and combining produce coming to be, and dissolving produce passing away. For they affect and are affected insofar as they happen to make contact. For in this they are not one. And when they combine and become entangled (*periplekomena*) they produce coming to be. But from what is truly one a plurality could not come to be, nor from what is truly many one—but this is impossible" (*GC* I 8 325ᵃ28–36 = DK67 A7 = TEGP 14). See also *Cael.* III 4 303ᵃ8–9n.

It is by the interweaving—that is, the combination—of the primary ones that all things will come to be: Reading ἐπαλλάξει with DP and the better mss. for Moraux περιπαλάξει.

Note 452

In a certain way these thinkers too make all the beings be numbers and composed of numbers: In other words, they are like Pythagoreans: "For it is impossible for a substance to be composed of substances that are actually present in it. For things that are actually two in this way are never actually one, although if they are potentially two, they can be one. For example, the double line is composed of two half lines, at any rate potentially. For their actuality separates them. And so if the substance is one, it will not be composed of substances present in it and present in the way that Democritus rightly states. For he says that it is impossible for one to be composed of two or two of one. For he makes the indivisible magnitudes the substances. It is clear therefore that the same will hold in the case of number, if indeed number is composed of units, as some people say. For two is either not a one, or there is no unit actually present in it" (*Met.* VII 13 1039ª3–14).

Note 453

Of what sort (*poion*) and what (*ti*) the shape is of each of the elements: The account or definition of something consists of its genus and its differentiae (*Met.* VII 12 1027ᵇ29–30), of which the genus is stated first: "the genus is intended to signify the what-it-is, and is placed first of the things said in the definition" (*Top.* VI 5 142ᵇ27–29). Sometimes both are included in the what-it-is or essence: "genera and differentiae are predicated in the what-it-is" (*Top.* VII 3 153ª17–18; also *APo.* II 5 91ᵇ28–30, 13 97ª23–25). But sometimes the genus tells us what the thing is while the differentiae tell us what sort or quality of thing it is: "a thing's differentia never signifies what-it-is, but rather some quality (*poion ti*)" (*Top.* IV 2 122ᵇ16–17; also 6 128ª26–27, *Met.* V 14 1020ª33).

They have assigned a spherical shape to fire: "Some say that what causes movement is most of all and primarily soul. And thinking that what was not itself in movement could not possibly move something else, they took the soul to be a thing that is in movement. That is what led Democritus to say that the soul is a sort of fire. For the shapes and atoms are unlimited and those that are spherical he says are fire and soul—which are like the so-called motes in the air that appear in the sunbeams that come through our windows. The universal seedbed of such shapes (*panspermian*), he says (and likewise Leucippus), are the elements of the whole of nature, while those of them that are spherical are the soul, because being of such a shape they are especially capable of moving through everything and—being themselves moving—of moving the rest, on the supposition that the soul is what imparts movement to animals. That is why, too, they make breathing the defining mark of being alive. For when the surrounding air compresses their bodies it squeezes out those atomic shapes which, because they are never at rest themselves, impart movement to animals. Then aid comes from outside by the entry of other similar atoms in breathing. For these prevent the squeezing out of those that are already inside, helping to counteract what is doing the compressing and solidifying. And life continues just so long as they are capable of doing this" (*DA* I 5 403ᵇ28–404ª16).

Note 454

The others they determine by greatness and smallness, regarding these (*autôn*) as a sort of a universal seedbed (*panspermian*) for all the elements: The *panspermia* is a "universal seedbed of shapes" (*Ph.* III 4 203ª21–22). Thus, *autôn* refers not to elements but to greatness and smallness, which serve as seeds for the shapes (see Verdenius, p. 283). The earth, water, fire, and air, which others regard as elements, are composites for Leucippus and Democritus, since "each of them is a universal seedbed (*panspermian*) for the homoeomerous things" (*GC* I 1 314ª28–ᵇ1).

Note 455

It is necessary to be in conflict with the mathematical sciences in speaking of indivisible bodies: See III 1 299ª4n, also III 7 306ª26–30.

Reputable beliefs (*endoxa*): "*Endoxa* are things that seem to be so (*dokounta*) to everyone, by the majority, or by the wise—either by all of them or by most or by the most notable and most *endoxos* (reputable)" (*Top.* I 1 100ᵇ21–23; repeated 101ᵃ11–13). Appeals to *endoxa* mark a discussion as dialectical in nature; appeals to truth mark it as scientific (I 14 105ᵇ30–31). Nonetheless, since reputable beliefs typically have some—albeit often partial and often un-perspicuously expressed—truth in them, they are "like" the scientific truth (*Rh.* I 1 1355ᵃ14). See Introduction, pp. xlvii–xlviii.

The [accounts] concerning time and movement: Especially, *Ph.* VI 1–2.

Note 456

The greatest bodies will always come to an end in being segregated out: What happens when water and air turn into earth is not that they literally become earth, but rather that atoms large enough to constitute earth get segregated out from them and then become aggregated in such a way so as to constitute perceptible earth. Aristotle's point is that segregation must eventually deplete the store of atoms large enough to do the job.

Note 457

All shapes are composed of pyramids, rectilinear ones of rectilinear ones, and the sphere of its eight parts: All plane figures are composed of triangles, all solid ones of pyramids—or, in the case of the sphere, of the pyramid-like ones that result from its symmetrical tri-division into eight parts.

Note 458

Some suppose that it is water, others air, others fire: Thales (water); Anaximenes (air); fire (Heraclitus). See III 1 298ᵇ29–33n.

Others something finer-grained than water and denser than air: It is unclear who held this view, which is also mentioned without specific attribution at *Ph.* I 4 187ᵃ14, *GC* II 1 328ᵇ35, 5 332ᵃ21, *Met.* I 7 988ᵃ30.

Note 459

Those who make this one element water, air, or something more fine-grained than water but denser than air, and have other things come to be from these by rarefaction and condensation, all fail to notice that they themselves are making something that is prior to the element in question: "The result for those who say that there is one only, and then generate the others by condensation and rarefaction, is to make the starting-points two: the rare and the dense, or the hot and the cold. For these are what play the role of craftsmen, while the one underlies them as matter" (*GC* II 3 330ᵇ9–13).

Note 460

Coming to be from their elements is composition, they say, and the one back into the elements, dissolution, so that it is necessary for the finer-grained one to be prior in nature: Things come to be by rarefaction and condensation. So progressive dissolution must lead to the most fine-grained (most rarified) element, whatever it is, and so the existence of the others presupposes its existence, but not vice versa, make it prior in nature to them. See I 2 269^{a}19n.

Note 461

For those distinguishing things in this way the result will be to say that all things are relatives, and that fire, water, and air will not unconditionally be, but rather the same thing will be fire relative to one thing, but air relative to another: The things that are unconditionally are substances (I 1 268^{a}3n). If, however, the substance (= essence) of fire, water, and air is defined by greatness and smallness, these things will not be substances, and so will not be starting-points or elements, since they will depend for their existence on other things. For greatness and smallness is in the category of relation, not in that of substance: "The great and the small, and the other things of that sort, must be relative to something. But the relative is least of all a nature or substance, and is posterior to quality and quantity. Also, the relative, not its matter, is an attribute of quantity, as was said, since another thing is [matter] for both the relative generally, and for its parts and kinds (*eidos*). For there is nothing either great or small, many or few, or, in general, relative to something, that is not great or small, many or few, or relative to something by being another thing. A sign that the relative is least of all a substance and a being is that of it alone there is neither coming to be nor passing away nor movement, as with respect to quantity there is growth and withering, with respect to quality alteration, with respect to place spatial movement, with respect to substance simple coming to be and passing away. But with respect to the relative there are none of these. For, without being moved or changed, a thing will be now greater and now less or equal, if the other thing has moved with respect to quantity. Also, the matter of each thing, and so of substance, must be what is potentially that sort of thing. But the relative is neither potentially nor actively substance. It is absurd, then, or rather, impossible, to make what is not a substance an element in, and prior to, substance, since all the categories are posterior to substance" (*Met.* XIV 1 1088^{a}22–^{b}4). See also, *Cat.* 6 5^{b}11–29.

Note 462

The more simple-minded ones . . . the ones more subtle in argument: The identity of these thinkers is unclear. "Heraclitus said that fire was the element of the other things but did not say that fire is pyramidal, whereas the Pythagoreans said that fire was composed of pyramids, but did say that it was the element of the other things" (Simp. 621.8–10). Compare *Plant.* II 7 827^{b}37–38: "fire is pyramidal in its own material and becomes light [and so moves upward]."

Note 463

As if they were growing together (*sumphusômenou*) **specks of dust** (*psêgmatos*): The word *psêgma* occurs again at IV 6 313^{a}20, where it refers to specks or motes floating in the air. Growing together, though it may sometimes be a completely natural process (*Met.* V 4 1014^{b}20–26), resulting in a natural unity (IX 1 1046^{a}28), as it probably is intended to be here, may also be a process that can lead to such things as Siamese twins: "Most monsters (*terata*) are due to embryos growing together" (*GA* IV 4 773ᵃ3–4). We might think of the way specks of soot in a flame, or motes in a sunbeam, seem to hang together.

Note 464
If they make the primary body indivisible, the arguments stated previously will come back again against their hypothesis: See III 4 303ᵃ20–24.

Note 465
Those who wish to get a theoretical grasp on things in a way appropriate to natural science: See III 1 298ᵇ18n.

Note 466
If there is more air than water, and, in general, more of a fine-grained one than of a coarse-grained one: See III 7 305ᵇ11–16, *Mete.* I 3 340ᵃ8–13, where this is said to be based on observation of what happens when, for example, water turns into air.

Note 467
A pyramid is not composed of pyramids: That is, not every part of a pyramid is itself a pyramid.

Note 468
If indeed [1] every body is divisible, and [2] the one with the smallest parts is their element: The combination of [1] and [2] is initially confusing, but the idea is this. For any part of a body you pick, there will be a smaller one, so whichever one you pick as your element on the basis of its size, there will be another smaller than it, and so prior to it.

Note 469
It has been determined previously that there are several natural movements: In I 2.

Note 470
We must investigate whether the elements are eternal or are coming to be and passing away: Reading γινόμενα φθείρεται with Moraux and most eds.; DP read γινόμενα ("eternal or coming to be") with ms. E as *lectio difficilior*.

Note 471
The body at which it stops will be either indivisible or, as Empedocles seems to wish to say, divisible though in fact never divided: = DK A43a = TEGP 216.

Note 472
Indivisible it will not be, because of the arguments stated previously: See III 1 299ᵃ2–11n, 4 303ᵃ20–24n, 7 306ᵃ26–30.

Note 473
A smaller body is more easily destroyed (*euphthartoteron*) **than a larger one:**
That is, more easily caused to pass away (the usual translation of *phthartos*,
phtheiresthai).

Note 474
A separated void: Reading κεχωρισμένον κενόν with Moraux (following
Simp. 629.19); ms. E, followed by Longo, has γεννώμενον; Allan conjectures
ἀφωρισμένον (notice κενὸν εἶναι ἀφωρισμένον a few lines later at III 6 305ᵃ21);
other mss., followed by DP, have κενόν alone. On separated void, see III 2 302ᵃ1n.

Note 475
There will be two bodies in the same place: "It is impossible for two bodies to be
together [in exactly the same place]" (*Ph.* IV 6 213ᵇ20).

Note 476
It is necessary for there to be a definite (*aphôrismenon*) **void:** A definite void is
one that fits the body that is coming to be in it like a glove, and so is separated from
other voids and bodies by its perimeter.
But that this is impossible was shown previously: At III 2 301ᵇ33–302ᵃ9.

Note 477
Balance-weight: See II 1 284ᵃ25n.
Immovable and mathematical: In other words, an abstraction. See II 1 299ᵃ16n.

Note 478
Together (*hama*): In its temporal sense, the adverb *hama* means (1) "at the same
time," or "simultaneously." But it also means (2) "together [in the same place]"
(see III 6 305ᵃ19n) or "at once," without direct reference to time. Its meaning in
contexts like this seems to be a mixture of (1) and (2).

Note 479
Those who dissolve them into planes: See III 1 299ᵃ2–3n.

Note 480
The finest-grained one comes to be in a bigger place: See III 5 303ᵇ27–29.

Note 481
When a liquid becomes vaporized (*diatmizomenou*) **or pneumaticized** (*pneumatoumenou*): The verbs *diatmizein* and *pneumatoun* are near synonyms in ordinary
Greek, but the latter has a somewhat technical meaning for Aristotle, as correlative
with the noun *pneuma*. "Boiling is due to liquid being pneumaticized (*pneumatoumenou*) by heat. For it gets swelled up (*hairetai*) because its mass becomes greater"
(*Resp.* 26 (20) 479ᵇ31–32). The growth of eggs and grubs and the expansion of yeast

in fermentation have a similar cause: "The increase in size of an egg is like that of larvae. For those animals that produce larvae give birth to a small thing at first and this increases in size because of itself and not because of being naturally connected to the parent in any way. The cause is similar to that in the case of yeast. For yeast also becomes great in size from a small beginning as the more solid part liquefies and the liquid becomes pneumaticized (*pneumatoumenou*). This is the handiwork (*dēmiourgei*) in the case of living things of the nature of the soul-involving heat (*psuchikou thermou*), in the case of yeast, of the humor (*chumos*) blended with it" (*GA* III 4 755ᵃ14–21). But what causes it to increase its mass and swell is the *pneuma* with which the heat imbues it: "[*Pneuma*] is evidently well disposed by nature to impart movement and supply strength. At all events, the functions of movement are pushing and pulling, so that its instrument (*organon*) must be capable of expanding and contracting. And this is just the nature of *pneuma*, since it contracts and expands without constraint, and is able to pull and push for the same reason" (*MA* 10 703ᵃ18–23). Thus "it makes perfect sense, indeed, for nature to make most things using *pneuma* as instrument. For just as some things have many uses where the crafts are concerned—for example, the hammer and the anvil in blacksmithing—so does *pneuma* in those constituted by nature" (*GA* V 8 789ᵇ8–12). Hence, despite the contrast drawn between larvae and grubs, there is *pneuma* even in utterly inanimate things: "in water *pneuma* is present, and in all *pneuma* there is soul-involving [= formative] heat (*thermotēta psuchikēn*), so that in a way all things are full of soul" (III 11 762ᵃ18–21). Even when *pneuma* is identified with "hot air" (II 2 736ᵃ1), the air itself is not just air heated up, but air involving soul-involving, formative heat.

Note 482

There is not a void and bodies cannot expand, as those who say these things claim: "There are some people who, because of the rare and the dense, think that it is evident that a void exists. For if rare and dense do not exist, it is impossible to contract and be compressed. But if this is not possible, either there will be no movement at all, or the whole universe will bulge, as Xuthus said, or change, for example of air and water, must always be into equal amounts (I mean, for example, that if air comes to be from a cup of water, then at the same time from an equal amount of air a cup of water must have come to be), or a void must exist. For compression and expansion are not possible otherwise" (*Ph.* IV 4 216ᵇ22–30). Little is known about Xuthus, who may have been a Pythagorean from Croton, or an atomist, or a mix of the two. But both horns of the argument require the existence of void: either within the universe, allowing for rarefaction and condensation, or outside the universe (if that is a possibility at all!), into which the excess volume of the universe can bulge.

Note 483

Or by dissolution into planes, as some people say: See III 1 299ᵃ2–3n.

Note 484

Those defending their theses (*theseis*) in [dialectical] arguments: "A thesis is: a contradoxical supposition of someone notable for philosophy—for example, that contradiction is impossible (as Antisthenes used to say), or that everything moves (in accord with Heraclitus), or that what is is one (as Melissus says). For to give thought to it when some random person declares things contrary to our beliefs is simpleminded. Or: something contrary to our beliefs for which we have an argument. For example, that not everything that is either has come to be or is eternally, as the sophists say: for a musician who is grammatical is so without having become so or being so eternally. For even if someone does not believe this, he might believe it because of having an argument. A thesis, then, is also a problem, but not every problem is a thesis, since some problems are such that we have no belief about them either way. But that a thesis is a problem is clear. For it is necessary from what has been said either that ordinary people dispute with the wise about a thesis, or that one or the other lot disputes among themselves, since a thesis is a contradoxical supposition. As thing stand, though, pretty much all dialectical problems are called theses" (*Top.* I 11 104^{b}19–35).

Note 485

Productive science (*poiêtikês epistêmês*): "There is no craft that is not a productive state involving reason and no such state that is not a craft, a craft is the same as a productive state involving true reason" (*NE* VI 4 1140^{a}8–10).

In that of natural science what appears to be so to perception has the controlling vote (*kuriôs*) **in every case** (*aei*): This is because the induction leading to natural science is based on a grasp of particulars, "which perception already controls" (*NE* VII 3 1147^{a}26). On "controlling vote," see II 13 293^{b}2n, and, on *aei*, Verdenius, p. 283.

Note 486

Earth alone is incapable of dissolving into another body: The argument seems to rely on the fact that an element for Plato is a scalene right triangle. The problem is that earth, which gets assigned a cube shape, is not dissolvable into such triangles, if its components are required to reform only into cubes, as *Ti.* 56d (Appendix) seems to require. For an account of why Plato selects the scalene right triangle as an element, see Cornford, pp. 224–239. The drifting about is what Aristotle is about to refer to as "dangling" (III 7 306^{a}21).

Note 487

"Dangling" (*paraiôrêsis*) **of the triangles . . . happens whenever one thing is transformed into another, because of the numerical inequality of the triangles that compose them:** When something composed of n+m triangles is dissolved into something composed of m triangles, n triangles will be left dangling, not composing any body at all. This is unreasonable because non-bodies cannot occupy space or drift around in it.

Note 488

The most exact sciences: See I 3 269^{b}21n.

Note 489

The mathematical [sciences], suppose even an intelligible [body] to be divisible: When a mathematician draws a particular equilateral triangle ABC in chalk on a blackboard, he uses it to represent an abstract particular equilateral triangle <ABC> whose sides are perfectly straight, exactly equal mathematical lines that have length but no breadth. <ABC> is an intelligible mathematical object. When he draws a second equilateral triangle DEF in order to prove that <ABC> and <DEF> are congruent, what distinguishes these two abstract mathematical triangles from each other is not their form or shape, which is the same in both, but their distinct parcels of matter, and which are the abstract analogues $<m_1>$ and $<m_2>$ of the different parcels of perceptible matter, m_1 and m_2, consisting of chalk and areas of blackboard, that distinguish ABC from DEF (*Met.* VII 8 1034^a5–8). <ABC> and <DEF> are particular abstract triangles, just as Callias and Socrates are particular non-abstract humans. And as the universal human is a sort of compound of this form (defined by the account of human) and this matter taken universally (1035^b27–30), so the universal mathematical triangle is a compound of the form (defined by the account of equilateral triangle) and something else. And this something else is not $<m_1>$ or $<m_2>$, which are distinct parcels of intelligible matter (*hulê noêtê*)—this being the sort that is "in perceptible things but not insofar as they are perceptible" (10 1036^a11–12). Instead it is the abstract universal material of which they are instances—the analogue, in other words, of the non-abstract universal material of which m_1 and m_2 are distinct instances. It is this universal analogue—intelligible matter taken universally—that *Met.* VIII 6 describes: "Some matter is intelligible, and some perceptible, and of the account always one part is the matter and the other the actuality [= the form]—for example, the circle is shape + plane (*ho kuklos schêma epipedon*)" (1045^a33–35). Since "shape" is a common equivalent of "form," we may infer that plane is the universal material component of the account or definition of the universal circle, and so of the universal equilateral triangle as well. It is thus a special case of intelligible matter. For what mathematicians leave behind when they do their abstracting from perceptibles is "only the quantitative and the continuous, sometimes in one, sometimes in two, sometimes in three dimensions, and the attributes of things insofar as they are quantitative and continuous" (XI 3 1061^a32–35). Intelligible matter taken universally, then, is the continuous—the abstract analogue of physical space that the quantitative divides up (notice "lines and the continuous" at VII 11 1036^b9–10), and so make intelligible mathematical objects divisible. See also *Cael.* I 7 275^b10n.

Note 490

The result will be that the whole will not be filled up: Yet, Plato denies that there is empty space (void): "Once the circumference of the universe has comprehended the [four] kinds, then, because it is round and has a natural tendency to gather in upon itself, it constricts them all and allows no empty space to be left over" (*Ti.* 58a).

Note 491

Among plane figures three shapes seem to fill the [whole of] place, triangle, square, and hexagon: If the polygons are regular, this is correct.

And among the solids two only, pyramid and cube: If the tetrahedra are regular, this is false, although they can come very close to filling it; just how close remains an unsolved problem (see Lagarais). Moreover, "the question of which tetrahedra fill space and which do not is still unresolved" (Senechal, p. 242).

Note 492

In this condition it would be most capable of receiving shape, like the all-receptive (*to pandeches*) **written about in the *Timaeus*:** See Plato, *Ti.* 50b–c (Appendix).
Matter: See I 3 270ª24n.

Note 493

Since fire is most capable of movement, and also is capable of heating and of burning, some people made it a sphere: Namely, the atomists. See III 4 303ª14n.
Others a pyramid: Plato, *Ti.* 56b (Appendix).

Note 494

For Democritus indeed even the sphere is a sort of angle: = DK 68 B155a = TEGP 157 F42. To get the idea, start with a straight line. As soon as you bend it you have a sort of (blunt or curved tip) angle; bend it sharply and you have an angle proper: "Bending is a change from what is straight to what is curved or angular; straightening is the change of either of these to what is straight" (*IA* 9 708ᵇ22–24). A sphere, on this showing, is a solid (curved) angle.

Note 495

The elements will differ [only] in the more and less (*to mallon kai hêtton*): The more and less corresponds to our notion of degree, and so is connected to the notion of increasing and decreasing—tightening and loosening (*epiteinein kai aniê-sin*). Thus as a musician tightens or loosens his instrument's strings until a certain target note is struck (*Pol.* IV 3 1290ª22–29), so too with vocal cords, sinews, and other string-like things (*GA* V 7 787ᵇ10–24). Hence Aristotle employs the notion of tightening and loosening wherever a certain tripartite structure is thought to exist, consisting of a continuous underlying subject (*to mallon kai hêtton*), a pair of opposed attributes that can vary in degree, and a target, typically a mean condition of some sort, that can be achieved by tightening or loosening the underlying subject to change the degree of the attributes. As a result, he speaks of tightening and loosening in characterizing a wide range of phenomena, from the parts of animals to political constitutions (*Pol.* V 9 1309ᵇ18–31, *Rh.* I 4 1360ª23–30). In the case of noses and other such parts, the continuous underlying subject is flesh and bone (or its shape), the pair of opposite attributes is hooked and snub, and the target— which lies somewhere in between the two, and so (as in political constitutions) in a mean of some sort—is being a straight nose, or at the very least a nose of some sort. In the case of colors, too, while many are constituted out of white and black in some definite ratio, others are constituted in "some incommensurable ratio of excess or deficiency," and so are apt for tightening and loosening (*Sens.* 3 439^{b}30). Because *to mallon kai hêtton* is found in many different genera, it cannot be the subject matter of any of the first-order sciences, since these are restricted to a single genus (*Rh.* I 2 1358^{a}10–17). Some idea of the importance of the notion when it comes to defining species and their essences may be gleaned from the following text: "Of the animals, some have all their parts mutually identical, whereas some have different ones. Some parts are identical in form [or species] (*eidei*)—for example, one human's nose and eye are identical to another human's nose and eye, one's flesh to the other's flesh, one's bone to the other's bone; and the same applies to the parts of a horse and of such other animals as we say are identical in form [species]. For as the whole is to the whole, so each part is to each part. In other cases—those whose genus is the same—they are indeed identical [in form], but they differ in excess or deficiency. By genus I mean, for example, bird and fish. For each of these exhibits difference with respect to its genus, that is, there are numerous species both of fish and of birds. Now the differences of most of the parts in animals lie in the contrarieties of their attributes (for example, of colors and shapes), in that some have the same things more others less, and additionally in greater or fewer number, and larger or smaller size—that is, to put it generally, in excess or deficiency. Thus in some the texture of the flesh is soft, in others firm; some have a long bill, others a short one; some have many feathers, others few. Further, even in the cases we are considering, it happens that different ones have different parts—for example, some have spurs, others do not, some have crests and others do not. But (one might almost say) most of the parts and those out of which the mass of the body is composed, are either identical [in species or form] or differ by way of their contrarieties, that is, by way of excess or deficiency. For the more and less may be taken to be a sort of excess or deficiency. Some animals, however, do have parts that are neither identical in species nor [different] in excess or deficiency, but are [merely] analogous—for example, as bone is to fish-spine, nail to hoof, hand to claw, feather to scale. For what the feather is in a bird, the scale is in a fish" (*HA* I 1 486^{a}14–^{b}22).

But it is evident that this is false: Even on Plato's own view, the elements are different in genus, which is a deeper difference than one merely of degree. See previous note.

Note 496
Intrinsic . . . coincidental: See I 2 268^{b}15n.

Note 497
They should have looked toward both the aggregating and the segregating when they assigned [fire a shape] or, better, toward the aggregating: Because aggregating is an intrinsic attribute of it; segregating a coincidental one.

Note 498
No shape is contrary to a shape: Reading οὐθὲν δ' ἐναντίον ἐστὶ σχῆμα σχήματι ("no shape is contrary to a shape") with Moraux, Longo (notice σχῆμα δὲ σχήματι οὐ δοκεῖ εἶναι ἐναντίον at *Sens.* 4 442^{b}19–20); Allan, Guthrie, Kouremenos, Stocks,

read οὐθὲν δ' ἐναντίον ἐστὶ σχήματι ("nothing is contrary to a shape"), which DP translates. Here is the background argument: "Shape is a sort of magnitude" (*DA* III 13 425ᵃ18); "a quantity is a plurality if it is countable, a magnitude if it is measurable" (*Met.* V 13 1020ᵃ8–10); a quantity (for example, four-foot or five-foot) has no contrary (*Cat.* 6 5ᵇ11–14). Shape, though, in contrast to *a* (specific) shape, is in the category of quality (8 10ᵃ11)—hence the contrary notion of shapelessness: "the statue, or anything else that is shaped, comes to be from shapelessness (*aschêmosunê*)" (*Ph.* I 5 188ᵇ19–20). A similar contrast between generic and specific is found in the case of scientific knowledge: "Scientific knowledge, a genus, is said to be just what it is, *of* another thing (it is said to be scientific knowledge of something), but none of the particular cases is said to be just what it is *of* another thing—for example, grammar is not said to be grammar of something or music music of something. If they too are said to be relative to something at all, it is with reference to the genus—for example, grammar is said to be scientific knowledge of something, not grammar of something, and music is said to be scientific knowledge of something, not music of something. So the particular cases are not relatives" (*Cat.* 8 11ᵃ24–32).

Note 499
What has large particles, they say, is cold, because it compresses and cannot pass through the ducts: Plato, *Ti.* 62a–b (Appendix).

Note 500
The most controlling differences: See II 13 293ᵇ2n.

Book IV

Note 501
Things are heavy or light in virtue of their being capable of being moved naturally in a certain way: Reading τῷ δύνασθαι with Moraux, Longo, and some mss.; DP and other mss. read τὸ δύνασθαι.

Note 502
To the activations of [light and heavy], though, names are not assigned, unless it was thought that "balance-weight" is such: On activation see I 12 281ᵇ22n, and, on balance-weight, II 1 284ᵃ25n.

Note 503
Heavy and light, then, are said of things unconditionally and in relation to something else: See II 13 293ᵇ4n.

Note 504
There is no up and down, they say, if indeed it is similar in every direction, and from whatever point he traverses it a given person will come to his own antipodes: See Plato, *Ti.* 62b–63e (Appendix).

Note 505

The extremity of the universe is up, both up as regards position and by nature primary: See I 2 269^{a}19n.

Note 506

Ordinary people (*hoi polloi*): Sometimes Aristotle uses *hoi polloi* (literally, "the many," "the multitude") to refer simply to a majority of people of whatever sort—to most people. But quite often, as here, he uses it to refer to the vulgar masses (*NE* I 5 1095^{b}16) in contrast to cultivated, sophisticated, or wise people (1095^{a}21). "Ordinary people" often seems to convey the correct sense.

Note 507

Some of them speak of lighter and heavier in the way one finds it written about in the *Timaeus*: At 63c–e (Appendix).

Note 508

From up to down a smaller quantity of fire is spatially moved faster, and a larger one more slowly: That is, when it is moved by force contrary to its natural movement.

Note 509

If the proportion of solid will exceed that of void, it will not be lighter: On the translation, see Verdenius, p. 283.

Note 510

Of those denying the existence of a void: "Those, then, who try to show that a void does not exist in fact refute not what people mean by 'void,' but what they in error say about it, as Anaxagoras does and those who try to refute it in this way. For they show that air is something, by twisting wineskins and showing how strong the air is, and by trapping it in clepsydras" (*Ph.* IV 6 213^{a}22–27). Empedocles denies the existence of a void at DK B13–14 = TEGP 38–39 F17–18a-b; F17, F18a = *Xen.* 976^{b}22–27.
Some have determined nothing about light and heavy—for example, Anaxagoras and Empedocles: Empedocles does not seem to mention heavy and light at all. Anaxagoras refers to them as mixed together at DK B10 = TEGP 28.

Note 511

Larger and a smaller quantity of fire will contain the same ratio (*logos*) **of solid to void:** Since they are determined by the fixed relation in which they stand to each other. See IV 2 309^{b}15–16.

Note 512

Due to what cause do plenum and void not stand apart from each other: That is, what causes there to be bodies that are a mixture of plenum and void.

Note 513
It is not void alone that is moved, but the solid as well: The solid = plenum. See IV 2 309ᵃ31.

Note 514
The things intermediate between the unconditionally heavy and unconditionally light ones: Namely, water and air.

Note 515
Nothing is unconditionally light or spatially moves upward, except [1] by being passed by other things or [2] being squeezed out: In [1] X appears to move unconditionally upward, but really it is just being passed by other things moving downward; in [2] X's upward movement is genuine, but due to force, since it is being pushed or squeezed upward by other things.

Note 516
Heavy and light and the coincidental attributes (*sumbainontôn pathêmatôn*) **pertaining to them:** The attributes in question are the intrinsic coincidents or *per se* accidents that follow from the differentiae defining the essence (notice *diaphoras kai ta sumbainonta* at IV 4 311ᵃ15), but are not parts of it. See I 2 268ᵇ15n.

Note 517
There are three sorts of movement (with respect to size, with respect to form (*kat' eidos*), **and with respect to place):** Since these correspond to increase and decrease, alteration, and spatial movement (IV 3 310ᵃ27–29), it seem that *kat' eidos* should be understood as meaning "with respect to quality," and not with respect to (substantial form). For the latter would be a case of coming to be or passing away, which is not strictly speaking a movement. See *Ph.* V 6 225ᵃ25–27. Nonetheless, the choice of *eidos* is significant. For in the case of an element its proper place, as we are about to see (*Cael.* IV 3 310ᵃ34), is—or is relevantly like—the substantial form of a matter-form compound.

Note 518
The spatial movement of each body toward its own place is spatial movement toward its own form: "The activity of the light is to be somewhere (namely, up) and it is prevented whenever it is in the contrary place" (*Ph.* VIII 4 255ᵇ11); "It is evident that the substance and the form are activity" (*Met.* IX 8 1050ᵇ2–3).

Note 519
Like spatially moves to like: See *NE* VIII 1 1155ᵃ34–35.

Note 520
If one were to displace the earth to where the moon is now, each of its parts would spatially move not toward it, but to just where it in fact is now: Because

a part of the whole is "attracted" to its own proper place, not to where the whole happens to be: "The spatial movements of the simple natural bodies—for example, fire, earth, and the like—make it clear not only that place is something but also that it has a certain capacity (*tina dunamin*)" (*Ph.* IV 1 208^{b}8–11). No causal efficacy, however, is being attributed to place as such: "of what in beings could one suppose place to be the cause? For not one of the four causes is present in it. For it is neither a cause as matter for the beings (since nothing is composed of it), nor as form and account of things, nor as end, nor does it cause the beings to move" (209^{a}18–22). Instead it is place insofar as it is "in a certain way (*tropon tina*)" (*Cael.* IV 3 310^{b}10) form that has a certain capacity. For insightful discussion, see Matthen.

Note 521

Place is the limit of what encompasses: "Place is . . . the limit of what encompasses something at which it is in contact with what is encompassed" (*Ph.* IV 4 212^{a}5–6a).

The extremity and center (*to meson*) encompass all the things moving upward and downward: See I 5 273^{a}17–19n.

Note 522

It is possible to reverse the intermediate ones, but not the extremes—for example, air is like water, water is like earth. For the relation of each higher body to the one falling below it is that of form to matter: "[The intermediate bodies] are given form by the extreme bodies, and thus mediately determined by the 'place.' Instead of saying 'are given form' or 'are determined' Aristotle says 'are like'; being entitled to do so by the meaning just given to 'like.' The like to which earth moves is that from which it receives its form, and the like to which water and air move is the extreme body—earth in the one case, fire in the other—from which each receives its form. Thus 'like' means 'receptive of form from.' In this sense water is like air which is like fire, and air is like water which is like earth; but the extremes themselves are like nothing but their places. The relation of likeness is reciprocal (i.e. determination is mutual) only between the intermediates; and the chain of resemblance breaks off in each direction short of the extreme. Starting from the center, we find in the three terms, water, air, fire, a gradual approximation (ἀεὶ γὰρ τὸ ἀνώτερον) [IV 3 310^{b}14] to the form realized in fire; starting from the extremity, we find in the terms air, water, earth, a gradual approximation to the form realized in earth. (Of these two complementary statements Aristotle gives only the first; but the second is necessary to complete the argument.) Therefore the intermediate bodies, as well as the extremes, may be said in moving to their places to attain their form" (Stocks, 310^{b}15n). This is almost but not quite right. For when up is associated with form and down with matter (IV 4 312^{a}15–16), we need to recognize that earth is least formed (and so is closer to matter), water more formed than earth (and so closer to fire and the upward place), air yet more formed, and fire most formed.

Note 523

Since (*epei*) **[all that is so], to investigate . . . :** The *epei* comes from IV 3 310ª23, which begins the statement of a long protasis, which ends here with the apodosis.

Note 524

It moves (*pheretai*) **toward health:** *Pheresthai* is usually "spatially move," but here, as at IV 3 311ª9, seems not to have primarily spatial connotations.

It is [capable of being made] diseased (*noseron*): *Noseron* usually means "diseased," "unhealthy," but here, as at IV 4 312ª19, it seems to refer to the capacity to be made or to become diseased.

Note 525

Their matter is closer to substance: "Air is *already* actually light as soon as it has been generated [come to be]. Motion to its own place does not alter the nature of air (its lightness), but expresses and enhances it. At the same time, natural locomotion [spatial movement] is intimately connected with elemental being, more so than it is for living organisms whose lower functions (nutrition and perception) are crowned by locomotion. The elements are incomplete because what controls their natural motion lies outside them, and is still outside them, even if an element arrives at its own place. An element is constantly active, but that unflagging motion cannot compensate for the fact that an element's form is and remains external to it" (Gill, p. 158).

Note 526

Spatial movement belongs to independent things, and in coming to be is the last of the movements: Before a thing can spatially move it must first have come to be as the sort of thing it is, and so has acquired the form responsible for its being a thing of that sort.

So that this movement would be primary with respect to substance: "The things that are posterior in coming to be are prior in form and in substance—for example, man to boy and human to seed (for the one already has the form, while the other does not)—and because everything that comes to be proceeds toward a starting-point and an end (for the for-the-sake-of-which is a starting-point, and the coming to be is for the sake of the end), and the activity is the end, and it is for the sake of this that the capacity [or potentiality] is acquired" (*Met.* IX 8 1050ª4–10).

Note 527

When, then, air comes to be from water and light from heavy, it progresses upward. And at the same time it *is* light, and is no longer becoming so, but in that place *is*: The idea is that when light air comes to be from heavy water, it moves upward, and in that place (namely, up) it is no longer *becoming* (something) light, but *is* (something light).

Note 528

It is evident, then, that being potentially, going toward actuality, it is progressing to that place (ἐκεῖ) **quantity, and quality where** (οὗ) **the actualization of its**

quantity and quality and place lie (καὶ ὅπου): Mss. EJH read καὶ ὅπου, which I have followed; Moraux, other mss., and most eds., seclude it, as either (1) "an unintelligent repetition of οὗ" (Guthrie, p. 348 n1) or (2) "inserted by someone who mistook οὗ = *ubi* [= 'where' in Latin] for the genitive of the relative [ὅς]" (Stocks). But neither reason seems compelling. Ἐκεῖ ("that place") invites but does not answer the question, "what place?" The οὗ clause answers the question: "The place where its quantity, quality, and place (that is, the place proper to it) are actualized." Remember, the proper or natural place of fire is "the limit of what encompasses" (IV 3 310ᵇ7) it, where "it" refers to the totality of fire. Thus that place (as a whole) is actualized only when or if the totality of fire is in its proper place. On actualization, see I 12 281ᵇ22n.

Note 529

What causes the movement is what produces it at the start, what removed the hindrance, or from which the thing rebounded, as was said in our first accounts, in which we determined that none of these things moves itself: The reference is to the following passage in *Ph.* VIII 4: "And yet this is what is being inquired into, namely, why it is that the light and the heavy do move to their own place. And the cause is that it is natural for them to be somewhere, and this is the being for the light and the heavy, the one being determined by up and the other by down. Things, though, are potentially light and heavy in many ways, as has just been said. For when something is water it is in a way at least potentially light, and when it is air it is still potentially light, for something may impede it from being up. But if the impediment is removed, it becomes active and moves always upward. In a similar way a quality too changes to being active. For scientific knowing changes at once to contemplating, if nothing prevents it. And a [compressed] quantity is at once expanded, if nothing prevents it. And the one who removes what supports or prevents in a way causes movement and in a way does not—for example, the one who pulls away a supporting pillar or removes a stone from [holding down an air-filled] wineskin in the water. For he moves the thing coincidentally, just as the ball that bounced back was moved not by the wall but by the thrower. It is clear, therefore, that none of these things moves itself. However, each does have a starting-point of movement, not of causing movement or of affecting, but of being affected" (255ᵇ13–31). Thus "what produces it at the start" refers to things like the thrower of a ball that bounces, or the remover of a supporting pillar.

Note 530

The differentiae and the coincidental attributes (*ta sumbainonta*) **pertaining to these:** The attributes in question are the intrinsic coincidents or *per se* accidents that follow from the differentiae defining the essence, but are not parts of it. See I 2 268ᵇ15n.

Note 531

By "unconditionally," I mean looking to the genus, and not to those things to which both heavy and light belong: In an essential definition, which consists of genus and differentiae, the genus, which is stated first tell us what the definiendum is, the differentiae, which come next, tell us what it is like. See *Top.* I 8 103ᵇ15–16, V 3 132ᵃ12–13.

Note 532
Non-composite parts: That is, elementary parts.

Note 533
It is about the non-composite parts of heavy and light things that we must speak, since the other bodies follow along with the primary ones. Which is just, as we said, what those thinkers should have done who say that heaviness is due to the plenum and lightness due to the void: See IV 2 309ᵇ17–24.

Note 534
A talent of wood is heavier than a mina of lead: A talent ≈ 57 lbs.; a mina ≈ 1 lb. 5 oz.

Note 535
It is not the case, as some people think, that all bodies have heaviness: The atomists, for whom a body is a plenum, that is, something full, and fullness is heaviness, are an example.

Note 536
For other people too think that there is something heavy, that is (*kai*), that always spatially moves toward the center: That is, people other than Aristotle himself.

Note 537
For we see, as was said previously, that earthy bodies sink below everything else and spatially move toward the center: See IV 4 311ᵃ19–21.

Note 538
The center is definite: See I 6 273ᵃ10–12.

Note 539
Fire is observed to spatially move upward even in air itself, the air remaining at rest: So that the air cannot be forcing it upward.

Note 540
Fire spatially moving upward, and earth and everything having heaviness in their spatially moving downward, are observed to do so at similar angles: See II 14 296ᵇ18–21n.

Note 541
Whether the resulting movement is toward the center of the earth or toward that of the universe, since of these it is the same point, is for another account: See II 14 296ᵇ9–18.

Note 542
The intermediate is in a way extremity and center of both: Reading ἀμφοτέρων τὸ μεταξύ with DP and some mss. for Moraux and other mss. ἀμφοτέρων ἐστὶ τὸ μεταξύ.

Note 543
What encompasses pertains to form, what is encompassed to matter: "As the matter and the unlimited are what are encompassed and inside, the form is what encompasses" (*Ph.* III 7 207ᵃ35–ᵇ1); "Something is said to be a whole if [among other things] . . . it is what encompasses the things it encompasses in such a way that they are one . . . as together composing one thing" (*Met.* V 26 1023ᵇ26–29). See also, *Cael.* III 8 306ᵃ9–10.

Note 544
Genus: The primary genera are the categories (quantity, quality and so on), which are referred to as such at *APo.* II 13 96ᵇ20–21, *Met.* VII 9 1034ᵇ9.

Note 545
For in [the category] of quality as in of quantity, there is what is more the way form is, and what is more the way matter is: "We might say that there are three starting-points—the form and the lack [of form] and the matter. But each of these is distinct for each genus—for example, in colors they are white [form], black [lack of whiteness], and surface [matter], or light [form], darkness [lack of light], and air [matter], out of which day and night come to be" (*Met.* XII 4 1070ᵇ19–21); "There must, surely, be a matter for each genus, except it cannot be separable from substances" (XIV 2 1089ᵇ27–28).

Note 546
Up pertains to what is defined: "The definition is . . . of the form" (*Met.* VII 11 1036ᵃ28–29).
Up pertains to what is defined, down pertains to matter: See IV 3 310ᵃ8–15n.

Note 547
It is the same matter, but its being is not the same [in the two cases]: See I 9 278ᵃ8n.
As in what is capable of being made diseased and what is capable of being made healthy: "To have the potential to be healthy and to have the potential to be sick are not the same, since if they were, to be sick and to be healthy would be the same. The underlying subject, though, whether it is healthy or diseased, whether it is moisture or blood, *is* one and the same" (*Ph.* III 1 201ᵃ35–ᵇ3). According to the Hippocratic author of *On Ancient Medicine*, for example, the human body contains a blend (*chrêsis*) of moist substances or humors (*chumoi*), each with a capacity (*dunamis*) to cause a specific effect: "These, when mixed and blended with one another are neither manifest nor cause the human being pain; but when one of them separates off and comes to be on its own, then it is both manifest and

causes the human being pain" (14.4 Schiefsky). Plato adopts a somewhat similar view, with imbalances in the blood playing an important role in causing certain diseases (*Ti*. 81e–86a).

Note 548
What has other sorts of matter than these, but ones having in relation to each other what these themselves have unconditionally, has both upward and downward spatial movements: Reading φερόμενα with DP; Guthrie and Longo read φερομένας, which Moraux secludes.

Note 549
There is one matter common to all of them—especially if they come to be from each other—though its being is distinct: See IV 4 312ᵃ18–21n.

Note 550
There is nothing to prevent there being one or more intermediates between the contraries, as in the case of colors: See III 1 299ᵃ21–22n.

Note 551
"Intermediate" and "center" are said of things in many ways: See II 13 293ᵇ4–8. **Said of things in many ways** (*pollachôs legetai*): "Something is said to be in many ways, however, but with reference to one thing and one nature—that is, not homonymously. Rather, just as what is healthy all has reference to health, one by safeguarding it, another by producing it, one by being a sign of health, another because it is a recipient of it, and what is medical all has reference to the craft of medicine (for one thing is said to be medical by possessing the craft of medicine, another by being naturally well disposed to it, another by being a result of the craft of medicine), and we shall find other things that are said to be in ways similar to these, so, too, something is said to be in many ways, but all with reference to one starting-point. For some things are said to be because they are substances, others because they are attributes of substances, others because they are a route to substance, or else by being passings away, lacks, or qualities of substance, or productive or generative either of substance or of things that are said to be with reference to substance, or denials of one of these or of substance (that is why we say even of not being that it *is* not being)" (*Met*. IV 2 1003ᵃ33–ᵇ10).

Note 552
Just as water is drawn up when its surface becomes one [with that of air]: As in the case of evaporation. "The exhalation from water is vapor; that from air to water is cloud. Mist is the residue of the condensation of air into water" (*Mete*. I 9 346ᵇ32–33).

Note 553
Earth, on the other hand, is not thus affected, because its surface is not one [with that of water]: There is nothing between earth and water analogous to

water vapor (a sort of air) forming on the surface of water as it is heated by the sun. Simp. 723.36 suggests that the roughness of the earth's surface is what prevents its surface from becoming one with that of water, but "this fact seems to be accidental [coincidental]" (Elders, p. 359, IV 5 312ᵇ12n). More than that, it seems simply false, since water's lower surface will take its shape from the upper surface of the earth below it. But perhaps the idea is that the earth's dryness does not provide the cohesion necessary for forming unified entities, so that the element above it cannot exert an influence on it like that of air drawing up water.

Note 554

What is relatively heavy sinks as far as its own space or as the body in which it rises, because of the similarity of matter: See IV 4 318ª18–20n.

Note 555

Either nothing will be unconditionally light: The expected second disjunct is missing.

If everything causes a balance to incline more (*rhepei mallon*) downward due to the size or number of its constituent bodies, or because there are plenums: One meaning of *rhepein* is "cause a balance or weighing scale to incline one way or the other," so the claim is that a thing's balance-weight (*rhopê*) depends solely on the factors mentioned. On balance-weight, see II 1 284ª25n.

We see this, though, and it has been shown, that in the same way as there is something that spatially moves always and everywhere downward, there is something that does so always and everywhere upward: See IV 4 311ᵇ13–29.

Note 556

In a large quantity of air there will be more [1] triangles, or [2] solids, or [3] small [particles] (*mikra*): We start with three options: "if there is a single matter for all things (for example, [a-i] void or [a-ii] plenum, or [b] magnitude, or [c] triangles)" (IV 5 312ᵇ20–22). Since [1] = [c], we are left with [2] and [3]. Most probably, [2] maps onto [b], and [3] onto [a-ii].

Note 557

Meaning by "the surge (*ton soun*)" the movement of the spatially moving bodies upward: The noun *sous* (*soun* is the acc.), from the verb *soumai* ("clash"), does not occur elsewhere in Aristotle. But Plato tells us that "*Sous* . . . is what the Spartans call a rapid advance" (*Crat.* 412b).

Note 558

The smaller the quantity in each genus the more easily it is divided and dispersed: The genera referred to are in particular the easily bounded elements, water and air, which are the ones in which bodies of one shape float, while those of a different shape sink.

Note 559

Those having breadth remain in place because of covering so large a surface, and because the large quantity is less easily dispersed: The large quantity in question is probably that of the supporting water. Compare II 13 294^{b}24–30.

Note 560

Concerning heaviness and lightness, then (*men oun*), **and the coincidental attributes pertaining to these, let things be determined in this way:** *Men* here is answered by *de* in the opening sentence of *Mete.*, indicating that the latter comes next in the series.

Appendix

Plato, *Timaeus* 50b–57d, 61c–64a*

We must always refer to [that nature which receives all the bodies] by the same term, since it does not depart from its own capacity in any way. Not only does it always receive all things, it has never in any way whatever taken on any shape similar to any of the things that enter it. Its nature is to be available for anything to make its impression upon, and it is modified, shaped and reshaped by the things that enter it. These are the things that make it appear different at different times. The things that enter and leave it are imitations of those things that always are, imprinted after their likeness in a marvelous way that is hard to describe. This is something we shall pursue at another time. For the moment, we need to keep in mind three kinds of things: that which comes to be, that in which it comes to be, and that after which the thing coming to be is modeled, and which is the source of its coming to be. It is in fact appropriate to compare the receiving thing to a mother, the source to a father, and the nature between them to their offspring. We also must understand that if the imprints are to be varied, with all the varieties there to see, this thing upon which the imprints are to be formed could not be well prepared for that role if it were not itself devoid of any of those characters that it is to receive from elsewhere. For if it resembled any of the things that enter it, it could not successfully copy their contraries or things of a totally different nature whenever it were to receive them. It would be showing its own face as well. This is why the thing that is to receive in itself all the elemental kinds must be totally devoid of any characteristics. Think of people who make fragrant ointments. They expend skill and ingenuity to come up with something just like this [that is, a neutral base], to have on hand to start with. The liquids that are to receive the fragrances they make as

50c

50d

50e

---

*The translation is that of Donald J. Zeyl, *Plato: Timaeus* (Indianapolis, 2000), lightly edited for consistency.

odorless as possible. Or think of people who work at impressing shapes upon soft materials. They emphatically refuse to allow any such material to already have some definite shape. Instead, they'll even it out
51a and make it as smooth as it can be. In the same way, then, if the thing that is to receive repeatedly throughout its whole self the likenesses of the intelligible objects, the things which always are—if it is to do so successfully, then it ought to be devoid of any inherent characteristics of its own.* This, of course, is why we shouldn't call the mother or receptacle of what has come to be, of what is visible or perceivable in every other way, either earth or air, fire or water, or any of their compounds or their constituents. But if we speak of it as an invisible and characterless sort of thing, one that receives all things and shares in a most perplexing way in what is intelligible, a thing extremely difficult
51b to comprehend, we shall not be misled. And insofar as it is possible to arrive at its nature on the basis of what we've said so far, the most correct way to speak of it may well be this: the part of it that gets ignited appears on each occasion as fire, the dampened part as water, and parts as earth or air in so far as it receives the imitations of these. . . .

Since these things are so, we must agree that that which keeps its
52a own form unchangingly, which has not been brought into being and is not destroyed, which neither receives into itself anything else from anywhere else, nor itself enters into anything else anywhere, is one thing. It is invisible—it cannot be perceived by the senses at all—and it is the role of understanding to study it. The second thing is that which shares the other's name and resembles it. This thing can be perceived by the senses, and it has been begotten. It is constantly borne along, now coming to be in a certain place and then perishing out of it. It is apprehended by belief, which involves sense perception. And the third type is place, which exists always and cannot be destroyed. It provides
52b a fixed state for all things that come to be. It is itself apprehended by a kind of bastard reasoning that does not involve sense perception, and it is hardly even an object of conviction. We look at it as in a dream when we say that everything that exists must of necessity be somewhere, in some place and occupying some space, and that that which doesn't exist somewhere, whether on earth or in heaven, doesn't exist at all.

We prove unable to draw all these distinctions and others related to them—even in the case of that unsleeping, truly existing reality—because our dreaming state renders us incapable of waking up and
52c stating the truth, which is this: Since that for which an image has

---

*Accepting the insertion of *noêtôn* before *pantôn* in 50a1.

come to be is not at all intrinsic to the image, which is invariably borne along to picture something else, it stands to reason that the image should therefore come to be in something else, somehow clinging to being, or else be nothing at all. But that which really is receives support from the accurate, true account—that as long as the one is distinct from the other, neither of them ever comes to be in the other in such a way that they at the same time become one and the same, and also two.   52d

Let this, then, be a summary of the account I would offer, as computed by my "vote." There are being, space, and becoming, three distinct things which existed even before heaven (*ouranon*) came to be.

Now as the wet-nurse of becoming turns watery and fiery and receives the shape of earth and air, and as it acquires all the affections that come with these characters, it takes on a variety of visible aspects, but because it is filled with capacities that are neither similar   52e nor evenly balanced, no part of it is in balance. It sways irregularly in every direction as it is shaken by those things, and being set in movement it in turn shakes them. And as they are moved, they drift continually, some in one direction and others in others, separating from each other. They are winnowed out, as it were, like grain that is sifted by winnowing sieves or other such instruments. They are carried off and settle down, the dense and heavy ones in one direction, and the rare and light ones to another place.   53a

That is how at that time the four kinds (*genê*) were being shaken by the receiver, which was itself agitating like a shaking machine, separating the kinds most unlike each other furthest apart and pushing those most like each other closest together into the same region. This, of course, explains how these different kinds came to occupy different regions of space, even before the universe (*to pan*) was set in order and constituted from them at its coming to be. Indeed, it is a fact that before this took place the four kinds all lacked proportion and measure, and at the time the ordering of the universe was undertaken, fire, water, earth, and air initially possessed certain traces of what they are   53b now. They were indeed in the condition one would expect thoroughly god-forsaken things to be in. So, finding them in this natural condition, the first thing the god then did was to give them their distinctive shapes, using forms and numbers.

Here is a proposition we shall always affirm above all else: The god fashioned these four kinds to be as nobly beautiful and excellent as possible, when they were not so before. It will now be my task to show you what structure each of them acquired, and how each came to be.   53c My account will be an unusual one, but since you are well schooled in the fields of learning in terms of which I must of necessity proceed with my exposition, I'm sure you'll follow me.

First of all, it is clear to everyone, I'm sure, that fire, earth, water, and air are bodies. Now everything that has bodily form also has depth. Depth, moreover, is of necessity comprehended within plane, and any plane bounded by straight lines is composed of triangles. Every triangle, moreover, derives from two triangles, each of which has one right angle and two acute angles. Of these two triangles, one [the isosceles right-angled triangle] has at each of the other two vertices an equal part of a right angle, determined by its division by equal sides; while the other [the scalene right-angled triangle] has unequal parts of a right angle at its other two vertices, determined by the division of the right angle by unequal sides. This, then, we presume to be the starting-point of fire and of the other bodies, as we pursue our likely account in terms of Necessity. Starting-points yet more ultimate than these are known only to the god, and to any man he may hold dear.

We should now say which are the most nobly beautiful four bodies that can come to be. They are quite unlike each other, though some of them are capable of breaking up and turning into others and vice versa. If our account is on the mark, we shall have the truth about how earth and fire and their proportional intermediates [water and air] came to be. For we shall never concede to anyone that there are any visible bodies more nobly beautiful than these, each conforming to a single kind (*genos*). So we must whole-heartedly proceed to fit together the four kinds of bodies of surpassing noble beauty, and to declare that we have come to grasp their natures well enough.

Of the two [right-angled] triangles, the isosceles has but one nature, while the scalene has unlimitedly many. Now we have to select the most nobly beautiful one from among the unlimitedly many, if we are to get a proper start. So if anyone can say that he has picked out another one that is more nobly beautiful for the construction of these bodies, his victory will be that of a friend, not an enemy. Of the many [scalene right-angled] triangles, then, we posit as the one most nobly beautiful, surpassing the others, that one from [a pair of] which the equilateral triangle is constructed as a third figure. Why this is so is too long a story to tell now. But if anyone puts this claim to the test and discovers that it isn't so, his be the prize, with our congratulations. So much, then, for the selection of the two triangles out of which the bodies of fire and the other bodies are constructed—the [right-angled] isosceles, and [the right-angled] scalene whose longer side squared is always triple its shorter side squared [i.e., the half-equilateral].

At this point we need to determine more perspicuously something that was not stated perspicuously earlier. For then it appeared that all four kinds of bodies could come to be from each other by successive stages.* But the appearance is wrong. While there are indeed four kinds of bodies that come to be from the [right-angled] triangles we have selected, three of them come from triangles that have unequal sides, whereas the fourth alone is fashioned out of isosceles triangles. Thus not all of them have the capacity of breaking up and turning into each other, with a large number of small bodies turning into a small number of large ones and vice versa. There are three that can do this. For all three are made up of a single sort of triangle, so that when once the larger bodies are broken up, the same triangles can go to make up a large number of small bodies, assuming shapes appropriate to them. And likewise, when numerous small bodies are fragmented into their triangles, these triangles may well combine to make up some single massive body belonging to another kind.

54c

54d

So much, then, for our account of how these bodies come to be from each other. Let us next discuss the form that each of them has come to have, and the various numbers that have combined to make them up.

Leading the way will be the primary form [the tetrahedron], the tiniest structure, whose elementary triangle is the one whose hypotenuse is twice the length of its shorter side. Now when a pair of such triangles are juxtaposed along the diagonal [i.e., their hypotenuses] and this is done three times, and their diagonals and short sides converge upon a single point as center, the result is a single equilateral triangle, composed of six such triangles. When four of these equilateral triangles are combined, a single solid angle is produced at the junction of three plane angles. This, it turns out, is the angle which comes right after the most obtuse of the plane angles.** And once four such solid angles have been completed, we get the primary solid form, which is one that divides the entire circumference [of the sphere in which it is inscribed] into equal and similar parts.

54e

55a

The second solid form [the octahedron] is constructed out of the same triangles which, however, are now arranged in eight equilateral triangles and produce a single solid angle out of four plane angles. And when six such solid angles have been produced, the second body has reached its completion.

---

*See 49b–c.

**The solid angle is the conjunction of three 60° plane angles, totaling 180°.

55b

Now the third body [the icosahedron] is made up of a combination of one hundred and twenty of the elementary triangles, and of twelve solid angles, each enclosed by five plane equilateral triangles. This body turns out to have twenty equilateral triangular faces. And let us take our leave of this one of the elementary triangles, the one that has begotten the above three kinds of bodies and turn to the other one, the isosceles [right-angled] triangle, which has begotten the fourth [the cube]. Arranged in sets of four whose right angles come together at the center, the isosceles triangle produced a single equilateral quadrangle [i.e., a square]. And when six of these quadrangles were combined together, they produced eight solid angles, each of which was

55c

constituted by three plane right angles. The shape of the resulting body so constructed is a cube, and it has six quadrangular equilateral faces.

One other construction, a fifth, still remained, and this one the god used for the universe, embroidering figures on it.*

Anyone following this whole line of reasoning might very well be puzzled about whether we should say that there are unlimitedly many cosmoses or a limited number of them. If so, he would have to con-

50d

clude that to answer, "infinitely many," is to take the view of one who is really "unfinished" in things he ought to be "finished" in. He would do better to stop with the question whether we should say that there's really just one or five and be puzzled about that. Well, our "probable account" answer declares there to be but one, a god—though someone else, taking other things into consideration, will come to a different belief. We must set him aside, however.

Let us now assign to fire, earth, water, and air the structures which have just been given their formations in our speech. To earth let us give the form of a cube, because of the four kinds of bodies earth is the most

55e

immobile and the most pliable—which is what the solid whose faces are the most secure must of necessity turn out to be, more so than the others. Now of the [right-angled] triangles we postulated at the start, the face belonging to those that have equal sides has a greater natural stability than that belonging to triangles that have unequal sides, and the plane that is composed of the two triangles, the equilateral quadrangle [the square], holds its position with greater stability than does the equilateral triangle, both in their parts and as wholes. Hence, if we

56a

assign this solid figure to earth, we are preserving our "likely account." And of the solid figures that are left, we shall next assign the least

---

*The remaining one of the regular solids is the dodecahedron. It approaches most nearly a sphere in volume, which is the shape of the universe, according to Timaeus.

mobile of them to water, to fire the most mobile, and to air the one in between. This means that the tiniest body belongs to fire, the largest to water, and the intermediate one to air—and also that the body with the sharpest edges belongs to fire, the next sharpest to air, and the third sharpest to water. Now in all these cases the body that has the fewest faces is of necessity the most mobile, in that it, more than any other, has edges that are the sharpest and best fit for cutting in every direction. It is also the lightest, in that it is made up of the least number of identical parts. The second body ranks second in having these same features, and the third ranks third. So let us follow our account, which is not only likely but also correct, and take the solid form of the pyramid that we saw constructed as the element or the seed of fire. And let us say that the second form in order of generation is that of air, and the third that of water.

56b

Now we must understand all these bodies as being so small that due to their small size none of them, whatever their kind, is visible to us individually. When, however, a large number of them are clustered together, we do see them in mass. And in particular, as to the proportions among their numbers, their movements and their other capacities, we must understand that when the god had brought them to complete and exact perfection (to the degree that Necessity was willing to comply obediently), he arranged them together proportionally.

56c

Given all we have said so far about the kinds of elemental bodies, the following account [of their transformations] is the most likely: When earth encounters fire and is dissolved by fire's sharpness, it will drift about—whether the dissolution occurred within fire itself, or within a mass of air or water—until its parts meet again somewhere, refit themselves together, and become earth again. The reason is that the parts of earth will never pass into another form. But when water is broken up into parts by fire or even by air, it could happen that the parts recombine to form one corpuscle of fire and two of air. And the fragments of air could produce, from any single particle that is dissolved, two fire corpuscles. And conversely, whenever a small quantity of fire is enveloped by a large quantity of air or water or perhaps earth and is agitated inside them as they move, and in spite of its resistance is beaten and shattered to bits, then any two fire corpuscles may combine to constitute a single form of air. And when air is overpowered and broken down, then two and one half entire forms of air will be consolidated into a single, entire form of water.

56d

56e

Let us recapitulate and formulate our account of these transformations as follows: Whenever one of the other kinds is caught inside fire and gets cut up by the sharpness of fire's angles and edges, then if it is

57a

reconstituted as fire, it will stop getting cut. The reason is that a thing of any kind that is alike and uniform is incapable of producing any change in, or being affected by, anything that is similar to it. But as long as something involved in a transformation has something stronger than it to contend with, the process of its dissolution will continue non-stop. And likewise, when a few of the smaller corpuscles are surrounded by a greater number of bigger ones, they will be shattered

57b and quenched. The quenching will stop when these smaller bodies are willing to be reconstituted into the form of the kind that prevailed over them, and so from fire will come air, and from air, water. But if these smaller corpuscles are in process of turning into these and one of the other kinds encounters them and engages them in battle, their dissolution will go on non-stop until they are either completely squeezed and broken apart and escape to their own likes, or else are defeated, and, melding from many into one, they are assimilated to the kind that prevailed over them, and come to share its abode from then on. And, what is more, as they undergo these processes, they

57c all exchange their regions of space: for as a result of the Receptacle's agitation the quantities of each of the kinds are separated from each other, with each occupying its own place, but because some parts of a particular kind do from time to time become unlike their former selves and like the other kinds, they are carried by the shaking toward the place occupied by whatever masses they are becoming like to.

These, then, are the sorts of causes by which the unalloyed primary bodies have come to be. Now the fact that different varieties are found within their respective forms is to be attributed to the constructions of each of the elementary triangles. Each of these two constructions

57d did not at the start yield a triangle that had just one size, but triangles that were both smaller and larger, numerically as many as there are varieties within a given form. That is why when they are mixed with themselves and with each other they display an infinite variety, which those who are to employ a likely account in their study of nature must take note of.

61c . . . We have now pretty much completed our presentation of the kinds of bodies that are distinguished by their multifarious shapes, their combinations and their transformations into each other. Now we must try to shed some light on what has caused them to come to have the affections they do. First, we need at every step in our discourse to appeal to the existence of perception, but we have so far discussed neither the coming to be of flesh, or of what pertains to flesh, nor the part of the soul that is mortal. It so happens, however, that we cannot give an adequate

61d account of these matters without referring to perceptual affections, but neither can we give an account of the latter without referring to the former, and to treat them simultaneously is all but impossible. So we must start by assuming one or other, and later revisit what we have assumed. Let's begin by taking for granted for now the existence of body and soul. This will allow our account of these affections to follow after the account we've just given of the elemental kinds.

First, then, let us see what we mean when we call fire *hot*. Let's look at it in this way: We notice how fire acts on our bodies by dividing and cutting them. We are all well aware that the affection is a sharp one. The fineness of fire's edges, the sharpness of its angles, the minuteness of its parts and the swiftness of its movement—all of which make fire severely piercing so that it makes sharp cuts in whatever it encounters—must be taken into consideration as we recall how its shape came to be. It is it, more than any other, that divides our bodies   62a
throughout and cuts them up into small pieces, thereby giving us the property (as well as the name [*kermatizein*]) that we now with perfect sense call *hot* [*thermon*].

What the contrary to these [affections of fire] is, is quite clear; nonetheless, we should not leave out anything needed from our account. As the larger parts of the moisture surrounding our bodies penetrate our bodies and push out the smaller parts, but cannot take up the places vacated by those smaller parts, they compress the moisture within us and congeal it by putting it in a state of motionlessness in place of a state of moving non-uniformity, by virtue of the uniformity and com-   62b
pression so introduced. But anything which is being unnaturally compressed has a natural tendency to resist such compression, and pushes itself outward, in the opposite direction. This resistance, this shaking is called "shivering" and "chill," and the experience as a whole, as well as what brings it about, has come to have the name *cold*.

Hard we call whatever our flesh gives way to; soft, whatever gives way to our flesh. And this is how they are relative to each other. Whatever stands upon a small base tends to give way. The form composed of quadrangles, however, is the least liable to being displaced because its bases are very stable, and that which is compacted to its maximum   62c
density is particularly resistant to being displaced.

Heavy and *light* can be most clearly explained if we examine them in conjunction with what we call above and below. It is entirely wrong to hold that there are by nature two separate places, divorced from and entirely contrary to one another, the one "below," toward which anything that has natural mass tends to spatially move, and the other "above," toward which everything makes its way only involuntarily. For given that the whole heaven is spherical, all the points that are situated

62d as extremes at an equal distance from the center must by their nature be extremes of just the same sort, and we must take it that the center, being equidistant from the extremes, is situated at the point that is the opposite to all the extremes. Now if this is the universe's natural constitution, which of the points just mentioned could you posit as "above" or "below" without justly giving the appearance of using totally inappropriate language? There is no justification for describing the universe's central place either as a natural "above" or a natural "below," but just as "at the center." And the region at the circumference is, to be sure, not the center, but neither is one of its parts so distinguished from any other that it is related to the center in a specific way more so than any of the parts opposite to it. What contrary names could you apply to something that is by nature all alike in every direction? How could you think to use such names appropriately? If, further, there is something solid and evenly balanced at the center of the universe, it

63a could not move to any of the extreme points, because these are all similar in all directions. But if you could travel around it in a circle, you would repeatedly take a position at your own antipodes and call the very same part of it now the part "above," and then the part "below." For the whole universe, as we have just said, is spherical, and to say that some place is its "above," and another its "below," makes no sense. The origin of these names and the things to which they really apply, which explain how we have become accustomed to using them in dividing the world as a whole in this way, we must resolve by adopting the fol-

63b lowing supposition: Imagine someone stepping onto that place in the universe that is the particular province of fire, where the greatest quantity of fire is gathered together, and toward which other fire moves. Imagine, further, that he has the power to remove some parts of the fire and place them on scales. When he raises the beam and drags the fire into the alien air, applying force to it, clearly the lesser quantity of

63c fire somehow gives way to his force more easily than the greater. For when two things are raised by one and the same exertion, the lesser quantity will invariably yield more readily and the greater (which offers more resistance) less readily, to the force applied. And so the large quantity will be described as *heavy* and moving *downward*, and the small one as *light* and moving *upward*. Now this is the very thing we must detect ourselves doing in our own region. When we stand on the earth and weigh out one earth-like thing against another, and sometimes some earth itself, we drag these things by force, contrary to their natural tendency, into the alien air. While both of them tend to cling to what is akin to them, nevertheless the smaller one will yield sooner and more

63d readily than the larger one to the force we apply that introduces it into

the alien stuff. Now this is what we call *light*, and the region into which
we force it to go we call above; their contraries we call *heavy* and *below*.
Now the things [having any of these designations] necessarily differ
relative to one another, because the various quantities of the elemental
kinds of body occupy contrary places: what in one place is light, heavy,
below, or above will all be found to become, or to be, totally contrary   63e
to, or at an angle to, or in any and every different direction from, what
is light, heavy, below, or above in the contrary place. In fact, this is
the one thing that should be understood to apply in all these cases:
the path toward its own kind is what makes a thing moving along it
"heavy" and the region into which it moves, "below," whereas the other
set of terms ["light" and "above"] are for things behaving the other way.
This, then, concludes our account of what causes [things to have] these
affections.

As for *smooth* and *rough*, I take it that anyone could discern the
cause of those properties and communicate it to someone else: roughness results from the combination of hardness with non-uniformity,
while smoothness is the result of uniformity's contribution to density.   64a

Further Reading

Detailed and regularly updated bibliographies of works on Aristotle's natural philosophy (compiled by Istvan Bodnár) and on his philosophy generally (compiled by Christopher Shields) are available online at:

https://plato.stanford.edu/entries/aristotle-natphil/
http://plato.stanford.edu/entries/aristotle/

Thesaurus Linguae Graecae (http://www.tlg.uci.edu) has excellent searchable Greek texts and English translations of Aristotle's writings, with linked dictionaries and grammars.

Editions of *De Caelo*, translations of it, and commentaries on it are listed under Abbreviations at the beginning of the present volume.

The following are further works that I have found especially worthwhile:

Aristotle Life and Works

Natali, C. *Aristotle: His Life and School* (Princeton, 2013).
Shields, C. (ed.). *The Oxford Handbook of Aristotle* (Oxford, 2012).

Books and Papers

Algra, K. *Concepts of Space in Classical and Hellenistic Greek Philosophy* (Leiden, 1959).
Bodnár, I. "Movers and Elemental Motions in Aristotle." *Oxford Studies in Ancient Philosophy* 16 (1997): 81–117.
Bolton, R. *Science, Dialectique et Ethique Chez Aristote* (Louvain-la-Neuve, 2010).
Freudenthal, G. *Aristotle's Theory of Material Substance: Heat and Pneuma, Form and Soul* (Oxford, 1995).
Matthen, M. "Holistic Presuppositions in Aristotle's Cosmology." *Oxford Studies in Ancient Philosophy* 20 (2001): 171–199.
Morison, B. *On Location: Aristotle's Conception of Place* (Oxford, 2002).

Owen, G. E. L. *Logic, Science, and Dialectic* (Ithaca, 1986).

Solmsen, F. *Aristotle's System of the Physical World* (Ithaca, 1960).

Thorp, J. "The Luminousness of the Quintessence." *Phoenix* 36 (1982): 104–123.

White, M. *The Continuous and the Discrete: Ancient Physical Theories from a Contemporary Perspective* (Oxford, 1992).

Wildberg, C. *John Philoponus' Criticism of Aristotle's Theory of Aether* (Berlin, 1988).

Relevant Works of Mine

Substantial Knowledge: Aristotle's Metaphysics (Indianapolis, 2000).

Action, Contemplation, and Happiness: An Essay on Aristotle (Cambridge, Mass., 2012).

"Aristotle's Method of Philosophy." C. Shields, (ed.), *The Oxford Handbook of Aristotle* (Oxford, 2012): 150–170.

Aristotle: Metaphysics (Indianapolis, 2016).

Aristotle: De Anima (Indianapolis, 2017).

Aristotle: Physics (Indianapolis, 2018).

Aristotle: A Quick Immersion (New York, 2019).

Aristotle: On Coming to Be and Passing Away & Mete. I 1–3, IV (Indianapolis, forthcoming).

Aristotle: Topics and Sophistical Refutations (Indianapolis, forthcoming).

Index

Note: In page numbers the initial 2 or 3 is omitted—for example, 268ᵃ = 68ᵃ and 300ᵃ = 00ᵃ. Line numbers are to the Greek text and are approximate in the translation. References are typically to key doctrines or discussions in the text and, when in bold, in the associated notes.